IAN S. FORRESTER QC LL.D.
A Scot without Borders

Liber Amicorum - Volume I

Editors

Sir David Edward
Jacquelyn MacLennan
Assimakis Komninos

60 Broad Street, Suite 3502, NY 10004, New York, USA
www.concurrences.com
contact@concurrences.com
Printed in United Kingdom
First Printing, 2015
ISBN 978-1-939007-25-4

Cover and book design by Yves Buliard, www.yvesbuliard.fr

Concurrences Books

Competition Digest – A Synthesis of EU and National Leading Cases — 2nd Edition
Frédéric Jenny • 2015

Antitrust in Emerging and Developing Countries
Eleanor Fox - Harry First • 2015

Consumer's Choice: The Emergence of a Powerful Concept in Competition Law
Paul Nihoul • 2015

Google, la presse et les journalistes – Analyse interdisciplinaire d'une situation de coopétition
Guillaume Sire • 2015

Les grands arrêts du droit de la concurrence
Laurence Idot • 2015

Les pratiques restrictives – L'application de l'article L. 442-6 du code de commerce à travers la jurisprudence
Erwann Kerguelen • 2015

William E. Kovacic: An Antitrust Tribute – Liber Amicorum (Vol. II)
Nicolas Charbit - Elisa Ramundo • September 2014

Competition Law on the Global Stage: David Gerber's Global Competition Law in Perspective
Nicolas Charbit - Elisa Ramundo • January 2014

Day to Day Competition Law: A practical Guide for Businesses
Patrick Hubert, Olivier Lecroart, Marie Leppard • March 2014

A quoi sert la concurrence ?
Martine Behar-Touchais, Nicolas Charbit, Rafael Amaro • October 2014

William E. Kovacic: An Antitrust Tribute – Liber Amicorum (Vol. I)
Nicolas Charbit - Elisa Ramundo • January 2013

All books are published in print and electronic format.

Foreword

Sir David Edward
Jacquelyn MacLennan
Assimakis Komninos

It is a great honour and a special delight to be able to present this Liber Amicorum to Ian Stewart Forrester QC LL.D. on the occasion of his 70th birthday.

Ian comes from a formidable family of Scottish Presbyterian ministers and professors of divinity in whose footsteps he has followed as an elder and regular preacher at St Andrew's Church of Scotland in Brussels. While firmly rooted in the faith of his ancestors, the intellectual rigour of David Hume and Adam Smith, and the civil law traditions of Scots law, he has, like so many Scots down the ages, sought broader horizons – mainly in Brussels, but now in Luxembourg, with more than a passing dalliance with the common law in New York and London, as well as the cultural life of Japan and the byways of Serbian politics. His endless good spirits and quirky sense of humour have made him friends as well as professional connections all over the world.

Ian was born in Glasgow in 1945, the son of a well-loved and respected schoolmaster and outstanding cricketer – one talent that Ian did not, as far as we know, inherit. The youngest child of the family, who lost his mother tragically early, he was educated at Kelvinside Academy and Glasgow University where he took the traditional Scottish general arts degree (MA 1965) followed by a degree in law (LL.B. 1967). This was a glittering period in the annals of the University, marked by debating successes with the late Alan Rodger (Lord Rodger of Earlsferry) and later, in a North American debating tour, with James Douglas-Hamilton (Lord Selkirk of Douglas). He continued his studies at Tulane University (MCL 1969), Louisiana being carefully selected as a civil law island within a common law sea. Ian returned there to teach on many occasions. It was in New Orleans that he met Sandra Keegan, who became his wife.

Before returning to Scotland after Tulane, Ian spent some time as an intern with Davis Polk in New York, and then returned to prepare for the Scots Bar as the 'devil' (pupil) of David Edward. But his time with Davis Polk had brought him into a case involving a Palestinian hijacked plane, which continued to take him to places like Beirut in the

1970s. This was somewhat disconcerting for his devil-master, while opening new casements onto the foam of international practice. Despite these distractions, Ian was admitted to the Scots Bar in 1972, and 'took silk' (becoming a QC) in 1988. In the meantime, he took the New York Bar in 1977, and he was later admitted to the English Bar in 1996.

Ian had moved in 1973 to Cleary Gottlieb in Brussels as one of the first generation of UK lawyers who arrived there when the UK joined the European Communities. For the next forty-two years Brussels was to be his home. It is where he raised a family, together with Sandra, becoming the proud father of two sons, Alexander and James, both of whom have resisted the law to date, despite bedtime stories which, Ian confessed, were a soporific means for him to find the clearest expression of his arguments in the case before him at the time.

Meanwhile, he moved from Big Law to Boutique Law, creating Forrester & Norall with Chris Norall, later joined by Alastair Sutton, and then back to Big Law when Forrester Norall & Sutton merged with White & Case. His appointment to the Luxembourg bench will round off Ian's illustrious career as a practitioner.

Ian belongs to the generation that 'made' the English-speaking competition law bar in Brussels, until then the monopoly of a few continental law professors and some Belgian French-speaking lawyers. He was fortunate to participate in many of the leading cases in the formation of key principles of EU law, particularly EU competition law. Examples are *Bosman* on freedom of movement in sport; *Bullock (Distillers)* on restricting exports through discriminatory pricing; *GSK* on parallel trade of pharmaceutical products; *Servier* and *Pfizer* on the precautionary principle; *Magill*, *IMS Health* and *Microsoft* on the interface of competition law and intellectual property law, and in particular, on compulsory licensing; *Rambus* on standard setting bodies and Article 102; *Intel* on unilateral conduct/discounts; *Chalkor* on the standard of judicial review of Commission decisions; and Servier on what promises to be a defining case in EU law on reverse settlements.

Ian has not just lived these cases professionally but also academically. He toured the amphitheatres and debated these and other cases with students, professors and researchers. There was never a conference he declined, to the despair of his faithful secretary and PA, Pauline Tart, who had to manage an unmanageable calendar.

Ian is also a prolific writer of seminal articles. His 'Laicisation of Community Law - Self Help and the Rule of Reason: How Competition Law Is and Could be Applied', co-authored with Chris Norall and published in 1984, remains a must-read for students of EU competition law. His articles on the modernization of EU competition law, when Regulation 1/2003 was being prepared, and on due process in EU competition law enforcement have also been influential, and he has written about the EU judicial system from a comparative law perspective.

Ian is generous with his time and talents and has been a mentor to many younger lawyers. A typical scene is Ian in an office full of papers and books surrounded by younger colleagues discussing a case. He has had a long association with the Jessup Moot Court and has also been the head of White & Case's global pro bono practice. He has also been a trustee and strong supporter of the European Baroque Orchestra, and recently embarked on a new career side line as narrator in 'The Snowman' concert and Master of Ceremonies at the Brussels Christmas Carol Concert.

His many qualities have been recognized in his appointment as Honorary Professor of European Law and the award of an LL.D. at his alma mater the University of Glasgow, and as an Honorary Bencher of the Middle Temple.

This Liber Amicorum is an occasion to mark the outstanding merits of a remarkable man and express the long lasting, deep, affectionate friendship by three generations of colleagues in this preface and in the contributions themselves. In this point of transition in an extraordinarily full professional life, we wish Ian all the best for an ever fruitful and rewarding time at the EU Bench.

David, Jacquelyn and Makis

Contributors

Cecilia Álvarez Rigaudias
Pfizer

Josef Azizi
University of Vienna

Barry Baines
State of New York

Jacques Bourgeois
Sidley Austin, College of Europe

Merijn Chamon
University of Gent

Claus-Dieter Ehlermann
WilmerHale

Alfonso Gutierrez
Uría Menéndez

Patrick Hugg
Loyola University College of Law

Sir Francis G. Jacobs
King's College London

Colin MacKay
BBC Radio Scotland

Jacquelyn MacLennan
White & Case

Paul Mahoney
European Court of Human Rights

Niamh Nic Shuibhne
Edinburgh Law School

Isao Noishiki
Matsushita Electric Industrial Co.

Christopher Norall
Forrester Norall & Sutton

José Pérez Santos
Uría Menéndez

Robert Reich
University of California at Berkeley

Konrad Schiemann
European Court of Justice

Dean Spielmann
European Court of Human Rights

Pauline Tart
White & Case

Mathieu Vancaillie
Ashurst

Michel Waelbroeck
Université Libre de Bruxelles

Jo Weiss
White & Case

Table of Contents

Part III - Human Rights - Intellectual Property - Other

IAN S. FORRESTER
QC LL.D.
Biography

I. Career

Ian S. Forrester QC LL.D. is a teacher, author and practitioner specialising in European law. He is partner at White & Case LLP (to September 2015), based in its Brussels office, and head of the Firm's worldwide pro bono practice. He has lectured widely on EU legal and policy topics and published extensively on these themes, particularly competition, customs, dumping, pharmaceuticals, sport, the precautionary principle, and human rights. Several articles concentrate on due process in competition cases.

Honorary Professor and Honorary Doctor of Laws at Glasgow University since 2009, he is a member of the Faculty of Advocates (the Scottish Bar) since 1972; he is also a member of the bars of England (1996), Belgium (1998) and New York, to which he was admitted in 1977 after examination, under special order of the New York Court of Appeals, following a challenge to the constitutional propriety of excluding non-resident aliens from bar membership. He was appointed Queen's Counsel in 1988, and Bencher, Middle Temple in 2012.

His early career was spent with Maclay, Murray & Spens in Scotland; Davis Polk & Wardwell in New York; and Cleary Gottlieb Steen & Hamilton in New York and Brussels. He co-founded the boutique firm Forrester & Norall in 1981, which enlarged to Forrester Norall & Sutton in 1989, and merged with White & Case in 1998.

Professor Forrester has appeared before the European Courts, European Commission and national courts and agencies in several leading cases, including *Magill* (compulsory licensing); *Bosman* (football transfers); *Microsoft* (compulsory licensing); *IMS* (compulsory licensing); *Pfizer Animal Health* (the precautionary principle); *Government of Gibraltar v Council* (status of Gibraltar Airport); *Glaxo Spain* and *Syfait et al v GlaxoSmithKline* (parallel trade in pharmaceuticals); *Les Laboratoires Servier* (settlement of patent disputes); *Chalkor* (due process and judicial review); *Canon* (dumping); *A and Others v. National Blood Authority* (can a blood transfusion be a 'defective' 'product'); *Bellona Foundation v EFTA* (environmental protection).

He is a Trustee of the European Union Baroque Orchestra; a Member of the Dean's Advisory Board, Tulane University School of Law; a Member of Glasgow University School of Law's Advisory Committee; and a Member of the Board of Trustees, Academy of European Law, Trier.

II. Education

Attended Kelvinside Academy, Glasgow; graduated from Glasgow University (MA 1965; LLB 1967; LL.D. honoris causa 2009); received an MCL from Tulane University of Louisiana (1969).

III. Selected publications

Books

'The German Civil Code, a translation and introduction', 1975

'The German Commercial Code', 1979

'The German Marriage Law', 1976, North Holland/Kluwer/Fred Rothman (co-author)

'The German Legal System', 1971, pamphlet, Rothman (co-author)

Articles and Papers

'Maintaining Trade Secrecy', *Georgia Law Review*, 1970; reprinted, *Patent Law Review*, 1970

'Jurisdiction of National and Community bodies in competition matters after SABAM', *Common Market Law Review*, 1974

'Distribution and Agency Agreements in EEC Competition Law', *Revue Suisse du Droit International de la Concurrence*, 1978, and *Journal of the Law Society of Scotland*, 1978

‘EEC Customs Law: Rules of Origin and Preferential Duty Treatment’, *European Law Review*, 1980

‘Developments in EEC Competition Law’, chapter on decisions of the EC Commission and judgments of the European Courts in the field of competition in the *Yearbook of European Law*; annual survey (1981-1996); biennial survey (1997 to date); Clarendon Press-Oxford (22 chapters to date) (co-author)

‘Legal Professional Privilege: Limitations on the Commission’s Powers of Inspection following the AM & S Judgment’, *Common Market Law Review*, 1983

‘The laicization of Community law: selfhelp and the rule of reason: how competition law is and could be applied’, *Common Market Law Review*, 1984; also in Fordham Corporate Law Institute, Matthew Bender & Company Inc., New York, 1984 (co-author). Reprinted in *EC Competition Law Reform*, Fordham Corporate Law Institute, Juris Publishing, Inc., Huntington, NY, 2003

‘Software Licensing in the Light of Current EC Competition Law Considerations’, *European Competition Law Review*, 1992

‘EC Intellectual Property Law and the Single Market’ (co-author) in *The Regulatory Affairs Journal*, Vol 5, No 7, July 1994

‘European Law and its implications for football’, paper presented to the Scottish Council for Civil Liberties and the Scottish Trades Union Congress Conference on ‘Football, the Law and Civil Liberties’, Glasgow, March 1996 (unpublished)

‘Pharmaceuticals: Test Bed for European Themes on Trademarks & Free Movement of Goods’, paper presented at the Fifth Annual Conference on International Intellectual Property Law and Policy at Fordham University School of Law, April 1997, *Fordham Intellectual Property, Media & Entertainment Law Journal*, Volume VIII, Autumn 1997, Number 1 (co-author)

‘The Repackaging of Trademarked Pharmaceuticals in Europe: Recent Developments’, paper presented at the Eighth Annual Conference on International Intellectual Property Law and Policy at Fordham University School of Law, April 2000, *European Intellectual Property Review 2000*, Issue 11, p. 512

‘The EU and Japan: Priorities and Prospects for the Coming Decade’, published in Japanese in *JMC Journal*, February 2001

‘The Reform of the Implementation of Articles 81 and 82 Following Publication of the Draft Regulation’, in *Legal Issues of Economic Integration* 28(2), 173-194, 2001

'Compulsory licensing of intellectual property rights in Europe: a rare cure to aberrant intellectual property rights', paper presented at the US Department of Justice/Federal Trade Commission Hearings on Competition and Intellectual Property Law and Policy in the Knowledge-Based Economy: Comparative Law Topics, May 22, 2002. Published in October 2002 in English in the Chinese *International Business Daily* (web edition). Published in Chinese in 2003 in *The Forum of Politics and Law*. Published in Japanese in two parts in the *CIPIC Journal*, Vol 134 (2003/3) and Vol 136 (2003/5), under the title 'Yohroppa niokeru kyousei raisensingu mondai nituite: ikinaikoku no ijyoutomoieru chitekizaisanken no enyou o naosu ryouyaku to naruka'.

'Trademark Exhaustion in Europe', published in Japanese in the *CIPIC Journal*, Vol 139 (2003/8), under the title 'Yohroppa niokeru syouhyou no syoujin mondai nituite' (co-author)

'The EFTA Court confronts re-labelling (*Paranova AS v Merck & Co., Inc. and Others*, Judgement of the EFTA Court of 8 July 2003, Case E-3/02)', in *European Law Reporter* 7-8/2003 at 278

'The exhaustion of trademark rights in the EU and the possible action against pirated and counterfeit goods' (published in Japanese only in the *CIPIC Journal*, Vol 142 (2003/11), under the title 'Ousyu-niokeru heikou-yunyu-mondai oyobi mohouhin/kaizokuban no torishimari nituite' (co-author)

Contribution to 'Roundtable on *Trinko*', *Global Competition Review*, Volume 7, Issue 2, March 2004

'Competition Law and Intellectual Property in Europe', Twelfth St. Gallen International Competition Law Forum 2005, University of St. Gallen, published in *Neueste Entwicklungen im europäischen und internationalen Kartellrecht, Zwölftes St. Gallen Internationales Kartellrechtsforum 2005*, Helbing & Lichtenhahn Verlag, Basel, 2006

'Precaution, Science and Jurisprudence: An Evaluation', *Journal of Risk Research*, Vol 9, No 4, 297-311, June 2006 (co-author)

'Regulating Intellectual Property Via Competition? Or Regulating Competition Via Intellectual Property? Competition and Intellectual Property: ten years on, the debate still flourishes', *European Competition Law Annual 2005: The Interaction between Competition Law and Intellectual Property Law*, Hart Publishing, 2008

'How The Monopolist Gained More Power By Abjuring Its Monopoly', paper delivered to the *Swedish Journal of European Law*/Swedish FIDE Association conference on The modernisation reform of EC antitrust enforcement and its effects in the national legal order, Stockholm, 2 December 2005, *Europarättslig Tidskrift*, Nummer 3 2006 Årgång 9, November 2006

'The judicial function in European law and pleading in the European Courts', Third Annual Wendell Gauthier Lecture, Tulane Law School, 2006, 81 *Tul. L. Rev.* 647, 2006

'Agenda de Lisbonne et droit de la concurrence', Editorial in *Concurrences* 3-2006 (co-author)

'Ex-post assessment of Regulation 1/2003', *Global Competition Policy*, October 2008, Release 2

'Exceptional approval of major mergers: London and Brussels compared', *Global Competition Policy*, May 2009, Release 1

'Due Process in EC competition cases: a distinguished institution with flawed procedures', (2009) 34 *E.L. Rev.* 817

'Google: The Benign Monopolist?', *GCP: The Antitrust Chronicle*, October 2009 (Release 2)

'A European Paradox: Imposing Market Reform 'Voluntarily'', paper delivered at the 1st Annual Concurrences Conference, 'New Frontiers of Antitrust', Paris, February 15, 2010; *Concurrences* No 2-2010

'Due process in competition proceedings: a practitioner's view from Brussels', *Concurrences* No 3-2010

'Obstacle to creation of EU-wide patent court', *World Intellectual Property Report*, BNA International, October 2010 (co-author)

'European Competition Law and the Indian Experience: A practitioner's view from Brussels', *Competition Law Reports (Commemorating the 1st Anniversary of the Competition Appellate Tribunal)*, Vol 1, New Delhi, 2010

'A Challenge for Europe's Judges: The Review of Fines in Competition Cases' (2011) 36 *E.L.Rev.* 185

'Google Books: Game and Set to the Sceptics; the Match Continues', *Competition Policy International Antitrust Chronicle*, June 2011 (2)

'Antitrust judicial review: Highlights of EU and national case laws', *Concurrences* N° 2-2011

'In Praise of "A Safe and Honourable Dispute"', presented at the International Rounds of the Philip Jessup Moot Court competition, 31 March 2012, Washington DC; *ILSA Quarterly*, volume 20, issue 4, May 2012

'Competition Law: the unpredictable ally of business', foreword to *Asian-Mena Counsel Special Report, Anti-Trust & Competition*, Vol. 10, Issue 4, 2012

'Is Common Sense Doomed? Choosing Between Rigid Clarity and Flexible Unpredictability', Social Science Research Network 19th St. Gallen International Competition Law Forum 2012 (ICF)

'A dangerous practice? Settling patent litigation is not such a bad idea', *Competition Law Insight*, 15 April 2014

'To Seek Leniency or Not To Seek Leniency: That Is The General Counsel's Question,' paper delivered at the Seminário sobre Compliance e Defesa da Concorência, 28 August 2014, Conselho Administrativo de Defesa Económicà/Centro de Estudos de Direito Econômico e Social, São Paulo, 2015

Chapters

EEC Section in *A Lawyer's Guide to International Business Developments*, edited by W. Surrey, Philadelphia, 1980 (co-author)

'EEC Competition Law on Agency' in *A Survey of Commercial Agency*, edited by H. Lidgard, Sacramento, 1984

Chapter on 'Distribution' in *International Anti-trust Law, Vol II*, edited by Julian Maitland-Walker, ESC Publishing Limited, 1984

'Recent Developments in EEC Trade Law' in *Legal Aspects of International Business Transactions II*, edited by D. Campbell and C. Rohwer, North-Holland, 1985 (co-author)

'EEC Trade Law and the United States', in *Annual Proceedings of the Fordham Corporate Law Institute*, Matthew Bender & Company Inc., New York, 1987

'Le rôle des avocats dans ce domaine: le lobbying' in *Union des Avocats Européens Conference Papers: Le Rôle du Parlement Européen pour la Défense des droits des opérateurs Economiques et citoyens communautaires*, 1993

'Sports and the EC' in *Sports Law & Finance*, IBC Legal Studies Publishing Ltd., Vol 2, Issue 3, September/October 1994

'The End of Innocence' in *Rules of Origin in International Trade: A Comparative Study*, edited by Edwin Vermulst, Paul Waer & Jacques Bourgeois, University of Michigan Press, 1994

'Opening the Procedure and its Effects: Notification of Complaints - the Statement of Objections' in *Droits de la défense et droits de la Commission dans le droit communautaire de la concurrence / Rights of defence and rights of the European Commission in EC Competition Law*, Bruylant, Bruxelles, 1994

'Competition Structures for the 21st Century', *Annual Proceedings of the Fordham Corporate Law Institute*, Matthew Bender & Company Inc., New York, 1994

'Le Lobbying' in *L'entreprise dans le marché unique européen*, Travaux de la CEDECE, La Documentation française, Paris, 1995

'The Role of the Lawyer' in *Robert Schuman Centre Annual Conference on European Competition Law 1996*, Kluwer Law International, 1997

Chapters on 'Costs, Legal Aid, Discontinuance, Service, Time Limits and Stay of Proceedings' in *European Courts Practice and Precedents*, Sweet & Maxwell, London, 1997 (co-author)

Chapter on 'Community Customs Law' in *Practitioners Handbook of EC Law*, Bar European Group/Trenton Publishing/Bar Council, 1998 (co-author)

'Current Goals of EC Competition Law', in *European Competition Law Annual 1997: Objectives of Competition Policy*, Hart Publishing, Oxford, 1998

'Modernisation of EC Competition Law', paper presented at the 26th Annual Conference on International Antitrust Law & Policy, Fordham Corporate Law Institute, October 1999, Fordham Corporate Law Institute 2000, Juris Publishing, Inc., New York, 2000; *Fordham International Law Journal*, Volume 23, April 2000, Number 4; reprinted in *EC Competition Law Reform*, Fordham Corporate Law Institute, Juris Publishing, Inc., Huntington, NY, 2003

'Regulating Deregulation: Achieving and safeguarding conditions for fair and efficient competition in the telecommunications industry: to whom should the task be entrusted?', in *European Competition Law Annual 1998: Regulating Communications Markets*, Hart Publishing, Oxford-Portland Oregon, 2000

'The Modernisation of EC Antitrust Policy: Compatibility, Efficiency, Legal Security', *European Competition Law Annual 2000: The Modernisation of EC Antitrust Policy*, Hart Publishing, 2001

Chapter on 'The European Law Background', in *European Employment Law and the U.K.*, Sweet & Maxwell, London, 2001 (co-author)

'The role of comparative law in the development of European law', paper on Intellectual Property aspects presented at the Swiss Institute of Comparative Law colloquium, April 2000 (*Publications de l'Institut suisse de droit comparé*, Volume 43, Schultheiss Zürich 2002)

'The Dangers of Too Much Precaution', chapter in *A True European: Essays for Judge David Edward*, Hart Publishing, 2003

'The use of comparative law in *A & Others v. National Blood Authority*', chapter in *Comparative Law Before the Courts*, British Institute of International and Comparative Law, 2004 (co-author)

'Diversity and Consistency: Can They Cohabit?', *European Competition Law Annual 2002: Constructing the EU Network of Competition Authorities*, Hart Publishing, 2004

'Modernisation: an extension of the powers of the Commission?' chapter in *Modernisation and Enlargement: two major challenges for EC competition Law*, D Gerardin Ed., Intersentia, 2004, pp. 83-97 (paper presented at Global Competition Law Centre, Bruges, First Annual Competition Conference 2004)

'Article 82: Remedies in Search of Theories?', paper presented at the 31st Annual Conference on International Antitrust Law & Policy, Fordham Corporate Law Institute, October 2004, 2004 *Fordham Corp. L. Inst.* 167, Juris Publishing, Inc., New York, 2005; and *Fordham International Law Journal*, Vol 28, Juris Publishing, Inc., New York, 2005

Chapters on 'Customs Valuation' and 'Customs Classification' in *The World Trade Organization: Legal, Economic and Political Analysis, Vol I*, 2005 Springer Science & Business Media Inc. (co-author)

'EC competition law as a limitation on the use of IP rights in Europe: is there reason to panic?', *European Competition Law Annual 2003: What is an Abuse of a Dominant Position?*, Hart Publishing, 2006

'Where law meets competition: is Wouters like a Cassis de Dijon or a platypus?', *European Competition Law Annual 2004: The Relationship Between Competition Law and the (Liberal) Professions*, Hart Publishing, 2006

'The Tension Between Regulation and Competitive Market Forces in Europe', chapter in *Companions and Crossroads: Essays in Honor of Shael Herman*, Tulane European & Civil Law Forum, Volume 21, 2006 (co-author)

'Beneath the Cherry Tree, in the Garden: European Thoughts on How to Enhance the Task of Uncovering and Thereby Deterring', *European Competition Law Annual 2006: Enforcement of Prohibition of Cartels*, Hart Publishing, 2007

'Remedies and Sanctions for Unilateral Conduct in Competition Cases', paper presented at the 34th Annual Conference on International Antitrust Law & Policy, Fordham Corporate Law Institute, October 2007, 2007 *Fordham Corp. L. Inst.* 559, Juris Publishing, Inc., New York, 2008

'Sector-Specific Price Regulation or Antitrust Regulation – A Plague on Both Your Houses?', *European Competition Law Annual 2007: A Reformed Approach to Article 82 EC*, Hart Publishing, 2008

'L'Europe des juges. Recent criticism of ECHR and ECJ judgments; the American debate on judicial activism versus judicial restraint', paper delivered to the Europaïsches Forum Alpbach/University of St. Gallen conference on 'The Role of International Courts', Salzburg, May 3-4, 2007; published in *The Role of International Courts,* German Law Publishers 2008

Chapter on 'Competition Law Adjudication', for American Bar Association 6-volume publication, *The Administrative Law of the European Union*, August 2008 (co-author)

'Parallel trade in prescription medicines in the European Union: the Age of Reason?', *Yearbook of Antitrust and Regulatory Studies (2008)*, Centre for Antitrust and Regulatory Studies, Warsaw University School of Management

'On Remedies, Abuses and the Links Between (Article 82 EC and Structural Remedies after Microsoft)', in *Current Developments on European and International Competition Law*, Carl Baudenbacher (Editor), Fifteenth St. Gallen International Competition Law Forum, University of St. Gallen, Helbing & Lichtenhahn Verlag, Basel 2008

'Creating new rules or closing easy cases? Policy consequences for public enforcement of settlements under Article 9 of Regulation 1/2003', *European Competition Law Annual 2008: Antitrust Settlements Under EC Competition Law*, Hart Publishing, Oxford and Portland Oregon, 2010

'*Victa placet mihi causa*: the Compulsory Licensing Part of the *Microsoft* Case', chapter in *Microsoft on Trial: Legal and Economic Analysis of a Transatlantic Antitrust Case*, L Rubini (Editor), Edward Elgar Publishers, 2010

'Compulsory Licensing in European Competition Law: The Power of the Adjective', chapter in *Intellectual Property and Competition Law: New Frontiers*, S Anderman and A Ezrachi (eds.) Oxford University Press, 2010 (co-author)

'Due process after *Menarini* and *Halcor*: is there any more to say?', *Guide to the World's Leading Competition and Antitrust Lawyers/Economists*, Euromoney Institutional Investor PLC, March 2010

'L'oralité devant les cours du Royaume Uni et européennes', paper delivered at the colloquium organised by the Ordre des avocats au Conseil d'état et à la Cour de cassation, Paris, 15 December 2008, published in *Thème et commentaires*, Dalloz, Paris 2011

'A Bush in Need of Pruning: the Luxuriant Growth of 'Light Judicial Review'', *European Competition Law Annual 2009: The Evaluation of Evidence and its Judicial Review in Competition Cases*, Claus-Dieter Ehlermann and Mel Marquis (Editors), Oxford and Portland Oregon 2011

'*Magill* Revisited', chapter for Liber Amicorum in honour of Jacques Bourgeois, Edward Elgar, 2011

'Arbitrating Competition Law Matters in Pharmaceutical Matters', chapter in *EU and US Antitrust Arbitration*, G Blanke and P Landolt (eds.) Wolters Kluwer, 2011 (co-author)

'The Interplay Between Standardization, IPR And Competition Law', in *Competition Law and Intellectual Property: A European Perspective*, ICLS-50, M Tavassi, G Muscolo, G Caggiano eds. Wolters Kluwer, 2012

'Facts are chiels that winna ding', paper presented at the 38th Annual Conference on International Antitrust Law & Policy 2011, 2011 *Fordham Corp. L. Inst.*, B. Hawk (Ed.), Juris Publishing, Inc., New York, 2012

'A Challenge for Europe's Judges: The Review of Fines in Competition Cases', The Role of the Court of Justice of the European Union in Competition Law Cases, *GCLC Annual Conference Series*, M Merola and J Derenne (eds.) Editions Bruylant, 2012

'*Post plures unum*: Streamlining and Simplifying Merger Procedures in an Era of Multijurisdictional Merger Filings', *European Competition Law Annual 2010: Merger Control in European and Global Perspective*, Philip Lowe and Mel Marquis (eds.) Hart Publishing, 2013

'Market Forces and Private Enforcement: A Start but some Way Still to Go', *European Competition Law Annual 2011: Integrating public and private enforcement of competition law. Implications for courts and agencies*, Philip Lowe and Mel Marquis (eds.) Hart Publishing, 2014 (co-author)

'Public enforcement and remedies in EU antitrust law', *Rights & Remedies in a Liberalised and Competitive Internal Market*, Eugène Buttigieg (Ed.), Gutenberg Press, Hal Tarxien, Malta, 2012

'Judicial review and competition law', *2013 Competition Case Law Digest* (N Charbit, E Ramundo, M Op-Courtaigne (eds.) Institute of Competition Law, 2012

'From Regulation 17/62 to Article 52 of the Charter of Fundamental Rights', *General Principles of EU Law and European Private Law*, Ulf Bernitz, Xavier Groussot & Felix Schulyok (eds.) Wolters Kluwer, 2013

'Judging the judgments: official creativity and judicial quality control', *Focus on Competition/Trends & Developments 2013-2014*, Karanovic/Nikolic, Belgrade, 2013

'Competition Law and Public Policy Considerations', *European Competition Law Annual 2012: Competition law, public policies and economic insecurity*, Philip Lowe and Mel Marquis (Editors), Hart Publishing, 2014

'*Quis custodiet ipsos custodies*? Assessing the judicial role in a lawful system of competition enforcement', *European Competition Law Annual 2013: Effective and Legitimate Enforcement*, Philip Lowe and Mel Marquis (eds.) Hart Publishing, 2014

'In Honour of the 20th Anniversary of the EFTA Court: The Style of the EFTA Court', chapter for inclusion in the EFTA Court's *20th Anniversary Festschrift*, Hart Publishing, 2014

'Quinquennial Thoughts: 2009-2014', 41st Annual Conference on International Antitrust Law & Policy 2014, 2014 *Fordham Comp. L. Inst.* 345, B Hawk (Ed.), Juris Publishing, Inc., 2015 (co-author)

'The European Commission and the ECN: Imagining the New Era – I would not start from here', *European Competition Law Annual 2014: Institutional Change and Competition Authorities,* Philip Lowe and Mel Marquis (eds.) Hart Publishing, 2015

'Trade policy in 2015 -- delivery time?', *Euromoney International Trade Expert Guide 2015* (co-author)

'Leniency: The Poisoned Chalice or the Pot at the End of the Rainbow?', *The Leniency Religion: Anti-Cartel Enforcement in a Contemporary Age,* Prof. Caron Beaton-Wells (Ed.), 2015 (co-author)

Part I

Salutations Tributes

Tribute

FRANCIS G. JACOBS

It is a real pleasure to contribute this tribute to a book in honour of Ian Forrester QC.

He is one of the most remarkable European lawyers of our time.

My own contacts with Ian started more than 40 years ago. Like many Scots, he sought to make his way outside his homeland, while remaining ever faithful to his native culture.

The accession of the United Kingdom to the then European Community in 1973 gave him what proved the perfect opportunity to hone his legal skills in Brussels with one of the leading US law firms, Cleary Gottlieb, at a time when I was a *referendaire* at the European Court of Justice in Luxembourg.

In 1981, Ian took a brave and, in the event, successful step: he co-founded with Christopher Norall the Brussels EC law firm of Forrester & Norall. That firm developed a substantial practice and a fine reputation. It subsequently became (with the participation of Alastair Sutton) Forrester Norall & Sutton. It merged with the leading law firm White & Case in 1998.

Throughout, Ian developed his practice and established himself as one of the leading practitioners, notably in antitrust and anti-dumping law, but also in many other fields of European Union law and international trade law. He has had a string of outstanding clients, in many parts of the world, and some outstanding successes in leading cases.

His practice has led him to reflect on issues of principle. Such issues seem constantly to arise in the application of antitrust and international trade law. The enormous level of fines in antitrust law, and the severe sanctions that may arise in international trade law, can cause increasing concern: and in Europe it is now accepted that, in particular, measures imposing such severe penalties can be justified only under stringent procedural and substantive guarantees. So for example the European Commission, in developing EU antitrust law as it may be entitled to do, may nevertheless be precluded from imposing fines if the type of conduct in issue has not previously been regarded as unlawful. Or new procedural safeguards may be required of officials responsible for enforcement. Those being investigated may be entitled to further protection: new rights of access to documents, or to opportunities to rebut allegations, may be properly invoked.

These matters have increasingly been of concern to Ian, not only in his advocacy, but also in papers he has published and lectures and seminars. They reflect his overriding concern for fairness.

But a tribute to Ian cannot rest on an account of his career and his professional achievements alone. Some more personal remarks are appropriate.

Ian's characteristic approach to a legal problem is to think it through aloud with those he consults, as in conversation. Indeed, his advocacy in court has sometimes followed the same conversational method. His cogitations seem to demonstrate his very essence as a reflective lawyer: perhaps a kind of juristic *cogito ergo sum*.

Sometimes, one reflection would lead rather circuitously to another, and it has been fascinating to follow such explorations, even if occasionally it might be thought to be taken too far - leading to the feedback, after one notable interview, that he was 'not concise'.

Ian has always been the most delightful company, with abundant conversation, and indeed cogitations, on law and other matters. Discussions have often been over meals, sometimes lengthy, but always instructive; stimulating and enjoyable at the same time. My memory goes back many years to a post-conference meal in New York, where after a considerable excursion by taxi I was first introduced to 'dim sum' – although that meal was not the origin or justification of the apophthegm *dim sum ergo non cogito*. Then there was 'fusion cooking', including some allegedly edible volcanic ash, in Tallinn. There was lunch on 'high table' at the Middle Temple in London.

Ian has done much in the public interest. He has taught EU law at universities and delivered many papers at seminars. As mentioned, he has taken seriously the need for respect for fundamental rights in the enforcement of the law – notably in the field of antitrust – and has published several searching articles in law journals on this subject.

He has also taken a lead on *pro bono* work: indeed he is head of White & Case's global *pro bono* practice. He has been involved in *pro bono* work for more than 45 years, although given his ever-youthful demeanour that may seem statistically improbable: he worked on the successful appeal to the US Second Circuit Court of Appeals 45 years ago on behalf of Louis Henry Burns, who was wrongly convicted on the basis of a coerced confession: see *Burns* v. *LaVallee*, 436 F.2d 1352 (2d Cir. 1970).

More generally, Ian has constantly and consistently demonstrated a concern for justice and fairness in the application of the law.

Pre-lunch oration from Saturday 27th June 2009

(The day after the award of his LLD by the University of Glasgow)

COLIN MACKAY

My Lords, Ladies and Gentlemen… I'd like to say a few words about my old and dear friend, Ian Stewart Forrester.

As Time's Wingèd Chariot Hurries Near bearing sweetmeats, pomegranates and goodness knows what further cornucopias of succulent goodies, these comments are few in number — and should therefore not lead to the situation of which the late Lord Justice of Appeal Lord Birkett (Norman Birkett) said he didn't mind if, during one of his after-dinner speeches, people occasionally glanced at their watches — but he did object when they shook them violently to make sure they were still going.

I cannot say what first drew me to Ian as a friend — it was perhaps his *debonair insouciance*, his ability to wear the Kelvinside Academy cap at a rakish angle, I cannot remember … but I suspect it had to do with our finding the same things funny to the point of mild hysteria. I remember attempts by our English master to introduce us to the *Pickwick Papers,* which were always doomed to failure because we kept dissolving in a fit of the giggles, drowning out his readings. This presented him with the problem that he could hardly tick us off for finding funny that which Dickens *meant* to be funny — but it was the start of a zany friendship which has endured for the best part of sixty years.

Pre-lunch oration from Saturday 27th June 2009
(The day after the award of his LL.D. by the University of Glasgow)

Ian and I both arrived at Kelvinside Academy on the same day in September 1949, along with Alan Rodger, who is disappointed not be able to be here today. We were all to go on to Glasgow University, then Alan went to Oxford … Ian went to New Orleans … and, like most journalists, I went to the pub. Most of you know his career, so I won't spell it out — but I pause only to remind you that he is a member of the Scottish Bar, the English Bar, the New York State Bar, and the Brussels Bar, that he has been a Q.C. for over twenty years, and that yesterday's richly-deserved honorary degree from his Alma Mater, Glasgow, is perhaps not even the peak — yet — of a career as a European competition lawyer whom his peers regard as being at the top of his tree, and as a Visiting Professor at the university of his youth. When I read the titles of his scores of learned publications, I have to go and lie down in a darkened room for a bit, because even the titles alone give me the hot flushes. What are we to make of 'Ex post assessment of Regulation 1/2003'? Or 'The interface between regulation, antitrust and consumer protection — is price regulation the answer?' (Just say yes — it's easier!) Or 'Beneath the Cherry Tree in the Garden — European thoughts on how to enhance the task of uncovering and thereby deterring.'

How did it all come about? When Ian was about 12 or 13 — I'm not very sure of the precise age — we first got a whiff of the formidable brain which was destined to collect facts, marshal them ruthlessly into incontestable arguments, sweeping all before them, and expertly concealing all the smoke and mirrors billowing and flashing their *faux messages* which is the art and craft of the truly gifted advocate. He proved, beyond peradventure, not a jot or tittle of doubt remaining, honest Guv, straight up, that *he was the King of Scotland* — or, rather, as Scots historians know, the King of Scots. '*Rex Scotorum*' were the proud words which lay beneath every one of his signatures. As in, 'I'm going to see Armstrong's *Last Goodnight* at the Citizens Theatre on Saturday afternoon. Do you want to come? Regards, Ian — *Rex Scotorum*.' Reams of paper, page after page after page, were produced in Ian's distinctive handwriting to prove his case. I have made a career of holding politicians to account in television and radio studios, including a Vice-President of the United States (Hubert Humphrey), eight Prime Ministers, twenty Secretaries of State for Scotland, and all four First Ministers — and Alan is a Lord of Appeal in Ordinary, used to casting a sceptical laser beam across every argument — yet he and I were *duped* to the point that, even when Ian *wasn't there*, we would refer, quite unironically, to 'The King' or to 'His Majesty'. Anyone listening in to our telephone conversations — 'The King is going to Copland and Lye in Sauchiehall Street to buy some more cufflinks' — might have suspected that these messages had the same earthshaking significances as those BBC wartime broadcasts: 'And now a message for our friends in Belgium — the storks are flying tonight', which meant a major combined ops assault was about to take place on the Flemish coast.

Another signature activity of I.S.F. is *travel* — lots and lots of it. I should say here that, in his Glasgow childhood, Ian lived in Cecil Street, Hillhead — which he was quick to tell one had previously been Sardinia Terrace. Very much in *Rex Scotorum* mode, he was as likely to refer to it by this rather raffish title as by the more prosaic

Cecil Street. I don't know whether you know this, Ian, but James 'Paraffin' Young, who made a colossal fortune for himself by discovering how to extract paraffin oil from shale, had a house in Sardinia Terrace — could it indeed have been yours? — to which he once invited Dr Livingstone, the explorer. So, maybe by a process of bricks-and-mortar property osmosis, the good doctor's *wanderlust* passed to you.

Anyway … Ian was still at University when he went to Afghanistan overland with Comex, the Commonwealth Expeditionary Force, as I suppose one might call it, under the legendary and charismatic Colonel Lionel Gregory. When still working with American law firms, he was negotiating with Yasser Arafat amongst others, at the time of Western airliners being blown up in the desert after being hijacked (in those innocent days there were not people still inside them). He found time to take tennis lessons with the professional at the Hotel Georges Cinque in Beirut. He once phoned me from Austria and said, 'I'm in Vienna -- and I haven't much time.' I faded up the Harry Lime *Third Man* theme in my head, wondering who were closing in on him in this *mitteleuropäische* cloak-and-dagger nightmare, until he said 'I've only six *schillinge* left and this operator won't take travellers' cheques.' And, in most recent times, an email is as likely to be replied to by BlackBerry from some Tokyo park.

Anyone who has been the recipient of the stunning hospitality of Sandra and Ian knows how much fun they extract from life, and how active they are, and how thorough in everything they do. It gave my wife Olive and me such a thrill to watch you being given an honorary degree in front of scores of young people about to graduate with law degrees — what an example you are to them. Your gentle affability was well summed up for me by the daughter of one of Olive's closest friends, who wanted, and gained from you, experience of working in an office specializing in European law. She is now carving out a formidable career of her own. I said, 'What did you make of Ian?' She said, 'He's just a lovely cuddly teddy bear.' I'm not sure you want to make that too public, in case those you oppose in court mistakenly think they can take you for a ride… but many will know what she meant.

But even cuddly teddy bears have to eat — so, in linking Sandra and the boys, and his sisters and the rest of the great clan:

I GIVE YOU A TOAST — DOCTOR IAN FORRESTER

Starting a law firm with Ian Forrester: a memoir

CHRISTOPHER NORALL

How do you start a law firm? I don't know if there's a recipe, but here's how Ian and I started ours. One Saturday in late July 1981, Ian invited me to lunch in his recently acquired gothic palace in Square Marie Louise. We had known each other for years, socially and as colleagues. I think each of us was vaguely aware that the other might be looking for something new, but in my recollection, it was just to be a nice social lunch, with no agenda, and no inkling of what direction the conversation would take. However it started, by the end of it, we had pretty much decided to start a new firm, subject to fleshing out what today would be called a business plan.

We were both leaving on vacation but when we got back in late August, we sat down together and jotted down a few calculations on a yellow pad. We kept the question simple — what would the expenses be, and how much work would we need to be sure we could live without being in penury? The answer was surprisingly easy: limit the initial investment to essentials, borrow a little working capital (which my parents generously provided and which we repaid well ahead of schedule), and we could keep our heads comfortably above water with relatively little work — something between a third and a quarter of the number of hours which we had been accustomed to billing. It was a no-brainer. We set November 2 for the opening.

September and October were fraught. We rented modest office space at 32 Rue Joseph II, which was being vacated by a down-at-heel travel agency. The trusty and indefatigable Pauline Tart bravely agreed to join the new venture as manager and secretary. Ian located a second hand Wang word processing system. We scoured shops for used furniture. An Italian carpenter who had previously worked for my mother knocked together and painted some basic office fittings. I bludgeoned and cajoled the telephone company into giving us lines (no small feat in those days). And many an evening Ian, Sandra and I dined at the 'Little Bones' restaurant down near the Gare du Midi, where you could get a decent Greek meal for a small price.

We opened on November 2. Ian brought two appeals in the European Court of Justice, one for the activist conservative MEP Lord Bethell, who was using litigation to try to persuade the European Commission to liberalize air transport, and the other for Control Data Corporation challenging the Commission's refusal to accord duty free treatment to the company's supercomputers. Then we were retained by Outboard Marine Corporation in an antidumping complaint targeting Japanese imports, a case which ran on for years.

Today, trade and customs law has become more of a niche practice, but then it was a very important part of the activity and policy of the EU, and especially important for Japanese and US multinationals. It made a huge contribution to the glittering client roster which we rapidly accumulated — Panasonic, Toshiba, Minebea, Toyota, Dupont, US Steel, to name but a few. It led naturally to assignments in areas such as competition law for these and other companies. Ian built on this platform to make particularly original and lasting contributions to the development of the law regarding parallel trade in the pharmaceutical sector, and on the interface between competition and intellectual property law.

We were also able to deliver some hefty blows in the debate on the evolution of competition law. Our 1984 article 'The Laicization of Community Law: Self-Help and the Rule of Reason: How Competition Law is and could be Applied' was, I believe, the first systematic account of how substantive interpretation and enforcement procedure could be restructured to allow the law to be applied by national courts and agencies, not just by the Commission. It generated great interest inside the Commission, and not a few protests that the time was not ripe. Eighteen years later the time was ripe, and our position was implemented pretty much lock, stock and barrel in Regulation 1/2003.

So we grew and prospered. In 1988 we were joined by Alastair Sutton, who, fresh from his service in Lord Cockfield's cabinet, provided us with enhanced credentials in dealing with the Commission. We trained up many able young lawyers and in due course were able to make some of them partners.

But times were changing, and so was the workplace for EU law in Brussels. The gospel of internationalization swept over the law firm world, especially the English-speaking part of it. The massive public relations effect of the Commission's 1992 programme made Brussels a must-have location for big UK and US firms, a trend that was accelerated by the adoption of the Merger Regulation in 1989. Like all the other boutiques in Brussels, we received many offers, and finally accepted to join White & Case in 1998.

My years of practice with Ian were halcyon years. We were in the right place at the right time. We were lucky — but we were also good. We were able to deliver excellent, clearly-focussed service to clients, value for money, and, for younger lawyers, rigorous training, useful experience and a clear career path — things which large firms in 2015, with their massive infrastructure, their bureaucracy, and their financial targets, sometimes struggle to achieve.

I salute Ian for his achievements, in some of which I was able to share. Perhaps the pendulum is swinging back a bit towards the kind of firm we started in 1981. Perhaps some young lawyers are having interesting conversations at lunch as I write. I hope so.

Tribute

ROBERT B. REICH

I have had the great privilege of knowing Ian S. Forrester QC for many years, even before he was dubbed a QC, which to my American ears sounds vaguely like a mathematical formula. Ian and I shared an office at a law firm that shall go unmentioned during the long summer of 1972, in a respectable-looking building in Brussels. At the time, I knew very little about the law, and I suspected Forrester QC knew even less. But I also had the misfortune of knowing almost no French, which was the language in which most legal discussion in the office was undertaken, while Forrester QC knew more of the *lingua franca*. As a result, we were equally incompetent, but clever enough to delude our superiors into thinking we were spending our time thinking great thoughts.

In the summer of 2001, we found one another again, this time in Edinburgh, where my family and I were vacationing, and where Forrester QC then had one of his homes. He invited us to dine in his ancient quarters, with his delightful American wife. Not only did he look precisely the same as he had almost three decades before, but he had also retained his wit and his charm. We vowed to stay in closer touch because if we waited another three decades we wouldn't dine together again until 2031, by which time his bright countenance, wit, and charm might have somewhat dimmed. But as I am prone to do, I got overly involved in American politics, while Forrester QC no doubt got overly involved in a wide array of issues, so that I now write without knowledge of what great feats he has achieved in the interim. Notwithstanding, I raise a glass here on the West Coast of the United States, in praise of a wonderful man and true friend, who deserves all the recognition and honour he can possibly muster.

An unfinished journey

PAULINE TART

I resisted editorial and other insistence that I offer a contribution to this tribute to Ian. I am not a writer, I pleaded, not a lawyer, or an erudite, celebrated and learned person from the judicial or other sphere, not a proper addition to the illustrious list gathered together to produce this book. But, they insisted, it will not be complete without something, anything from you. So I set on the journey to think where it started and where it has led.

1976, June: the start of a long, very hot summer in Belgium. I arrived with two suitcases, followed by a metal trunk, to begin a job with Cleary, Gottlieb, Steen & Hamilton, as secretary to two people, one Scottish, the other German, the common language English. Mr Forrester was young, with copper-coloured hair and beard, and drove, I later learned, a yellow Triumph Spitfire.[1] At my interview, he had drily remarked that the job would be boring, lots of repetition, re-drafting, sometimes long hours. An unappetising introduction, perhaps, but definitely intriguing, and I accepted. On my first day, Ian was not in Brussels but in New York, a city ever since a routine part of his life. I was therefore put at the disposal of partner Richard Webster, known for his ruthless insistence on perfectly-typed texts, no error admitted. Those were the days of IBM golf-ball typewriters, real cutting-and-pasting, carbon copies on flimsy paper — yellow, pink and blue — for different files. Any mistake meant delicate erasing with a typing rubber on the original and on each of the carbon copies, a fastidious task and one to be avoided. I managed and, once initiated to the language of the legal world in which I was to move, turned into a fast, accurate typist.

One of Ian's duties was regularly to contribute to producing the firm's EEC Reporting series on trade developments and competition developments, for dispatch to clients and potential clients. Lomé Convention, the Maghreb, GATT soon were familiar vocabulary. 1976 was the year of European Commission competition decisions in *Hoffmann-La Roche (Vitamins)*, *CSV*, *Pabst & Richarz*, *Reuter/BASF*, *Miller*, *Junghans*,

1 Thanks to my husband for pointing out that a Spitfire is an aircraft, and a Triumph Spitfire a car.

Theal-Watts followed in 1977, among others, by *De Laval-Stork*, *Hugin/Liptons* and – closer to a Scottish heart – *Distillers*. The Court of Justice, meanwhile, kept us busy in 1976 with judgments in *SABAM*, the *Sugar* cases, *EMI/CBS*, *Terrapin/Terranova*. Ian would dictate lengthily, pausing frequently for reflection, telephone calls would interrupt; I listened, taking down his musings in shorthand interspersed with longhand for the unknown and new names, glad he spoke slowly.

Ian's first plunge into writing for publication was before my time, in 1970, 'Maintaining Trade Secrecy', followed in 1971 by a pamphlet on 'The German Legal System', in 1974 by 'Jurisdiction of National and Community Bodies in Competition Matters after *SABAM*', then a translation and introduction to the German Civil Code, the German Commercial Code, and German Marriage Law, which led me to think that Ian must be fluent in German. Not quite so, he had a co-author, but an example of his refusal not to take up any challenge. He still refers to the 'BGB', pronounced in the German fashion, and ends sentences saying '*Punkt*'. I arrived at the tail-end of that project, but learnt the importance of keeping track of names, telephone numbers, bits of paper, a habit that would serve me and others well over the years. He had already participated in the writing of two-inch-thick tomes for Japanese clients on the application of the EEC's competition rules to imports from Japan, distributorship and agency agreements under the EEC's competition rules, the rules on mergers, joint ventures and acquisitions, and negative clearance and exemptions. This first contact with Japan developed into a keen interest and deep love for that country, its traditions, culture and people.

My first real taste of Ian's liking for the learning and the development of theories through writing articles came with a piece on 'Distribution and Agency Agreements in EEC Competition Law', then we moved on to customs law, the rules of origin and preferential duty treatment. Dry stuff, but the charming introduction relates not facts, rules and regulations, but the reflections of Lady Grisell Baillie, a fearless Scottish noblewoman, who — not in the prime of youth - embarked in 1731 on the Grand Tour of Europe, and left to her heirs a guide to travel around Continental Europe, in which she offered advice on dealing with 'the searchers', the customs and like agents responsible for collecting duties and tolls and enforcing currency controls. The opening paragraphs show the care, still exercised, given to writing to attract and retain attention. Few of Ian's articles have appeared without some historical reference, a witness to his love of language and history, while allowing no supporting evidence to go unexplored. They are used as a tool not only to keep his own knowledge sharp, but to educate younger lawyers in the art of writing attractively, seeking unusual theories, ensuring any argument is substantiated, and not being afraid to be provocative as long as the proposition is defensible. Some have succeeded moderately, some brilliantly, but I suggest that no *protégés* have forgotten Ian's contribution to their futures, whether or not as member of the legal profession, and that all hold their mentor in affectionate respect.

Court pleadings, oral hearings, public and private conferences, contributions to books and, in more recent times, sermons for the Church of Scotland, have all become outlets for intense writing episodes.[2] It may be that the sermons, with perhaps the least number of pages, require the most effort and energy. They are the fruit of long ruminations, exchanges with the fertile minds of family and friends, much reading, and a last minute rush of energy in the week before the day. Ian has confessed that the most challenging part of leading a service is not, however, the sermon (for the adults), but the children's address, since children are unpredictable, and there is no knowing in advance how they might respond to a question. He has, with the inventiveness shown also in the many unprepared and improvised speeches he has given in varied circumstances, never to my knowledge been flummoxed.

His career of writings, spanning over a hundred published pieces, has taken us through kilos of paper, large quantities of pencils, hours of drafts, re-writing, proof-reading, foot-note verification, correction. Drafts have been reviewed on flights, in airports, on his rare real holidays, in a vast array of countries. Ian not only travels with pleasure, but has rarely the heart to say no to an invitation to address a conference, a high-level meeting, give a lecture, speak to a group of students, join in a university gathering. Travel arrangements have consumed many hours. Despite the innumerable flights taken I cannot recall more than one or two missed ones, one of which was his first visit during my career to India. I had omitted to check visa requirements, so Ian arrived at the airport for the flight to New Delhi without a visa and, for once despite his ability to talk his way out of difficulties, was not allowed on the flight. Expected for the first time there as a speaker at a large conference, and in my absence by then on holiday, he deployed all his resourcefulness, gained entry to consular officials in Brussels out-of-hours, a time when no ordinary person would have prevailed, obtained his visa in record time, and flew into New Delhi to take the platform at the appointed hour. Ian's kindness towards human failing meant that I was not chastised, but I was embarrassed. A lesson was learnt too, not only to check visa requirements, but that personal skills and amicable relations can make a very big difference to the success of an enterprise.

The journey has included upheavals, too: reaching the end of five years with Cleary Gottlieb, five in those days being a minimum to look good on one's *curriculum vitae* (fewer being indicative of lack of skills, unsuitability for the job, unreliability or instability), I envisaged a change of tack. Thoughts turned to a job with a Belgian company in Algeria, which seemed more adventurous than Brussels. I proffered my notice to Ian, who refused it, whispering that he had ideas of moving on, setting up his own boutique firm, and would I be part of the team? I still reflect on which was the wisest course. Life in Brussels was quite different then to what it is today; the 'international' community mingled little with the locals; European Commission staff were a nation apart; there were in general many fewer outsiders working in the city. Life in Algeria would also have been in a compound, but a decidedly more restricted one. Ian's powers of persuasion prevailed, and on 1 November 1981, a public holiday, Ian, Chris Norall, our part-time accountant/bookkeeper, and I gathered in our new

2 His favourite Bible reading, Luke 24: 13-31, tells also of a journey, that of the disciples on the road to Emmaus.

offices at 36 rue Joseph II to stick stamps on piles of envelopes announcing the opening of 'the establishment of the legal practice of Forrester & Norall, specializing in the law of the European Economic Community and International Transactions.' We had a postal address, a telephone number and a telex number. No fax, and certainly no e-mail in those times. Life was dire when the telephone line was cut off, and again maintaining personal relationships was precious; the man at the telephone company was an indispensable ally. It was a great day, too, when the first cheque in payment of fees arrived through the post. There were multinational names among those first clients, several of which remain in the fold to this day.

Individuals and small enterprises had their importance, too. Lord Bethell's application to the Court of Justice (against the European Commission's failure to act on his request to take action with respect to the observance of the competition rules in the air transport sector) had been submitted in September 1981, whilst Ian was still at Cleary Gottlieb, with now long-time friend Mario Siragusa. Ian pled the case in Luxembourg on 18 March 1982: the outline for his argument runs to 13 A4 pages in 1.5 spacing. Despite his eloquence, we lost that case, but another day in court came soon thereafter on 17 June 1982, arguing on behalf of a large corporation that the product 'Corian' should be classified for customs purposes as artificial stone. Samples of different materials were required, some of which still have a place among the memorabilia in Ian's office.

Before those two cases, Ian had indicated his strong leaning towards fair competition and justice for all, in taking up the defence of a tiny whisky distiller, Bulloch, as an intervening party in the European Commission's action against the giant Distillers Company in 1978. I had the privilege of attending the Court hearing in January 1980. Sitting at an animated dinner table the night before the hearing with Sandy Bulloch and the team, I recall hoping all would be fresher and sharper of tooth for the next morning's hearing than I myself was likely to be. Suffice it to say that, much to our pleasure, our side won.

In 1989, Forrester & Norall enlarged with the arrival of Alastair Sutton, a European Commission official on the case team leading a dumping investigation in Japan. Forrester Norall & Sutton moved to new, larger premises in the Tour Madou, where the panoramic view from our offices on the 27th floor and a desk facing east gave me the recompense for long and hard days of some magnificent sunrises in the morning, and in the evening from the other side of our floor a similar view of sunsets over the Grand'Place. Fire drills were an interesting interlude, with descent from the 27th floor by the metal safety stairs outside, sometimes in wild and windy weather. On occasion, infrequently but grimly, there were suicides from the top of the building. Then came *tractations* with the landlord, whose intention was to renovate the building. First, it was to be that office space would be ours during the works; later it transpired that could not be the case. The hunt for new premises opened. We needed offices near the European Commission, with the possibility for expansion, easy for public transport access (staff always kept in mind), and corresponding to budgetary requirements. We officially moved to 62 rue de la Loi on 28 May 2001, at a time of labour unrest in Brussels, with the result that our new home was the target of egg-throwing. Once calm was restored, a thorough clean-up rendered it once again red and white. The Tour Madou was in the meantime stripped of all but the structure and now, to my amusement at least, my former view is enjoyed by European Commission officials in DG Competition, some of whom had indeed walked its floors as Forrester Norall & Sutton associates or trainees.

Then, in 1998, came a big change, the 'marriage' of Forrester Norall & Sutton with White & Case, an association which was to offer to both wider opportunities for interesting and profitable business opportunities. The transition was not easy; understanding the formalities required by a large American infrastructure was hard for our relatively relaxed European habits, much effort, much paperwork, many hours were consumed, but the hard work led to a continuingly successful and, I suggest, mutually rewarding practice.

From the offices of Cleary Gottlieb at rue de la Loi 23, to Forrester & Norall in rue Joseph II to the Tour Madou back to rue de la Loi 62 has been an adventure with too many twists and turns, hills and vales to be recounted here, even were my memory to allow. These few lines cannot do true justice to the many people who have come and gone, some to the Commission, some to other law firms, some to set up their own firms, some to industry, to teaching, to many places around the world. I believe they have all taken away the memory of a satisfying, stimulating professional and personal experience, due much in part to the leadership of Ian and his insistence on people as human beings who will give of their best there where they are perhaps pushed hard, but equally encouraged to take up challenges, motivated to go beyond what they imagine being capable of and, always, his open door, his invitation to develop skills in the written and the spoken word, his wise advice on the vast range of anxieties brought to his attention.

The adventure has not quite yet ended, and at the time of writing may take another twist, and another direction. Ian has never been of a mind to pronounce that he would retire one day, rather that he would not. I shall, one day, but what will remain is the memory of very full, demanding years, which have often challenged me, but which have invariably been rewarded with words of thanks, gestures of affection and appreciation, and brought recompense in many forms, not least being surrounded each day by a warm, articulate, intelligent, deeply human set of people. Few on this planet have that advantage, and I am hugely indebted, enormously grateful to Ian for his making it mine.

Ian has in recent years been invited on several occasions to contribute to a *Festschrift* or a *Liber Amicorum* or an Essay to honour a friend. He has taken the task always seriously, but with always with particular pleasure. Probably, I felt, he hopes one day to be the recipient of such a work. I seem to recall, when the idea was first whispered of, that Makis Komninos asked, "Do you really think he would like that?" I could answer, wholeheartedly and truthfully, that yes indeed, he would. I know he will be deeply touched by this tribute to his career, to his personal talents, and to his professional legacy. May he enjoy reading it, too.

Part II

EU Law & Policies

Should the EU judiciary be decentralized?

JOSEF AZIZI*

I. Prologue

The present contribution can certainly not be more than a sketch of some personal reflections. But it is meant symbolically as homage to Ian Forrester: indeed, I had the pleasure to witness his skills, intellect and wisdom both as a pleading barrister in Court and as an academic teacher. Having furthermore the privilege to be on amicable terms with him, I hope he will accept this wee personal tribute with benignity.

II. Introduction of the topic

1. Basic idea

To start with, just a point of clarification: the following fleeting glimpse firmly bases itself on the premise that the European Union as it stands today is on the whole sensible, absolutely necessary and geared to the future. In the same vein, there cannot be any serious challenge to the fact that the Union, in order to realize and to maintain the overall concept of a unique supranational legal order, needs a minimum of centralized legislative, executive and judicial authorities of its own.

However, it not infrequently happens that the European Union is criticized for shaping its citizens' lives by means of centralistic and unilateral decisions. Thus, one might ask oneself to what extent in particular the judicial system of the Union could be the

* The author would like to thank Fiorentina Azizi for critically reading through the manuscript.

object of criticism as to certain centralistic features, and, if so, whether this should give rise to a less centralized structure or functioning.

2. Terminological clarifications

Before starting this brief overview, it would seem appropriate to outline the main elements of our topic.

(a) The 'EU judiciary'

The Court of Justice has frequently defined and refined the characteristics of a 'court or tribunal of a Member State' in the sense of Article 267 TFEU.[1] Roughly speaking, those characteristics of such a judicature would be that it is independent (its members must not be given instructions, removed or relocated), that it is established by law, that it is permanent, that its jurisdiction is compulsory, that it has an *inter partes* procedure and that it applies rules of law.

It would seem that these characteristics might well be generalized to define any kind of judiciary in an EU law context.[2] Hence, from a *functional* point of view, the EU relevant judicature includes any judicial body endowed with the power of deciding, in principle with final *res iudicata* effect, questions of EU law. Within this judicial universe, however, from an *organizational*[3] point of view, a clear distinction has to be made between the national[4] courts of the Member States, on the one hand, and the judiciary of the European Union, on the other hand. In the latter sense, the EU judiciary is identical with the *Court of Justice of the European Union*, which–pursuant to Article 19, para 1, TEU[5]–is the collective term for all courts of the European Union: it includes the Court of Justice ("ECJ"), the General Court ("EGC") and specialized courts.[6] It is in this strictly organizational sense that the term 'EU judiciary' shall be used throughout the following remarks.

(b) The term 'decentralization'

Equally, it would seem adequate to outline, for the purpose of our discussion, the term 'decentralization' in a judicial context, and even more specifically with regard to EU law. The following short essay shall distinguish between the terms 'centralization' or 'decentralization' on the one hand and 'concentration' or 'deconcentration' on the other. To this effect, a judicial task or competence would be *centralized* to the extent

---

1 See Consolidated versions of the Treaty on European Union (TEU) and the Treaty on the Functioning of the European Union (TFEU), OJ 2012 C 326 of 26 October 2012, p. 01 (http://eur-lex.europa.eu/legal-content/EN/TXT/?uri=uriserv:OJ.C_.2012.326.01.0001.01.ENG#C_2012326EN.01004701).

2 However, there does not seem to be a strict requirement of a full fetched '*inter partes* procedure' as to ECJ proceedings under Articles 218 or 267 TFEU.

3 I.e., as to the establishment of a court, the appointment of its members and its (budgetary and administrative) maintenance.

4 Or multinational: see, e.g., the Benelux Court of Justice.

5 See *supra* note 1.

6 At present established: the European Union Civil Service Tribunal (ECST): see the decision published in OJ L 325 of 12.12.2005, p. 1.

to which one single court would have, at the same instance level, exclusive jurisdiction on a certain matter or type of proceedings. By contrast, *decentralization* would mean that a plurality of courts is, at the same instance level, competent to deal with a certain matter or type of proceedings. Equally, there would be a *concentration* of judicial tasks or competences, if only one single court is the first and the last instance for a certain matter or type of proceedings. On the contrary, judicial tasks or competences are *deconcentrated*, if there is more than one level of judicial review for a certain matter or type of proceedings.

It goes without saying that these distinctions refer to the *external* position of the respective court within the overall system of legal remedies, and this is the sense in which these terms shall be employed here further on. But for the sake of completeness, let us add that within one particular court, the judicial work might be also *internally* more or less 'decentralized' or 'centralized', to the extent to which cases are attributed to single judges, small or larger chambers or to the plenary.

3. The relevance of judicial decentralization in an EU law context

As a matter of principle,[7] the Member States' judiciaries are by definition located in the various Member States. They are obviously *decentralized* with regard to the application of EU law, in as much as they exercise in parallel competences of jurisdiction not exceeding the territory of their respective Member States. Yet, whether and to what extent, *within* a Member State, the judicial powers of the national judiciary are centralized or decentralized, respectively concentrated or deconcentrated, depends on the relevant internal legal order.

As for the EU judiciary, it is equally obvious that it is wholly *centralized*: indeed, each of the EU Courts in Luxembourg[8] has exclusive jurisdiction, at its instance level, for certain EU matters and/or for certain types of EU judicial proceedings. The EU judiciary is nonetheless deconcentrated inasmuch as, for actions falling within the scope of jurisdiction of the EGC according to Article 256, para. 1, TFEU, the EGC is acting as an autonomous first instance court under appeals review by the ECJ. The same is true for matters intrusted at first instance level to the ECST, as specialized court, with the EGC acting as second instance court[9] (and with the exceptional possibility of a further review by the ECJ[10]). The relevant Treaty provisions presently in force would, for the future, *allow greater deconcentration* through the creation of additional specialized courts[11] and through the possible transfer of any present ECJ competences to the EGC[12] (including preliminary rulings in specific areas[13]). By contrast, they leave *no room for decentralizing* the EU judiciary.

---

7 I.e., *mutatis mutandis* for multinational Member States' courts, see *supra* note 4.

8 See Sole Article, lit d), of Protocol (No 6) TFEU on the location of the seats of the institutions and of certain bodies, offices, agencies and departments of the European Union.

9 Cf. Art. 256, para. 2, subparagraph 1, TFEU.

10 Cf. Art. 256, para. 2, subparagraph 2, TFEU.

11 Cf. Art. 257, paras. 1 and 2, TFEU.

12 Cf. Art. 256, para. 1, subparagraph 1, second sentence, TFEU.

13 Cf. Art. 256, para. 3, TFEU.

4. Our issue

(a) General statement

(i) EU related tasks of Member States' judiciaries

In quantitative terms, it should be recalled that the national courts are in charge of the vast majority of EU-relevant cases.[14] Indeed, the implementation and application of EU law lies mostly within the competences of the Member States and, moreover, the legality of their behaviour[15] is in the first place to be reviewed by the respective national judiciary.

(ii) Tasks of the EU judiciary

Nonetheless, it is the *EU judiciary* which *ensures the homogeneity and uniformity of legal practice under the Treaties*, by having the final say as to the legality of the interpretation and application of EU law.[16]

In performing its tasks, the EU judiciary has, on the one hand, to review the legality of the behaviour set (or envisaged[17]) by the institutions and other organizational entities[18] *of the Union*. This concerns both the appraisal of the validity of general and individual EU legal acts in the framework of preliminary ruling proceedings[19] as well as, on the basis of direct actions, the legal review of general or individual legal acts adopted[20] (or envisaged[21]) by EU bodies, respectively of their alleged inaction.[22] Also with respect to EU bodies, the EU judiciary has inter alia jurisdiction concerning non-contractual damages allegedly caused by them[23] and pursuant to arbitration clauses.[24]

---

14 As is well known, the national judge is frequently characterized in this functional sense as the 'first European judge' or as the 'ordinary judge of the Union'. This characterization is a consequence of the pertinent case law of the ECJ (cf. e.g., Judgment in *Amministrazione delle Finanze dello Stato v Simmenthal SpA*, C-106/77, EU:C:1978:49).

15 I.e., the behaviour of Member States' legislative, administrative and judicial authorities.

16 See Art. 19, para. 1, second sentence, TEU.

17 See Art. 218, para. 11, TFEU, concerning the ECJ competence to give an opinion on the compatibility of draft agreements with the Treaties.

18 Like 'bodies, offices or agencies of the Union' (cf. Art. 263, para. 1, TFEU).

19 Cf. Art. 267 TFEU.

20 See Art. 263 TFEU.

21 See Art. 218, para. 11, TFEU, concerning the ECJ competence to give an opinion on the compatibility of draft agreements with the Treaties.

22 See Art. 265 TFEU.

23 See Arts. 268 and 340, para. 2, TFEU.

24 See Art. 272 TFEU.

Apart from this, the EU judiciary is entrusted with assessing directly (in the course of infringement proceedings[25]) or indirectly (as a side effect of preliminary ruling proceedings or of certain direct actions[26]) the legality *of Member States*' behaviour.

Last but very importantly, the EU judiciary is called upon to give a uniform interpretation of EU law in answer to requests by Members States' courts for preliminary rulings.

Thus, the jurisdiction of the EU judiciary encompasses, together with its overall competence to give a uniform interpretation of EU law, the review of legality under EU law, for the Union as well as for its Member States, of their respective behaviour.

Whereas notably preliminary rulings proceedings and infringement proceedings are part of the ECJ's jurisdiction, most[27] direct actions fall–on first instance level - under the jurisdiction of the EGC.

(b) Outline of the problem at stake

Against this background, a question one might ask oneself is whether and to what extent the present structures and division of responsibilities amongst the different bodies of the EU relevant judicature could or even should be examined under the aspect of structural and substantive weight redistribution. More precisely: does the entirely centralized character of the EU judiciary meet the needs of an adequate judicial system in a Union of at present 28 Member States?[28]

A profound analysis of this question would undoubtedly go well beyond the scope of the present contribution. But this does not exclude a brief overview of some possibly relevant aspects.

(c) Possible arguments for decentralizing the EU judiciary

In favour of decentralizing the EU judiciary, substantially the following general points might be put forward, most of which correlating in one way or another with factors of propinquity: the geographical distance, language problems, little confidence in the judiciary because of an alleged lack of understanding for national particularities as well as because of an alleged lack of participation in and lack of transparency of its proceedings. In addition, these and other points might be raised under the aspect of efficiency in order to advocate calls for decentralization.

25 See primarily Arts. 258-260 TFEU.

26 E.g., concerning State Aid.

27 N.B. with the important exceptions foreseen in Art. 51 of the Statute. Notably the fact that Member States' actions against acts of EU legislation are exclusively entrusted to the ECJ seems to clarify its role as an 'EU constitutional court.'

28 If not: should a decentralization of the EU judiciary be realised through the establishment of decentralized EU courts or by a transfer of jurisdiction to national/multinational Member States' judiciaries?

Nevertheless, it should already be specified from the outset that, as a rule, arguments invoking *subsidiarity*[29] in favour of decentralizing the EU judiciary would not have their place in this context. Indeed, the subsidiarity principle only applies to areas which do not fall within the Union's exclusive competence.[30] Yet, on the one hand, legislating on the EU judicature falls by definition in the exclusive competence of the Union.[31] On the other hand, decentralizing the EU judiciary would in any case need a modification of EU primary law (thus potentially overriding or limiting anyhow other[32] rules of that same normative level, of which the principle of subsidiarity).

(d) Possible ways of decentralizing the EU judiciary

(i) Legislative measures

As a matter of fact, since the essentials of the EU judiciary's present shape[33] are fixed in the Treaties, any alteration as to their wholly centralized character would require a prior *Treaty amendment*. To what extent and which other legal bases would have to be amended depends on the model of decentralization envisaged.

(ii) Possible models of decentralization

There would be various possible models for an eventual decentralization of the EU judiciary: On the one hand, decentralization could be achieved by the creation of *regional EU Courts*, i.e., by parallel judicial bodies of the European Union which are competent to exercise jurisdiction under EU law in a regionally limited district. Such regional EU Courts would in *organizational terms*[34] *as well as in functional terms*, be *part of the judicature of the Union*. On the other hand, a judicial decentralization would also be achieved if present tasks of the EU judiciary were transferred to *national courts of the Member States* or to *inter-Member States' courts*.[35] In such a context, these would then be-*organizationally* speaking–*Member States' courts* which would *functionally* act as *EU Courts*.[36]

29 N.B.: Generally speaking, in conformity with the principle of subsidiarity, the lowest or least centralised authority which is capable of addressing an issue effectively should do so. Specifically for the relationship between the European Union and its Member States, the subsidiarity principle has found its very particular shaping in Art. 5, para. 3, TEU.

30 Cf. Art. 5, para. 3, subparagraph 1, TEU.

31 This is even true in areas of law which fall in the concurrent competence of the EU and its Member States: indeed, as soon as the Union brings up substance legislation in such an area, the competence of legislating on the competent judiciary would, in parallel, fall within the Union's jurisdiction. Needless to add that, moreover, the judiciary competent to judge the legality of such legislation under EU law would anyway be the EU judiciary.

32 So called 'substantive Derogation' ('*materielle Derogation*'. See, for many others: Benjamin Kneihs, *Verfassungs- und Allgemeines Verwaltungsrecht*, Facultas Verlags- und Buchhandels AG Vienna 2008, p. 30; Theo Mayer-Maly, *Einführung in die Rechtswissenschaft*, Springer Verlag 2013, p.11.).

33 Including, inter alia, the centralized seat of the EU judiciary in Luxembourg (see note 8 *supra*).

34 See *supra* note 3.

35 Like the Benelux Court of Justice.

36 As to the different categories of merely *functional* EU Courts, see Josef Azizi, 'Ausgewählte Aspekte der Gerichtsbarkeit der Europäischen Union: Grundlegende Prämissen und aktuelle Entlastungsfragen', in: F.Leidenmühler/J.Eder/L. Leingartner/C.Winkler (edts.), *Grundfreiheiten – Grundrechte – Europäisches Haftungsrecht; Beiträge zum 11. Österreichischen Europarechtstag 2011* in Linz, nwv Neuer Wissenschaftlicher Verlag, Wien/Graz (2012), pp. 23ff (29-32).

III. Possible assessment criteria

Before having a look at our question, it seems adequate to define parameters for assessing whether it would be appropriate to somewhat decentralize the EU judiciary.

1. The overall standard: basic functionality of the judicial power and judicial legitimacy

(a) The essential function of a judiciary and its link with judicial legitimacy

In the context of our focus, the essential function of any judiciary and the suitability of a judicature to comply with this function's requirements would constitute the overall standard for assessing that judicature's degree of centralisation or decentralization in terms of legitimacy and adequacy. Indeed, any legal measure concerning the shaping and competences of the judiciary must in the first place be examined as to whether it is in line with or serves at the best a judiciary's overall purpose and central judicial function. Otherwise, if the measure envisaged risks to harm this function, it would seem advisable not to take it. In case the measure was completely neutral with respect to these criteria, other considerations, such as budgetary factors, might be decisive.

The *basic functionality of the judicial power* could, roughly speaking, be seen as *safeguarding or re-establishing social peace and legal certainty by resolving conflicts of interest without recourse to violence*.[37] Ideally, this basic durability or lasting effect of resolving conflicts through judicial activities should be twofold: it should not only put an end to the matter of litigation decided (remedying effect), but it should also clarify the litigious legal question in such a way that future similar conflicts might be prevented both between the parties of the case decided as well as beyond that individual case (preventive effect). This latter element is of particular importance for realizing the EU judicature's task to ensure uniform interpretation and application of EU law.

Trying to achieve and put constantly into practice this basic functional aim is a highly demanding and never ending exercise requiring permanent efforts. Its lasting success in social reality depends ultimately to a large extent on the acceptance and legitimacy, for the general public, of the judicial system. Hence, the legitimacy of an operative judiciary is at the same time not only a useful effect, but also an essential precondition of long term judicial functionality.

Similarly, as a consequence, it can be said that, on the one hand, durably effective legal protection is certainly a result of the willingness to accept judicial decisions and is thus a consequence of judicial legitimacy. But, on the other hand, effective legal protection is also in itself an essential tool for reaching and maintaining judicial legitimacy.

---

37 *Mutatis mutandis*, this legal security factor applies not only to litigations between parties, but also to any judicial proceedings on the 'abstract' assessment and–possibly–annulment or invalidation of general norms outside of litigation proceedings.

(b) Factors of efficiency ensuring the legitimacy of judicial activities[38]

(i) General remark

Under articles 13 and 6 (1) of the European Convention on Human Rights[39] and article 47 of the Charter of Fundamental Rights[40] ('Right to an effective remedy and to a fair trial') the following criteria for an *effective legal protection* have been recognized in the relevant case-law: independence and legal foundation of the tribunal, public character of the proceedings, rights of the defence and similar procedural rights, reasonable time-frame, rights to adjacent procedural measures. Each of these crucial criteria has been developed, explained and nuanced in numerous decisions.

Yet, on the whole, it is even quite beyond these established criteria of effective legal protection that *factors of efficiency*[41] contribute in an essential manner to the legitimacy of judicial activities. These legitimating factors could be roughly classified in the following categories.

(ii) Categories of efficiency related factors for judicial legitimacy

1. Judicial legitimacy and efficiency through the convincing quality[42] of judicial decisions[43]

2. Independence- and impartiality-related organizational elements of judicial legitimacy and efficiency[44]

---

38 See, e.g., Josef Azizi, 'Direktklagen und Sonderbereiche beim Gericht erster Instanz', in Everling/Müller-Graff/Schwarze (eds.) *Die Zukunft der Europäischen Gerichtsbarkeit nach Nizza*, EuR Beiheft 1-2003, pp. 87ff (91) ; *in extenso* Jean-Marc Sauvé, 'Les critères de la qualité de la justice', in *Cour de Justice de l'Union européenne (ed.), De 20 ans à l'horizon 2020 — Bâtir le Tribunal de demain sur de solides fondations, Célebration des 20 ans du Tribunal de première instance des Communautés européennes* (2010), pp. 30 ff (30 f passim) with further references.

39 Convention for the Protection of Human Rights and Fundamental Freedoms (ECHR) [www.echr.coe.int/Documents/Convention_ENG.pdf].

40 Charter of Fundamental Rights of the European Union (CFR), OJ 26.10.2012, Nr. C 326/391 [EUR-Lex - 12012P/TXT - EN]. Explanations: OJ 14.12.2007, Nr. C 303/17 [EUR-Lex - 32007X1214(01) – EN].

41 As to factors of judicial efficiency with regard to intellectual property law, see Thomas Jäger, *System einer europäischen Gerichtsbarkeit für Immaterialgüterrechte*, Springer-Verlag Berlin/Heidelberg (2013), passim (p. 567f): In this respect, he advocates essentially priority for the following factors, in terms of clout, for a judicial system of powerful efficiency ('*effektives Durchsetzungssystem*'): clearly defined judicial competences, uniform interpretation, high professional qualification and swift proceedings.

42 It goes without saying that the realization of high standard judicial decisions is intimately linked to the professional qualification of judges (see note 44 *infra*).

43 In terms of rationality and reasonable thinking, the ultimate achievement conveying legitimacy on a judiciary would be the *convincing quality of judicial decisions*. In order to match with these postulates, a judicial decision should have the following characteristics: the judicial decision should have a sufficiently *predetermined legal frame* (as to the organizational, procedural and substantial rules to be applied), including in particular fundamental rights, allowing for the *foreseeability* of judicial action. The *reasoning* of the judicial decision should be clear, coherent and complete. It should allow to understand and to justify the operative part of a judgment by dealing with the essential arguments and facts of the case in light of the legal frame. It should also show, to the greatest possible extent, coherence with the existing case law. The *operative part* of the judgment should be unambiguous and complete.

44 Inter alia with regard to the core requirement of judicial independence and impartiality, the legitimacy of a judiciary depends on a range of *organizational features* entailing the basic image of its efficiency for a wider public. *First*, the *personal legitimacy* of the judges: this includes the absence of any obstacles to their independence and impartiality, as well as their professional qualification. These requirements must be insured beforehand through thorough

3. Judicial legitimacy through procedural efficiency[45]

- In the context of our topic, *procedural efficiency* is an aspect liable to promote judicial legitimacy which seems particularly relevant to evaluate certain arguments advocating a decentralization of the EU judiciary. This comprises notably:
- effective access to justice,[46]
- the swiftness of judicial proceedings,[47]
- the transparency of judicial proceedings,[48]
- safeguarding the parties' procedural rights,[49]
- leading an adequate dialogue with the parties on essential questions,
- the possibility of appeal against first-time judicial decisions,
- the enforceability of judicial decisions.[50]

---

and credible selection proceedings and–later on–secured by appropriate rules of conduct. *Second*, legitimacy must equally be achieved through clear *organizational rules* predefining the external and internal structures and competences of the judiciary at issue. Amongst others, this would include fixed rules on the composition of a judicial body, like the 'lawful judge'-principle ('*gesetzlicher Richter*'), and rules for the attribution of cases.

45 The element of procedural efficiency is clearly adjacent to the 'Right to an effective remedy and to a fair trial' under Art. 47 CFR, see pt. III.1.b.i. *supra*. See also, in this respect, e.g., Matthias Pechstein, *EU-Prozessrecht*, 4th ed., Mohr Siebeck Tübingen (2011), pp.14 ff.

46 N.B.: The feature 'effective access to justice' may have more than one aspect: it encompasses the absence of prohibitive obstacles to accede in an efficient manner to the judiciary. Such obstacles could be as well of a legal nature (e.g., legal bars for admissibility to bring an action) as of a factual or physical nature (e.g., long distance, language problems).

47 Deciding a case within a reasonable period of time is a core element of effective legal protection under Article 6, para. 1, ECHR resp. Article 47, para. 2, CFR ('*bis dat qui cito dat*'; 'justice delayed is justice denied'); cf. in the specific context of the EU judicature: Alison McDonnell, 'Time is Money?

Reasonable Duration of the Procedure before the European Courts as an Aspect of Effective and Timely Judicial Protection', in T.Baumé/E.Oude Elferink/P.Phoa/D.Thiaville (eds.) *Today's Multilayered Legal Order: Current Issues and Perspectives, Liber Amicorum in honour of Arjen W.H. Meij*, Paris publishers, Zutphen (2011), p. 183 ff.

48 In terms of judicial legitimacy, the transparency principle (cf. Art. 15, para. 1, TFEU) corresponds, for the EU judicature, by and large to the well-known principle, 'Not only must Justice be done; it must also be seen to be done' (*R v Sussex Justices, Ex parte McCarthy* ([1924] 1 KB 256, [1923] All ER 233), towards the parties to a case, as well as *vis-à-vis* third persons. In proceedings before the EU Courts, this concern for legitimating transparency is seen inter alia in the announcement of all pending cases and judgments in the Official Journal, in the normally public character of hearings, in the public rendition of judgments and their accessibility on the Internet (even if not always in all official languages) and in the publication of selected judgments in all languages. See also the fundamental requirement to hold a 'public hearing' under Art. 47, para. 2, CFR resp. under Art. 6, para. 1, first sentence, ECHR. As to the possible tension between the principle of judicial independence, on the one hand, and the eventual request for full transparency of judicial proceedings before the EU courts, in the other hand, see Josef Azizi, 'Unveiling the EU Court's internal Decision-Making Process: a case for dissenting opinions?', in: W.Heusel/J.-P. Rageade (eds.) *A European Law Practitioner — Liber amicorum John Toulmin*, ERA Forum Volume 12, Supplement 1, May 2011, 49ff.

49 Cf. the safeguards comprised in the procedural guarantee of a 'fair trial' under Art. 6 ECHR, like the equality of arms principle, the right of access to the file and the right to be heard and the right to a statement of reasons. See, in this respect, i.e., Frank Schorkopf, 'Recht auf ein faires Verfahren', in: S.Heselhaus/C.Nowak (eds.) *Handbuch der Europäischen Grundrechte* (2006), p. 1414 ff. (1420 ff.); Hanns Peter Nehl, *Recht auf rechtliches Gehör*, ibid. p. 1442 ff.; Hanns Peter Nehl, *Recht auf Akteneinsicht*, ibid. p. 1468ff.

50 As well as adequate sanctions for the failure to respect judicial decisions.

IV. Judicial legitimacy through the completeness of judicial protection[51]

1. The pertinence of arguments for decentralizing the EU judiciary as seen in the light of judicial efficiency

(a) General

The possible arguments put forward in favour of decentralizing the EU judiciary may now constitute the object of a closer examination. To that end, in the first place, the facts alleged to support arguments favouring decentralization must be verified. In a second move, if these facts prove to be correct, their implications in terms of judicial efficiency respectively legitimacy would have to be looked at. Finally, their possible relevance for the question of centralization or decentralization of the EU judiciary might be examined.

In this exercise, the previously addressed criteria of judicial functionality might, as far as possible, serve as benchmarks for assessing the adequacy of the present legal frame for the EU judiciary in terms of centralization or decentralization.

(b) The argument of geographical distance

The often considerable distance between the residence of the parties in various Member States and the seat of the EU Courts in Luxembourg[52] is not unlikely to be invoked as an argument for decentralizing the EU judiciary. In terms of judicial efficiency, this argument might amount mainly to asserting an impediment to effective access to justice. Indeed, this circumstance might be seen as generating difficulties impeding direct communication with the EU Courts and, more specifically, as an obstacle for participation in oral hearings.

Nevertheless, arguments of geographical distance do not really withstand close examination: Nowadays, electronic and other technical means at hand[53] allow smooth communication and exchange of information irrespective of any geographical distance. It may be true, though, that – inasmuch as the presence of parties to a hearing is required – the travel could be cumbersome and could give rise to specific expenses which will only be reimbursed to the winner of the action. This factor will indeed have to be weighed against possible advantages of a centralized EU judiciary. However, it must not be overlooked that even within the territory of some Member States huge distances

51 The efficiency-bound credibility and thus the legitimacy of the judiciary also depend on the watertight character of the system of legal remedies. Therefore, in line with the postulate of *completeness of judicial protection*, no illegality should fall outside judicial control.

52 See note 8 *supra*.

53 Like 'e-Curia', the electronic communication system of the EU judiciary. [http://curia.europa.eu/jcms/upload/docs/application/pdf/2011-10/en08602.pdf].

must be covered to reach high level courts in the respective capital.[54] Moreover, one should consider that, in the near future, even participating in hearings might be possible via video technology.[55] Besides, empirically speaking, so far parties to EU Court proceedings do not seem to be deterred from participating in oral hearings.

Finally, as stated initially, there can be no doubt that if the unique character of the EU legal order is to be kept, a minimum of centralization of the Union's judicial authority is indispensable (like for its legislative and executive authorities) . In this sense, it is obvious that the geographical distance is only a necessary and unavoidable secondary feature (side effect) of any centralized EU organ or body. In our discussion of the appropriateness of a decentralization of the EU judiciary, geographical distance therefore is only an additional argument of merely ancillary nature helping to support eventual main substance arguments in favour of decentralization. Taking all this into account, demands for a decentralization of the EU judiciary based on arguments of geographical distance do not seem to be very convincing.[56]

(c) Language-related arguments

For the *language aspect*, at any rate two different lines of critical argumentation could be thought of: one might be found in the concern that, due to the supranational/ multinational character of the EU judiciary, language aspects would, as such, form a *barrier for access to the EU Courts*; the other could consist in the reproach that the language regime of the EU judiciary *impairs the swiftness of proceedings* (principle of procedural economy). What about the validity of those arguments concerning possible repercussions of the language aspect for proceedings before the EU Courts?

As things stand, the language situation[57] at the EU judiciary is the following: applicants and referring national courts are free to choose and use any[58] of the–at present 24 - official languages of the Union in their applications or requests for preliminary rulings[59] and their choice in principle determines the procedural language for the respective

54 Like for appeals against judicial decisions rendered by judicial bodies in the French overseas departments and territories, the Netherlands Antilles or the British Overseas Territories.

55 N.B. provided this was considered compatible with the principle of procedural immediacy.

56 See also the by and large similar view expressed by Thomas Jäger, System einer europäischen Gerichtsbarkeit für Immaterialgüterrechte, Springer-Verlag Berlin Heidelberg (2013) 721.

57 For the language regime before the EU Courts see, inter alia, Eleanor V. E. Sharpston, (29 March 2011), '*Appendix 5: Written Evidence of Advocate General Sharpston*', *The Workload of the Court of Justice of the European Union* (House of Lords European Union Committee), retrieved 27 August 2013.

58 In contrast to the proceedings before the European Court of Human Rights, the parties' choice is not limited to English or French.

59 In preliminary ruling proceedings, the language of the case is–save for possible exceptions–the language of the referring court or tribunal (cf. Article 37, para. 3, ECJ Rules of procedure, see references below).

case.[60] [61] This language choice has several legal consequences: it means inter alia that the persons concerned have the right to present their written and oral contributions to the competent EU Court in the language they had chosen; it means furthermore that they would be entitled to be served with a version in that same language of other parties' and interveners' contributions, where needed even by means of translation for submissions in writing and by means of interpretation for oral statements. And last but not least, only the version of a judgment in the chosen language of the proceedings shall be authentic. Thus, all in all, the EU judicial system apparently ensures to the greatest possible extent that there are no language barriers for *access to the EU judiciary*.

Yet, the practical consequences of this legal situation for the *duration of proceedings* are more complex and at first sight perhaps not equally reassuring. First, it should be pointed out that the high number of official languages of the Union gives rise to specific problems for the internal work organization of the EU judiciary: on the one hand, evidently, the members of the EU Courts cannot possibly master all official EU languages; on the other hand, direct communication and deliberation is absolutely vital for smooth decision finding amongst judges. For these reasons, following a long-established, but merely internal practice, the EU Courts use in principal one single working language, which (for mainly historical reasons) is French.[62] Consequently, whenever French is not the language of an EU Court proceeding, all submissions or otherwise essential documents have to be translated into this internal working language.[63] Similarly, the final judgment will, in principle, have to be translated into the language of the proceeding–and, for cases out of the ordinary–in all other official languages. As a result, in spite of the–in general excellent–performance of its translation service,[64] due to this constant need for translations, the EU judiciary's proceedings regularly

---

60 Cf. Arts. 36 – 42 ECJ Rules of procedure [Rules of Procedure of the Court of Justice of 25 September 2012 (OJ L 265, 29.9.2012, p. 1), as amended on 18 June 2013 (OJ L 173, 26.6.2013, p. 65)]; Arts. 35 – 37 EGC Rules of procedure [Rules of Procedure of the Court of First Instance of the European Communities of 2 May 1991 (OJ L 136 of 30.5.1991, p. 1, and OJ L 317 of 19.11.1991, p. 34 (corrigenda) as last amended on 19 June 2013 (OJ L 173 of 26.6.2013, p. 66)]; these latter provisions apply also to the ECST [see Art. 29 Rules of Procedure of the European Union Civil Service Tribunal of 25 July 2007 (OJ L 225 of 29.8.2007, p. 1, with corrigendum OJ L 69 of 13.3.2008, p. 37)]; see also Arts. 44-49 of the presently finalized draft new EGC Rules of procedure [http://www.statewatch.org/news/2014/nov/eu-cjeu-draft-rules-of-procedure-general-court-5628-14.pdf].

61 Where the defendant is a Member State, the applicant must choose an official language of that Member State (Article 37, para. 1, lit. (a) ECJ Rules of Procedure).

62 Three historical explanations can be given for the choice of the French language as internal working language of the EU judiciary:

1. At the time of the foundation of the European Communities, French was the official language used in the largest number 0f Member States [i.e., in 3 of the 6 founding Member States (Belgium, France and Luxembourg)].
2. From the start, the seat of the EC judiciary has always been Luxembourg, which is precisely one of those Member States having French as official language.
3. The very first Treaty (i.e., the ECSC-Treaty), which was the legal point of departure and central object of interpretation for the ECJ at the time of the foundation of the European Communities, was the one and only instrument of primary law to be authentic merely in one single language, and that language was French.

63 Advocates General may work and draft their opinions in any official language, as they do not take part in any deliberations. These opinions, destined to benefit judges and their deliberations, form then also part of the procedural documents which have to be translated into French (cf. Art. 38, para. 8, ECJ Rules of procedure).

64 In point of fact, on the whole, qualitatively as well as quantitatively speaking, the translation services of the Court of Justice of the European Union have constantly provided over the years a most remarkable performance.

suffer from considerable additional delays in comparison with national courts. By contrast, at Member States' level, as a matter of principle mostly only one official language would be used in court.

Hence, it would come as no surprise if, in order to speed up proceedings, some users, under the aspect of the need for translations, preferred a decentralization in whole or in part of the EU judiciary. Nonetheless, on closer examination, delays due to a need for translations do not seem to be a major obstacle for the reasonable length of preliminary rulings proceedings.[65] This may be due to the fact that, on the whole, the national courts limit their requests for preliminary rulings to some questions relevant for their case, that judgments in such cases are mostly rather succinct, the ECJ limiting the answers to be translated to the questions relevant for the homogeneity of EU law[66] and that, more and more frequently, the translation is limited to the language of the case. By contrast, actions for annulment before the EGC normally entail the translation of a considerable amount of texts, both for the often voluminous written pleadings and submissions to the Court as well as for the final judgment, which must often analyse and answer a vast number of complex factual and legal questions. It does not seem astonishing that, at worst, solely the translation of such a judgment might take several months. Now, as a matter of fact, within the institution 'Court of Justice of the European Union,'[67] the translation of ECJ judgments is normally given priority over the translation of GCE documents. This may seem understandable in as much as the duration of preliminary ruling procedures, which are only an intermediate phase within the main proceedings before the referring national court, adds to the overall length of these proceedings. But this explanation certainly could not seem satisfactory or reassuring to parties involved in GCE direct action proceedings.[68]

Accepting and maintaining[69] in equal measure all 24 official languages of the Union as languages for EU Court proceedings is a crucial political decision based on fundamental considerations. Above all, European citizens should, to the maximum extent possible, feel welcome and at home within the European Courts.[70] Even if the impact of translations for the overall duration of some EU Court proceedings is a fact, it might still be seen as a mere spin-off effect of a multilingual unique judiciary. It would only receive some major relevance for the question of decentralization if the translation

---

65 E.g., the overall duration of preliminary rulings proceedings between 2010 and 2014 oscillated between 16.3 and 15.0 months (cf. *Court of Justice of the European Union Annual Report 2014*, p. 72, http://curia.europa.eu/jcms/upload/docs/application/pdf/2015-03/en_ra14.pdf).

66 Along these lines also Thomas Jäger, *System einer europäischen Gerichtsbarkeit für Immaterialgüterrechte*, Springer-Verlag Berlin Heidelberg (2013) 577.

67 Cf. Art. 13, para. 1, TEU.

68 As a matter of fact, this problem is much less acute for the ECST, where French is, for the vast majority of staff cases, the language of the proceedings (71.92% in 2014), followed by English (14.65%) German (5.73%) and Italian (5.10%): see Court of Justice of the European Union, *Annual Report 2014*, p. 227 [http://curia.europa.eu/jcms/upload/docs/application/pdf/2015-04/en_ecj_annual_report_2014_pr1.pdf].

69 See in this respect Article 64 of the Statute of the Court of Justice of the European Union.

70 Obviously for similar considerations, the EU judiciary up to now charges in principle no court fees [cf. Article 90, GCE Rules of procedure (and Article 139 of the new GCE draft rules of procedure, see note 60 *supra*), Article 143 ECJ Rules of procedure].

time needed was considered so exaggerated that it would severely and persistently prevent, hamper and jeopardize the fulfilment of the EU judiciary's tasks. However, until now, even with all possible criticism as to needed translation time, this factor would not seem so massively detrimental as to provoke calls for decentralization. Obviously, the most appropriate solution would simply be to raise the EU judiciary's budgetary means in order to increase the number of staff and thus reinforce the capacities of the EU Courts' translation service. Apart from that, if ever multilingualism were seen as a real problem (*quod non!*), less radical measures than decentralizing the EU judiciary could still be thought of.[71]

(d) Arguments drawn from an alleged lack of understanding for national particularities

(i) Overview

Occasionally, use has been made of a range of arguments tending to suggest that the EU judiciary, and more particularly EU judges, were not able to live up to the legal or traditional standards or expectations present in at least part of the EU Member States. Such a sentiment of uneasiness or even distrust might, ultimately, inspire ideas of at least partly decentralizing the EU Court's activities by transferring them to national judiciaries.

For instance, for the preconditions to become a judge or advocate general at the ECJ or EGC, the respective provisions of the TFEU refer in part to the national law of the Member States. Yet, it was sometimes faulted that as to the required ability to accede to high[72] or highest[73] level judicial responsibilities and functions in the various Member States, the qualification requirements to be met were far from being similar or even equivalent. As is well known, in Member States with a Common law tradition, judges are selected for appointment on the basis of a long-lasting outstanding career as a legal practitioner. By contrast, in other Member States, judicial functions may be accessible to persons of a comparatively very young age and limited experience. On the other hand, in some Member States, it is possible to accede to certain judicial functions without a law degree or thorough legal training, whereas in others a university degree and, in addition, intensive post-university professional training and/or practice are both imperative preconditions for becoming a judge. It might be argued that members of the EU judiciary who would not comply with the appointment standards of certain Member States might encounter less confidence in their judicial work from parties with that origin.

---

71 Like, e.g., at worst, measures tending to reduce the number of languages which could be used in proceedings.

72 Cf. Art. 254, para. 2, TFEU : '… persons […] who possess the ability required for appointment to high judicial office.'

73 Cf. Art. 253, para. 1, TFEU : '… persons […] who possess the qualifications required for appointment to the highest judicial offices in their respective countries.'

Another reproach could be that EU judges know little about the relevant facts and legal rules or about the traditional legal thinking in Member States other than their own. Parties might tend to feel difficulty in having to explain at EU Court level what otherwise would have been well known to a national judge in their home country.

Conversely, parties to EU Court proceedings might also feel uncomfortable with the circumstance that the applicable rules of procedure of the EU judiciary sometimes significantly differ from their national procedural law.

And again, these and similar perceptions might ultimately prompt some national lawyers or interested citizens to question the appropriateness of a centralized EU judiciary as it stands today. Hence, it would seem appropriate to review those arguments with due attention.

(ii) Review of those arguments

First, as to arguments alleging that members of the EU Courts are less credible than national judges, the following should be kept in mind: the whole Union is built on the understanding that the EU and all Member States respect the fundamental values mentioned in Article 2 TEU[74] and, more specifically, fundamental rights have been solemnly recognised, consecrated and enshrined in primary law,[75] including the basic guarantees for a high standard[76] judiciary,[77] both at EU level and at Member State level. In addition, for the ECJ and the EGC, the Treaties not only impose specific substantive personal qualifications[78] to be met by future EU judges, but they also foresee, by instituting the pre-selection panel under Article 255 TFEU, a formidable procedural means of proven efficiency to safeguard compliance with those requirements.[79] Unless there was an intention to put into doubt the basic premise of commonly understood and respected high judicial standards, and thus to rock the very foundations of the Union, arguments of distrust in the qualification of EU judges must consequently be considered as a nonstarter.

Second, regarding the argument that EU judges have but little information on the relevant national facts and national legal rules or about the traditional legal thinking in Member States other than their own, the following can be said:

To start with, as to establishing the relevant facts, even at national level the parties to a case normally would have to fully cooperate with the competent court by providing

74 Including inter alia the respect for human dignity, freedom, equality, the rule of law and respect for human rights, as well as non-discrimination, tolerance, justice, solidarity and equality between women and men.

75 See Art. 6, paras. 1 – 3, TEU.

76 See e.g., Title 6 ('Justice') CFR and Articles 5 and 6 ECHR.

77 Not to mention the serious possible sanctions threatening Member States infringing those standards (c.f. Art. 7 TEU).

78 Cf. Arts. 253 and 255 TFEU in conjunction with Art.19, para. 2, subparagraph 3, TEU.

79 See Third Activity Report of the Panel provided for by Art. 255 of the Treaty on the Functioning of the European Union, 13 December 2013, [http://curia.europa.eu/jcms/upload/docs/application/pdf/2014-02/rapport-c-255-en.pdf].

it with all relevant information and evidence. Therefore, in this respect, there does not appear to be a significant difference only because additional background information on facts specific to certain Member States might be appropriate.

Furthermore, concerning the call for full knowledge of relevant national law by EU judges: in this respect, it has to be recalled, that, in proceedings before the EU judiciary, *national legal rules have in principle*[80] *only the character of mere facts relevant for the application of EU law.*[81] Therefore, for EU Courts, the adage '*iura novit curia*' would in principle only apply to EU law, not to national law. This being said, the infrastructure of the EU judiciary is well equipped to provide the EU Courts upon request with any suitable background information, for a pending case, as to the existing legal situation and standards in one or several Member States or even–if need be–in third countries[82] and/or international organizations.[83] Seen from this angle, independently from their national origin, the members of the EU judiciary are, whenever needed, fairly well informed in that respect.[84]

Aside from that, any possible allegation that the EU judiciary was not representative of the legal thinking and legal traditions of the Member States could hardly seem valid: if the EU Treaty foresees that the ECJ shall consist of one judge from each Member State[85] and that the General Court shall include at least one judge per Member State,[86] this is certainly not meant to make judges an extension and mouthpiece of national political and/or economic lobbies of their respective home countries. Indeed, any such view would be clearly incompatible with the fundamental idea of judicial independence and impartiality. In contrast, these Treaty provisions must be reasonably interpreted as simply ensuring, for the work of the EU judiciary, the presence of the legal traditions and legal thinking specific to each Member State. It might be added that, at the EGC, traditionally chambers of three judges are composed in such a way as to avoid, within the same chamber, the presence of judges from closely related legal traditions.[87] In

80 Save for an express *renvoi* to national law by EU law (e.g., Art. 19, para. 4, of the Statute).

81 This is true not only in the context of actions for infringement, but also wherever national legal acts give rise at least indirectly to EU Court proceedings, like in preliminary ruling proceedings or even in the context of various direct actions.

82 Like e.g., of a State which is a party to the Agreement on the European Economic Area, or, where appropriate, of any other third State.

83 It is indeed part of the tasks of the 'Research and Documentation Directorate', which comprises a specialized unit for the national legal order of each Member State, to furnish, where required, brief assessments of specific legal questions from the perspective of national law.

84 By the way, at present, the legal orders of the Member States have reached such a scope and high degree of complexity that, in principle, no single lawyer could pretend to be up to date with the whole national law even of his own home country.

85 Cf. Art. 19, para. 2, subparagraph 1, first sentence, TEU.

86 Cf. Art. 19, para. 2, subparagraph 2, TEU.

87 E.g., as far as possible, the judge from Ireland and the judge from the United Kingdom would not sit in the same chamber of three judges. Ditto for the judges from France and Luxembourg, or from Austria and Germany, or from two Nordic Member States.

this truly enriching fashion, the Court tends to maintain, even for very small panels, maximal representativeness of the Member States' various legal traditions.[88]

Third, attention could be given to the possible argument that parties to EU Court proceedings might feel uncomfortable with the circumstance that the applicable rules of procedure of the EU judiciary sometimes differ from their national procedural law: it indeed does not seem unlikely that in one or the other respect the rules of procedure of the EU Courts would substantially differ from those of the Member States' courts. However, the very fact of having autonomous EU Courts entails the necessity of enacting specific rules of procedure for them, many of which are tailor-made to suit the specific types of EU judicial competences. And even neglecting this important circumstance: given the number of Member States, it would not be surprising if one or the other EU procedural rule was effectively somewhat different from national procedural law. It follows from these considerations that possible differences between national procedural rules and EU Court rules of procedure are only a direct consequence of the autonomous character of the EU judiciary. Arguments based on those circumstances prove therefore to be ineffective for the discussion of the eventual opportunity to decentralize or not the EU judiciary, inasmuch as they are of an entirely secondary and ancillary nature.

(e) Arguments drawn from an alleged lack of participation and transparency in EU Court proceedings

(i) General introduction

Still in a context of propinquity bound criticism, the EU judiciary might be blamed for not being sufficiently close to the citizens. In this sense, it might be alleged that persons interested in the outcome of a judicial proceeding were not sufficiently involved in the procedure and that they should be more closely associated with it. Likewise, it might be suggested that EU Court proceedings were not sufficiently transparent.[89] Along similar lines, a general aloofness of the EU judiciary and its members might even be put forward.

---

88 Conversely, as a matter of fact, the comparatively small number of judges at the ECST would not lend itself to a similar approach. But its jurisdiction being limited to EU staff cases, a quick glance at the particular nature of its clients (most of whom reside near the main EU institutions) and of its specifically Union-bound litigation matters shows that any argumentation for decentralizing that Court would be void of purpose.

89 Under a very vague and diluted concept of democracy, any means allowing private persons to be in some way associated with public activities or structures could be considered 'democratic', at least by getting information [see Josef Azizi, Multilevel Governance: a Way to increase Democratic Legitimacy of the Judiciary?, in A. Balthasar/ J.W. Pichler (edts.), 'Multilevel Governance – from Local Communities to a True European Community,' *Proceedings of the Conference on European Democracy 2014* (EuDEM 2014), Klein publishing, Vienna (2015) pp. 25-50, at p. 26 (pt. II.A.1.c)]. On that note, such arguments amount to a democracy-related criticism of the EU judiciary.

(ii) Assessment of these arguments

First, as to the argument that interested parties are not sufficiently involved in EU Courts' proceedings, as a matter of principle, access to EU Courts is provided in various ways.

Direct actions, mainly actions for annulment, can be brought by interested (natural or legal) persons if they fulfil the–even if partly restrictive[90] - preconditions enounced in the TFEU. Persons which can establish an interest in the result of a case submitted to the EU judiciary are entitled to participate as interveners,[91] save for cases between Member States, between institutions of the Union or between Member States and institutions of the Union. Main parties have a right to express themselves and exchange their arguments and they have to answer the questions of the competent EU Court (mainly the EGC) both in writing and–where foreseen–in an oral hearing. Their active participation in the proceedings is not only foreseen, but even essential for the whole procedure in light of the basic functions of the judiciary and with respect to fundamental principles of law including fundamental rights. *Mutatis mutandis*, this is also true for preliminary ruling proceedings, in as much as the parties to the main proceedings are closely associated[92] to the proceedings before the ECJ.[93] It therefore can hardly be upheld that interested private parties would not have adequate opportunities to participate in EU Court proceedings.

Second, as to the transparency of EU Court proceedings, above all the main parties' right of *access to the file*, notably to the documents relating to the case either produced by the parties or addressed to them by the respective Court, must be emphasized. Besides, as to the public character of EU Court proceedings, it should be recalled that for each case pending before an EU Court, for the sake of general information, a note is published in the Official Journal at the moment of the beginning of the proceedings. In the same manner, notice is given as soon as the decision terminating the proceedings has been delivered. Moreover, these notices and any prior information as to dates relevant for an ongoing proceeding[94] are provided on the official website of the Court of Justice of the European Union.[95] Equally, as soon as a judgment or an Advocate General's opinion is delivered, the full text is electronically published in all language versions available. Often, in addition, the content of the judgment is also resumed in

---

90 Under Art. 263, para. 4, TFEU, in order to be admitted as having *locus standi* before the EGC, they would, if they are not the addressee of the contested legal act, have in principle to prove that they are *directly* and *individually* concerned by it, unless it is a regulatory act which is of direct concern to them and does not entail implementing measures.

91 Cf. Art. 40, para. 2, of the Statute.

92 In conformity with standing case law, 'the system of references for a preliminary ruling is based on a dialogue between one court and another' (Judgment in *Willy Kempter KG v Hauptzollamt Hamburg-Jonas*, C-2/06, EU:C:2008:78, paragraph 42). Along these lines, all the referring national court's arguments including its own opinion as to the answer to the submitted question and - subject to their inclusion by the referring national court -also the arguments of the parties to the main proceedings, are brought to the ECJ's attention.

93 Cf. Art. 23, paras. 1 and 2, of the Statute, and Articles 96, para. 1, and 97, ECJ Rules of procedure.

94 Like the date of an oral hearing or of the delivering of an Advocate General's opinion or of the judgment.

95 http://curia.europa.eu/.

a more easily comprehensible short press release. So, for the greater public, the transparency and public character of court proceedings is at any rate preserved, in principle, at least through public access to hearings and to judgments.[96] It is true that with regard to the basic principle of transparency, under Article 15, para. 3, TFEU, the general right of access to documents granted to citizens and residents of the Union applies to the Court of Justice of the European Union only when it exercises its administrative tasks. Nonetheless, like all exceptions, this rule has to be given a very strict interpretation.[97]

By contrast, what remains inaccessible to the parties and the greater public is any information on the internal decision making of the EU Courts in a particular case. More specifically, the secrecy of deliberations, as expressly foreseen,[98] can be seen inter alia as contributing to the overall protection of judicial independence, especially in connection with a limited but renewable term of office for the judges.[99] Therefore, in EU Courts, the issuing of dissenting opinions outside the judgment would be contrary to the secrecy of deliberations and is not admitted. Besides, unveiling dissenting opinions of panel members in cases which have not been concluded on the basis of a unanimous decision would be wholly counterproductive for legal certainty, especially in the frame of preliminary ruling proceedings. Indeed, the main purpose of such proceedings is to provide, in an unambiguous way and potentially even for a larger public, legal security through a uniform interpretation of the EU law provision at issue. The presenting of a dissenting opinion would obviously go in the opposite direction and in this way jeopardize the very function of any preliminary ruling proceeding. Thus, the secrecy of deliberations, as foreseen, indeed puts a limit to the application of the general principle of transparency in the field of the EU judiciary. However, this limitation would seem justified, on the one hand, for protecting the independence of the judges from any external pressure on them, even if exercised in the name of democracy or by democratically legitimated actors. On the other hand, it seems equally justified in order to preserve the core efficiency of preliminary ruling proceedings. Finally, one should not close one's eyes to the fact that in the vast majority of Member States, for all or almost all national courts the publication of a dissenting opinion is neither foreseen nor allowed. For all these reasons, even from the angle of the principle of transparency, the mere fact that within the EU judicature the issuing of dissenting opinions is prohibited does not seem to justify any kind of decentralization of the EU judiciary.

---

96 Subject to the specific structural and functional requirements of any judiciary, this would, for the EU judiciary, also fit with Art. 1 para. 2 TEU, which invokes 'an ever closer union among the peoples of Europe, in which decisions are taken as openly as possible and as closely as possible to the citizen'.

97 See e.g., Judgement of 27 February 2015, *Breyer v Commission*, T-188/12,EU:T:2015:124.

98 E.g., Art. 35 read in conjunction with Art. 53, para. 1 of the Statute of the Court of Justice of the European Union as well as Art. 4, ECJ Rules of procedure, Art. 4, paragraph 1, EGC Rules of procedure and Art. 5 of the new draft EGC Rules of procedure.

99 See Josef Azizi, 'Unveiling the EU Courts' Internal Decision-Making Process: A Case for Dissenting Opinions?', in: W. Heusel/J.-P. Rageade (eds.) *A European Law Practitioner. Liber amicorum John Toulmin*, ERA Forum (2011) 12: pp.49-68 (at p.55 passim).

Third, as to a putative general aloofness of the EU judiciary and its members: it is not excluded that, in the context of a specific judicial proceeding, a participant might have experienced disappointment, in the course of exchanges with the registry or during a hearing. But even if this were the case, this would certainly not allow generalizing in an abstract manner such a personal experience and its maybe subjective and emotional perception. In any event, similar experiences and perceptions might also be generated by national judiciaries.

Hence, on the whole, it does not seem that 'democracy related'[100] arguments drawn from insufficient opportunities for participation in EU Court proceedings, from a lack of transparency or from an alleged aloofness of the EU judiciary could serve as a valid basis for claims to somewhat decentralize the EU judiciary.

(f) Arguments drawn from an alleged insufficient working capacity of the EU Courts

(i) Introduction

From time to time, the overall length of proceedings before the EU judiciary has given rise to criticism. This problem is certainly not a phenomenon with a single cause, but is due to various factors which often are juxtaposed, like the increasing number of cases, inadequate staffing, cumbersome procedures,[101] little cooperation on the part of counsel,[102] etc. Consequently, problem solving could hardly limit itself to one single solution. Depending on the type of proceedings concerned, over time various solutions

---

100 See note 89 *supra*.

101 E.g., sometimes double exchange of written pleadings, confidentiality problems following interventions, occasionally unproductive but unavoidable oral hearings, etc.

102 As a matter of fact, lawyers could speed up litigation e.g., *before the EGC* by the following means:

1. Use of e-curia: lawyers would be very welcome not to continue to refuse the use of e-curia.
2. Respecting the procedural requirements (including soft law 'Practice Directions to parties'), in particular those connected to the language regime.
3. Choosing carefully the language of procedure.
4. Respecting the indicated length of pleadings.
5. Limiting the number of pleas for annulment to the most promising ones.
6. Limiting the number of pleadings.
7. Using clear and concise language, avoiding repetitions (beware: need for translation!).
8. Limiting the use of annexes.
9. Avoiding unnecessary interim- or preliminary issues, such as asking for or objecting to confidential treatment, etc.
10. Abstaining from (ab-)using Court proceedings merely as a convenient starting basis for exercising psychological pressure before conducting negotiations with the adverse party (e.g., in trademark cases).
11. Not applying for interim measures and/or expedited procedure without solid reasons.
12. Not asking for an annulment or postponement of hearings without serious reasons.

In order to disencumber proceedings *before the ECJ*, given the often important help offered by lawyers for the preparation of references, they could e.g., work so as to keep to a minimum irrelevant, premature or poorly-prepared references and those which concern only the specific application of Community law and not its interpretation.

formed the subject of a public debate, some of them relating to a possible partial decentralization of the EU judiciary.

(ii) Preliminary ruling proceedings

a. Starting point of discussion

Preliminary ruling proceedings, over a number of years before and after the turn of the century, specially suffered from a considerable and even steadily increasing duration.[103] In view of this serious threat, and given the evident immediate repercussion of this fact on the total length of the main proceeding before the referring national court, several proposals were made. One of these was the suggestion to introduce an intermediate level of preliminary ruling courts whose decisions might in one way or the other be reviewed by the ECJ. The following is meant to give a small extract of some arguments discussed at that time.[104]

b. The Community Courts' discussion paper ('document de réflexion')

In their common discussion paper of May 1999,[105] the Court of Justice and the Court of First Instance[106] analysed possible advantages and disadvantages of such a system of regional preliminary ruling courts, albeit without taking a firm stand on the question.

Following that discussion paper, the main advantages of such a system with regional preliminary ruling courts would be a greater closeness to the national legal system and judiciary as well as avoiding bottle necks at the EU judiciary's translation service.[107]

All the same, the paper identifies '*major drawbacks as regards the maintenance of uniformity in the interpretation and application of Community law*'. On that note, the document acknowledges a serious *risk of break up for the fundamental unity of EU law*. It states: 'Any reorganisation of the preliminary ruling procedure on a national or regional basis, regardless of whether jurisdiction is conferred on national or on Community courts, *involves a serious risk of shattering the unity of Community law, which constitutes one of the cornerstones of the Union and which will become still more vital and vulnerable as a result of enlargement of the Union.*[108] Jurisdiction to determine the final and binding interpretation of a Community rule, as well as the

---

103 E.g., preliminary rulings average duration of: 21.4 months in 1998, 21.2 months in 1999, 21.6 months in 2000, 22.7 months in 2001, 24.1 months in 2002, 25.5 months in 2003.

104 For a more detailed presentation of the historical discussions see e.g., Hannes Rösler, *Europäische Gerichtsbarkeit auf dem Gebiet des Zivilrechts: Strukturen, Entwicklungen und Reformperspektiven des Justiz- und Verfahrensrechts der Europäischen Union*, Mohr Siebeck Tübingen 2012, p. 304 ff. See also, inter alia, Francis G. Jacobs, Recent and ongoing measures to improve the efficiency of the European Court of Justice, EL Rev. 2004, pp. 823-830.

105 The Future of the Judicial system of the European Union – Court of Justice and Court of First Instance discussion paper (*L'avenir du système juridictionnel de l'Union européenne - Document de réflexion de la Cour de justice et du Tribunal de première instance*), Annex to Council document ST 8208 1999 INIT, at pp. 37-39 (English version: pp. 28-29).

106 (CFI, today: EGC).

107 Ibid., p. 37 (English version: p. 28).

108 (emphasis mine).

validity of that rule, should therefore be vested in a single court covering the whole of the Union.'[109] The document also identifies problems due to the close link of such new preliminary ruling courts to the different national legal systems. It suggests – if ever such a solution was envisaged – to endow exclusively supreme courts with preliminary ruling competences, but subject to control by the ECJ, which could be seized either by those courts on their own motion or by means of an 'appeal in the interest of the law.'[110]

c. The initiative of Judge Hirsch

Conversely, a little later, Günter Hirsch, then a judge at the ECJ, in an academic article[111] clearly advocated a reform of the EU judicial system in order to bring about such adecentralization by transferring competences in the field of preliminary rulings to Member States' courts. According to him, the main argument militating in favour of such a structural change was to speed up preliminary ruling proceedings and to reduce the workload of the ECJ. As to the model of decentralization proposed by him, rather than instituting – in several or in all Member States – new EU Courts and charging them with preliminary ruling tasks,[112] he preferred endowing *national supreme courts* with the competence to give preliminary rulings only on the *interpretation*, but not on the validity, of EU law. Besides the obvious relief of workload for the ECJ, Hirsch invoked the elimination of time, staff and finance related problems in the language and translation context. He also assumes that a national preliminary ruling court would be in a better position than the ECJ for ascertaining the question referred in the context of the relevant national legal order.[113] As to the compatibility of his proposal with the existing basic Treaty concept for preliminary ruling references, Hirsch recalled the following: already in accordance with that concept as it stands, any national lower instance court is by all means entitled to interpret EU law, without there being any possibility for the ECJ to review, for the sake of legal coherence, that interpretation.[114] Thus, according to him, his proposal is in perfect conformity with everyday legal routine.

In order to preserve, in spite of it all, the necessary unity and homogeneity of EU law, Hirsch proposed to let the ECJ exercise a last instance jurisdiction for preliminary rulings on the interpretation of EU law. Accordingly, in his view, the Commission and the respective Member State, and – subject to authorization by the national court -

109 Ibid., pp. 37-38 (English version: p. 28).

110 Ibid., pp. 37-38 (English version: pp. 28-29): '*appel dans l'intérêt de la loi*'(point of general legal interest). This specific right of appeal resembles the First Advocate General's right, under Art. 62 of the Statute (later on introduced by the Treaty of Nice), to propose review, by the ECJ, of certain types of EGC decisions under Art. 256, paras. 2 and 3, TFEU].

111 See Günter Hirsch, *Dezentralisierung des Gerichtssystems der Europäischen Union?*, ZRP 2000, p. 57 ff.

112 Pursuant to his rather opaque explanation [ibid. (see precedent note), p.59], in his opinion the relationship between the ECJ and such new Community Courts would pose 'problems which would clearly outweigh the advantages'.

113 Hirsch also asserts, without further precision, that this model would 'reinforce the desirable integration and coherence of national law with Community law' [ibid. (see precedent note)].

114 Ibid. (see precedent note).

possibly also the parties to the main proceedings should have a right of appeal. In addition, when needed to avoid divergences, or for questions of fundamental importance, the national preliminary ruling instance should be obliged to refer the questions to the ECJ. Hirsch concluded by saying that his proposal is not intended to weaken the EU judiciary, but rather to enhance a greater 'Europeanisation' of the national judiciaries.

d. The Working Party's report

In obvious contrast to this opinion, in its report, the Working Party on the Future of the European Communities' Court System[115] clearly and severely rejected one variant of that proposal already at the very outset.[116] Indeed, the Working Party 'considered that national courts could not be left to settle all questions of Community law by themselves, with the parties being entitled merely to bring the national judgment before the Court of Justice in a sort of longstop appeal claiming breach of Community law. The Working Party felt that national courts and tribunals should be able to deal with issues of Community law arising in the exercise of their national jurisdiction, by being entitled or obliged to submit questions to the Court of Justice without having to pass through a hierarchy of national courts. Such a proposal would debase the entire system of cooperation established by the Treaties between national courts and the Court of Justice - a system that has proved its worth. Its implementation, indeed, would constitute a significant reform, which would imply that a radical change to the Union's structure had been decided in advance.'

Even so, the Working Party admitted that the setting up of new, devolved courts at national level[117] would have 'the twofold advantage of relieving the ECJ of examining those preliminary questions which are not specially significant for Community law and of reducing the administrative costs and time lags currently caused by the translation of the documents for the proceedings.'

Nevertheless, in the Working Party's opinion, this advantage would be clearly more than offset by serious disadvantages: 'A reference for a preliminary ruling is a dialogue between the national court hearing the principal action, which is the only court fully familiar with the case, and the Community court, which is alone capable of securing a uniform interpretation of Community law. To interpose another national court between them *would jeopardise the uniform application of Community law,*[118] even if that court were obliged to refer specially significant questions to the Court of Justice. What would happen is that the same problem would be considered by three courts in succession,

115 This group, created upon an initiative of the European Commission, was presided over by former ECJ president Ole Due and comprised inter alia José Luís da Cruz Vilaça, former president of the Court of First instance (CFI) ['Due Committee'].

116 See *Report by the Working Party on the Future of the European Communities' Court System*, January 2000, p. 13 ff [http://ec.europa.eu/dgs/legal_service/pdf/due_en.pdf] (also known as 'Due-report').

117 As a matter of fact, the Working Group examined and rejected in parallel the following three models: 1. The setting up by Member States of devolved judicial bodies specializing in preliminary rulings. 2. The authorizing of the ECJ to select certain questions from among those referred to it. 3. The conferring of extended jurisdiction on the Court of First Instance to give preliminary rulings [ibid. (see precedent note), at pp. 20-22].

118 Emphasis mine.

thus prolonging the proceedings. The outcome would be similar, moreover, if all questions were first submitted for assessment by the Court of Justice, which would then remit the less important ones to the devolved court. Such a system could of course provide a degree of uniformity, but it would lose most of the advantages of devolution.' On top of it, the Working Party finally added that, in its view, the administration of devolved courts would entail high costs for Member States and could distort the national court structure.

e. Brief assessment

There is little to be added to this last statement. Indeed: if the essential goal of safeguarding and strengthening of the unity and coherence of EU law is to be maintained, there must be a possibility for a centralized EU judiciary to give definitive guidance as to the interpretation of EU law in view of the specific overlap of supranational[119] and national law. With all due respect for the benefits of creating new and/or putting in charge existing regional courts competent for giving preliminary rulings, in addition to the crucial disadvantages mentioned both in the Community Courts' discussion paper and in the Working Party's report (see above), there would seem to be another major drawback to this model: if the judges of such a regional court, be it a national or an EU Court, would originate from that region, there is a high likelihood, given the sometimes considerable differences between the various legal traditions of the Member States, that such regional courts might tend (intentionally or not) to develop within their jurisdiction some kind of specific *'regional EU law'*.[120] Such a surreptitious development, under the shield of a seemingly unique and coherent overall legal system, is not unlikely, over the years, to corrode and dilute the unity of EU law. Yet, with respect to the European Union's core idea and identity, any possible alteration adversely affecting the fragile unity and coherence of Union law must be absolutely excluded.

Nonetheless, it has to be emphasized that, for obvious reasons, the discussion was always limited to referrals concerning the *interpretation, not* the *validity* of EU law. In view of possible horizontal legal repercussions of validity rulings throughout the whole Union area, and given the fundamental character of such judicial decisions, it would not make sense to decentralize and thus transfer that competence even to several parallel courts. Indeed, under the crucial aspect of legal certainty, the non-validity of an EU act, declared with definitive effect, has, so to speak, an existential character for the EU legal order as such, beyond the individual case.[121]

119 Indeed, EU law is a specific legal order *sui generis*, characterised inter alia by its autonomy and supremacy: Judgment in *Costa v E.N.E.L.*, C-6/64, EU:C:1964:66, point 1 of the operative part and para. 12.

120 E.g., something like a regional 'Nordic EU law', a regional 'Common law EU law' or even, more specifically 'national regional EU law', like 'French EU law' or 'German EU law', might quickly develop in various directions, thus clearly reducing the homogeneity in the interpretation and application of EU law.

121 See, as to the *erga omnes* effect of preliminary rulings on validity: Koen Lenaerts/Ignace Maselis/ Kathleen Gutman/ Janek Tomasz Nowak, *EU Procedural Law*, Oxford University Press, Oxford 2014, p. 472, with reference *i.a.* to Judgment in *International Chemical Corporation v Amministrazione delle fianze dello Stato*, C-66/80, EU:C:1981:102, at p. 1269.

Fortunately, the difficulties that had given rise to proposals for decentralizing the ECJ's preliminary ruling tasks could in fact be answered successfully and are therefore – for the time being - not present any more. Indeed, thanks to a whole set of measures,[122] the ECJ was finally able to stabilize and even gradually cut down the length of its preliminary ruling proceedings.[123] Some of these measures were of a procedural, others of a more structural nature.[124] As a matter of fact, in consequence of the average duration of proceedings in references for a preliminary ruling (judgments and orders), which before had been constantly increasing over the years,[125] has dropped from a dramatic 25.5 months in the year 2003 to the more defensible 15.0 months in the year 2014.[126]

Hence, having regard to the crucial disadvantages of decentralization in the field of preliminary references, as outlined above, and for as long as the problem of excessive duration of proceedings remains contained, there does not seem to be a valid reason to call for a decentralization of the EU judiciary in this field.

(iii) Direct actions

a. Actions for annulment or for failure to act

Actions for annulment or for failure to act are directed against institutions, bodies, offices or agencies of the Union. Consequently, for as long as these are centralized, there is no point in decentralizing the competent EU judiciary. [127]

However, insofar as the tasks and activities of EU institutions, bodies, offices or agencies would be decentralized, there might be repercussions on the competence for their judicial review. If this were to include a transfer of executive or legislative authority to the Member States, direct judicial control would no longer be a competence of the EU judiciary, but would fall within the competences of the Member States' national judiciaries. Indeed, such review of acts[128] of authorities, by the EU Courts, is strictly

122 Many of these measures were inspired by proposals contained in the Working Party's Report and/or by suggestions contained in the common ECJ and EGC (then: CFI) discussion paper ('*document de réflexion*'), see *supra*.

123 In addition, measures destined to better inform and prepare national courts as to preliminary ruling proceedings may also have been and would continue to be helpful.

124 Let us mention, inter alia, the following examples: a more generalized introduction of the possibility, in principle, for the Court to proceed without oral hearings in a large number of cases; reduction of the number of translations in many cases; case management through permanent monitoring on the basis of internal deadlines; the obtaining of considerable extra staff for the ECJ, inter alia as measures accompanying the introduction of an expedited or accelerated procedure and (for references for a preliminary ruling relating to the area of freedom, security and justice) of an urgent procedure; establishment of new electronic tools allowing immediate transfer of documents and exchanges between cabinets, registry, and various internal administrative services; introduction of e-curia, allowing for an efficient exchange of documents with the parties; more frequent use of smaller chambers, etc.

125 E.g., 21.2 months in 1999, 21.6 months in 2000, 22.7 months in 2001, 24.1 months in 2002.

126 For urgent preliminary ruling procedures under Art. 23a of the Statute and Arts. 107-114 ECJ Rules of procedure (a category introduced only at a later stage) the average duration, in 2014, was even only 2.2 months.

127 Besides, the fact that actions for annulment are always expressly aimed at a substantial modification of EU law somewhat recalls the reflections above on the appropriateness of decentralizing the competence for validity rulings (see point IV.F.2.5. *supra*).

128 (respectively, of failures to act).

limited, to acts[129] of the Union. This means that, in procedural terms, the defendant is exclusively defined *ratione personae*, namely as comprehending only organizational entities of the Union. Therefore, in this respect, the competence for judicial review is of a purely incidental or ancillary character (*'caractère accessoire'*) and has to follow the author of the behaviour[130] in question. As soon as the behaviour to be reviewed is adopted by a Member State's authority, this necessarily implies that that behaviour is attributable to that Member State. Consequently, its review belongs to the Member State's judiciary. For example, when part of the Commission's competences for the enforcement (administration and application) of EU competition law were shifted to Member States' national competition authorities, judicial review of their activities *ipso jure* followed that shift and joined the national judiciaries' competences.[131] Thus, the fact of partly decentralizing the enforcement of competition law obviously caused an important decentralization of judicial competences, away from the EU judiciary towards the judiciaries of the Member States.[132] Conversely, entrusting former national enforcement competences to the Union has a centralizing effect by adding to the EU judiciary's review competences.[133]

All in all, strictly speaking, decentralizing the EU judiciary as such in the field of actions for annulment or for failure to act would make little sense. So, inasmuch as the average duration of such proceedings is often found to be excessive, this problem will have to be addressed by a set of adequate other measures. From the point of view of judicial architecture, it has also to be emphasized that, in the possible event that certain legal matters give rise to a large mass of proceedings, the TFEU would foresee the possibility to shift judicial competences for this domain to a Specialized Court.[134].In any event, if ever a shift of administrative/executive enforcement competences from the Union to the Member States were to be put into effect, the respective EU judiciary's tasks in that field would, as a consequence, end up with the national jurisdictions.

---

129 (respectively, of failures to act).

130 I.e., acts or failures to act.

131 Council Regulation (EC) No 1/2003 of 16 December 2002 on the implementation of the rules on competition laid down in Arts. 81 and 82 of the Treaty, OJ L 1, 04.01.2003, pp.1-25, in force 1 May 2004. This Regulation inter alia grants national competition authorities and national courts the power to grant exemptions under Art. 81(3) EC, a domain previously exclusively reserved to the European Commission.

132 See, e.g., Koen Lenaerts/Damien Gerard, 'Decentralisation of EC Competition Law Enforcement: Judges in the Frontline', *World Competition* 27(3), 2004, pp. 313-349.

133 This has been the case, e.g., as to the protection of trademarks: with the creation of the Office for Harmonisation in the Internal Market, Trade Marks and Designs (OHIM), judicial review was shifted to the EGC. The same view is expressed by Sacha Prechal/R.H. van Ooik/J.H. Jans/K.J.M. Mortelmans, '"Europeanisation" of the Law: Consequences for the Dutch Judiciary', de Rechtspraak, Raad vor de Rechtspraak, Research Memoranda nr. 2, vol. 1, Colofon The Hague, June 2005, p. 9.

134 See Arts. 257 and 256, para. 2, TFEU and Art. 19, para. 1, TEU.

b. Other direct actions

For actions for damages[135] as well as for arbitration[136] cases there would not seem to be any particular argument in favour of decentralizing these activities of the EU judiciary. The comparatively moderate number of such proceedings has in any event, up to now, not given rise to particular concern.

The defendant in actions for non-contractual damages under Article 340, para.2, TFEU, as defined *ratione personae*, is always the European Union, whereas the judicial competence for contractual damages follows the rules applicable to the specific contract.[137] Anyway, given the unique character of EU compensation law for non-contractual damage caused by the Union, properly specific as to its standards by comparison with national compensation law, there is no point in diversifying the respective judicial competences by transferring them to the national judiciaries.

As for proceedings pursuant to arbitration clauses, if ever the parties to a contract were not satisfied with the EU judiciary's usual treatment of arbitration proceedings, they are simply free not to foresee in an arbitration clause jurisdiction for the EU judiciary to give judgment. Hence, there would not seem to be the least reason for decentralizing in any way the EU judiciary in this regard.

(iv) Other classes of proceedings

a. Actions for infringement

It would seem utterly inconceivable to transfer the EU judiciary's competence for actions for infringement to a decentralized set of courts, even if they were eventual regional EU Courts. The infringement, by a Member State, thus by a Lord of the Treaties, of the EU legal order is of specific gravity and its appreciation should follow identical standards. It may not be excluded that part of this judicial competence one day would be attributed to the EGC,[138] but that would still be a centralized EU Court. On the whole, no plausible reason for decentralizing the EU judiciary in this field seems to exist.

b. Other proceedings

Proceedings before the ECJ on the compatibility of an envisaged agreement[139] with the Treaties have most obviously a constitutional dimension. Indeed, such an agreement, if is not compatible with the Treaties, might create major tensions between the Union's obligations under public international law (*'pacta sunt servanda'*) on the one hand and

135 Arts.268, 340, para. 2, TFEU.

136 Art. 272 TFEU.

137 Cf. Art.340, para. 1, TFEU.

138 Cf. Art. 256, para. 1, last sentence, TFEU.

139 Cf. Art. 218, para. 11, TFEU.

the legal impossibility, under the Treaties, to implement it. It would seem highly unjustifiable to attribute jurisdiction for such proceedings to a decentralized judiciary.

V. Overall assessment

1. Preliminary statement

Taking into consideration several, in one or the other way efficiency bound criteria of judicial legitimacy, a cursory review of some possible arguments in favour of decentralizing the EU judiciary has not shown convincing results in support of this idea. This mere fact in itself may already speak in favour of not pursuing this approach. And what's more, anyway, certain advantages of a centralized EU judiciary, notably in the light of legal certainty, may be taken into account: the centralised character of judicial protection and enforcement assures a high degree of uniformity of case law, and this factor is of particular relevance under the overall aim of assuring a uniform interpretation and application of EU law. Besides, in the interest of the parties, it allows for a single set of procedural rules and it offers one single point of reference.

Yet, a few additional considerations would not seem out of place.

2. Nature of arguments

(a) Envisaged categories of arguments

The arguments in favour of decentralizing the EU judiciary are different in nature: Some may be more psychological, others more technical or legal. It may be worthwhile briefly looking at these different groups of arguments.

(b) Psychological arguments

Several arguments,[140] which not always are documented in writing, seem indeed primarily to reflect various apprehensions, not so much of a legal, but of a somewhat psychological overtone, points revealing a fear of estrangement or exclusion resulting from the unfamiliarity or maybe even from an aura of otherness of the EU judiciary for many national lawyers.[141] These apprehensions of feeling distanced from the EU Courts are probably mostly due to a lack of sufficient information on the EU judiciary. Closing this information gap continues to constitute a permanent challenge. In the past, the EU judiciary has not ceased to struggle actively against this perception at different levels. On the one hand, members of the EU Courts frequently participate and take the

140 E.g., arguments drawn from the differences in legal culture, proceedings or language. The argument of geographical distance may also, frequently, be more of a psychological than of a financial nature.

141 This apprehension of national lawyers seems to match with the fact that a sizable number of the lawyers pleading before the Union Courts work as EU law specialists for big - mostly international - law offices in Brussels, rather than for law offices situated in their respective home countries.

floor at multiple occasions in all Member States in order to fully inform a larger public about the EU judiciary's functioning and activities. On the other hand, the EU Judiciary's Protocol, Visits and Press and Information Directorate takes care of informing inter alia professionally interested persons and national courts by various means.[142] With the growth and deepening of the Union, these and similar efforts will probably have to further diversify and intensify, particularly in the context of professional training through specialized institutions, such as the European Law Academy (ERA).[143]

(c) Legal/legal-political arguments

Some of the critical arguments underlying calls for a decentralization of the EU judiciary are of a more legal or legal-political nature, mostly concerning, in one way or another, the EU Court's rules of procedure and/or even the Statute. As has been shown, it would be incongruous for the EU judicature not to have its own procedural and organizational rules. But this does not exclude incorporating into them, as far as possible, provisions responding to largely spread and expressed needs, provided they are in line with the right to an effective remedy and to a fair trial (Article 47 CFR). This could be the case e.g., for arguments drawn from an alleged lack of participation or of transparency in EU Courts' proceedings. However, as already set out, such arguments tend essentially to have little basis in fact.

(d) Technical arguments

Other arguments in favour of decentralizing the EU judiciary may be characterized as being of a more technical nature, yet mostly with financial implications, like arguments relating to infrastructural aspects. Such infrastructural problems could concern both the EU judiciary[144] as well as its 'clientele', i.e., lawyers and citizens.[145] As far as the EU judiciary is concerned, the overcoming of infrastructural problems will frequently be a mere question of acquiring adequate working capacities[146] and technical devices, facilities etc., subject to the provision of the necessary budgetary means, thus depending above all from the competent budget authorities of the Union. Parties to the EU Court proceedings will have to bear their own costs, unless otherwise decided,[147] but – as already mentioned and in contrast to the situation in most Member States – they will have to bear no legal fees for the assertion of their cause in Court.

---

142 E.g., through organizing and managing diverse information events, such as the 'Annual Meeting of national judges', seminars for national judges, study visits for legal professionals and law students. Each year the EU Courts receive visits from approximately 4,000 legal professionals (national judges, advocates, university professors, in-house lawyers, etc.) and some 10,000 other visitors, mostly law students: see http://curia.europa.eu/jcms/jcms/Jo2_12525/, retrieved April 2015.

143 Europäische Rechtsakademie Trier.

144 E.g., insufficient working capacity in the Court's translation service.

145 E.g., problems related to travelling or to means of communication.

146 Especially in getting adequate numbers of highly skilled staff in the EU Courts, e.g., translation staff, or law clerks/legal secretaries both in cabinets and registries of the EU Courts.

147 E.g., through a decision in the operative part of the judgment or by order allowing for legal aid (cf. Arts. 115-118 and 185-189 ECJ Rules of Procedure; Arts. 94-97 EGC Rules of Procedure).

(e) Sham argumentation?

An entirely different aspect should not be fully neglected either: it is common knowledge that in its case law, the EU judiciary, while implementing specific methodological features,[148] has time and again given rise to an often unexpected and dynamic impact and reinforcement of EU law. On and off, such jurisprudence has received quite unfavourable comments in various Member States. It therefore should not be entirely ruled out that some of the arguments presented in favour of decentralizing the EU judiciary effectively only serve as a pretext, whilst cleverly disguising neither more nor less than a grim determination to weaken the EU judiciary.

3. Considerations based on the Treaties' present approach for a centralized EU judiciary

(a) Preliminary ruling proceedings

(i) Introductory remarks

The application of EU law is overwhelmingly decentralized. Consequently, if the preliminary ruling proceedings are to serve most efficiently their purpose of safeguarding the uniform interpretation of EU law, they can best do so if performed by a centralized EU judiciary which holds equally accessible jurisdiction for the whole Union and thus, in the interest of legal unity and consistency, outbalances the highly likely centrifugal tendencies in the interpretation and application of EU law. In this sense, at least in theory, the optimal solution would be the exercise of all – or at least of all similar - preliminary ruling competences by one and the same EU Court. In this case, the main concern for a Union-wide approach would be on the one hand the internal coordination between the chambers of that Court in order to preserve, in a harmonized manner, the continuity and uniformity of its case law; on the other hand, as to the practical use of such proceedings by national courts, even if the right balance must be struck between discouragement and abuse, it remains essential for the overall functioning of the system that all Member States' courts really feel free to make references. On the whole, preliminary ruling proceedings are a tool of rare elegance and efficiency.[149]

---

148 Like the use of systematic-teleological interpretation and the development of specific methodological tools, such as the '*effet utile*' or the 'general principles of EU law'.

149 For the sake of completeness, it may be added that the first preliminary ruling proceedings in Europe – albeit limited to the validity of legal acts - were already foreseen in the Austrian Federal Constitution in 1920: under Article 140 B-VG, the OGH (Supreme Court of Cassation) and the VwGH (Supreme Administrative Court) could interrupt pending proceedings in order to ask the VfGH (Constitutional Court) to review and annul a parliamentary law deemed unconstitutional.

(ii) *Possible future EGC preliminary ruling competence*

a. The pertinent provision

Within the EU judiciary, these tasks until now fall under the exclusive competence of the ECJ. However, Article 256, para. 3, TFEU, allows for the EGC[150] to have 'jurisdiction to hear and determine questions referred for a preliminary ruling under Article 267 [TFEU], in specific areas laid down by the Statute'.[151] That provision also foresees that for cases requiring a 'decision of principle likely to affect the unity or consistency of Union law', the EGC may transfer the case to the ECJ. In addition, still in the vein of maintaining the ECJ's crucial function as the last and overall judicial instance safeguarding the unity of EU law, Article 256, para. 3, TFEU, permits an *ex officio* exceptional review, by the ECJ, 'where there is a serious risk of the unity or consistency of Union law being affected'.

b. Assessment

In this sense, the authors of the Treaty of Nice, which introduced this provision, have still clearly opted for a *centralized* model for the EU judiciary's role in preliminary ruling proceedings. Nevertheless, they have added an element of *flexibility,*[152] permitting the transfer, limited to specific legal domains, of preliminary ruling competences from the ECJ to the EGC.[153] That model, once activated, would still be *centralized*, because it would be part of the jurisdiction, for the whole Union, of one single Court, namely the EGC. But, at the same time, the judicial preliminary ruling competences would be *deconcentrated*, since part of these competences would be dealt with by a Court other than the ECJ, albeit under its ultimate control.

(b) Other proceedings

(i) *Residual transfer possibility*

In addition, by virtue of Article 256, para. 1, second sentence, TFEU, other competences of the ECJ may be transferred[154] to the EGC: here again, the concept of a *centralized* EU judiciary is preserved, but judicial competences are shifted from one *centralized* Court to another one.

---

150 Extremely favourable even as to a future general transfer of preliminary ruling competences to the EGC see Sacha Prechal, 'National Courts in EU Judicial Structures', *Yearbook of European Law* (2006) 25 (1), p. 429-450 (at p. 440).

151 See in this respect e.g., Josef Azizi, 'Opportunities and Limits for the Transfer of Preliminary Reference Proceedings to the Court of First Instance', in I.Pernice/ J.Kokott/ C.Saunders (eds.) *The Future of the European Judicial System in a Comparative Perspective*, Baden-Baden Nomos 2006, 241-256.

152 I.e., by means of a modification of the Statute (cf. Art. 281 TFEU).

153 Such a transfer would seem particularly opportune for matters where the competence for direct actions has been shifted to a specialized court under Art. 257 TFEU: see e.g., for matters of intellectual property law, Josef Azizi, 'Opportunities and Limits for the Transfer of Preliminary Reference Proceedings to the Court of First Instance', (see *supra*), at p. 256; Thomas Jäger, *System einer europäischen Gerichtsbarkeit für Immaterialgüterrechte*, (cited *supra*), at p. 573.

154 Also by means of a modification of the Statute.

(ii) Transfer possibility for direct actions

Also in the field of *direct actions* normally falling within the EGC's competence, the Treaty legislators have chosen a similar model of flexibility for *deconcentration* whilst maintaining the fundamentally *centralized* character of the EU judiciary. Indeed, Article 257 TFEU offers the possibility to establish *specialized courts* to 'hear and determine at first instance certain classes of action or proceeding brought in specific areas'. In such cases, the EGC will have jurisdiction over appeals, again under exceptional review by the ECJ in the event of 'a serious risk of the unity or consistency of Union law being affected'. In this fashion, again, exclusive competences of one centralized EU Court (here: the EGC) are transferred to another centralized EU Court with exclusive competence (i.e., a specialized Court). Thus, the treatment at first instance of certain matters is deconcentrated, whilst there would still be in principle two, exceptionally even three judicial instances with successive review competence for the same legal domain. Hence, in a flexible manner,[155] deconcentration would go in parallel with maintaining the centralized character of the EU judiciary, but allowing for more efficiency thanks to specialization. At the same time, the ECJ's role in keeping the unity and consistency of EU law is nonetheless basically confirmed and preserved.

(c) General assessment

What conclusions can be drawn from these provisions as to the judicial architecture foreseen by the Treaties? The Treaty legislators obviously favour a centralized EU judiciary. Nevertheless, they have allowed for a flexible system of work relief by cascades, to some extent in parallel with deconcentration: the (centralized) EU judiciary is conceived in the form of a pyramid, with, at its top, the ECJ, in the middle the EGC and at the bottom possible specialized courts. To reduce, if necessary, the workload of the ECJ, the Treaties foresee the transfer of competences to the EGC. In parallel, whenever needed, an excessive workload of the EGC can be transferred to new specialized Courts ('cascading work relief').[156]

Indeed, the creation of specialized Courts is specifically foreseen for the purpose of coping with large mass proceedings. By systematically discharging the EGC[157] from large mass proceedings, it might, in turn, potentially relieve the ECJ.

155 I.e., by means of regulations of the European Parliament and the Council, acting on a proposal from the Commission after consultation of the ECJ or at the request of the ECJ after consultation of the Commission (cf. Art.257, para. 1, TFEU).

156 By contrast, any increase in the number of judges at the EGC leads inevitably to increasing difficulties for the internal coordination, to ensure the uniform character of the case law. An increase of the number of judges should therefore only be taken into consideration if all other means of discharging the EGC of its work burden have been exhausted (additional judges only as last resort, '*ultima ratio*').

157 Under the Treaty of Nice and still under the Treaty of Lisbon, the EGC is intended to be the General (Administrative) Court of the EU, in contrast to the ECJ as Constitutional Court and the specialized courts. Its basic function is the uniform safeguarding of the general principles of EU law across all fields of EU law. It cannot be the EGC's task to cope in first instance with large mass proceedings.

VI. Conclusion

It would seem, that – at least at the present stage – decentralizing the EU judiciary would not be an appropriate answer to possible problems, of whatever nature, of the EU judiciary. However, the main answer provided by the Treaties to face difficult situations, liable to imperil the adequate functioning of the EU Courts, would be *deconcentration, not decentralization* of the EU judiciary[158], and this seems to be a workable concept.

Yet, if ever the present or potential[159] competences of the EU judiciary were to be treated in a decentralized manner, in the interest of safeguarding the unity and consistency of EU law, two main tools for assuring a uniform case law will have to come into play, both related to the crucial functions of a centralized judicature: on the one hand, in cases of an attribution of tasks of the EU judiciary to a national judiciary, *preliminary ruling proceedings* will remain the classical – though indirect - way to insure a uniform interpretation and application of EU law.[160] On the other hand, if at some future stage regional EU Courts exercising parallel competences were to be established, a homogeneous case law enhancing the uniform interpretation and application of EU law in the sense of Article 19, para. 1, TEU, will have to be preserved by means of an efficient *right of appeal*, possibly complemented by some other system of *efficient legal review by a centralised EU Court*, i.e., a Court with jurisdiction for the whole Union (centralization through legal remedies).

Even if, on the whole, the question remains open as to how much uniformity would be really needed,[161] a legal situation which would completely exclude[162] such access to the remaining centralized EU judiciary would not seem compatible with the *effet utile* of Article 19, para. 1, TEU.

Inversely, it might well be that in the future, in one way or another, national judicial competences would either be centralized by switching to the EU Judiciary[163] or be transferred to still decentralized regional inter-Member States' courts. In the latter case, in order for them to be admissible to submit references for preliminary rulings, the organization and the tasks of such interstate courts will have to comply with the basic requirements identified by the ECJ. More particularly, such an interstate court would only be compatible with EU law if it is a court common to a number of Member States, situated, consequently, within the judicial system of the European Union, and if its

---

158 See pt. V.C. above.

159 Like e.g., in legal domains which up to now are not or not entirely falling within the scope of EU law.

160 In this context, the Member States' obligation to 'provide remedies sufficient to ensure effective legal protection in the fields covered by Union law' (Art. 19, para. 1, TEU) should be mentioned.

161 As to examples for possible 'inherent' divergences in the implementation and application of EU law see Sacha Prechal, 'National Courts in EU Judicial Structures', *Yearbook of European Law* (2006) 25 (1), pp. 429-450 (at p. 438).

162 At national or at EU level.

163 Like in the case of trademark law, see above.

decisions were subject to mechanisms capable of ensuring the full effectiveness of the rules of the European Union, as is the case for the Benelux Court.[164] It would have to be ensured[165] that the activities of such interstate courts would be attributable to the respective Member State signatories of the agreement establishing them: in case of a breach of EU law by such a court, those Member States would have to be liable in terms of proceedings for EU State liability before national courts and for infringement before the ECJ.[166] They would have to apply EU law and it would have to be warranted that the ECJ would have a binding last word on the question referred. The interstate agreement, on which such a partly decentralized judicial system would be based, would have to ensure that it does not have an adverse effect on the autonomy of the EU legal order and the primacy of EU law.

All in all, it seems that the workload of the EU Courts does not justify, at the present and still fragile evolutionary stage of European integration, either a general or even a partial decentralization of the EU Judiciary by creating regional EU Courts or by charging Member States' or inter-Member States' courts with present tasks of the EU judiciary. However, it is not excluded that arising new interstate models might bring new aspects to be further analysed in the context of specific legal matters not yet fully covered by EU law, but likely to be in the near future. Yet, at this stage, the creation of some kind of regional inter-Member States' courts would seem more appropriate – if ever – for newly emerging matters of EU law, rather than putting at risk the stability and continuity of already existing achievements.[167]

---

164 Judgment in *Parfums Christian Dior v Evora*, C-337/95, EU:C:1997:517, paragraphs 21 to 23; equally: ECJ opinion 1/09 of 8 March 2011, EU:C:2011:123, concerning the creation of a unified patent litigation system, paragraph 82.

165 Besides the necessary characteristics of any judiciary, see point II.2.a. *supra*.

166 See, e.g., ECJ opinion 1/09 of 8 March 2011, EU:C:2011:123, concerning the creation of a unified patent litigation system. More recently, with an expression of deep anxiety and preoccupation as to preserving exclusivity for the authoritative role of the ECJ in interpreting EU law with respect to another international judiciary: ECJ Opinion 2/13 of 18 December 2014, Opinion on a draft agreement concerning the Accession of the European Union to the European Convention for the Protection of Human Rights and Fundamental Freedoms EU:C:2014:2454 .

167 See Josef Azizi, Multilevel Governance: a Way to Increase Democratic Legitimacy of the Judiciary? in: A. Balthasar/J.W. Pichler (edts.), "Multilevel Governance - from Local Communities to a True European Community", Proceedings of the Conference on European Democracy 2014 (EuDEM 2014), Klein publishing, Vienna (2015) p. 25-50, at p.50.

The Union interest: a hidden persuader?

JACQUES BOURGEOIS AND MERIJN CHAMON

I. Introduction

We are grateful for the honour of contributing to this *Liber Amicorum*. Ian Forrester's prose and speech have always been elegant and on occasion, when needed, also barbed. In Court pleadings he once described the position taken by the European Commission as a jellyfish: it has no backbone yet it stings. The following musing over a concept that could deserve the same qualification is offered to Ian Forrester, a barrister/academic and a gentleman.

Legal practitioners working in the fields of trade or competition law will be familiar with what used to be called the Community interest and should now be called the Union interest. While the notion plays a prominent role in the Commission's assessment of complaints on alleged anti-competitive practices under Articles 101 or 102 TFEU and in decisions under the Common Commercial Policy (CCP), its function in these two fields at first sight seems rather different.

II. The Union interest in the common commercial policy…

While the Union relies on several trade defence instruments in the CCP, we will limit ourselves to looking at the measures taken under the Anti-Dumping Regulation.[1] Article 5 of that Regulation provides that proceedings will be initiated following complaints on behalf of the domestic EU industry, while Articles 7 and 9 of the Regulation provide that even if the Commission indeed concludes there is dumping and injury, duties may only be imposed if this is in the Union interest. Article 21(1) of the Regulation clarifies that various interests (of domestic industry, users and consumers) need to be assessed to verify whether it is in the Union interest to intervene by adopting anti-dumping measures. The first paragraph then further provides that such measures may not be adopted when this is 'clearly […] not in the Community interest.' The wording, unaltered since the introduction of this provision in secondary EU law,[2] is rather strange, since the logic of the paragraph's first sentence seems to be that the Union interest needs to be shown, while in its third sentence intervention seems to be the default course of action unless the Union interest militates against it. In any event, regardless of whether the Union interest is implicitly assumed or whether it should be explicitly shown, it is a necessary pre-condition under the Anti-Dumping Regulation in order for the Commission to act. While the Regulation refers to various interests, it only refers to the economic interests of three groups (domestic industry producing the goods in question, domestic users of those goods, and consumers). The Union interest thus only appears to be the EU's economic interest.

III. Is different from the Union interest in the EU's competition policy…

This is different for the notion of Union interest in the EU's competition policy. Article 7(2) of Regulation 1/2003 provides that any natural or legal person who can show a legitimate interest is entitled to lodge a complaint with the Commission for alleged violations of the competition rules laid down in Articles 101 and 102 TFEU. While the Commission is under a clear obligation to seriously examine every complaint with the necessary care,[3] this does not amount to a duty to start investigations on every complaint received. The Commission's discretion here is in large part covered by the

1 Council Regulation (EC) N° 1225/2009 of 30 November 2009 on protection against dumped imports from countries not members of the European Community, OJ 2009 L 343/51.

2 Although the Community interest had figured earlier in the Commission's decisional practice and in the Regulation itself, this provision was first introduced with the adoption of Regulation 3283/94, see Council Regulation (EC) N° 3283/94 of 22 December 1994 on protection against dumped imports from countries not members of the European Community, OJ 1994 L 349/1. Its wording was (and still is) virtually identical to the Commission's original proposal. See European Commission, COM (94) 414 final, p. 206.

3 Judgment of 18 September 1992, *Automec v. Commission*, T-24/90, EU:T:1992:97, para. 78.

notion of the Union interest,[4] commanding the Commission only to pursue those cases if this is warranted by said interest. The Union interest is not referred to in Articles 101 or 102 TFEU and, unlike the EU's anti-dumping policy, neither is it developed in the secondary legislation giving effect to these provisions.[5] Instead it has been elaborated in the Commission's enforcement practice and sanctioned by the General Court in the *Automec II* judgment[6] and by the Court of Justice in the *Ufex* case,[7] and the Commission has hence amply referred to it in its guidelines.[8] Further, while the Union interest in the anti-dumping regime functions as a necessary precondition to act, the Union interest in competition enforcement is a merely optional ground on which the Commission can rely to justify its decision not to investigate a complaint. Lastly, the Union interest in competition policy seems to be a broader notion than the notion in the EU's trade policy. While the latter, as noted, refers to *various* interests, the appreciation of the Union interest predominantly appears to require the Commission to assess the effects of an anti-dumping measure on all relevant *market* operators.

This of course has to do with the economic ambiguity of anti-dumping measures: while they may be beneficial to the competing domestic industry, downstream industry may instead benefit from lower prices on the upstream market and so may final consumers. All these interests, however, are economic interests. This is different for the Union interest in competition policy where the Commission has inter alia[9] identified the following criteria relevant in its assessment: (i) the possibility for the complainant to bring an action before a national court; (ii) the duration and extent of the alleged anti-competitive behaviour as well as its effect on competition in the EU; (iii) the significance of the alleged infringement for the functioning of the internal market; (iv) the probability of finding an infringement and the scope of the investigation required therefor; (v) the stage of the investigation and whether the alleged infringement has ceased or where the undertakings concerned have made commitments, etc.[10] Some of these criteria are clearly not strictly economic and also relate to the specific bureaucratic interest of the Commission and the general efficiency of enforcement proceedings.

---

4 For a more extensive discussion of the reasons for rejecting complaints, see Luis Ortiz Blanco (ed.), *EU Competiton Procedure*, Oxford, Oxford University Press, 2014, p. 558 et. seq.

5 Regulation 1/2003 does refer once to the Community interest in the 18th recital of its preamble. However, that recital clarifies Article 13 of the Regulation to the effect that the Commission cannot be forced to take up a case, in the event that no national competition authority has indicated its intent to deal with it, if it finds this is not in the Union interest. That the Commission may rely on the notion to reject investigating a complaint in the first place is not actually provided for. See Council Regulation (EC) N° 1/2003 of 16 December 2002 on the implementation of the rules on competition laid down in Articles 81 and 82 of the Treaty, OJ 2003 L 1/1.

6 Judgment in, *Automec v. Commission*, footnote 3 above, EU:T:1992:97, *op. cit.*

7 Judgment in *Ufex v. Commission*, C-119/97 P, EU:C:1999:116.

8 See *e.g.*, European Commission Notice on the handling of complaints by the Commission under Articles 81 and 82 of the EC Treaty, OJ 2004 C 101/65.

9 On the grounds for rejecting a complaint generally, see the Commission notice on best practices for the conduct of proceedings concerning Articles 101 and 102 TFEU, OJ 2011 C 308/6, paras 135-138.

10 Ibid., para. 44.

IV. But both may conceal 'hidden persuaders'

Even if the two policy fields concerned are rather distinct, it is still remarkable that the notion of Union interest may have such different interpretations, especially given the fact that both fields still fall squarely in the area of economic law, and that both frameworks in which the notion functions are strikingly similar: market operators lodging a complaint at the Commission for competition-distorting practices. Subscribing to Bomhoff's qualification of the EU legal order as being perfection-seeking,[11] the lack of coherence between these two distinct but related areas indeed seems one of those 'gaps', 'blind spots' or exceptions in an otherwise perfectionist EU legalism.[12] While we would not qualify it as an element in the perfection-seeking dynamics of EU law, we suggest that the two notions of Union interest may still share a similarity, having the function, in the decision-making process, of a hidden persuader.

The term hidden persuader was originally coined by Vance Packard in his discussion of the use of psychological techniques to engineer consumer preferences,[13] and takes up a slightly different function in our present argument. The working hypothesis proposed here is that the Union interest functions as an obscure criterion, determining the outcome in a procedure resulting from a complaint on either dumping or anti-competitive behaviour. The Union interest may be a hidden persuader in anti-dumping decisions in the sense that its formal assessment may cover only part of what leads to a decision *not* to impose anti-dumping duties or to impose lower ones than would actually be needed to remove the injury.[14] In competition law, the Commission's reliance on the Union interest may be a hidden persuader in the sense that the Commission may opt to reject a complaint for lack of Union interest, pursuant to Article 7 of Regulation 773/2004,[15] rather than on grounds relating to the intrinsic merits of the complaint.[16] The Commission would have reason to do so because the legal review of such a decision is only marginal compared to the review of a Commission decision finding there is no evidence of anti-competitive behaviour. In addition, it is doubtful that a Commission decision rejecting a complaint for lack of Union interest is a decision within the meaning of Article 16 of Regulation 1/2003 that is binding on national competition authorities (NCAs). Yet under our working hypothesis, the Commission would indeed consider that such a rejection decision pre-empts intervention by NCAs much the same way as

11 Jacco Bomhoff, 'Perfectionism in European Law', (2012) 14 *Cambridge Yearbook of European Legal Studies*, p. 83.

12 Ibid., p. 99.

13 See Vance Packard, *The Hidden Persuaders*, Harmondsworth, Penguin Books, 1962.

14 We leave aside the question of whether, during pre-lodging contacts with the Complaints office, prospective complainants might be advised not to file a complaint in politically sensitive cases.

15 Commission Regulation (EC) N° 773/2004 of 7 April 2004 relating to the conduct of proceedings by the Commission pursuant to Articles 81 and 82 of the EC Treaty, OJ 2004 L 123/18.

16 Such as those mentioned in the Commission notice, cited *supra* in fn. 9.

it would by finding there is no sufficient evidence of an infringement of competition rules. While the pre-emption in such a case would not be complete, an NCA would only have the possibility to apply national competition law and then only in so far as its decision does not contradict that of the Commission.[17]

V. Identifying the hidden persuader in practice

The embryonic argument presented above should not be interpreted as a contention that the Commission relies on the notion of Union interest to hide a *détournement de pouvoir*. Instead, it is argued that the discretion afforded to the Commission under that notion should be delineated more precisely, something which does not even necessarily imply a restriction of the Commission's discretion.

1. The common commercial policy

It is also precisely this discretion which makes the persuader hidden and hard to reveal in the Commission's decisional practice in the two fields concerned. An important case in the field of the CCP confirming the Commission's far-reaching discretion was *Fediol*.[18] In that 1988 case, the European association of seed crushers and oil processors challenged the Commission's decision not to impose duties against soy imports from Brazil, even after finding Brazil had indeed granted subsidies, since this would not have been in the Community's interests. At that time however, the Anti-Dumping Regulation[19] only provided that the Community interest needed to be taken into account by the Council when fixing definitive duties and by the Commission when fixing provisional duties. *Fediol* relied on these provisions and an *a contrario* reasoning to argue that the Commission could then not invoke the Community interest to simply terminate proceedings.[20] The Court however noted that 'although it is true that the Commission is under a duty to establish objectively the facts concerning the existence of subsidization practices and of injury caused thereby to Community undertakings, it has a *very wide* discretion to decide, in terms of the interests of the Community, whether or not to terminate the proceeding.'[21]

As noted above, the current Article 21 of the Anti-dumping Regulation now expounds on the Union interest but in a rather vague manner. While the Commission's bureaucratic interest is not explicitly recognized as coming under that Union interest, it may well

17 See *in fine* Judgment in *Toshiba Corporation e.a.*, C-17/10, EU:C:2012:72, paras 69-92.

18 Judgment in *Fediol v. Commission*, C-188/88, EU:C:1988:400.

19 Council Regulation (EEC) No 2176/84 of 23 July 1984 on protection against dumped or subsidized imports from countries not members of the European Economic Community, OJ 1984 L 201/1.

20 Judgment in *Fediol v. Commission*, EU:C:1988:400, *op. cit.*, paras 33-34.

21 Ibid., para. 40 (emphasis added).

be a legitimate interest to take up in the equation. The same goes for the EU's general interests in its external relations, especially in light of Article 21 TEU and the necessary coherence in its external action: does it not follow from this Treaty provision that the EU's decision in the CCP should take into account the EU's general objectives in its external relations? One could even apply this to the *Fediol* case of 1988, since in 1985 Brazil had just transitioned to a civilian government. Since the EU is now under a duty to advance democracy 'in the wider world' would it not be advisable to refrain from imposing duties on a frail democracy, even if from a purely economic perspective such duties would be justified?

This question has so far been kept off the table. In its 2006 green paper on trade defence instruments, the Commission proposed to come to a more transparent (re-)weighing of the industry/users/consumers' interests, further suggesting to take into account other interests (such as the impact on the EU's development policy),[22] but the reform process failed. In the currently pending review process,[23] the Commission has re-confirmed that the 'Union interest test ensures that the overall *economic* interests of the EU are considered before measures are imposed'[24] while further suggesting to adopt guidelines on the Union interest test.[25] While such guidelines would be welcome from a transparency perspective, the basic features of the Union interest test should still be laid down in legislation, in light of Article 290 TFEU, if they are to be considered as essential elements in the EU's trade defence policy.

Apart from these legitimate economic interests, linked to the objectives of the EU, which could be taken up in the Union interest test, the latter's clarification could also be seized to address wider policy interests that are now playing a role of hidden persuaders in the decision-making process. Above, it was noted that despite there being injurious dumping and Union interest, the duties imposed may be lower than the injury margin. Member States which are represented in the Advisory Committee might not share the Commission's view on the Union interest. Rather than meeting these Member States' concerns and reviewing its assessment of the Union interest, the Commission could then simply opt to change the level of the duty as a compromise.

---

22 See European Commission, Global Europe - Europe's trade defence instruments in a changing global economy, COM (2006) 763 final, p. 7.

23 See the proposal of the European Commission on the modernasiation of trade defence instruments, COM (2013) 192 final.

24 European Commission, Impact Assessment accompanying the proposal on the modernisation of trade defence instruments, SWD (2013) 106 final, p. 4 (emphasis added).

25 Ibid., p. 31 *iuncto* p. 36.

The injury margin used being too low to reflect the actual injury margin, is also made possible by the lack of transparency and the difficult methodology used.[26] However, the fact that definitive duties are not fixed by the Council any more, now that the CCP has been integrated in the general comitology regime,[27] should place a special responsibility on the Commission, guardian of the *common* European interest, to ensure duties are imposed (or not) in line with the *Union* interest.

The Union interest as employed by the Commission in anti-dumping proceedings should be subject to a more profound debate. It should for instance be explored whether the Union interest in some cases might require the Commission not to impose measures, even if this would make sense from a purely economic view. While this could sound like blasphemy to some, it should be repeated that the CCP is not an island, detached from the EU's general objectives and its duties to contribute to a prosperous, stable and democratic world. At the same time, clarification of the Union interest should confirm it is the *common* Union interest and does not serve to hide purely national interests. For this, the elimination of the Council's role in the adoption of anti-dumping measures would serve as a stepping stone.

2. The EU's competition policy

As explained above, the hidden-persuader function of the Union interest in competition law seems different from its function in the CCP. Indeed, while the latter requires clarification and a debate on its broadening, the Union interest in competition law would seem to require clarification and a narrowing of the Commission's discretion afforded pursuant to that notion.

Today the Union interest has become the key concept in the Commission's decisional practice.[28] The concept's primordial role is in part due to its flexibility and open-endedness. The criteria composing the Union interest[29] therefore do not constitute an exhaustive list and the Courts have further confirmed that the Commission may almost cherry-pick amongst the criteria in the motivation of its decisions rejecting a complaint for lack of Union interest.[30] While this large, judicially-sanctioned discretion is very interesting for the Commission, it should be equally clear that it is less so for the

26 See Edwin Vermulst & Paul Waer, 'The Calculation of Injury Margins in EC Anti-Dumping Proceedings', (1991) 25 *Journal of World Trade* 6, pp. 6-7. For a general discussion of the fixing of the amount of the anti-dumping duty, see Ivo Van Bael & Jean-François Bellis, *EU anti-dumping and other trade defence instruments*, Alphen aan den Rijn, Kluwer Law International, 2011, pp. 401-408.

27 This was eventually done through Regulation (EU) N° 37/2014 of the European Parliament and of the Council of 15 January 2014 amending certain regulations relating to the common commercial policy as regards the procedures for the adoption of certain measures, OJ 2014 L 18/1. The post-Lisbon rules on comitology are laid down in Regulation (EU) N° 182/2011 of the European Parliament and of the Council of 16 February 2011 laying down the rules and general principles concerning mechanisms for control by Member States of the Commission's exercise of implementing powers, OJ 2011 L 55/13. For a discussion of the reduced executive function of the Council, see *i.a.* Claude Blumann, 'Un Nouveau Départ Pour la Comitologie : le Règlement n° 182/2011 du 16 février 2011', (2011) 47 *Cahiers de droit européen* 1, pp. 35-36; Paul Craig, 'Delegated Acts, Implementing Acts and the New Comitology Regulation', (2011) 36 *European Law Review* 5, pp. 685-686.

28 Lorenzo Federico Pace, *European Antitrust Law*, Cheltenham, Edward Elgar, 2007, p. 234.

29 See *supra* at fn. 10.

30 See *i.a.* Case C-450/98 P Judgment in *IECC v. Commission*, C-450/98 P, EU:C:2001:276, paras 58-59.

individual complainant. Certainly, the latter would be better off if the Commission were required to exercise its far-reaching material discretion in a more structured fashion. Exactly this argument was made in the *Ufex* case on appeal by the appellants who argued that in *Automec II,* the Court of First Instance had ruled that '[t]he Commission should in particular balance the significance of the alleged infringement as regards the functioning of the common market, the probability of establishing the existence of the infringement and the scope of the investigation required in order to fulfil, under the best possible conditions, its task of ensuring that Articles 85 and 86 are complied with.'[31] They inferred from this that those criteria should all be looked at by the Commission before taking a decision on the Union interest and that the criteria could 'only be supplemented according to the circumstances by other particulars of the case.'[32] Otherwise, the appellants argued, the Union interest would 'become a vague concept defined on a case-by-case basis by the Commission itself.'[33]

The Court however noted that accepting such an argument 'would rigidify the case-law.'[34] And as a result the notion of Union interest remains a very malleable concept in the hands of the Commission. While the Court cannot be faulted with its rejection of the appellant's argument in *Ufex*, since it would otherwise indeed have codified the criteria to be taken into account to determine the Union interest, there nonetheless remains scope for requiring the Commission to follow a more structured approach in its assessment.

Incidentally, this could also be to the benefit of the Commission, since its large discretion has already backfired on occasion. In the *Watch repairers* case, the Commission had found that there was insufficient Union interest to continue its investigations into the alleged anti-competitive practices. The Commission had invoked four reasons to this end: (i) the market concerned was of limited size, (ii) the Commission could not establish the existence of an agreement or concerted practice, (iii) no dominant position in the market could be found (and hence the question of abuse did not pose itself) and (iv) there would be little likelihood to establish an infringement of competition rules.[35] However, these considerations were to a great extent linked, and depended on the Commission's definition and assessment of the relevant market (and its size). Since the Court found that the Commission had erred on the latter point, the Commission's rejection based on lack of Union interest collapsed like a house of cards.[36] In addition, the *Watch repairers* case also set at least one further limit to the discretion of the Commission when assessing the Union interest: whereas it is accepted that the

---

31 Judgment in *Automec v. Commission*, footnote 3 above, EU:T:1992:97, *op. cit.*, para. 86.

32 Judgment in *Ufex v. Commission*, EU:C:1999:116, *op. cit.*, para 76.

33 Ibid.

34 Ibid., para. 81.

35 See Judgment of 15 December 2010, *CEAHR v. Commission*, T-427/08, EU:T:2010:517, para. 163.

36 Ultimately, the annulment of the Commission's decision by the General Court did not really help the complainants. While the Commission reopened the case, it again concluded in 2014 that there was only a limited likelihood of finding an infringement, thus closing the case. See http://ec.europa.eu/ competition/antitrust/cases/dec_docs/39097/39097_3089_3.pdf.

Commission may refer to the possibility to bring proceedings at the national level, if the complainant's rights may be safeguarded at national level, the Court clarified that this possibility does not suffice if the practices complained of exist in several (*in casu* five) Member States, since that would make the Commission the appropriate authority.[37] Does the Union interest then not also impose a special responsibility on the Commission?

The decentralization of the enforcement of competition rules following Regulation 1/2003 also warrants a renewed look at the concept of the Union interest. In those cases where the Commission rejects a complaint for lack of Union interest, the complainant should indeed have the possibility to turn to the national competition authority, in accordance with the decentralization which Regulation 1/2003 puts in place. The latter's presence in the European Competition Network, together with the Commission, should allow a more efficient and effective handling of the complaint.

If the Commission follows a structured approach in its assessment, the complainant will be able to properly assess whether it could be fruitful to file a complaint at the NCA. Legal certainty and the efficiency of competition law enforcement would gain from such a structured approach. Conversely, it is more difficult for a complainant to appreciate the reasons behind a rejection if the Commission continues to apply the current concept of Union interest. In addition it may undermine the Commission's legitimacy if parties might believe that the Commission relies on the malleable concept of Union interest all too freely and that it in reality may have had other reasons for rejecting a complaint.

Again transparency is an issue here as well. The Commission's Annual reports on Competition Policy are not as voluminous as they used to be, and in the past the Commission only reported on the number of complaints received and the number of complaints rejected, without specifying whether it did so by relying on the (then) Community interest.[38] Furthermore, we have reached out to several NCAs querying whether market operators had lodged complaints with them following a rejection decision by the Commission for want of Union interest. Here the rules on confidentiality in those Member States proved to be very disparate and overall lacking in transparency. In all, the impression is that the potential of the concept of Union interest as a mechanism to come to an effective and transparent division of labour within the European Competition Network (ECN) is not being realized.

Taking the example of cooperation within the ECN: if the Commission rejects a complaint for lack of Union interest, because the conduct complained of is largely restricted to a single Member State or because there is insufficient significance for the functioning of the internal market, should the Commission not link this by default to the criterion whereby an NCA is better placed to conduct investigations? The NCA in turn could benefit from the first assessment of the Commission but could evidently not invoke the lack of Union interest to reject a complaint itself. While the Commission

37 *Judgment in CEAHR v. Commission*, fn.35 above, EU:T:2010:517, *op. cit.*, para. 176.

38 See for instance European Commission, Report on Competition Policy, Volume 2, 2004, p. 7.

has rightly noted that a rejection of a complaint at national level does not mean that the complaint will have sufficient Union interest,[39] this should then surely work both ways. The fact that a complaint was rejected for want of Union interest could never as such be invoked by an NCA. This was also recently recognized by the Belgian Competition Authority in the *Spira* case, but it still qualified the Commission's opinion as an 'important argument'.[40] It should be clear that whether this is the case depends on the quality of the Commission's reasoning and how it relies on the Union interest in its assessments.

Precisely this issue was also contested in the *Spira* case before the General Court,[41] but the latter followed its traditional approach to scrutinizing the Commission's assessment of the Union interest. The fact that the practices complained of had an EU- (and even world-)wide scope, was not found to be sufficient by the Court to prove Union interest. While the Court is evidently right on this point, an approach such as the one taken in the *Watch repairers* case might have resulted in special scrutiny by the Court: because the Commission would be the best-placed competition authority, it must be very sure that there is no Union interest, since recourse to the NCAs would not be a genuine alternative.

The Union interest as used by the Commission in its enforcement of Competition rules should be subject to a more profound debate. It should for instance be explored whether the Union interest in some cases requires the Commission to act, like in the CCP, instead of allowing the Commission not to (further) act (on complaints). The Union interest's potential in clarifying the division of tasks with the ECN, to the benefit of market operators and the efficiency of enforcement in general, also merits further consideration.

VI. Concluding remarks

In the Common Commercial Policy and in Competition Policy, the notion of Union interest plays an important role. While one might think that the Union interest in both fields would be one and the same, we found that their content and function is radically different even if there may be a sting to both.

However, in the ever self-perfecting EU legal order, greater coherence between these notions is possible and worthy of pursuing. A more profound debate on the Union interest would allow it to reflect the *genuine* Union interest, expelling such hidden persuaders as may exist now that are alien to it. Depending on the case, the Union interest might then require the Commission to act or refrain from acting. In both the

39 See Commission européenne, Affaire COMP/38863/B2 – Décision de rejet de plainte, 03/11/2007.

40 Decision, nr.BMA-2015-P/K-08 of 25 March 2015, para. 103 (http://economie.fgov.be/nl/binaries/BMA-2015-PK-08_PUB%20_tcm325-265454.pdf).

41 Judgment of 11 July 2013 *Spira v. Commission*, joined cases T-108/07 and T-354/08, EU:T:2013:367, para. 190.

fields of the CCP and the EU's Competition Policy, elements of the Union interest's current function in the other field could be introduced.

Greater transparency in the Commission's reliance on the Union interest would then also be in the interest of market operators, allowing them to better understand the Commission's reasoning and to make a more considered assessment of their case before filing a complaint at the Commission.

The outer limits of the competences under Article 114 TFEU

CLAUS-DIETER EHLERMANN*

I. Introduction

During his long and intensive career as one of the first and most experienced lawyers specialising in EU law, Ian Forrester's extraordinary reputation has – at least in my view – become more and more associated with competition law. But his professional experiences extend to other areas of EU law as well. The four fundamental freedoms, and, more generally, the internal market, are no exception. I feel therefore encouraged to contribute to this *liber amicorum,* in honour of Ian Forrester, a reflection on the evolution of an old friend of mine, i.e., the core EU power for the establishment and the functioning of the internal market, i.e., Article 114 (1) TFEU.

Article 114 (1) TFEU is one of – if not *the* – most important and frequently invoked provision conferring competences on the European Union (EU). It is therefore useful to explore the outer limits of this provision. At the same time, it is interesting to look at its evolution: is this provision, as interpreted by the Court of Justice of the EU (CJEU), very different from the original proposal of the Commission, which led, through the Single European Act (SEA), to the insertion of Article 100a into the EEC

---

* The author wishes to thank Philippe Claessens, Senior Associate at WilmerHale, for his assistance in documentary research.

Treaty (EECT)? Or is Article 114 TFEU – in spite of differences in wording – rather close to these original ideas?

The following text will try to answer these questions. It will demonstrate that, in practice, as interpreted by the CJEU, the remaining gap between the original proposal of the Commission of what became, through the SEA, Article 100a (1) EECT, and is now Art. 114 (1) TFEU, is rather narrow. The (more or less near) future will show whether a gap remains or whether it will totally disappear.

The analysis will be limited to Art. 114 (1) TFEU and its predecessors. The analysis will thus not extend to the subsequent paragraphs of Article 114, which were among the most controversial points of discussion during the Intergovernmental Conference leading to the SEA. This limitation applies in particular to the 'opt out' clause of paragraph 4 of Article 100a EECT (Art. 114 (5)), on which agreement was only reached after hours of discussion and drafting by the Heads of State and Government *in personam* at the European Council in Luxembourg on 2 and 3 December 1985. It is surprising that, in practice, these latter, highly controversial provisions have given much less rise to controversy than the – relatively uncontroversial – paragraph 1 of Article 114 and its scope of application.

In the same vein, the following analysis will not cover issues of proportionality and subsidiarity. It is well known – and often criticized – that the CJEU rarely finds that the Community legislature has violated the principle of proportionality, while measures of the Member States are often found wanting in this respect. Even more reluctant is the CJEU to engage in a discussion of the subsidiarity principle.

II. The genesis of Article 114 TFEU

The earliest version of Article 114 TFEU was introduced, through the SEA, as Article 100 A of the EEC Treaty. The Intergovernmental Conference, leading to the adoption of SEA, started on 9 September 1985.

The first suggestion of the Commission to the Intergovernmental Conference, dated 16 September 1985, which finally became Article 100a (1), read:

Article 2

> The Council, acting by a qualified majority on a proposal from the Commission and after consulting the European Parliament and the Economic and Social Committee, shall adopt all necessary measures for the establishment and functioning of the internal market…
>
> NB. Article 2 will have to be amended with the greater role to be given to Parliament in the legislative process.

A second Commission paper, dated 23 September 1985, explained the relationship of the proposed new article with the EEC Treaty as follows:

> Article 2 is an enabling provision, empowering the Community to take the measures necessary to achieve the objectives of Article 1 [defining the Internal Market]...
>
> It is also a procedural provision aimed at facilitating the decision-making process, with a view to the implementation of Article 1, by permitting recourse to a qualified majority vote...
>
> (1) Insofar as it implements Article 1, Article 2 is a *lex specialis* in relation to the relevant provisions of the Treaty:
>
> - which provide for unanimity: Articles ... 100 and 235.

Less than two weeks later, the Commission presented a revised suggestion, dated 5 October 1985, which was worded as follows:

> 'By way of derogation from Articles 100 and 235, the measures necessary to ensure the establishment and functioning of the internal market in respect of goods and services shall be adopted by the Council acting by a qualified majority.'

The Intergovernmental Conference translated this into Article 100a (1) EECT which read:

> By way of derogation from Article 100 and save where otherwise provided in this Treaty, the following provisions shall apply for the achievement of the objectives set out in Article 8a. The Council shall, acting by qualified majority on a proposal from the Commission in cooperation with the European Parliament and after consulting the Economic and Social Committee, adopt the measures for the approximation of the provisions laid down by law, regulation or administrative action in Member States which have as their object the establishment and functioning of the internal market.

Through the consolidation of the Treaty on European Union and of the Treaty establishing the European Community according to the Treaty of Nice, Article 100a became Article 95 of the Treaty establishing the European Community (TEC). The Treaty of Lisbon gave it today's wording. Article 114 (1) TFEU reads:

> Save where otherwise provided in the Treaties, the following provisions shall apply for the achievement of the objectives set out in Article 26. The European Parliament and the Council shall, acting in accordance with the ordinary legislative procedure and after consulting the Economic and Social Committee, adopt the measures for the approximation of the provisions laid down by law, regulation or administrative action in Member States which have as their object the establishment and functioning of the internal market.

Before I comment briefly on the discussions leading to the introduction of Article 100a (1) EECT through the SEA, it is useful to retrace, also briefly, the genesis of the provision defining the internal market, to which Article 100a (1) EECT and its successors refer.

The already-mentioned first document, submitted by the Commission to the Intergovernmental Conference leading to the SEA, dated 16 September 1985, contained the most radical definition of the internal market. Article 1 of this document read:

> The Community internal market shall be progressively established during the period expiring on 31 December 1992.

It shall comprise an area without borders in which persons, goods, service and capital shall move freely under conditions identical to those obtaining within a Member State. The revised Commission contribution to the Intergovernmental Conference, dated 5 October 1985, maintains this wording.

The text of Article 8a EECT, introduced through the SEA, is apparently more complex and less ambitious. It reads:

> The Community shall adopt all measures with the aim of progressively establishing the internal market over a period expiring on 31 December 1992 in accordance with the provisions of this Article and of Articles ... 100a ... and without prejudice to the other provisions of this Treaty.
>
> The internal market shall comprise an area without internal frontiers in which the free movement of goods, persons, services and capital is ensured in accordance with the provisions of this Treaty.

Through the consolidation of the Treaties, according to the Treaty of Nice, Article 100a EECT became Article 95 of the TEC. The Treaty of Lisbon gave it today's wording. Article 26 TFEU reads:

1. The Union shall adopt measures with the aim of establishing or ensuring the functioning of the internal market in accordance with the relevant provisions of the Treaties.
2. The internal market shall comprise an area without internal frontiers in which the free movement of goods, persons, services and capital is ensured in accordance with the provisions of the Treaties.
3. ...

To sum up:

The definition of the internal market has remained the same since its introduction through the SEA. The date for the establishment of the internal market has been dropped, since 31 December 1992 has long passed.

Also the conferral of competences through Article 100a (1) EECT, Article 95 (1) TEC and – now – Article 114 (1) TFEU has remained the same. Only in one respect does 114 (1) TFEU differ notably from its predecessors. Corresponding to its true importance and weight among the provisions attributing powers to the EU, Article 114 TFEU is not anymore conceived and presented as a derogation from the general power of approximation of laws, regulations and administrative provisions of the Member States, contained in a preceding provision of the TFEU. The TFEU therefore changes the traditional order of EU competences to harmonize. While Article 100a EECT (and Article 95 ECT) followed Article 100 EECT (respectively Article 94 TEC), Article 114 TFEU precedes Article 115 TFEU, thus relegating the original general power to an almost secondary role.

Before turning to the main part of this inquiry about the outer limits of Article 114 (1) TFEU, i.e., the case law of the CJEU, it is useful to go back to the genesis of Article 100a (1) EECT. Why does this provision in addition to the definition of its purpose, i.e., the achievement of the objectives set out in Article 8a EECT (in simpler terms, the establishment of the internal market as defined in Article 8a), refer to the approximation of laws, regulations and administrative actions of the Member States? Would the definition of the purpose not have been enough to circumscribe and limit the new conferral of competences, encapsulated in Article 100a (1) EECT? That was – as we have shown earlier – the position expressed in Article 2 of the first contribution of the Commission to the Intergovernmental Conference of 16 September 1985. Why was this position not sufficiently precise and acceptable for the Intergovernmental Conference?

It is impossible to answer this question satisfactorily today. Already in the autumn of 1985, representatives of different Member States would probably have given different answers.

It is however surprising, that even in the earliest comments on Article 100a (1) EECT, made soon after the end of the negotiations on the SEA, the question was not raised, although the problems resulting from the requirement of approximation of laws, regulations and administrative actions of Member States were properly identified and discussed.

On reflection, the explanation for the requirement of approximation of Member States' rules seems relatively simple. I still remember the observation of one of the participants in the Intergovernmental Conference, who explained that it would be easier for his government and his national parliament to accept a derogation from the existing Community competence to harmonize national law than a completely new, and therefore totally unknown, Community power to adopt provisions for the establishment and functioning of the internal market. From a psychological point of view, this position – which prevailed – is easily understandable. Article 100 EECT was a well-known source of Community competence; since the entry into force of the EECT, it had served as a legal base for a multitude of Directives. In other words, negotiators of the SEA preferred to operate in previously explored territory rather than venture into the unknown.

III. The interpretation of the CJEU

Having traced the history of Article 114 TFEU, it is appropriate to turn now to the interpretation of this provision – and that of its predecessors – by the CJEU. In view of the limited purpose of this paper, the reader should not expect an exhaustive list of

CJEU judgments; instead, our analysis will focus on those CJEU decisions, which seem relevant to answer our question.

A further warning is appropriate: conclusions of Advocate Generals will only be mentioned exceptionally. References to conclusions will be made mainly in cases in which there is a marked difference between the conclusions and the judgment.

The first notable case is the decision in the famous titanium dioxide case, more precisely the decision on the application for the annulment of Council Directive 89/428 of 21 June 1989 'on procedures for harmonizing the programmes for the reduction and eventual elimination of pollution caused by waste from the titanium dioxide industry'.[1] The action was brought by the Commission, supported by the EP, against the Council. At issue was the legal basis of the Directive. The original proposal of the Commission was based on Articles 100 and 235 EECT. The proposal followed a well-established practice frequently used prior to the entry into force of the SEA: Article 100 EECT covered the harmonization of conditions of production; recourse to Article 235 EECT was considered to be necessary, because the EECT contained no powers with respect to the protection of the environment. Following the entry into force of the SEA, the Commission changed its proposal and substituted Article 100a in place of Articles 100 and 235 EECT. The Council then amended the Commission's proposal, by replacing Article 100a by a reference to Article 130s. Like Article 100a, Article 130s was also introduced into the EEC Treaty by the SEA. According to Article 130s EECT, one of the provisions of the new Title VI 'Environment' of the EEC Treaty was, 'the Council, acting unanimously on a proposal from the Commission and after consulting the European Parliament and the Economic and Social Committee, shall decide what action is to be taken by the Community.'

The differences between Articles 100a and 130s EECT are obvious. Article 100a is satisfied if the Council decides by qualified majority, Article 130s requires unanimity; Article 100a associates the EP via the cooperation procedure, Article 130s limits the role of the EP to a simple consultation.

The choice of the right legal basis was not a new issue for the institutions involved in the titanium dioxide case. Normally, the correct legal basis is determined by the 'centre of gravity' of the measure at issue; if it is impossible to determine *one* single centre of gravity, because the measure has *several* equally important components, the legal bases for these components have to be *combined*. In practice, this combination entails that the stricter requirements prevail.

The litigation strategies of the Commission and the Council were determined by the established jurisprudence on the choice of the correct legal basis: for the Commission, the centre of gravity of the Directive was the establishment of the internal market through the harmonization of conditions of competition, thus Article 100a EECT. Conversely, the Council argued that the centre of gravity of the Directive was the

---

1 Judgment in *Commission of the European Communities v Council of the European Communities*, C-300/89, EU:C:1991:244.

elimination of the pollution caused by waste from the titanium dioxide manufacturing process, thus Article 130s EECT.

It is obvious that the benefits of Article 100a EECT for the Community decision-making process would have been destroyed if the CJEU had accepted the position of the Council. These benefits would also have been squandered if the CJEU had required recourse to both Article 100a and Article 130s EECT, (a requirement which was not even advanced by the Council).

Instead, the CJEU sided with the Commission. The CJEU considered that Article 100a EECT alone was the correct legal basis. However, the CJEU arrived at this result without accepting that the 'centre of gravity' was the establishment of the internal market through the harmonization of conditions of competition.

The CJEU started its analysis with a familiar statement: the legal basis for a measure may not depend simply on an institution's conviction as to the objective pursued but must be based on objective factors which are amenable to judicial review. Those factors include in particular the aim and the content of the measure.

Already, Advocate General Tesauro had considered 'it is impossible to identify in the Directive one main or predominant component and another which is merely incidental or secondary, but there are two components which are both essential and are inseparably linked'. In full agreement with the Advocate General, the CJEU found that 'according to its aim and content, as they appear from its actual wording, the Directive is concerned, indissociably, with both the protection of the environment and the elimination of disparities in conditions of competition'. The CJEU also found that the Directive at issue displays the features both of actions relating to the environment, i.e., Article 130s, and of a harmonizing measure, i.e., Article 100a.

However, the Court refused to apply its traditional jurisprudence, according to which the relevant measure has to be adopted on the basis of these two provisions. The CJEU stated that the use of both provisions as a joint legal basis 'would divest the cooperation procedure of its very substance', as unanimity, resulting from the use of 130s, would 'undermine the essential element of the cooperation procedure', the very purpose of which is to increase the involvement of the EP in the legislative process of the Community, reflecting 'a fundamental democratic principle'.

Therefore, a choice between Article 100a and Article 130s had to be made.

According to the CJEU, again in full agreement with Advocate General Tesauro, the correct legal basis in this case was Article 100a. The CJEU arrived at this conclusion in noting first that According to 130s (2) 'environmental protection requirements shall be a component of the Community's other policies'. Secondly, in the absence of harmonization of provisions relating to the protection of the environment, 'competition may be appreciably distorted. It follows that action intended to approximate national rules concerning production conditions in a given industrial sector with the aim of eliminating distortions of competition is conducive to the attainment of the internal market'. Finally, the CJEU observed that Article 100a (3) requires the Commission, in its proposals, to take as a base a high level of protection in matters of environmental protection.

It is interesting to note that the CJEU arrived at this conclusion without having recourse to concepts such as '*lex specialis*' or 'subject matter', which the Commission had invoked in support of its position. Instead, the CJEU referred to the horizontal character of environmental policy concerns (Article 130s (2)) and the obligations of the Commission resulting from Article 100a (3). This reasoning is of course transposable to sectors other than the environment (such as health, see *infra* 3), but also more nuanced than the concepts used by the Commission.

The second noteworthy case concerns the regulation No 1768/92 of 18 June 1992 concerning the creation of a supplementary protection certificate for medicinal products.[2] The regulation was issued on the basis of Article 100a EECT. Spain asked for its annulment. Spain argued (first) that the Community had no power to adopt the regulation at issue; it considered (second) that if such power were considered to exist, recourse to a unanimous vote by the Council, either on the basis of Article 100 or Article 235 EECT, would have been required.

In our context, only the reasoning of the CJEU dealing with Spain's second argument is of interest. The CJEU accepted the use of Article 100a, and thus rejected both Article 100 (as Article 100a derogates from Article 100) and Article 235 (as Article 235 may only be applied if no other provision of the Treaty gives the Community the necessary power to act).

The CJEU confirms its finding in the titanium dioxide case, in order to give full effect to the fundamental freedoms mentioned in Article 8a, that 'harmonising measures are necessary to deal with disparities between the laws of the Member States in areas where such disparities are liable to create or maintain distorted conditions in competition'.

In addition, the CJEU finds that harmonizing measures are necessary to deal with disparities between the laws of Member States in so far as such disparities are liable to hinder the free movement of goods within the Community. At the time the contested regulation was adopted, provisions concerning the creation of a supplementary protection certificate for medicinal products existed in two Member States and were at the draft stage in another State. The regulation thus aims to prevent the heterogeneous development of national laws leading to further disparities which would be likely to create obstacles to the free movement of medicinal products.

The regulation was thus validly adopted on the basis of Article 100a.

While the judgments in the titanium dioxide case and the supplementary protection certificate case are clearly 'Article 100a friendly', the third judgment, concerning the advertising and sponsorship of tobacco products, might be called 'Article 100a

2 Supplementary protection certificate case – Judgment in *Kingdom of Spain v Council of the European Union*, C-350/92, EU:C:1995:237.

unfriendly'.[3] At issue was an action for annulment, brought by Germany against Directive 98/42 of 6 July 1998 'on the approximation of the laws, regulations and administrative provisions of the Member States relating to the advertising and sponsorship of tobacco products'. The Directive contained an almost total prohibition of advertising and sponsoring. It had been based on Articles 57 (2), 66 and Article 100a EECT. Germany had voted against the adoption of the Directive.

The CJEU started its analysis in noting that the 'national measures affected are to a large part inspired by public health policy objectives'.

Since the entry into force of the Treaty of Maastricht, the Community had certain competences in the area of public health. However, the first indent of the new Article 129 (4) ECT excluded any harmonization of laws and regulations of the Member States designed to protect and improve human health. According to the CJEU, that provision did not mean that harmonizing measures adopted on the basis of other provisions of the Treaty cannot have any impact on the protection of human health. Such provisions may not, however, be used to circumvent Article 129 (4) ECT.

What follows is a detailed – and rather strict – analysis of Article 100a (1).

The CJEU states 'to construe that article as meaning that it vests in the Community legislature a general power to regulate the internal market would not only be contrary to the express wording ... but would also be incompatible with the principle ... that the powers of the Community are those specifically limited to those specifically conferred on it'.

A measure adopted on the basis of Article 100a must 'genuinely' have as its object the improvement of the conditions for the establishment and functioning of the internal market. If a 'mere finding of disparities' between national rules and of the 'abstract risk' of obstacles to the exercise of fundamental freedoms or of distortion of competition were sufficient to justify the use of Article 100a as a legal basis, 'judicial review of compliance with the proper legal basis might be rendered nugatory'. The Court must therefore verify whether the measure at issue 'in fact' pursues the objectives stated by the Community legislature.

The CJEU confirms its finding in the supplementary protection certificate case (*supra* 2) that recourse to Article 100a is possible if the aim is 'to prevent the emergence of future obstacles to trade resulting from multifarious development of national laws'. However, the emergence of such obstacles must be 'likely' and the measure in question must be 'designed' to prevent them.

The CJEU also confirms reasoning well known from the titanium dioxide case (*supra* 1), applied this time to public health. The Court notes that the third paragraph of Article 129 (1) provides that health requirements are to form a constituent part of the Community's other policies and that Article 100a (3) expressly requires that, in the process of harmonization, a high level of human health protection is to be ensured. Recourse to

3 Tobacco advertising I – Judgment in *Germany v Parliament and Council*, C-376/98, EU:C:2000:544.

Article 100a is thus not prevented on the grounds that public health protection is a 'decisive factor in the choices to be made'. In referring to a 'decisive factor', it is possible that this statement goes even a step further than the titanium dioxide judgment, where the Court had found the objectives of the protection of the environment and the elimination of disparities in conditions of competition to be 'indissociably' linked.

In applying these principles to the Directive at issue first to the free movement of goods and the freedom to provide services, the CJEU notes that with respect to periodicals, magazines and newspapers which contain advertising for tobacco products, though at present no obstacles exist to their importation, it is probable that such obstacles will arise in the future. In principle, a Directive prohibiting advertising in such media could therefore be adopted on the basis of Article 100a with a view to ensuring the free movement of press products.

However, the prohibition of advertising cannot be justified by the need to eliminate obstacles to the free movement of advertising media, or the freedom to provide services for 'posters, parasols, ashtrays and other articles used in hotels, restaurants and cafés, and the prohibition of advertisement spots in cinemas, prohibitions which in no way help to facilitate trade in the products concerned'.

Perhaps in anticipation of the next tobacco case, already pending (see *infra* 5), the CJEU accepts that a measure adopted on the basis of Article 100a may incorporate provisions which do not contribute to the elimination of obstacles to the exercise of the fundamental freedoms, 'provided that they are necessary to ensure that certain provisions imposed in pursuit of that purpose are not circumvented'. But the prohibitions mentioned in the preceding paragraph do not fall into that category.

With respect to the elimination of distortions of competition, the CJEU stresses, in referring to its earlier titanium dioxide judgment (*supra* 1), that the distortion has to be 'appreciable'. In the absence of such a requirement, the powers of the Community legislature would be practically unlimited.

The CJEU finds that the Directive at issue does not contribute to eliminating such distortions. As regards advertising agencies and producers of advertising media, undertakings established in Member States which impose fewer restrictions are unquestionably at an advantage in terms of economies of scale and increased profits. The effects of such advantages on competition are, however, 'remote and indirect'.

The CJEU accepts that differences between certain regulations on tobacco advertising through sponsorship may give rise to appreciable distortions of competition. These differences give rise, in particular, to certain sports events being relocated, with considerable repercussions on the conditions of competition for undertakings associated with such events. Such distortions could be a basis for recourse to Article 100a in order to prohibit 'certain forms of sponsorship'. But they are not such as to justify the use of Article 100a for an outright prohibition of advertising.

Finally, as regards distortions of competition in the market of tobacco products, for the CJEU, the Directive is likewise not apt to eliminate appreciable distortions of competition. Producers and sellers may be obliged to resort to price competition to influence their market share in Member States which have restrictive legislation. However, that does not constitute a distortion of competition, but rather a restriction of forms of competition which applies to all economic operators in those Member States.

The CJEU refuses to annul the Directive at issue in part, as partial annulment would entail amendment by the Court of provisions of the Directive. For the Court, such amendments are a matter for the Community legislature. The Court therefore annuls the Directive *in toto*.

The tobacco advertising I judgment was considered to be a landmark decision. It seemed to signal a change of paradigm. While the CJEU remained hesitant to control the respect by the Community legislature of the proportionality principle, and even more so of the subsidiarity rule, it exercised strict control over the use of legal bases of Community acts – in particular of a legal basis conferring rather broad powers to the Community institutions, and allowing recourse to a vote by qualified majority, such as Article 100a, thus protecting the Member States who did not agree with the view of other Member States.

However, examined more closely, the tobacco advertising I judgment does not reveal any new, revolutionary principle likely to restrict the use of Article 100a. Its requirements are dictated by common sense and, in so far as it refers to earlier jurisprudence, perhaps by greater clarity than the titanium dioxide and the supplementary protection certificate judgments.

Even more important is the observation that the tobacco advertising I decision has remained an isolated incident. We are not aware of any other CJEU decision which has found the recourse to Article 100a or its successor provisions (Article 95 ECT and Article 114 TFEU) by the Community legislature to be illegal. This – somewhat surprising – result is attributable in part to the capacity and willingness of the Community institutions to adapt their action to the requirements of the CJEU , but also to the flexibility of the CJEU with respect to the approximation requirement of Article 100a (Articles 95 ECT and 114 TFEU).

The fourth noteworthy case is 'Article 100a friendly' and comparable to the supplementary protection certificate case (*supra* 2). The Netherlands, supported by Italy, asked for the annulment of Directive 98/44 EC of 6 July 1998 on the legal protection of biotechnical inventions, adopted on the basis of Article 100a.[4] The Directive requires Member States, through their patent laws, to protect biotechnological inventions, whilst complying with their international obligations.

With respect to the use of Article 100a, the judgment seems to bring nothing new.

4 Judgment in *Kingdom of the Netherlands v European Parliament and Council of the European Union*, C-377/98, EU:C:2001:523.

In referring to its earlier jurisprudence (*supra* 2 and 3), the CJEU notes that recourse to Article 100a as a legal basis is possible if the aim is to prevent the emergence of future obstacles to trade resulting from the multifarious development of national laws, provided that the emergence of such obstacles is likely and the measure in question is designed to prevent them. According to the Court, in addition to the risk of divergent trends, at the time the Directive was adopted, marked differences with significant consequences were already apparent between national laws. The Directive therefore 'in fact aims to prevent damage to the unity of the internal market' which might result from the Member States' deciding unilaterally to grant or refuse protection.

However, the judgment diverges from the reasoning in the supplementary protection certificate case in expressly addressing the centre of gravity issue. For Italy, intervening in support of the Netherlands, the chief aim of the Directive is to support the industrial development of the Community and scientific research in the genetic engineering sector. Its legal bases should therefore have been Articles 130 and 130f ECT, instead of Article 100a ECT. The Court confirms its traditional jurisprudence that the legal basis on which an act must be adopted should be determined according to the main object of the act. For the CJEU, this main object is however the establishment of the internal market. 'Whilst it is common ground ... that the aim of the Directive is to promote research and development in the field of genetic engineering ... the way in which it does so is to remove the legal obstacles within the single market ... Approximation of the legislation of the Member States is therefore not an incidental or subsidiary objective of the Directive but is its essential purpose. The fact that it also pursues an objective falling within Articles 130 and 130f [ECT] is not, therefore, such as to make it inappropriate to use Article 100a [ECT] as the legal basis of the Directive'.

The fifth important case for the understanding of the limits of what is now Article 114 TFEU is again a tobacco case, but it pursues the line of 'Article 100a EECT/Article 95 ECT/Article 114 TFEU friendly' cases. Different from the third case which concerned advertising and sponsoring (*supra* 3), this case examines rules regulating the manufacturing, presentation and sale of tobacco products; more precisely, Directive 2001/37/EC of 5 June 2001 on the approximation of the laws, regulations and administrative provisions of the Member States concerning the manufacture, presentation and sale of tobacco products (tobacco manufacturing case). The Directive was based on Articles 95 and 133 ECT (common commercial policy) and aimed at recasting and amending two earlier Directives. The CJEU replied to a request for preliminary ruling, made by the High Court of England and Wales in proceedings brought by British American Tobacco (Investments) Ltd and Imperial Tobacco Ltd.[5]

With respect to Article 95, the CJEU repeats its findings in the tobacco advertising I case, that measures based on this article must genuinely have as their object the establishment and functioning of the internal market, and actually contributing to the elimination of obstacles to the free movement of goods or the freedom to provide services, or to the removal of distortions of competition. The Court also repeats its

5 Judgment in *British American Tobacco (Investments) and Imperial Tobacco*, C-491/01, EU:C:2002:741.

traditional jurisprudence that recourse to Article 95 is possible if the aim is to prevent the emergence of future obstacles to trade, provided the emergence of such obstacles is likely and that the measure in question is designed to prevent these obstacles. Finally, the Court reiterates its recent statement (in the tobacco advertisement I case) that the Community legislature cannot be prevented from recourse to Article 95 on the grounds that public health is a decisive factor in the choices to be made.

Contrary to the infamous posters, parasols, ashtrays, etc., mentioned in the tobacco advertisement I case, the market for tobacco products, especially cigarettes, in the Community is one in which trade between Member States represents a relatively large part. National rules laying down the requirements to be met by those products, in particular those relating to their designation , composition or packaging, are in themselves liable, in the absence of harmonization at Community level, to constitute obstacles to the free movement of goods. Differences between the Member States' laws, regulations and administrative provisions on the manufacture, presentation and sale of tobacco products, which create obstacles to trade, had already emerged, or were likely to emerge; the public being increasingly conscious of the dangers to health posed by consuming tobacco products, and the Member States responding to these concerns by adopting new rules intended to more effectively discourage consumption of those products by warnings and information appearing on their packaging, or to reduce the harmful effects of tobacco products by introducing new rules governing their composition.

While the preceding considerations of the CJEU derive from already well-known principles, the following findings are new.

First, the Court does not allow Article 95 to be called into question by the argument that, since the Community legislature had already established a fully harmonized regime applicable to the tar yields of cigarettes, it could not legislate afresh on the basis of that article or, in any event, it could only do so on the basis of new scientific facts.

The Court finds that 'the Community legislature can properly carry out its task of safeguarding the general interest recognised by the Treaty, such as public health, only if it has the freedom to amend the relevant Community legislation so as to take account of any changes in perception or circumstances. It follows that, even where a provision of Community law guarantees the removal of all obstacles to trade in the area it harmonizes, that fact cannot make it impossible for the Community legislature to adapt that provision in step with other considerations'. Article 95 can therefore be used again, even if no 'approximation of the provisions laid down by law regulation or administrative action in Member States' is any more at stake.

The Court adds that progress in scientific knowledge is not the only ground on which the Community legislature can decide to adapt Community legislation, since it must also take into account other considerations such as increased importance given to the social and political aspects of the anti-smoking campaign.

The Directive does not apply only to tobacco products manufactured for sale in the Community, but also to tobacco products manufactured for export to non-member States. The CJEU also accepts that this aspect of the Directive can be based on Article 95, in referring to its tobacco advertising I judgment.

The Court finds that although the prohibition of manufacture for export is not directly aimed at improving the conditions for the functioning of the internal market, the fact remains that a measure adopted on the basis of Article 95 may incorporate such a provision, as long as its purpose is to ensure that certain prohibitions concerning the internal market and imposed in pursuit of that objective are not circumvented. Such is indeed the intention of the Community legislature in the case at hand: it intends to prevent the undermining of internal market provisions in the tobacco products sector, which might be caused by unlawful reimports into the Community or by deflections of trade within the Community.

The Court holds that it was thus possible for the Directive, including the prohibition on the manufacture within the Community, for export to non-member countries of cigarettes, to be adopted on the basis of Article 95.

The reference to Article 133 was superfluous and a purely formal effect without consequences. The link to the implementation of the commercial policy was in any event 'secondary in relation to the content of the Directive as a whole, which was primarily designed to improve the conditions for the functioning of the internal market'.

The contribution of the judgments of the CJEU in joined cases C-465/00, C138/01 and C-139/01[6] is limited, but clearly 'Article 100a friendly'. At issue in these three cases is the interpretation of Directive 95/46/EC on the protection of individuals with regard to the processing of personal data and on the free movement of such data. The CJEU replied to requests for preliminary rulings from the *Verfassungsgerichtshof* and the *Oberster Gerichtshof* of Austria in proceedings brought by the Austrian *Rechnungshof* and two employees of the Oesterreichischer Rundfunk. The questions of the Austrian Courts related essentially to the interpretation of the Directive. The legal basis of the Directive, Article 100a, was only touched upon marginally.

The CJEU notes that the Directive is intended, as its title suggests, to ensure the free movement of personal data between the Member States through the harmonization of national provisions on the protection of individuals with regard to the processing of such data. The Court adds that recourse to Article 100a does not presuppose the existence of an actual link with free movement in every situation referred to by the measure. What matters is that the measure must actually be intended to improve the conditions for the establishment and functioning of the internal market.

The two following cases both deal with Article 8 of Directive 2001/37/EC, which was already examined in one of the preceding paragraphs (*supra* 5). Article 8 of the Directive obliges Member States to prohibit the marketing of tobacco for oral use.

6 Judgment in *Österreichischer Rundfunk and Others*, joined cases C-465/00, C-138/01 and C-139/01, EU:C:2003:294.

The CJEU replied to requests for preliminary rulings from the High Court of Justice of England and Wales in proceedings between Swedish Match AB and Swedish Match UK Ltd and the Secretary of State for Health[7] and from the *Verwaltungsgericht Minden* in proceedings brought by Arnold André GmbH.[8] The key passages of the two 'tobacco for oral use' judgments are worded identically.

The two judgments may be qualified again to be 'Article 95 ECT/Article 114 TFEU friendly'. We consider this qualification to be appropriate in spite of the fact that both judgments refer to 'direct effect' on the functioning of the internal market, thus alluding to a requirement of Article 100 EECT, which was deliberately deleted during the negotiations of the Single European Act on the new Article 100a EECT. It might be useful to recall that Article 100 EECT/Article 94 ECT/ Article 115 TFEU allow only the approximation of such laws, regulations or administrative provisions of the Member States 'as directly affect the establishment or functioning of the common/internal market'. However, 'direct effect on the functioning of the internal market' is not really an additional requirement, as such direct effect is said to be a logical consequence of the approximation of provisions of the Member States which obstruct the fundamental freedoms.

In addition, both 'tobacco for oral use' judgments contain a clarification that will be useful for future cases. The CJEU holds that the appropriate measures may consist in requiring all Member States to authorize the marketing of the products concerned, subjecting such an obligation of authorization to certain conditions, 'or even provisionally or definitely prohibiting the marketing of a product or products'.

The next relevant judgment falls into this category of measures. The judgment concerns Directive 2002/46/EC of 10 June 2002 on the approximation of the laws of the Member States relating to food supplements, adopted on the basis of Article 95 ECT. The CJEU replied to requests for a preliminary ruling from the High Court of Justice of England in Wales in proceedings brought by the National Association of Health Stores and Health Food Manufacturers Ltd and by the Alliance for Natural Health and Nutri Link Ltd.[9] The 'foods supplement' case repeats already well-known principles concerning the interpretation of Article 95, without adding any new insights of general importance.

The following case (the 'smoke flavouring' case[10]) resembles the foods supplement case. At issue was Regulation (EC) No 2065/2003 on smoke flavourings used or intended for use in and on foods. The regulation was based on Article 95 ECT. The United Kingdom asked for its annulment, as the regulation does not harmonize national laws but sets up a centralized procedure (a 'regulatory committee' procedure) at Community level for the authorization of smoke flavouring for foods. According to

7 Judgment in *Swedish Match AB and Swedish Match UK Ltd v Secretary of State for Health*, C-210/03, EU:C:2004:802.

8 Judgment in *Arnold André*, C-434/02, EU:C:2004:800.

9 Judgment in *Alliance for Natural Health and Others*, Joined cases C-154/04 and C-155/04, EU:C:2005:449.

10 Judgment in *United Kingdom v Parliament and Council*, C-66/04, EU:C:2005:743.

the United Kingdom, the legislative power conferred by Article 95 is a power to harmonize national laws, not a power to establish Community bodies or to confer tasks on such bodies, or to establish procedures.

The judgment of the CJEU, which pursues the line of 'Article 95 ECT/Article 114 TFEU friendly' decisions, clarifies the scope of Article 95 with respect to harmonization by implementing powers conferred on the Commission. After repeating some of the already well-known principles established by earlier jurisprudence, the Court observes that by the expression 'measures for the approximation' the authors of the Treaty intended to confer on the Community discretion as regards the harmonization technique most appropriate, 'in particular in fields which are characterized by complex technical features. That discretion may be used in particular to choose the most appropriate harmonization technique where the proposed approximation requires physical, chemical or biological analyses to be made and scientific developments in the field concerned to be taken into account.' The Court adds that where the Community legislature provides for a harmonization which comprises several stages, two conditions must be satisfied. First, the Community legislature must determine in the basic act the essential elements of the harmonizing measure in question. Second, the mechanism for implementing those elements must be designed in such a way that it leads to a harmonization within the meaning of Article 95. That is the case where the Community legislature establishes detailed rules for making decisions at each stage of such an authorization procedure, and determines and circumscribes precisely the powers of the Commission as the body which has to take the final decision. That applies in particular where the harmonization in question consists in drawing up a list of products authorized throughout the Community to the exclusion of all other products. The Court finds that all these conditions are fulfilled; it therefore approves the use of Article 95 as legal basis of the Regulation.

The so-called ENISA case[11] goes even further. The judgment is probably the most 'Article 95 ECT/Article 114 TFEU friendly' decision of the CJEU so far. At issue was Regulation No. 460/2004, adopted on the basis of Article 95. As its title suggests, the Regulation establishes a European Network and Information Security Agency (ENISA). According to the Regulation, the role of the Agency is to assist the Commission and the Member States, and in consequence cooperate with the business community, in order to help them to meet the requirements of network and information security, thereby ensuring the smooth functioning of the internal market. Preceding the adoption of the Regulation establishing ENISA, the Community had adopted a series of Directives relating to electronic networks.

The United Kingdom asked for the annulment of the Regulation. It submitted that Article 95 does not provide an appropriate legal basis, as none of the provisions of the Regulation approximates, even indirectly and in a very minor way, national legislation. The United Kingdom maintained that the regulation responds to the risk to the smooth functioning of the internal market arising from the complexity of the matter not by

11 Judgment in *United Kingdom v Parliament and Council*, C-217/04, EU:C:2006:279.

harmonizing national rules, but by creating a Community body with an advisory role. Giving non-binding advice cannot amount to an approximation of the provisions laid down by law, regulation or administrative action in the Member States within the meaning of Article 95. Moreover, according to the United Kingdom, the dissemination of such advice may in practice increase the disparities which exist between national laws. The only possible connection which might exist between the tasks of the Agency and the harmonization of law is the one which results from the fact that it assists the Commission. However, that role is too far removed from Community legislation seeking harmonization of national legislation.

Advocate General Kokott sided with the United Kingdom. The Regulation does not affect any approximation of laws. The Agency, ENISA, cannot adopt any provisions on the approximation of laws, nor does it take part in specific procedures for the adoption of such provisions. The potential contributions of ENISA to the approximation of laws are not sufficient for its establishment to be regarded as a measure for the approximation of the provisions laid down in Member States. It is not predictable whether and in what form ENISA will contribute to the approximation; the corresponding measures will not necessarily be based on Article 95. The ENISA Regulation is therefore not so much a step on the way to the approximation of laws of the Member States as a step into the uncertain. These considerations led Advocate General Kokott to propose to annul the Regulation.

Conversely, the Court approves the choice of Article 95 as a legal basis for the Regulation. Recalling its findings in the 'smoke flavouring' case, that the Community legislature enjoys discretion in regards to the method of approximation most appropriate for achieving the desired result, the Court notes that nothing in the wording of Article 95 implies that the addressees of measures adopted on the basis of that provision can only be individual Member States. The legislature may deem it necessary to provide for the establishment of a Community body responsible for contributing to the implementation of harmonization in situations where, in order to facilitate the uniform implementation and application of acts based on Article 95, the adoption of non-binding supporting and framework measures seems appropriate. However, the tasks conferred on such a body must be closely linked to the subject matter of the acts approximating provisions of law of the Member States. Such is the case in particular where the Community body thus established provides services to national authorities and/or operators which affect the homogeneous implementation of harmonizing instruments and which are likely to facilitate their application.

The Court finds that the tasks conferred on ENISA are indeed closely linked to the objectives pursued by the existing Community Directives in the area of network and information security. The Regulation does not constitute an isolated measure but forms part of a normative context circumscribed by these Directives and directed at completing the internal market in the area of electronic communications, an area in which technology is being implemented which is not only complex, but also developing rapidly. The Community legislature was therefore entitled to consider that the opinion of an independent authority providing technical advice at the request of the Commission and the Member States might facilitate the transposition of the Directives at issue into the laws of the Member States and the implementation of those Directives at national level. Consequently, the ENISA Regulation could be adopted on the basis of Article 95 and the action of the United Kingdom is dismissed.

A chronological examination of CJEU jurisprudence should discuss, at this stage, the 'European Cooperative Society' case. We prefer, however, to reserve this case for later analysis (*infra* 18). Instead, we mention, somewhat *en passant,* a case which might be considered to be remotely similar to the 'supplementary protection certificate' (*supra* 2) and to the 'biotechnical inventions' (*supra* 4) cases. At issue was Directive 2001/29/EC on the harmonization of certain aspects of copyright and related rights in the information society. The Directive is based, inter alia, on Article 95. The Court replies to a request for preliminary ruling of the *Ostre Landsret* in proceedings brought by Laserdisken ApS against the Danish Ministry of Culture.[12]

The CJEU finds that Article 95 is one of the appropriate legal bases of the Directive. The reasoning of the Court in this respect is very short. The Court notes that, according to its preamble, the proposed harmonization will help to implement the four freedoms of the internal market and that without harmonization at Community level, legislative activities at national level might result in significant differences in protecting the free movement of services and products incorporating, or based on, intellectual property.

The next case, 'tobacco advertising II' is an old acquaintance. At issue this time was Directive 2003/33/EC on the approximation of the laws, regulations and administrative provisions of the Member States relating to the advertising and sponsorship of tobacco products. Directive 2003/33/EC was adopted following the annulment by the Court of the preceding Directive 98/43/EC on the advertising and sponsorship of tobacco products. The new Directive was again based on Article 95. The plaintiff was once more Germany, which had again voted against the adoption of the Directive.

However, contrary to the tobacco advertising I case, the judgment of the Court this time approves the choice of Article 95.[13]

That result is not surprising, as the new Directive follows the lessons of the tobacco advertising I judgment.

The Directive is limited to press products, radio broadcasts and information society services, television advertising being already prohibited by an earlier Directive.

The Court notes that tobacco advertising by means of those media has a cross-border character which enables undertakings engaged in the production and sale of tobacco products to develop marketing strategies for the widening of their customer base outside the Member State from which they come.

---

12 Judgment in *Laserdisken ApS v. Kulturministeriet*, C-479/04, EU:C:2006:549.

13 Judgment in *Germany v Parliament and Council*, C-380/03, EU:C:2006:772.

For the Court, the already existing or likely future differences between the Member States also meant that there was an appreciable risk of distortions of competition.

The Court clarifies that when the existence of obstacles to trade has been established, it is not necessary also to prove distortions of competition.

Contrary to its predecessor, the Directive is designed and intended to apply uniformly throughout the Community. According to the express provisions of the Directive, Member States cannot prohibit or restrict the free movement of goods or the freedom to provide services which comply with the Directive.

The Court confirms that recourse to Article 95 as a legal basis does not presuppose the existence of an actual link with the free movement between the Member States in every situation covered by the measure founded on that basis. What matters is that the measure adopted on that basis is actually intended to improve the conditions for the establishment and functioning of the internal market.

Finally, the CJEU rejects the argument that since the true purpose of the prohibition is not to improve the conditions for the establishment and functioning of the internal market, the Community legislature infringed the prohibition laid down in Article 152 (4) (c) ECT, which excludes any harmonization of the laws and regulations of the Member States in the field of public health. The Court repeats that, provided that the conditions for recourse to Article 95 are fulfilled, the Community legislature cannot be prevented from relying on Article 95 on the ground that public health protection is a decisive factor in the choices to be made. The Court adds that Article 152 (4) (c) ECT does not mean that harmonizing measures adopted on the basis of other provisions of the Treaty cannot have any impact on the protection of human health.

The judgment in the 'retention of data' case[14] pursues the line of 'Article 95 friendly' cases. At issue was Directive 2006/24/EC on the retention of data generated or processed in connection with the provision of publicly available electronic communication services or of public communication networks, and amending Directive 2002/58/EC. The Directive was adopted on the basis of Article 95. Ireland, which had voted against the adoption of the Directive, asked for its annulment. According to Ireland, the sole objective or, at least, the main or predominant objective of the Directive is to facilitate the investigation, detection and prosecution of crime, including terrorism. Ireland submits that the centre of gravity of the Directive does not concern the functioning of the internal market. Therefore, the only legal basis for the Directive is Title VI of the EU Treaty.

The CJEU disagrees. Following the principles resulting from its earlier jurisprudence, the Court considers that the conditions for recourse to Article 95 are fulfilled. Legislative and technical disparities exist between the different national provisions governing the retention of data by service providers, with significant economic implications.

---

14 Judgment in *Ireland v Parliament and Council*, C-301/06, EU:C:2009:68.

By contrast, the measures provided by the Directive do not, in themselves, involve intervention by the police or law-enforcement authorities of the Member States. The Directive thus regulates operations which are independent of any police and judicial cooperation in a criminal matter.

It follows that the substantive content of the Directive is directed essentially at the activities of service providers, and therefore relates predominantly to the functioning of the internal market.

Having made clear that the action brought by Ireland related solely to the choice of legal basis and not to any possible infringement of fundamental rights, the CJEU consequently dismisses the action of Ireland.

Another high profile and very 'Article 95 ECT/Article 114 TFEU friendly' case is the famous 'Roaming Regulation' case.[15] At issue was the validity of Regulation (EC) No 717/2007 on roaming on public mobile telephone networks within the Community and amending Directive 2002/21/EC. The Regulation was adopted on the basis of Article 95. The Court replies to a reference from the High Court of England and Wales in proceedings brought by Vodafone Ltd and three other mobile telephone companies.

The Regulation amends the regulatory framework, established by the Community legislature through Directive 2002/21/EC, also adopted on the basis of Article 95. That framework established a mechanism allowing national regulatory authorities (NRAs), where there is no effective competition on a relevant market, to impose *ex ante* regulatory obligations on undertakings designated as having significant market power. The Regulation is the Community answer to the complaint that roaming rates for mobile telephony calls between Member States are excessively high. The Regulation caps the wholesale and retail charges terrestrial mobile operators may charge for the provision of roaming services on public mobile networks for voice calls between Member States.

At first sight, the Regulation is a measure of consumer protection. However, as a matter of consumer protection, the Regulation can only be adopted if the conditions of Article 95 are fulfilled, as Article 153 ECT allows other measures only if they support, supplement or monitor the policy pursued by the Member States.

At the centre of the case is thus the power of the Community legislature, already recognized in the tobacco manufacturing case (*supra* 5), to adapt existing Community rules to new perceptions or circumstances.

Advocate General Poiares Maduro discusses in detail the nature and the limits of this power of adaption and amendment. According to the Advocate General, amendments may supplement and complement a harmonizing measure. They may also change it. The need for amendment may arise precisely because particular harmonizing measures may come to be seen to be operating in unsatisfactory ways, and may therefore require an amendment inconsistent with the original approach. The amendment itself does

15 Judgment in *Vodafone and Others*, C-58/08, EU:C:2010:321.

not need to be justified by the need to eliminate obstacles to trade or distortions of competition, but the measure as amended must still serve the purpose of Article 95. For this, one has to consider what would be the situation in the absence of any Community regulation on the subject matter. Potential obstacles to trade arising from national price control measures can be prevented either by imposing limits on national regulations on prices or by regulating prices at Community level. The fact that the Community legislator may originally have chosen the first of these approaches to prevent obstacles to trade should not prevent the later adoption of a different approach if other policy goals so require.

The Advocate General then asks the question whether, in the present case, in the absence of Community legislation, there was indeed a risk of different national price control measures susceptible to create obstacles to trade and justify the adoption of Community price control measures. In his view, the Community legislator has not demonstrated, either at the time of the adoption of the original measure or of the amendment, that such a risk existed.

However, the Advocate General believes that the Community legislator could regulate roaming prices under Article 95 because the Regulation removes restriction to free movement arising from the behaviour of private parties which disfavour cross-border activity. The disfavouring of cross-border activities has the potential to impede the establishment of an internal market by discouraging customers from engaging in cross-border economic activity such as making use of roaming services. Actions, including those of private actors, which directly disfavour cross-border activities, can be characterized as impediments to the establishment of the internal market. To justify the application of Article 95 to actions of private parties, the Advocate General invokes the case law of the CJEU on the horizontal application of free movement rules.

We do not consider it necessary to take a closer look at the innovative and unusual reasoning of the Advocate General, as the CJEU follows the traditional road to examine and justify the legal basis of the Roaming Regulation. The Court notes that there was pressure for Member States to take measures to address the problem of the high level of retail charges for Community-wide roaming services. It follows for the Court that the Community legislature was actually confronted with a situation in which it appeared likely that national measures would be adopted aiming to address the problem of the high level of retail charges for Community-wide roaming services through rules fixing the rate of retail charges. Such measures, based on the residual competence of Member States as regards consumer protection rules, would have been likely to lead to a divergent development of national laws.

Taking into account the considerable interdependence of retail and wholesale charges for roaming charges, a divergent development of national laws seeking to lower retail charges only, without affecting the level of costs for the wholesale provision of Community-wide roaming services, would have been liable to cause significant distortions of competition and to disrupt the orderly functioning of the Community-wide roaming market. The Court therefore concludes that the object of the Roaming

Regulation is indeed to improve the conditions for the functioning of the internal market and that it could be adopted on the basis of Article 95.

The following case (Case C -137/12, judgment of 22 October2013) hardly tells us anything about the limits of Article 114 TFEU. It is more concerned with the exclusive competences of the EU to conclude agreements in the area of commercial policy. At issue is the Decision on the signing, on behalf of the Union, of the European Convention on the legal protection of services based on, or consisting of, conditional access. Prior to the negotiation of the Convention, the Community legislature had adopted Directive 98/84/EC on the legal protection of services based on, or consisting of, conditional access. While the Commission had proposed to adopt the Decision on the basis of Article 207 (4) TFEU, i.e., the special basis for commercial policy agreements, together with Article 218 (5) TFEU, the general basis for the signing of international agreements, the Council had substituted Article 207 (4) with Article 114 TFEU. The Commission, supported by the EP, opposed the reference to Article 114 TFEU and asked for the annulment of the Decision.

The CJEU agrees with the Commission. The Court finds that the objective of the Decision, by authorising the signing of the Convention on behalf of the EU, is intended to introduce similar protection to that assured by Directive 98/84/EC in European non-member countries, in order to promote the supply of such services to those countries by EU service providers. That objective, which can be seen to be the primary objective of the Decision, therefore has a specific connection with international trade in those services and can legitimately be linked to the common commercial policy. The Court recognizes that certain provisions of the Convention are also supposed to improve the conditions for the functioning of the internal market by clarifying the definitions of sanctions. For the Court, that objective is however purely incidental to the primary objective of the Decision; as a purely ancillary objective, it provides no justification for the adoption of the Decision on the basis of Article 114 TFEU.

The most recent and also most 'Article 114 TFEU friendly' case decided by the CJEU is the famous 'short selling' case.[16] At issue was Article 28 of Regulation (EU) No 236/2012 on short selling and certain aspects of credit default swaps. This article vests the European Securities and Market Authority (ESMA) with certain powers to intervene by way of legally binding acts in Member State financial markets, in the event of a threat to the orderly functioning and integrity of financial markets, or to the stability of the whole or part of the financial system in the Union. The action which ESMA is empowered to take under Article 28 of Regulation (EU) No 236/2012 includes the imposition on natural and legal persons of notification and disclosure requirements, and a prohibition on the entry into certain transactions or subjecting such transactions to conditions. The United Kingdom requested the annulment of this article for a variety of reasons. We will examine only one of these reasons, i.e., the alleged violation of Article 114 TFEU. For the United Kingdom, in as much as Article 28 of Regulation (EU) No 236/2012 empowers ESMA to adopt individual decisions that are binding on

16 Judgment in *United Kingdom v. Parliament and Council*, C-270/12, EU:C:2014:18.

third parties in the event of insufficient or inadequate action by relevant competent authorities of the Member States, Article 114 TFEU is an incorrect legal basis for the adoption of such measures.

Advocate General Jääskinen agrees with the United Kingdom. While the Advocate General, in following the jurisprudence of the CJEU in the ENISA case (*supra* 10), approves the use of Article 114 for the establishment of ESMA and the regulation of its tasks and powers, he considers that reliance on Article 114 as the sole legal basis for Article 28 of Regulation (EU) No 236/2023 is not supported by the Court's case law. For the Advocate General, the conferral of decision making powers under that article on ESMA, in substitution for the assessments of the competent national authorities, cannot be considered to be a measure for the approximation of the provisions laid down by law, regulation or administrative action in Member States, which have as their object the establishment and functioning of the internal market within the meaning of Article 114 TFEU. The decision making powers of ESMA with respect to disclosure, prohibitions or conditions relating to short selling go much further than the power to lay down measures relating to a specific product or class of products and, if necessary, individual measures concerning those products, recognized in earlier jurisprudence. The decision making powers of ESMA also go further than those recognized in the ENISA case (*supra* 10). In fact, Article 28 of Regulation (EU) No 236/2012 creates an EU level emergency decision-making mechanism that becomes operable when the relevant competent national authorities do not agree as to the course of action to be taken. Hence, the outcome of the activation of these ESMA powers is not harmonization, or the adoption of uniform practice at the level of Member States, but the replacement of national decision making with EU level decision making. The Advocate General therefore concludes that Article 28 of Regulation (EU) No 236/2012 goes beyond the limits of Article 114 TFEU.

The CJEU disagrees. It approves the choice of Article 114 TFEU as the legal basis of the Regulation. Its reasoning follows the precedents in the smoke flavouring case (*supra* 9), recognising the discretion of the EU legislature to determine the most appropriate method of harmonization for achieving the desired result, especially in fields with complex technical features, and in the ENISA case (*supra* 10), allowing the EU legislature to delegate to a Union body, office or agency powers for the implementation of the harmonization sought. The CJEU recalls further that according to its jurisprudence, the concept of measures for approximation of legislation encompasses the power of the EU legislature to lay down measures relating to specific products or a class of products as well as, if necessary, individual measures concerning these products, and that the addressees of these measures do not only have to be the Member States. Article 28 of Regulation (EU) No 236/12 is in fact directed at the harmonization of the Member States' laws, regulations and administrative provisions relating to the supervision of a number of stocks and the monitoring, in specific situations, of certain commercial transactions concerning these stocks. The EU legislature considered it appropriate to lay down a common regulatory framework with regard to the coordination and consistency between Member States where measures have to be taken in exceptional circumstances. Therefore, the harmonization is intended to prevent the creation of obstacles to the proper functioning of the internal market and the continuing application of divergent measures by Member States. Article 28 of Regulation (EU) No 236/12 thus satisfies all requirements laid down in Article 114 TFEU.

The most recent high-profile controversy in which the scope of Article 114 was marginally at stake concerns the EU regulation on 'bankers' bonuses'. The case (C-507/13) will however never lead to a decision by the CJEU, because immediately after the publication of the conclusions of the Advocate General,[17] the UK withdrew its request for annulment. It is only this rather peculiar and singular circumstance, i.e., the immediate withdrawal of the annulment action after the (unfavourable) conclusions of the Advocate General, which prompts us to mention the case.

At issue was, inter alia, the new Capital Requirements Regulation (EU) 575/2013 on prudential requirements for credit institutions and investment firms, and amending Regulation (EU) 648/2012. The legal basis of the Regulation is Article 114 TFEU.

The UK requested the annulment of certain requirements of disclosure of remuneration elements by financial institutions, contained in Article 450 of the Capital Requirements Regulation. The UK considered recourse to Article 114 (1) to be excluded by Article 114 (2) according to which Article 114 paragraph 1 shall not apply, inter alia, to provisions relating to the rights and interests of employed persons.

Advocate General Jääskinen rejected the UK's arguments without much ado. He said that he had difficulty in seeing how disclosure obligations contained in Article 450 (1) of the Capital Requirement Regulation could be considered to be provisions that are relevant to the rights and interests of employed persons, as Article 450 (1) of the Regulation only binds financial institutions and not its employees. The Advocate General proposed to reject the action for annulment.

Before drawing conclusions from this review of the jurisprudence of the CJEU, we need to come back to the 'European Cooperative Society' case[18] which we have already mentioned earlier (*infra* 11), but reserved for later analysis. At issue was Regulation (EC) No 1435/2003 on the Statute for a European Cooperative Society (SCE). The Regulation lays down a single statute applicable to the European cooperative society in order, inter alia, to remove all barriers to cross-border cooperation of companies while taking account of the special features of cooperatives. The proposal of the Commission for an SCE was based initially on Article 100a, and later, following the Treaty of Amsterdam, on Article 95 ECT. The Council amended the proposal and substituted Article 95 with Article 308 ECT. The EP, supported by the Commission, requested the annulment of the Regulation. According to the EP, Article 308 was wrongly chosen as the legal basis; the Regulation should be based on Article 95.

17 Opinion of Advocate General Jääskinen in *United Kingdom v. Parliament and Council*, C-507/13, EU:C:2014:2394.

18 Judgment in *United Kingdom v. Parliament and Council*, EU:C:2006:279.

The CJEU recalls that Article 308 ECT may be used as the legal basis for a measure only where no other provision of the Treaty gives the Community institutions the necessary power to adopt it. Having also recalled its jurisprudence with respect to Article 95 ECT, the Court notes that it is apparent from the content and the purpose of the Regulation that it aims to introduce a new legal form in addition to the national forms of cooperative societies. The SCE is a form which coexists with cooperative societies under national law. In those circumstances the Regulation, which leaves unchanged the different national laws already in existence, cannot be regarded as aiming to approximate the laws of the Member States applicable to cooperative societies, but has as its purpose the creation of a new form of cooperative society in addition to the national forms. The CJEU stresses that this finding is not affected by the fact that the contested regulation does not lay down exhaustively all of the rules applicable to SCEs and that, for certain matters, it refers to the law of the Member State in the territory of which the SCE has its registered office, since that referral is of a subsidiary nature. The Court concludes therefore that Article 95 could not constitute an appropriate legal basis for the adoption of the Regulation which was correctly adopted on the basis of Article 308 ECT.

IV. Conclusions and outlook

After this review of the case law of the CJEU, it is relatively easy to draw general conclusions and to indicate the limits of Article 114 TFEU.

The first comment concerns the judgments just examined. They impress the observer through their consistency. The CJEU seems to act like a mason who carefully puts one brick on another. The cases which interpret successively Article 100a EECT, Article 95 ECT and, finally, Article 114 TFEU, appear to result in a remarkably coherent construction. The fact that all the judgments reviewed have led to the CJEU deciding in the most representative form of deliberation, i.e., the 'Grand Chamber', may have contributed to this impressive result.

The second comment concerns the CJEU's general attitude to the Treaty articles just mentioned. The vast majority are what we have called 'Article 100 a EECT/Article 95 ECT/Article 114 TFEU friendly'. The 'tobacco advertising I' decision has remained an isolated case. Some observers regret this. We do not share this view. We accept that the Directive at issue in this case was excessive and that at least partial annulment was justified. But the reasons for annulment might have been found in a violation of the proportionality principle, instead of a violation of the limits of Article 100a EECT. However, the traditional reluctance of the CJEU to criticize the Community legislature for non-respect of the proportionality principle is well known; this reluctance might explain the recourse to annulment for overstepping the limits of Article 100a EECT.

The third comment concerns the attitude of the CJEU to the 'harmonization' requirement of Article 100a EECT/ Article 95 ECT/Article 114 TFEU. We have always considered this requirement to be superfluous for the purpose of limiting the conferral of powers to the Community legislature which these Articles entail. The requirement of the 'achievement of the objectives' of the internal market, set out in Article 8a EECT/ Article 14 ECT/Article 26 TFEU, would have been sufficient. However, whatever the merits of inserting the harmonization requirement may have been at the time of the SEA, that element has been maintained by the Lisbon Treaty. It exists and has to be respected.

The fourth comment concerns the flexibility which the Court has shown with respect to the harmonization requirement. In recognising this flexibility, we have less in mind the jurisprudence with regard to the likely adoption of future national laws, regulations or practices, as well as the possibility to apply Article 100a EECT/ Article 95 ECT/ Article 114 TFEU even when harmonization has taken place already, so as to allow the Community legislature to adapt the existing Community rules to new circumstances or perceptions. This kind of flexibility might be considered to follow from common sense considerations and therefore not to be particularly noteworthy. Instead, we want to highlight the remarkable respect which the CJEU has shown for the particular aspects of Community rule making, as demonstrated by the natural smoke flavouring case (*supra* 9), the ENISA case (*supra* 10) and the short selling case (*supra* 16). Is it surprising that all these cases (plus the bankers' bonuses case, which did not mature to a CJEU judgment), were brought by the UK? We do not believe so. For us, these actions are a sign of the profound EU scepticism which characterizes UK policy vis-à- vis the EU. In this context it might be noted that with four requests for annulment, the UK is not only the champion of direct actions targeting Community rules adopted under Article 110a EECT/Article 95 ECT/Article 114 TFEU, but that the UK also leads the list of requests for preliminary rulings: four of the seven requests for preliminary rulings examined above have been made by the High Court of England and Wales.

However, the harmonization requirement requires a price. The first price is the one which results from the European Cooperative Society case (*supra* 18). EU rules which do not harmonize national legislation, but which are strictly in addition to national rules, cannot be adopted under Article 114 TFEU. They cannot be adopted even under Article 115 TFEU, asking the Council to act unanimously, as Article 115 TFEU requires also 'the approximation of . . . laws, regulations or administrative provisions of the Member States'. The only available legal basis is thus Article 352 TFEU. It might be recalled that Article 352 (1)'s first sentence reads:

> If action by the Union should prove necessary, within the framework of the policies defined in the Treaties, to attain one of the objectives set out in the Treaties, and the Treaties have not provided the necessary powers, the Council, acting unanimously on a proposal from the Commission and after obtaining the consent of the European Parliament, shall adopt the appropriate measures.

At first sight, it is surprising that the adoption of EU rules which are additional to national rules, and thus exercise no constraint on national legislation, is more difficult than the adoption of EU rules which entail such constraints, because they oblige the national legislature to adapt national law. This position is supported by the new Article 118 paragraph 1 TFEU, inserted by the Lisbon Treaty, which reads as follows:

> In the context of the establishment and functioning of the internal market, the European Parliament and the Council, acting in accordance with the ordinary legislative procedures, shall establish measures for the creation of European intellectual property rights to provide uniform protection of intellectual property rights throughout the Union and for the setting up of centralised Union-wide coordination and supervision procedures.

However, Article 118 TFEU is a special provision for the creation of European intellectual property rights. It is therefore perfectly possible to hold the view that the addition of EU law to national law, without any consequences for national law other than the preference of private or legal persons for the solutions offered in the future by EU law, is a stronger interference with the autonomy of Member States than simple harmonization.

The legal basis chosen by the Commission for its proposal on a Common European Sales Law (OJ 2012 C 37/16), i.e., Article 114 TFEU, has therefore little chance to be retained by the Community legislature.

The second limit flows from the fact that harmonization of provisions laid down by law, regulation or administrative action in Member States requires the existence – or at least the likelihood of future existence – of such provisions, the harmonization of which is considered to be necessary for the establishment and the functioning of the internal market. In other words, the pretence to harmonize is void, if there is nothing to be harmonized. The EU is thus not entitled to introduce obstacles to the fundamental freedoms which are totally new, because such obstacles neither exist in one or several of the Member States, nor are they likely to be introduced by any of the Member States.

We recognize that this limit is more fragile than the preceding one. First, because the likely adoption of future legislation entailing hitherto unknown obstacles to the fundamental freedoms is a matter of appreciation. Secondly, because the CJEU has always held that individual provisions have to be considered in their overall context. It is therefore tempting to argue that an all-embracing regulation of a certain economic activity by the EU justifies – and perhaps even requires – a restriction which has not yet found its expression in national legislation. However, this argument would be incompatible with the fundamental finding of the CJEU in the tobacco advertising I judgment (*supra* 3) that 'to construe that article [Article 100a EECT, now Article 114 TFEU] as meaning that it vests in the Community legislature a general power to regulate the internal market would not only be contrary to the express wording of [that provision] . . . but would also be incompatible with the principle embodied in Article [5 TEU] that the powers of the Community are limited to those specifically conferred on it.'

A final – and in our view most justified – limit to the use of Article 114 TFEU results from its objective, the establishment and functioning of the internal market. We recall that the internal market is defined as 'an area without internal frontiers in which the free movement of goods, persons, services and capital is ensured in accordance with the provisions of the Treaties' (Article 26 TFEU). Ensuring the 'free movement of goods, persons, services and capital … in accordance with the provisions of the Treaties' entails in the first place the removal of obstacles to the fundamental freedoms; according to the settled case law of the CJEU starting with the titanium dioxide case (*supra* 1), it encompasses also the removal of appreciable distortions of competition. National provisions which neither constitute obstacles to one of the fundamental freedoms nor entail appreciable distortions of competition can therefore not be harmonized under 114 TFEU. Such provisions are also likely to escape harmonization according to Article 115 TFEU. They may even be beyond the reach of Article 352 TFEU. But whether that will be so is a matter of pure speculation.

Evolving constitutional pluralism in Europe: the judicial conversation advances?

PATRICK R. HUGG

'The dialogue between the two courts is henceforth entering a new phase.'[1]

I. Introduction

Legal actors in Europe today, and in most of the world, find themselves subject to an intricate mosaic of political, economic, and legal forces, representing a 'shift in the architecture of public power.'[2] Norms radiate from divergent sources in today's globalized world,[3] generating innovative forms of pluralistic governance, blending traditional hard law with various nuances of soft law[4] and other pressures,[5] yielding a

---

1 Mattias Wendel, 'Exceeding Judicial Competence in the Name of Democracy: The German Federal Constitutional Court's OMT Reference', 10 *Eur. Const. L. Rev.* 263, at 264.

2 Neil Walker & Stephen Tierney, 'Introduction, A Constitutional Mosaic? Exploring the New Frontiers of Europe's Constitutionalism', in *Europe's Constitutional Mosaic* 6, *passim* (2011). See generally, Klemen Jaklic, *Constitutional Pluralism in the EU* (2014) (for theoretical exploration of constitutional pluralism).

3 In contemporary discourse, the 'global-words' can be so widely overused that their meaningful use requires specific definition within its context. See e.g., Thomas Klak, *Globalisation and Neoliberalism: the Carribean Context 1* (1997) ('overused, abused, and . . . dangerous euphemism.', Id.).

4 '[T]hose regulatory instruments and mechanisms of governance that, while implicating some kind of normative commitment, do not rely on binding rules or on a regime of formal sanctions.' Anna di Robilant, 'Genealogies of Soft Law', 54 *Am. J.Comp. L.* 499, 499 (2006).

5 William Twining, 'Normative and Legal Pluralism: A Global Perspective', 20 *Duke J. Comp.& Intl L.* 473, 475 (illustrating the ubiquitous pressures in various parts of the world today, from WTO decisions, Islamic banking practices, to university library rules, and traditional norms of etiquette. Id. at 475).

'deep pluralism.'[6] Forms range broadly, from the powerful legal authority of national constitutions, to other national, regional and local legislation, on the one hand, to the different forms of authority agreed through international treaties establishing collaborations, such as the European Union, the Council of Europe, the United Nations, the World Trade Organization, and through scores of additional trade and other accords containing voluntary commitments to follow mutually agreed principles and rules.[7] Indeed, this strong, gradual diffusion of state-centered authority outward to other reference sources 'represents a defining and deepening feature of the contemporary age.'[8]

Virtually everywhere, the legal and governmental space is thus shared among these sources and degrees of power or influence. These authorities and influences may be independent, may complement or overlap one another, and sometimes they may conflict.[9] They are also subject to interpretation and enforcement by diverse governments, judicial organs and dispute resolution regimes. As a part of this, international courts, more than ever, have assumed a role hardly imagined in the past, as they 'increasingly speak to issues that used to fall exclusively within the national domain ... [issuing] literally thousands of international judicial rulings reviewing human rights and economic practices of governments ..., further evidence of evolving norms of state sovereignty.'[10]

The consequent legal pluralism sometimes includes interactions among different tribunals and regulatory authorities that can assume 'a dialectical quality' as they inform and influence one another.[11] At the highest level especially, 'constitutional pluralism' forms part of the mosaic, and its development has emerged as a ubiquitous topic in the public law academy, though it can be a vague term, meaning different things to different people.[12] In this article's analysis, the meaning is more straightforward,

6 Gráinne De Búrca, Robert O. Keohane, and Charles F. Sabel, New Modes of Pluralistic Governance, 45 *N.Y.U. J. Int'l L. & Politics*, 2013. ('The result is deep pluralism: the profusion within many domains of international organizations with partially complementary, but also partially competing purposes, representing differing values and accountable to distinct sets of authorizing actors—to the extent they are accountable at all.' Id. at 2). For insightful examination of globalism and legal pluralism, see, Ralf Michaels, 'Global Legal Pluralism', 5 *Annual Review of Law & Social Science* 1 (2009).

7 See generally, G. De Búrca and J.H.H. Weiler, *The Worlds of European Constitutionalism 1-3* (Cambridge University Press, 2012).

8 Neil Walker, *Intimations of Global Law 3* (Cambridge University Press, 2015).

9 Paul Schiff Berman, '[N]ormative conflict among multiple, overlapping legal systems is unavoidable and might even sometimes be desirable . . . .', 'Global Legal Pluralism', 80 *S. Cal. L.Rev.* 1155, 1155 (2007).

10 Karen Alter, *The New Terrain of International Law xv* (2013). 'Every national judge is bound to apply fundamental rights which are simultaneously provided by a plurality of legal regimes, with at least partially overlapping scopes of application: national constitutions/charters or statutory law, the EU (which includes the EU Charter and a steadily growing number of EU legislative measures), the ECHR, and a significant number of international treaties in force in the Member States.... At the same time, each system of fundamental rights protection (national, *supra*national, international) has its own court, empowered with exclusive jurisdiction to exercise judicial review of the specific legal act providing protection to fundamental rights.' *Judicial Interaction Techniques – Their Potential and Use in European Fundamental Rights Adjudication*, Center for Judicial Cooperation, European University Institute, at 14.

11 Berman, *supra* note 9, at 1197.

12 J.H.H. Weiler, 'Prologue: global and pluralist constitutionalism – some doubts', in *The Worlds of European Constitutionalism 8-9*, (G. De Búrca & J.H.H. Weiler eds., 2012).

referring to the repeated and competing claims of authority by different judicial organs in the EU and its Member States.

When various norms diverge or even conflict, the inevitable question arises: who defines and orders this complex source of governance? This article explores the more narrow inquiry challenging both jurists and scholars today: How is legal authority in the European Union (EU) shared, and how is this sharing negotiated and agreed?[13] Scholarly observation and thought on these topics is expansive.

In 2014, judicial assertions of authority at the national level and the EU level posed renewed opportunities for further discussion and perhaps some disharmony. The German Constitutional Court (*Bundesverfassungsgericht*, hereafter BVerfG) in 2014 submitted its 'truly historic'[14] first TFEU Article 267[15] reference to the European Court of Justice (hereafter ECJ)[16] – its first in the some sixty years of its uneven relationship with the ECJ, in what might be considered 'an invitation to a judicial dialogue.'[17] In that reference, the BVerfG's Second Senate posed questions to the ECJ and also suggested or, some say, presumed to instruct the ECJ as to the answer to its questions with attention to EU treaty requirements, and 'assuming the competence to interpret EU law,'[18] and then insisting that the German Court may not be bound by the ECJ decision anyway.[19]

From multiple directions, court watchers now anxiously await the ECJ's opinion, and subsequently the BVerfG's reception of it, raising the obvious and immediate uncertainties of the effects of a direct conflict, or shades of conflict, or of a compromise between the two courts, and possible ricochets from other Member State courts questioning EU and European Central Bank (ECB) actions. The unsurprising thesis of this article recommends the prudence of a repetition of past judicial accommodations. Particularly in 2015, with political instability and widespread disenchantment with

13 Neil Walker & Stephen Tierney, 'Introduction, A Constitutional Mosaic? Exploring the New Frontiers of Europe's Constitutionalism', in *Europe's Constitutional Mosaic* 11 (2011).

14 Mattias Wendel, 'Exceeding Judicial Competence in the Name of Democracy: The German Federal Constitutional Court's OMT Reference', 10 *Eur. Const. L. Rev.* 263, at 263.

15 Consolidated Version of the Treaty on the Functioning of the European Union art. 267, O.J. (C 326), 26/10/2012, at http://eur-lex.europa.eu/legal-ontent/en/TXT/?uri=CELEX:12012E/TXT.

16 BVerfGE, Case 2 BvR 2728/13 et al. *OMT*, order of 14 Jan. 2014. This decision was published on 7 Feb. 2014. EN translation available at: www.bundesverfassungsgericht.de/en/decisions/rs20140114_2bvr2813en.html. At the ECJ, the referral case is captioned: 'Case C-62/14 Peter Gauweiler, Bruno Bandulet, Wilhelm Hankel, Wilhem Nölling, Albrecht Schachtschneider, Joachim Starbatty, Roman Huber and Others, Johann Heinrich von Stein and Others, and Fraktion DIE LINKE im Deutschen Bundestag v Deutcher Bundestag (Request for a preliminary ruling from the Bundesverfassungsgericht (Germany)),' lodged on 10 February 2014.

17 Jürgen Bast, 'Don't Act Beyond Your Powers: The Perils and Pitfalls of the German Constitutional Court's Ultra Vires Review', 15 *German L.J.* 167, 173 (2014).

18 Dagmar Schiek, 'The German Constitutional Court's Ruling on Outright Monetary Transactions (OMT) – Another Step towards National Closure?', 15 *German L.J.* 329, 337 (2014)
('not so much as a reference but an assumption of competence' *Id.*).

19 *OMT Judgment*, at para. 103.

presiding governmental regimes at all levels in Europe,[20] the two prestigious courts should, and likely will, arrive at another pragmatic negotiated arrangement for sharing authority, clarifying further their historic, evolving relationship.

II. Context of this novel judicial relationship

The evolution of the European Union as a new model in international law has been the product of dynamic political and judicial leadership over the six decades from the first European Community treaty to the present.[21] Strong national leadership forged the original treaties that proposed the first peaceful, supranational collaboration on the continent, and subsequent treaties gradually advanced the integration project forward.[22] Early in this course of events, the judiciary of the then European Economic Community articulated a bold and novel vision of how this legal order must be interpreted and enforced if the principles and ambitions of the treaties were to be realized, creating a new, more powerful form of international collaboration,[23] 'without either precedent or imitation.'[24] Combining the radical innovations of the original treaties with the ECJ's equally radical interpretive doctrines, 'an *avant garde* international organization usher[ed] forth a new model of transnational discourse ... no longer governed by the general principles of public international law.'[25]

The story of these remarkable achievements retraces, of course, a well-worn path, heralded and criticized by scholars, jurists, and politicians. Perhaps a bit less well-known, except among constitutional specialists, is how the national governments and

20 See, e.g., Bruno Waterfield, 'How the European dream is dying, state by state', *The Telegraph*, 24 Jan. 2015, http://www.telegraph.co.uk/news/worldnews/europe/eu/11366613/How-the-European-dream-is-dying-state-by-state.html (24 March 2015) ('Europe is being swept by a wave of popular disenchantment and revolt against mainstream political parties and the European Union.' Id.).

21 See generally, P.J.G. Kapteyn, A.M. McDonnell, K.J.M.Mortelmans and C.W.A. Timmermans (eds.) *The Law of the European Union and the European Communities* 1-51 (Kluwer Law International, 2008.). National governmental leaders exercised bold leadership, seizing crucial opportunities to advance European integration, from French political economist Jean Monnet and Foreign Minister Robert Schuman to German Chancellor Konrad Adenauer and Belgian Paul-Henri Spaak and Italian Alcide De Gasperi in the founding of the first Communities. Norman Davies, *Europe: A History* 1083-85 (1996). For a detailed personal account, see Jean Monnet, *Memoirs passim.* (Doubleday, 1978). Similarly early on, the European Court of Justice's 'massively expansionist interpretation of the Treaties' established doctrines of supremacy and direct effect that would make effective the new legal order, in 'the most radical moment in the European integration project.' Bill Davies, *Resisting the European Court of Justice* 24, 1 (Cambridge Univ. Press 2012). See also, Karen J. Alter, *Establishing the Supremacy of European Law* 1-27, 2001 ('The transformation of the European Legal System was orchestrated by the ECJ through bold interpretations.'Id. at 1.).

22 Jeremy Rifkin, *The European Dream* 203-09 (2004). See also, John Gillingham, *Coal, Steel, and the Rebirth of Europe, 1945-55*, at 228-236 (For detailed description of the assertiveness of Monnet, Schuman, and Adenauer toward model-breaking collaboration between France and Germany. Id.).

23 Edward A. Tomlinson, 'Reception of European Law in France', 1 *Colum. J. Eur. L.* 183 (1995).

24 Dieter Grimm, 'The European Court of Justice and National Courts: The German Constitutional Perspective After the Maastricht Decision', *3 Colum. J. Eur. L.* 229, 229 (1997).

25 J.H.H. Weiler, 'The Transformation of Europe', 100 *Yale L.J.* 2403, 2407-07 ('The importance of developments in this early period cannot be overstated.' Id. at 2410.).

their judiciaries accepted these pronouncements in divergent ways.[26] While national political leaders often favoured or acquiesced in this European cooperation, some of their highest courts resisted intrusion into their jurisdiction to safeguard their national sovereignty and their national constitutions.[27]

For centuries, national constitutions have represented an almost *Lex Sacra*, a touchstone of authority 'central to the legitimate exercise of public power . . . dominat[ing] the modern liberal imagination since the Enlightenment. The ideal of limited collective self-governance has spawned a rich and highly diverse tradition of hard-fought national constitutions from the time of the Glorious Revolution in 1688 into the present.'[28] ECJ opinions exerting primacy over these traditional norms could seem adventurous, and their full dimension has spawned 'a key, if controversial, discourse and practice for those seeking to explain, justify and frame the progress of the new supranational polity and the challenges it poses to the state system.'[29]

In post-war Germany, the BVerfG was created as a special court with a special place and mission in time.[30] Because of the radical post-war political environment in which it was born, following World War II's human rights offences, this court would conceive its role as final guardian and defender of the identity of the new Germany in which human rights were tightly safeguarded through a form of a 'constitutional patriotism,' exercising an aggressive judicial stance as protector of the new Germany's 'militant democracy,' not just to protect human rights, but actively to promote human rights.'[31]

Noteworthy as well was, and is, the significance of the dialogue between the legal academy and its judges in Germany, termed the 'German juridical debate,'[32] that has played a role in the BVerfG's judgments. And the BVerfG would listen and respond in a manner to protect German notions of democracy and fundamental rights.[33]

Thus, well-known are the conflicting pronouncements about the full force of European Community law in the 1960s and 70s.[34] The ECJ's assertion of primacy and direct effect 'were not widely accepted in European legal communities in the 1960s. European judges are traditionally conservative in their interpretive approaches, adhering closely

26 Gerhard Bebr, *Development of Judicial Control of the European Communities* 614 et seq. (1981).

27 See, e.g., Paul Craig, 'The ECJ, National Courts and the Supremacy of Community Law', in *The European Constitution in the Making* 35 et seq.(Ingolf Pernice/Roberto Miccù eds., Nomos 2003).

28 Daniel Halberstam, 'Local, global and plural constitutionalism: Europe meets the world', in *The Worlds of European Constitutionalism* 150-151 (De Búrca & J.H.H.Weiler ed. 2011).

29 Walker & Tierney, *supra* note 2, at 2.

30 See generally, Donald P. Kommers, *The Constitutional Jurisprudence of the Federal Republic of Germany* 1 (2012) (The BVerfGE was created after the war as the guardian of political democracy, charged with enforcing 'constitutional morality' governing German law and politics. Id.).

31 Davies, *supra* note 21, at 11-14.

32 Miriam Aziz, 'Sovereignty Lost, Sovereignty Regained? Some Reflections on the Bundesverfassungsgericht's Bananas Judgment', 9 *Colum. J. Eur. L.* 109, 111 (2002).

33 See *Solange I*, *infra* at note 41.

34 See, e.g., Anthony Arnull, Alan Dashwood, Michael Dougan, Malcolm Ross, Eleanor Spaventa & Derrick Wyatt, *European Union Law* 139-42 (fifth ed. 2006).

to the wording of legal texts and leaving it to political bodies to create significant innovations in the law.'[35] Yet the creative, forceful doctrines proclaimed by the ECJ in the historic cases of *Van Gend en Loos*[36] and *Costa*[37] in 1963 and 64 challenged traditional notions of international law, and the full effect of these doctrines was disputed early on by the Italian Constitutional Court in its own 1964 *Costa* judgment,[38] and subsequently in 1973, in its *Frontini* decision, in which the court explained that it had accepted the general authority of the ECJ, but insisted that it must maintain jurisdiction to safeguard fundamental human rights and basic principles of the Italian Constitutional order.[39] Then 'famously'[40] in 1974, the BVerfG reversed its earlier acquiescence to the ECJ's claim of authority and issued its famous *Solange I* judgment,[41] unambiguously asserting its authority to protect the fundamental rights enshrined in the German constitution, as well as 'to declare *ultra vires* acts of Community organs as inapplicable in Germany.'[42] And the BVerfG is not just any Member State court:

> Being the constitutional court of a large founding Member State of the EU which possesses high intellectual and moral capital, the Karlsruhe body has been attracting the attention of other constitutional courts since decades, and it has been providing a ground for the political, legal and scientific discourse about constitutional relations between Member States.[43]

---

35 Alter, *supra* note 21, at 20.

36 Judgment in *Van Gend En Loos v. Nederlandse Administratie Der Belastingen*, C-26/62, EU:C:1963:1.

37 Judgment in *Flaminio Costa v. E.N.E.L*, C-6/64, EU:C:1964:66.

38 *Costa/ENEL*, Case 14/1964, Reported in Italian in (1964) 87 I Foro Italiano 465, 7 March 1964. Note that this decision preceded the ECJ's decision in the same case. *See also*, Patrick Del Duca & Duccio Mortillaro, 'The Maturation of Italy's Response to European Community Law: Electric and Telecommunication Sector Institutional Innovations', 23 *Fordham Int'l L.J.* 536, 538 (1999) (for the Italian Constitutional Court's gradual, though conditioned, acceptance of EU law).

39 ICC Case No. 183/1973, *Frontini v. Amministrazione delle finanze dello Stato* [1974] CMLR.372. The Italian Constitutional Court (ICC) had rejected the supremacy of the ECJ in the reference to it in the original *Costa* case. Alter, *Establishing the Supremacy*, *supra* note 21, at 19. Later in *Frontini*, the ICC softened its approach, accepting the general notion of ECJ primacy, but with the condition that the ICC itself would maintain its role as guardian of the fundamental human rights or basic principles of the Italian constitutional order. Giacinto della Cananea, 'SCRUTINY: The Italian Constitutional Court and the European Court of Justice: From Separation to Interaction?', 14 *European Public Law*, 523, 524 (2008).

40 Robert Schütze, *European Constitutional Law* 359 (Cambridge University Press 2012) ('Famously, the German Constitutional Court rejected the European Court's absolute vision and replaced it with the counter theory of relative supremacy of European law.' Id.).

41 Judgment in *Internationale Handelsgesellschaft von Einfuhr- und Vorratsstelle für Getreide und Futtermittel*, C11/70, EU:C:1970:114.

The BVerfGE had been sensitive to the intense public and academic debate, in the face of the German government's acquiescence to the ECJ, and its *Solange I* decision, taking a 'middle path in an increasingly entrenched and embittered argument.' Davies, *supra* note 21, at 43).

42 Torstein Stein, 'Always Steering a Straight Course? The German Federal Constitution Court and European Integration', 12 *ERA Forum* 219, 219-20 (2011).

43 See, Emö Várnay, *German Constitutional Court requests preliminary ruling from the European Court of Justice on the ECB Outright Monetary Transaction decision*, Lendület-HPOP's Research Group, MTA TK Lendület HPOPs-Policy Opportunities for Hungary in the European Union Research Group, 2 April 2014, available at http://hpops.tk.mta.hu/en/blog/2014/04/german-constitutional-court-request.

The BVerfG's reactions to the ECJ were especially influential in guiding the Hungarian and Polish constitutional courts in their reception of these EU doctrines.[44] The Polish constitutional court expressed its own strong stance within the broad parameters set by the German court and has used German case law to support its position in specific cases, and strongly guarding Poland's 'essential core of sovereignty.'[45] While recognizing that Community law constituted a new model of law, the Polish court maintained that the guarantees of the Constitution regarding individual rights and freedoms comprise an unsurpassable minimum standard that must be respected.[46] The Hungarian constitutional court's decisions regarding ECJ jurisprudence have also generally followed the principal concepts of the BVerfG's position.[47]

Other national constitutional courts, notably in Ireland, Denmark, Greece, Spain, and France, have also questioned, in various ways, the ECJ's assertion of authority.[48]

'The ECJ's assertion of doctrine, beginning in the 1960s, squarely posed problems to the national constitutional courts in considering the extent to which they would give effect to these doctrines, while retaining the sacrosanct nature of their domestic constitutions.'[49] These courts found themselves engaged in the unenviable task of balancing on the one hand the protection of domestic constitutional principles and values which they were sworn to defend and which they regard as so vital to state sovereignty with, on the other hand, the requirements of EU law as elucidated by the ECJ.[50]

While some Member State courts readily accepted the ECJ's doctrines, others rejected the primacy of EU law outright, and some have accepted the primacy of EU law, but not as an independent source of authority, rather insisting that EU law's authority comes from the delegation by the Member States, and that it is limited to the remit of that delegation, and subject to the supervision of the national courts.[51] Ultimately, the varied responses to full legal integration by the Member State courts have mostly 'led to a nonlinear acceptance of the ECJ's jurisprudence by national actors across time and geography,' producing across the EU a 'patchwork, contingent judicial settlement, in which different Member States impose differing conditions on the acceptance of legal primacy.'[52] Professor Bill Davies has produced documentary evidence of how the 'push back' by national judiciaries made an important impact on the constitutional

---

44 Allan F. Tatham, *Central European Courts in the Face of EU Membership* 5 (Brill 2013).

45 Id. at 6.

46 Krystyna Kowalik-Bańczyk, 'Should We Polish It Up? The Polish Constitutional Tribunal and the Idea of Supremacy of EU Law', 6 *German L.J.* 1355 (2005) at 1364.

47 Tatham, *supra* note 44, at 6.

48 Roman Kwiecién, The Primacy of European Law over National Law Under the Constitutional Treaty, 6 *German L.J.* 1479, 1486-87 (2005).

49 Id. at 1.

50 Id. at 2.

51 See e.g., Damian Chalmers, Christos Hadjiemmanuil, Giorgio Monti & Adam Tomkins, *European Union Law* 196 – 203 (Cambridge University Press, 2007) (categorizing numerous Member State national court stances. Id.).

52 Davies, *supra* note 21, at 7.

dialogue and ultimate settlement among the ECJ and the Member States.[53] Much of the conflict would dissipate over the ensuing years, as the judicial systems would respond, compromise, and a sort of convergence 'has taken place'[54] granting the EU law a qualified authority. At varying times, the courts and their rulings would simply coexist,[55] as issues may 'lie dormant for years,'[56] awaiting some accommodation to evolve or not.

Professor Karen Alter has observed that the evolution of the European legal system resulted from 'doctrinal negotiation' that yielded a 'negotiated compromise' between the ECJ and the national courts.[57] Both the ECJ, on the one hand, and the national courts, on the other, realized that neither had the ability to impose its will on the other, and so general agreement ensued that compromise was more favourable than the uncertainties of the potential legal chaos that might result.[58] 'The ECJ was unwilling to undermine its legitimacy by incurring the wrath of the Member States in an overly radical jurisprudence and lower national courts, working in their own self-interest vis-à-vis the higher national courts…, [and so] the ECJ was careful to avoid any kind of 'backlash' from Member State governments and rival higher national courts, as well as sceptical public opinion.[59] One could also reason that the ECJ was in a 'dialogue with national bureaucracies and academics and was fully aware of the media and public opinion context within the member states.'[60] Professor Weiler has suggested that the ECJ's early radical doctrines proffered in the Communities' foundational period were sustainable only because 'the Member States, severally and jointly, balanced the material and political costs and benefits of the Community.'[61]

In the specific case of Germany, the interactions between the BVerfG and European Community political leaders and judges illustrates a dynamic process of exchange. In response to public rumblings and later judicial decisions from Germany and some other Member States, Community actors endeavoured to elaborate and demonstrate a robust intention to increase human rights protection at the European level.[62] In 1969, in the landmark *Stauder* judgment,[63] the ECJ proclaimed a new-found doctrine by

53 Id.

54 Damian Chalmers, Gareth Davies & Giorgio Monti, *European Union Law* 222-23 (3d ed. 2014).

55 Since 1993, the BVerfG and the ECJ have coexisted in a sort of 'stand-off' over who has the final authority to resolve issues arising from conflicts in national and EU law. Gunnar Beck, 'The Lisbon Judgment of the German Constitutional Court, the Primacy of EU Law and the Problem of Kompetenz-Kompetenz: A Conflict between Right and Right in Which There is No Praetor', 17 *Eur. L.J.* 470 (2011).

56 J.H.H. Weiler & Ulrich R. Haltern, 'The Autonomy of the Community Legal Order', 37 *Harv. Int'l L.J.* 411, 413.

57 Alter, *supra* note 21, at 38.

58 Id.

59 Davies, *supra* note 21, at 36-37.

60 Id. at 37.

61 J.H.H. Weiler, *The Constitution of Europe: Do the New Clothes Have an Emperor* 30 (Cambridge University Press 1999).

62 Davies, *supra* note 21, at ix.

63 Judgment in *Stauder v City of Ulm*, Sozialamt, C-29/69, EU:C:1969:57.

which fundamental human rights protections were enshrined in the general principles of Community law that the ECJ would enforce.[64] The ECJ followed with successive judgments, notably its own *International Handelsgeschellschaft* decision in 1970, and *Nold* in 1974, further articulating fundamental rights protection.[65] But it was too late: as noted above, 'a fortnight after the *Nold* decision, the BVerfG decided to reserve for itself a right to review Community legislation pursuant to the fundamental rights of the German Constitution (Basic Law or *Grundgesetz*, hereinafter GG) 'as long as' the European Communities had no 'catalogue' of European fundamental rights upon which to rely,'[66] and thus the BVerfG issued its *Solange I* judgment[67] in 1974, pronouncing its own articulation of its judicial authority.

Three years after *Solange I,* in 1977, the principal EU political institutions adopted the *Joint Declaration by the European Parliament, Council and the Commission concerning the protection of fundamental rights and the ECHR*, which, after endorsing the case law of the ECJ, promised to protect the rights guaranteed by the constitutions of the Member States and of the *European Convention for the Protection of Human Rights and Fundamental Freedoms*.[68] Two years later, the first direct elections to the European Parliament occurred, enhancing its democratic legitimacy.[69] Then came elaboration in the ECJ's *Hauer* judgment in 1979, another step in incrementally and concretely articulating its expanding expression of human rights protection, ultimately pronouncing that the ECJ would safeguard the fundamental rights found in the constitutional traditions of all the Member States as well as in international agreements, including the *European Convention*.[70]

The German Court, in1986, 'completely reversed'[71] its *Solange I* position in *Solange II*,[72] recognizing that the ECJ has established an impressive standard for human rights review, and stating that the court would no longer actively exercise its jurisdiction to review EU legislation in human rights claims in German courts, except in extreme cases of a serious decline of Community fundamental rights protection.[73]

---

64 Elizabeth Shaver Duquette, 'Human Rights in the European Union: Internal versus External Objectives', 34 *Cornell Int'l L.J.* 363, 365-66 (2001) (To 'prevent a possible 'rebellion' by the national courts, the ECJ quickly announced a concept of EC human rights . . . .' Id. at 365-66.)

65 See generally, Ane Maria Røddik Christensen, *European Union and Human Rights* 28-33 (DJØF Publishing 2007).

66 Karl M. Meessen, 'Hedging European Integration: The Maastricht Judgment of the Federal Constitutional Court of Germany',17 *Fordham Int'l L.J.* 511, 513 (1993).

67 BverfGE, May 29, 1974, *Internationale Handelsgesellschaft mbH v. Einfur- und Vorratstelle* für Getreide und Futtermittel 37 BVerfGE 271, 2 C.M.L.R 540, 549-50 (1974).

68 O.J. C 103, 1977, at 1. See also, Brid Moriarty & Eva Massa, *Human Rights Law* (Oxford University Press 2008) (tracing the process from the 1969 *Stauder* holding through successive judgments restating and expanding fundamental rights protection, including European treaty expressions. Id. at 158 et seq.).

69 David Judge & David Earnshaw. *The European Parliament 38*, (2d ed. 2008).

70 Judgment in *Liselotte Hauer v. Land Rheinland-Pfalz*, C-44/79, EU:C:1979:290.

71 Stein, *supra* note 42, at 221.

72 *Wünsche Handelsgesellschaft*, BVerfGE 2, 197/83; 1987 3 CMLR 225.

73 BVerfGE 73, 339.

> This dramatic *volte-face* by the Constitutional Court was prompted by pervasive developments throughout the whole structure of the European Communities. These developments, in the aggregate, placed beyond any cavil the commitment in the Communities to the rule of law, the realization of democratic principles, and the thoroughgoing protection of fundamental human rights.[74]

However, the German Court did not really 'completely reverse' its position. While relaxing the exercise of its jurisdiction, the Court also left open to itself the authority to resume its active supervision if circumstances warranted.[75]

Seven years later, in 1993, in its so-called *Maastricht* judgment,[76] officially *Brunner v. Treaty on European Union*,[77] the BVerfG tacked to another course, professing a relationship of cooperation with the ECJ, but emphasizing its insistence that it maintains the sole authority to judge whether legal acts are in compliance with the GG (*Kompetenz-Kompetenz*).[78] The BVerfG repeated that it was satisfied with EU human rights doctrines and their enforcement, but expressly 'refused to recognize the primacy of Community law and the ECJ's prerogative to delimit the competences of the community in a given case.'[79] This 'powerful judgment . . . warned the EU institutions and the ECJ that Germany's acceptance of the principle of supremacy was conditional'[80] . . . and that the BVerfG intended to carefully watch and defend against any EU overreach of its authority as conferred in the treaties.[81] The Court also opened the topic, which would resurface later, of the importance of national democratic legitimization:

> [44] If the peoples of the individual States provide democratic legitimation through the agency of their national parliaments (as at present) limits are then set by virtue of the democratic principle to the extension of the European Communities' functions and powers. Each of the peoples of the individual States is the starting point for a state power relating to that people. The States need sufficiently important spheres of activity of their own in which the people of each can develop and articulate itself in a process of political will-formation which it legitimates and controls, in order thus to give legal expression to what binds the people together (to a greater or lesser degree of homogeneity) spiritually, socially and politically.

---

74 E. R. Lanier, 'Solange, Farewell: The Federal German Constitutional Court and the Recognition of the Court of Justice of the European Communities as Lawful Judge', 11 B.C. *Int'l & Comp. L. Rev. 1*, 22 (1988).

75 Id. at 29.

76 See, e.g., Frederick M. Abbott, 'The Maastricht Judgment, the Democracy Principle, and US Participation in Western Hemispheric Integration', 37 *German Yearbook Int'l L.* 137 (1994)('The Maastricht Judgment of the German Constitutional Court I has caused a considerable stir within the German legal community. The Judgment is perceived by some as a step backward in the European integration process, or at least as a halt, because it implies significant residual national constitutional constraints on the exercise of authority by Union institutions. Id.).

77 89 BVerfGE 155, 12 Oct. 1993, English translation in 33 I.L.M. 388, 422-23 (1994), and [1994] 1 C.M.L.R. 57.

78 Id. at para. 106. See also, J.H.H. Weiler & Ulrich R. Haltern, 'The Autonomy of the Community Legal Order – Through the Looking Glass', 37 *Harv. Int'l L.J.* 411, 413 (1996).

79 Stein, *supra* note 42, at 223.

80 Paul Craig & Gráinne de Búrca, *EU Law: Text, Cases, and Materials* 277 (Oxford Univ. Press 2011).

81 Id.

> [45] From all that it follows that functions and powers of substantial importance must remain for the German *Bundestag*.[82]

In 2000, the German Court seemed to reaffirm its *Solange II* reasoning in the *Bananas* judgment,[83] read by some as renewed 'evidence of a renewed cooperative relationship'[84] with the ECJ, that it was satisfied with the sufficient level of human rights protection in the Community and rejecting a reference from a lower German court challenging an EU regulation.[85] While re-emphasizing its *Solange II* position that it would not actively exercise its review jurisdiction, however, the BVerfG also reiterated 'its own evolution on the [*ultra vires*] question and in so doing merely reassert[ed] the now well established limitations it has imposed on the force of E.C. Law in Germany.'[86] Then, in its *Honeywell* judgment in 2006,[87] the Court seemed to take a small step back, stating a 'deep reticence . . . about going against EU law, ' explaining that any *ultra vires* act must be manifest and significant, and further, that the ECJ must have first had the opportunity to review the issue.[88]

But something changed in three years. In its elaborate (420 paragraph) 2009 *Lisbon* judgment,[89] the BVerfG offered 'the most comprehensive assessment of European integration since the Court's seminal *Maastricht* pronouncement . . . now postulating *constitutional limits* for further European integration.'[90] The BVerfG reached deeper than before, providing some more clarity and specificity regarding the Court's notion of its review and the demands of the German Basic Law. The judgment approved in principle Germany's ratification of the Lisbon Treaty, and the BVerfG repeated much of its previous doctrine, and then pivoted, venturing conceptually much further, concretely articulating an 'identity core' of the German constitution that must remain

---

82 Brunner, *supra* note 77, at paras. 44-45.

83 BVerfGE, Case No. 1 BVR 1036/99, 9 Jan. 2001. For background on this unusual litigation and German courts questioning of an EU regulation, see Norman Reich, 'European and German Constitutional Law Provoked by the Banana Litigation', 7 J. *Eur. J. Int'l L.* 103 (1996).

84 U. Elbers & N. Urban, 'The Order of the German Federal Constitutional Court of 7 June 2000 and the Kompetenz-Kompetenz in the European Judicial System', 7 *Eur. Pol. L.Rev.* 21, 32 (2001).

85 BVefGE 102, 104. See also, *Brid Moriarty & Eva Massa*, *supra* note 68, at 34.

86 Russell Miller, 'Federal Constitutional Court Concedes the Applicability of European Community Law in the Banana Case', 1 *German L.J.* 2, at http://www.germanlawjournal.com. See also, Erich Vrancs, 'German Constitutional Foundations of, and Limitations to, EU integration: A Systematic Analysis', 14 *German L.J.* 75, 105-06 (2013).

87 BVerfGE Case 2 BVR 2661/06, Decision of 6 July 2010, NJW 2010, 3422.

88 Damian Chalmers, Gareth Davies& Giorgio Monti, *European Union Law* 231 (Cambridge University Press, third ed. 2014).

89 BVerfGE, 2 BvE 2/08 from 30 June 2009, available at: http://www.bundesverfassungsgericht.de/entscheidungen/es20090630_2bve000208.html. For in-depth scholarly discussion of the *Lisbon Judgment*, see 'The German Constitutional Court's Lisbon Ruling: Legal and Political Science Perspectives', *Centre of European Law and Politics*, (Andreas Fischer-Lescano, Christian Joerges, Arndt Wonka eds. 2010).

90 Daniel Thym, 'In the Name of Sovereign Statehood: A Critical Introduction to the Lisbon Judgment of the German Federal Constitutional Court', 46 *Common Mkt. L. Rev.* 1795, 1795 (2009).

at the national level and may not permissibly ever be delegated to the EU.[91] The Court restated its own *Kompetenz-Kompetenz* jurisdiction as the final resort to review future EU treaty changes and transfers of powers to the EU on two distinct grounds: (i) '*Ultra- vires-Kontrolle*' (review), and (ii) '*Identitätskontrolle*' (identity review).[92] The *ultra vires* review refers to the *Maastricht* decision's notion that the transfer of powers to the EU must be properly approved by the Bundestag, respect fundamental rights, and be sufficiently legally certain.[93] The Court limited its *ultra vires* review to obvious transgressions, respecting the GG's 'openness towards European Law.'[94] Identity review questions respect for the national identity of the Member States, the 'non-transferable identity of constitutions, and a minimum core of sovereignty embedded in national political institutions.'[95]

The BVerfG observed that democratic legitimacy requires that national parliaments must retain the primary legitimizing function for as long as they represent identifiable and politically self-conscious peoples in the sense of a common political culture based on, among all things, shared language, culture, values and common collective historical experience.[96] And Member States must retain sovereignty over certain central areas of 'democratic formative action.'[97] The BVerfG identified six areas of competence where a further transfer of national power could seriously erode state sovereignty: 1) the military and police monopoly on the use of force domestically and abroad, 2) criminal law, 3) fundamental fiscal decisions, 4) the guarantee of a just social order, and 5) decisions that are important to the preservation of national culture, in particular family law, the school and education system and the status of religious communities, and finally a soon to be an ever so relevant sixth area of competence: budgetary autonomy, such that EU measures must not impose financial obligations on Member States that could effectively deprive them of their budgetary autonomy to effectively maintain their economic, cultural and social framework.[98]

---

91 BVerfGE, 2 BvE 2/08 (2009). See also, Henning Deters, 'National Constitutional Jurisprudence in a Post-National Europe: The ESM Ruling of the German Federal Constitutional Court and the Disavowel of Conflict', 20 *European L.J.* 204, 211 (2013)(analysis and criticism of the BVerfGE's rulings. Id. *passim*). The BVerfG also declared the German act regarding the involvement of the *Bundestag* and *Bundesrat* in EU decision-making unconstitutional, imposing an approval requirement that the government promptly complied with so as to allow the ratification of the Treaty. Philipp Kiiver, 'The Lisbon Judgment of the German Constitutional Court: A Court-Ordered Strengthening of the National Legislature in the EU', 16 *Eur. L.J.* 578, 578-79 (2010).

92 Id. at para. 233, 240, 241, 340. See, Gunnar Beck, *supra* note 55, (for incisive analysis of the *Lisbon* judgment).

93 Beck, *supra* note 92, at 471.

94 *Lisbon Judgment*, *supra* note 89, at para. 240.

95 Id. at para. 219, 226-29, 234, 235, 240-41.

96 Id. at para. 249.

97 Id.

98 Id. at paras. 250-60.

A year later, the BVerfG's perhaps anomalous 2010 *Data Retention Case*[99] addressed an EU Directive, and suggested perhaps another 'new approach.'[100] The Court annulled a German law implementing the Directive, a law that was partially written in the specific language contained within that Directive, leaving questions open about renewed fundamental rights review, and repeating the Court's concern over 'constitutional identity review.'[99]

III. The 2008 global financial crisis in Europe

This was at the same time as the global financial crisis was wreaking ruinous damage in many parts of the world, including notably in Europe where experts called it the 'deepest recession since the 1930s.'[100]

> Since 2009, the European Union . . . has been at the center of a major budgetary, financial, and economic crisis. . . , triggered and magnified by structural inadequacies of the Economic and Monetary Union, [and consequently] the EU institutions and member states reacted by introducing major changes to the . . . fundamental norms governing the action of EU institutions and member states in the fiscal domain.[101]

Greece would be hit especially hard by the financial crisis, and in 2010, eurozone Member States arranged loans for Greece.[102] As part of its significant role in the Eurozone group, the German legislature enacted its Monetary Union Financial Stabilisation Act, that authorized the German Finance Ministry to execute a €22.4 billion loan for Greece.[103] At the same time, the Eurozone political leaders authorized the European Commission to create a euro rescue package to help protect the common currency, which included two programs, the European Financial Stability Mechanism (EFSM) and the European Financial Stability Facility (EFSF) 'to handle bailouts and work in tandem with the European Central Bank to buy the bonds of countries like

99 Id.

100 István P. Székely & Paul van den Noord, 'Economic crisis in Europe: Cause, consequences, and responses – A report by the European Commission', *VOX CEPR's Policy Portal* (6 Oct. 2009), available at http://www.voxeu.org/article/economic-crisis-europe-cause-consequences-and-responses.

101 Federico Fabbrini, 'The Euro-Crisis and the Courts: Judicial Review and the Political Process in Comparative Perspective', 32 *Berkley J. Int'l L.* 64, 64 (2014)(cogent, in depth analysis of the measures taken and the judicial reactions to them, generally validating the measures, but often expressing dissatisfaction and imposing judicial restrictions on the new EMU measures. Id. at 120).

102 Sebastian Recker, 'Casenote – Euro Rescue Package Case: The German Federal Constitutional Court Protects the Principle of Parliamentary Budget', 12 *German L.J.* 2071, et seq. (2011).

103 Id.

Italy and Spain that are straining under high interest rates.'[104] The German *Bundestag* then authorized funding for this in the amount of €147.6 billion.[105]

Multiple constitutional complaints to the BVerfG were lodged, asking for a temporary injunction to prevent this from going into force, in petitions that, collectively, would be termed the *Aid Measure for Greece and Euro Rescue Package Case*.[106] In 2011, the BVerfG concluded that both German laws were constitutional, and the Court repeated its parliamentary budget autonomy requirements, finding them satisfied, with one further requirement that the *Bundestag's* budgetary committee specifically authorize the limits.[107] The Second Senate President, Justice Andreas Vosskuhle, issuing the ruling, commented that the judgment 'should not be misinterpreted as a constitutional blank check for further rescue packages.'[108] Yet one scholar observed that the 'judgment appears to follow a familiar pattern,'[109] with the BVerfG rolling out its doctrine stressing the primacy of the German Constitution over EU law, not to mention its own authority as the court of last resort to judge any transfers of powers or and finances to the EU, yet through cases over twenty-five years, the Court has proclaimed powers, but consistently 'deferred to the political authorities and approved the contested treaty extensions and other measures on each and every occasion.'[110] Numerous others have agreed: 'This 'yes, but . . .' pattern is well known from Karlsruhe's rulings concerning the European Union. Since the *Maastricht* case in 1993, the Court has never impeded but shown sensitivity for European integration . . . [and] has established an impressive track record calling for further involvement of the parliament in external relations and taxes and finance, including the taking of credit.'[111] The eminent Prof. Joseph Weiler penned the oft-quoted: '[T]he German Constitutional Court has a well-earned reputation of the Dog that Barks but does not Bite.'[112]

---

104 Nicholas Kulish & Melissa Eddy, 'In Victory for Merkel, German Court Ruling Favors European Bailout Fund', *N.Y.Times,* 12 Sept. 2012, available at http://www.nytimes.com/2012/09/13/world/europe/german-court-backs-euro-rescue-fund.html?_r=0.

105 Recker, *supra* note 105, at 2072.

106 Id. at 2071.

107 BVerfGE 7 Sept. 2011 (Euro Rescue Package Case), 2 BVR 987/10, at paras. 94, 119, available at http://www.bverfg.de/entscheidungen/rs20110907_2bvr098710.html.

108 'Ruling in Greek Aid: German Court Rejects Challenges to Euro Bailouts', *Spiegel Online International,* 7 Sept. 2011, available at http://www.spiegel.de/international/germany/ruling-in-greek-aid-german-court-rejects-challenges-to-euro-bailouts-a-784859.html.

109 Gunnar Beck, 'The German Constitutional Court versus the EU: self assertion in theory and submission in practice – Euro Aid and Financial Guarantees', eutopialaw.com blog, 24 to 27 October 2011, available at http://eutopialaw.com/2011/10/26/the-german-constitutional-court-versus-the-eu-self-assertion-in-theory-and-submission-in-practice-%E2%80%93-euro-aid-and-financial-guarantees-part-3/.

110 Id.

111 See e.g., Karsten Schneider, 'Yes, But . . . One More Thing: Karlsruhe's Ruling on the European Stability Mechanism', 14 *German L.J.* 53, 54 (2013).

112 J.H.H.Weiler, The Lisbon '*Urteil*,' 20 *Eur. J. Int'l L.* 3, 505-509, (2009).

Subsequently, in February, 2012, a treaty[113] under public international law among Eurozone members was signed to establish a new rescue organization, entitled the European Stability Mechanism (ESM), created as a permanent crisis resolution mechanism to provide stability support through a number of financial assistance instruments, to supersede the older, temporary EU bailout funding programs, the European Financial Stability Facility (EFSF) and the European Financial Stabilisation Mechanism (EFSM).[114]

As European financial and political leaders attempted to exercise effective remedial fiscal and monetary policy, the BVerfG would re-assert itself, 'reaffirming and reimagining the Basic Law's principle of democracy as a foundation of the German constitutional order and, therefore, as a limit on Germany's participation in European integration.'[115]

As would be expected, the usual litigants and others filed complaints in the BVerfG, challenging Germany's participation in the ESM, and one of the cases notably,'brought by Europolis, a eurosceptic think tank in Berlin, call[ed] on the German court to refer the matter to the ECJ, which ha[d] already been asked to rule on a separate case submitted by the Irish supreme court in Dublin.'[116] 'Some 37,000 people had signed a petition to the court asking it to block the ESM, and make it subject to a referendum. Since Germany is due to contribute 27% of the fund, it cannot proceed without German ratification.'[117]

On 12 September 2012, in an expedited proceeding, the 2012 *ESM (European Stability Mechanism) Temporary Injunction Case*,[118] the German Court refused to grant a temporary injunction prohibiting Germany from participating in the bailouts that would come from that EU rescue mechanism, but as it often has, the Court stipulated conditions.[119]

Just days before this, on 6 September 2012, the ECB had reacted further to the acute decline of confidence in the euro and the rising risk premiums for government bonds in the Eurozone, publicly announcing its Decision to consider a programme of buying

---

113 Treaty Establishing the European Stability Mechanism, 1 Feb. 2012, available at http://europa.eu/rapid/press-release_DOC-12-3_en.htm.

114 The ESM's website offers detailed information, available at http://www.esm.europa.eu/.

115 Russell A. Miller, 'Germany v. Europe: The Principle of Democracy in German Constitutional Law and the Troubled Future of European Integration', 54 *Va. J. Int'l L.* 579, 581 (2014).

116 Quentin Peel & Jamie Smyth, 'German lawsuit challenges rescue fund', *Fin. Times*, 13 August 2012, available at http://www.ft.com/intl/cms/s/0/fda2f444-e562-11e1-9a2f-00144feab49a.html#axzz3Vn7S8SXy.

117 'German court backs eurozone's ESM bailout fund', BBC, 12 Sept. 2012, available at http://www.bbc.com/news/world-europe-19567867.

118 See Miller, *supra* note 117, at 587 ('The history of the Court's intervention reads like a Michelin travel guide, with stops in Brussels, Maastricht, Amsterdam, Lisbon, and--with the ESM Temporary Injunction Case from 2009—Luxembourg.').

119 132 BVerfGE 195, 2 BvR 1390/12, 12 Sept 2012.

government bonds (Outright Monetary Transactions – OMT),[120] to do 'whatever it takes' to use its monetary instruments to support the Eurozone.[121] The ECB proclaimed that it was 'ready to use the programme to purchase on secondary markets government bonds issued by States in the euro area, subject to certain conditions . . . .'[122] The announcement itself quickly achieved its desired effect, calming markets and drawing public praise from the financial commentators as having been a strategic move by the ECB.[123] 'As a working rule, the shorter a statement, the more it says. A commitment made by the (ECB) in September 2012 runs to fewer than 500 words, but it was enough to send the bond vigilantes packing.'[124] Again, legal challenges promptly and predictably followed, as numerous politicians, professors, a journalist, and an NGO filed constitutional complaints in the BVerfG against the German federal government and the *Bundestag*, alleging that their fundamental rights had been violated because the German government had not challenged the ECB Decision, and that the TFEU's prohibition against purchasing government bonds of Eurozone Member States (TFEU Art. 263) had been violated.[125]

The legal challenges were expected because every step of the advance toward the euro's creation, beginning in 1993, had been the subject of attacks in the BVerfG, brought by claims against the Maastricht Treaty, then opposing Germany's participation in the second stage of the monetary union in 1998, the Lisbon Treaty in 2009, the bailout of Greece in 2010, leading up to the multiple suits in 2011opposing German participation in the European Stability Mechanism and the Treaty on Stability, Consolidation and Governance, and the EU legislation accompanying them.[126] The BVerfG has issued a total of eight rulings since the 'outbreak of the crisis in 2008.'[127]

---

120 Press Release, European Central Bank, 6 Sept. 2012, at http://www.ecb.europa.eu/press/pr/date/2012/html/pr120906_1.en.html.

121 Remarks by President of the European Central Bank, Maria Draghi, to the Global Investment Conference, 26 July 2012, at http://www.ecb.europa.eu/press/key/date/2012/html/sp120726.en.html.

122 *Peter Gauweiler et al v. Deutscher Bundestag, Opinion of Advocate General in Gauweiler and Others*, Case C-62/14, 14 January 2015.

123 See e.g., John Dizard, 'Beyond the bazooka of Eurozone bailouts', *Fin. Times,* 8 March 2013, http:/www.ft.com/intl/cms/s/0/6bd34000-6a32-11e2-a7d2-00144feab49a.html?siteedition=intl#axzz3UN5ugRlp ('an undoubted success.' Id.*)*. See also, Zsolt Darvas, 'The ECB's Magic Wand', *Intereconomics* 2012, ZBW - Leibniz Information Centre for Economics 5, ('a wise decision . . . . worked like a magic wand, as government bond yields have fallen without any actual intervention.' Id. at 267.).

124 'It isn't over', Economist, 15 Feb. 2014, available at http://www.economist.com/news/finance-and-economics/21596570-european-monetary-policy-has-not-been-given-reprieve-markets-believe-it-isnt.

125 Order of 14 January 2014 - 2 BvR 2728/13, *BVerfGE*, available at https://www.bundesverfassungsgericht.de/entscheidungen/rs20140114_2bvr272813en.html. As the case captions will reveal, German politician Peter Gauweiler has consistently served as a lead complainant in legal actions against Eurozone activities. See also, 'Prominent opponent of Merkel's euro bailouts quits leading post in German governing party', U.S. News & World Rep. 31 March 2015, available at http://www.usnews.com/news/business/articles/2015/03/31/euro-bailout-rebel-quits-senior-german-governing-party-job. ('Peter Gauweiler, who has repeatedly filed complaints to Germany's highest court against the bailout of Europe's strugglers,' resigned his seat in the *Bundestag* in March, 2015, protesting against 'pressure to vote in favor of a four-month extension to Greece's bailout in February.' Id.).

126 Schiek, *supra* note 18, at 329-330.

127 Schneider, *supra* note 113, at 54.

In September 2012, the BVerfG's Second Senate issued its initial opinion, 'clear[ing] the path for the next steps in [the] fast-moving 'rescue' situation.'[128] The Court denied the request for a temporary injunction against the ESM Treaty, but only on the condition that Germany's potential financial obligations were limited and that increased financial obligations would require the approval of both houses of the German parliament, which must be provided comprehensive information.[129]

But the additional challenges to the ECB Decision ultimately led the conflict forward to 2014, in a return to that often ambiguous conflict zone between the ECJ and BVerfG, this time presented in the context of the explosive financial pressure cooker in Europe. In this broad based suit in the BVerfG challenging the legality of the ECB's OMT Decision, the BverfG, as mentioned above, issued its first ever Article 267 Reference to the ECJ. And what a judgment! The BVerfG re-asserted its authority to exercise its *ultra vires* review, questioning 'a transgression of powers by an EU institution,'[130] and more. But commentators were mixed as to whether the referral was 'an act of submission under the judicial sovereignty of the ECJ, or . . . a strategy to pass the ball to the ECJ and postpone further involvement.'[131]

This 2014 judicial interchange between the two courts is even more noteworthy because it arrives in a sensitive context. The BverfG's referral returned to the combative stance of some earlier decisions, assertive in that it presumed to instruct the ECJ as to the proper decision of the referral issues, stating that the ECJ should declare the OMT Decision invalid under EU law, or at a minimum that it be narrowly interpreted[132] – not exactly a supplication for guidance.[133] Soon thereafter, this stage was made more dramatic by the similarly assertive judgment of the ECJ in December 2014, declaring the draft agreement between the European Commission and the Council of Europe regarding the EU's accession to the European Convention of Human Rights and Fundamental Freedoms invalid.[134] Thus in these concurrent, recent expressions of judicial authority, neither Court appeared reticent to defend its own authority.

---

128 Id.

129 BVerfGE, 2 BvR 1390/12, 12 Sept. 2012, available at http://www.bverfg.de/en/decisions/rs20120912_2bvr139012en.html.

130 Dieter Murswiek, 'ECB, ECJ, Democracy, and the Federal Constitutional Court's Referral Order From 14 January 2014', 15 *German L.J.*, 147, 147 (2014).

131 Klaus Ferdinand Gärditz, 'Beyond Symbolism: Towards a Constitutional Actio Popularis in EU Affairs? A Commentary on the OMT Decision of the Federal Constitutional Court', 15 *German L.J.* 183, 183 (2014)(posing 'questions of legal symbolism used in political communication.' Id.at 184).

132 See *OMT Judgment, infra* note, at paras. 69-100.

133 See, e.g., Samuel Dahan, Olivier Fuchs & Marie-Laure Layus, 'Whatever It Takes? Regarding the OMT Ruling of the German Federal Constitutional Court', 18 *J. Int'l Econ. L.* 137, 137 (2015)('In other words, the German decision implied that although the Bundesverfassungsgericht was extending its hand to the CJEU, it was doing so with a closed fist.' Id.). See also, Alexander Thiele, 'Friendly or Unfriendly Act? The "Historic" Referral of the Constitutional Court to the ECJ Regarding the ECB's OMT Program', 15 *German L.J.* 241 (2014)(directly posing the attitudinal question).

134 ECJ, Opinion 2/13, 18 Dec. 2014. Opinion of the Court (Full Court) of 18 December 2014.

Opinion pursuant to Article 218(11) TFEU - Draft international agreement - Accession of the European Union to the European Convention for the Protection of Human Rights and Fundamental Freedoms - Compatibility of the draft agreement with the EU and FEU Treaties.

In the OMT referral proceeding at the ECJ, Advocate General Cruz Villalón issued his Opinion in January, 2015, articulating his view, among many cogent observations, that the OMT programme is, in principle, compatible with EU law, but moreover that if the programme is ever actually implemented, certain conditions would have to be satisfied.[135]

So the legal observers await the ECJ's final judgment in summer 2015, and then the BverG's reception of it. Will the ECJ accommodate being told that a national constitutional court is the final arbiter of the application of EU law in a Member State, and that a national court, if dissatisfied with the ECJ's view, concretely plans to declare an EU measure inapplicable in that Member State, raising the glaring potential for twenty-eight different national receptions of EU law? Will the ECJ compromise and accept the BVerfG's escape option that a narrow interpretation of the ECB Decision might be possible as an offer to compromise? Will the ECJ refuse the case because the OMT option has never been implemented, or because the BVerfG stated that it may not follow the ECJ's reply to its question?[136] Italy, Spain, and the Netherlands, which offered submissions in the case at the ECJ, questioned the admissibility of the reference, and Italy argued that this is not *actually* an Art. 267 reference, but something difficult to find in the EU Treaties.[137]

The following analysis examines the OMT referral itself, and its potential conflict between these high courts, attempting to illuminate the dimensions of both courts' positions, and, as noted previously, this article recommends a further elaboration of the constructive path toward cohabitation of the overlapping judicial space, as constitutional pluralism evolves in Europe.

IV. The application to the BVerfG and its response

Upon news of the September 2012 ECB announcement of its OMT Decision, the claimants in the pending ESM and fiscal treaty case, on which the BVerfG had just refused to grant interim measures, supplemented new complaints in the proceedings against it, transforming the case 'into a tribunal on the ECB's OMT program.'[138] While the OMT technique pursues the same objectives as the ESM, i.e., upholding the liquidity of states in trouble, the German *Bundestag* has no say in the ECB's decisions.[139] Patently, this has the potential to circumvent the BVerfG's pronouncements protecting

---

135 Opinion of Advocate General, *supra* note 124, at para. 263.

136 Advocate General Cruz Villalón noted that 'a national court should not be able to request a preliminary ruling from the Court of Justice if its request already includes, intrinsically or conceptually, the possibility that it will in fact depart from the answer received.' Id. at para. 36.

137 Id. at paras. 35-51.

138 Franz C. Mayer, 'Rebels without a cause? A critical analysis of the German constitutional courts OMT reference', 15 German L.J. 111, at 114 (2014).

139 Id. at 113.

the essential democratic role of the German *Bundestag*. And while the IMF, the ECB, and the European institutions and Member States have sought to combat the contagion from the 2008 financial crisis, the BVerfG 'has been a persistent irritant throughout those efforts.'[140]

In its lengthy paragraph five of its subsequent judgment, the BVerfG summarized the substance of the complaints: the claimants asserted that the German government and the Bundestag 'are obliged to work towards repeal of the OMT Decision, or at least prevent its implementation, and that the German *Bundesbank* may not take part if the Decision is put into effect.'[141] They argued that the Decision constitutes an *ultra vires* act, not included in the ECB's mandate, as well as violating the TFEU Art. 123 prohibition against monetary financing.[142] Further, the Decision to purchase bonds of only select Member States for which no buyers are interested, amounts to a suspension of market mechanisms, also prohibited by the Treaty.[143] The ECB has neither 'sufficient democratic legitimation' nor a mandate to defend the euro by any means whatsoever, especially including economic redistributions between banks and taxpayers of different Member States, and because the potential liability and payment risks to the German federal budget are so huge and without approval by the German parliament, the GG's grant of budgetary responsibility to the parliament can be impaired, violating the GG's principle of democracy and infringing the constitutional identity of the GG.[144]

The ECB pled that its Decision is 'covered by its mandate and does not violate the prohibition of monetary financing,'[145] and that the economic situation of the bond markets was so severe that the Decision was necessary. The *Bundesbank* disagreed with the ECB (again),[146] citing the risk that 'the large-scale purchase of government bonds carries considerable risk and can lead to an ever-increasing amount of Member States' debts being assumed by the Eurosystem.'[147]

By order of 14 January 2014, though announced on 7 February 2014, as noted by so many commentators, in its first ever reference to the ECJ,[148] the BVerfG released its Art. 267 reference, requesting a preliminary ruling from the ECJ.[149] The German Court

140 Miller, *supra* note 117, at 586.

141 *OMT Judgment*, *supra* note 16.

142 Id.

143 Id.

144 Id.

145 Id. at para. 6.

146 Brian Blackstone, 'Bundesbank's Weidmann Criticizes ECB's Stimulus Measures', *Wall St. J.*, 7 Oct 2014, available at http://www.wsj.com/articles/bundesbanks-weidmann-criticizes-ecbs-stimulus-measures-1412693836.

147 *OMT Judgment, supra* note 16, at para. 14.

148 See e.g., Schiek, *supra* note 18, at 329-335 (2014) (The *BVerfGE*'s reference to the ECJ addressed only a part of seven overall claims that had been brought by the several claimants challenging Germany's participation in various aspects of the Eurozone stability programmes. *Id.*).

149 *OMT Judgment*, *supra* note 16, at para. 1.

first bowed to the ECJ and to the German Constitution's openness to European integration:

> The primacy of application of Union law is to be recognised , and . . . the powers of control which are constitutionally reserved for the BVerfG are only exercised in a manner that is cautious and friendly towards European law. This means the [BVerfG's] *ultra vires* review must in principle comply with the rulings of the Court of Justice as a binding interpretation of Union law. Prior to the acceptance of an *ultra vires* act by European bodies and institutions, the Court of Justice is therefore to be afforded the opportunity to interpret the Treaties, as well as to rule on the validity and interpretation of the legal acts in question, in the context of preliminary ruling proceedings according to Art. 267 TFEU.[150]

The BVerfG next plainly punched its 'invariably masters of the Treaties' ticket, observing again that 'the precedence of Union law . . . cannot be comprehensive.'[151] Then, the Court continued, the identity review exercised by the Court must insure that the overall budgetary responsibilities of the *Bundestag* must be safeguarded as 'a fundamental part of the ability of a constitutional state to democratically shape itself,' and that organ 'may not consent to automatism of bonds or benefits . . . not subject to strict specifications and whose effects are not limited.'[152] The *Bundestag* must individually approve every large-scale federal aid measure on the . . . European level.'[153]

Regarding the first question referred for the preliminary ruling, the German Court addressed whether the ECB Decision transgressed the central bank's monetary policy mandate or if it violated the prohibition of monetary financing of the budget.[154] The Court recited considerable precedent, and then stated that it 'considers the OMT Decision incompatible with [the] TFEU because it exceeds the mandate of the [ECB] and . . . encroaches upon the responsibility of the Member States for economic policy [and] encroaches upon the responsibility of the Member States for economic policy, . . . and appears to be incompatible with the prohibition of monetary financing of the budget enshrined in Art. 123 TFEU (2) .'[155] Though, it is possible, the Court said, that the OMT Decision 'could be interpreted in conformity with primary law.'[156]

The BVerfG judged the OMT Decision to be primarily an economic policy act, rather than an act of monetary policy, leaving 'considerable doubts as to its validity.'[157] As the *Bundesbank* has argued, varying interest rate spreads are intended in the TFEU as an expression of the independence of Member State national budgets, and these should

150 Id. at para. 24.

151 Id. at para. 26.

152 Id. at para. 28.

153 Id.

154 Id. at para. 38.

155 Id. at para. 55.

156 Id.

157 Id. at para. 69.

not permissibly be lowered by central bank bond purchases.[158] Trying to protect 'the current composition of the euro area currency with the OMT Decision . . . is obviously not a task of monetary policy but one of economic policy, which remains a responsibility of the Member States.'[159] The Decision's selective and conditional application also suggest its economic policy dimension.[160] The Court then elaborated its reasons why the Decision also violated TFEU Art. 123's prohibition of monetary financing.[161]

Finally, the Court offered its assessment that the Decision could yet be valid if it were 'interpret[ed] in conformity with Union law . . . comply[ing] with the above-mentioned conditions.' These require that it be limited so that it does not undermine the conditionality of the assistance programmes of the [EFSF and the ESM] and would only be of a supportive nature with regard to economic policies in the Union, further excluding the possibility of any debt cuts or unlimited government bond purchases, avoiding interference with price formation on the market.[162]

In a perhaps significant, though unusually awkward sentence, the Court then seemed to alert, or even caution, the ECJ: considering the BVerfG's obligation to grant preventive legal protection, the interpretation of EU law is relevant to the outcome of the claims in the case 'should the Court of Justice not qualify the OMT Decision as a suitable subject for a referral under Art. 267..., then the BVerfG would 'have to answer the preliminary question' regarding compatibility with EU law.[163]

The judgment concludes with the notation that the Senate decided with a six member majority, two judges dissenting.[164]

In her dissenting opinion, Justice Lübbe-Wolff stated that she feared the Court had exceeded its judicial competence, though only '[i]n an effort to secure the rule of law,' and she suggested that the claims should have been rejected as inadmissible.[165] She reasoned that the issues foremost represent a matter of political discretion, and the majority's rules are found neither in the GG or case law interpreting it.[166] She continued:

> The question is, whether the national perspective . . . is still the appropriate and the constitutional one where a decision may have legal and factual consequences of the magnitude and reach at issue here. That some few independent German judges -- invoking the German interpretation of the principle of democracy, the limits of admissible competences of the ECB following from this interpretation,

158 Id. at para. 71.

159 Id. at para. 72.

160 Id. at paras. 72-77.

161 Id. at para. 84 -89.

162 Id. at paras. 99-100.

163 Id. at para. 101.

164 Id. at para. 105.

165 Dissenting opinion, paras. 3, 11.

166 Id. at paras. 12-13.

> and our reading of Art. 123 et seq. TFEU -- make a decision with incalculable consequences for the operating currency of the euro zone and the national economies depending on it appears as an anomaly of questionable democratic character.[167]

Justice Gerhardt likewise considered the complaints to the OMT Decision inadmissible, finding that the majority's judgment expanded the possibilities of an individual to demand - without connection to a substantive fundamental right – 'a review of the acts of Union institutions by the Constitutional Court,' in a broad manner granting every citizen a form of *actio popularis* jurisdiction not contained in the GG.[168] He asked 'why is it not sufficient to work via the means that democracy provides – through the formation of political opinions within and outside Parliament and through elections – towards the system of powers being respected, or to demand that the consequences of a transgression of powers be accepted.'[169] Others agree, and especially with such broad jurisdiction to contest EU related matters,[170] fearing that the BVerfG's *Demokratieprincip* (principle of democracy) has become a 'profound barrier to European integration. . . . its rulings reveal [its] continuing willingness to intervene in and superintend the measures necessary for supranational integration.'[171]

V. Criticism

Diverse criticism of the BVerfG's judgment followed. First, of course, the glaring issue stands out of why the German Court so expressly articulated such a definitive view of the answer to the key Article 267 'question'[172] that it referred to the ECJ. One might reasonably ask whether this opinion in the form of a referral is actually a legitimate request for resolution of a legal issue. Second is the court's confrontational statement that it might itself declare the ECB programme invalid in Germany if the ECJ didn't satisfy its reasoning.[173] The damage to legal certainty in the EU would be existential if Member State tribunals actually exercised their claimed *ultra vires* review, variously striking EU measures. Third and equally significant, one of the two dissenting judges in the Second Senate suggested explicitly that, sometimes, '[i]n an effort to

167 Id. at para. 28.

168 Id. at para 5-6.

169 Id. at para. 8.

170 See Klaus Ferdinand Gärditz, 'Beyond Symbolism: Towards a Constitutional Actio Popularis in EU Affairs? A Commentary on the OMT Decision of the Federal Constitutional Court', 15 *German L.J.* 183, 183 (2014)('The extreme generosity of the Court to grant a broad standing in EU affairs foreshadows far reaching repercussions that might adversely affect the BVerfG's struggle for its own role in a competitive and complex field of European multi-level constitutionalism with a dwindling – albeit still vivid – weight of national constitutional law.' Id. at 186.).

171 Miller, *supra* note 117, at 581 (2014) (The German 'court has not shied away from serving as a master of European integration.' Id. at 581).

172 Art. 267 TFEU includes the word 'question' three times in defining its jurisdiction for preliminary rulings.

173 *OMT Judgment*, *supra* note 16, at para. 103.

secure the rule of law, a court may happen to exceed judicial competence.'[174] As one scholar expressed, 'It is a sad irony . . . that, in a doubtlessly well-intentioned effort to protect the principle of democracy against an alleged excess of competences at the EU level, the [BVerfG] itself exceeds the limits of its judicial mandate under German constitutional and EU law.'[175] Fourth, and addressing one of the specific issues raised by the Court, the ECB's OMT Decision actually was a monetary policy mechanism, carefully and successfully designed to re-establish the monetary transmission mechanism.

Scholarly and other commentary repeated these and other criticism of the OMT judgment. They argued that the BVerfG had exceeded its role, transgressing fundamental constitutional principles in accepting judicial challenges against the government and the parliament for not stopping the ECB's actions,[176] and that the BVerfG contradicted its promise in its *Honeywell* judgment to exercise its *ultra vires* review in a 'reserved' or 'modest' manner.[177] Others noted that the German Court's concern about the distinction between economic and monetary policy ignores that functional competences can overlap with other competences, and the BVerfG should have yielded more ground to the area of the ECB's expertise, allowing a broader margin of discretion to the central Bank.[178] One expert argued the BVerfG's ruling ignores the 'essentially . . . preventative nature' of Art. 123 TFEU, and that its insistence on strict compliance with narrow definitions 'at a time of acute, almost existential, crisis [that could] actively counteract the efforts of indebted Member States to return to fiscal discipline.'[179] Another critic worried that the German Court's decision 'reflects a serious misunderstanding of central banking' and the Court's conditions for the acceptable use of OMT would actually deny the programme its effectiveness, creating more risk of financial crisis.[180] Further, the BVerfG's deep exercise of its *ultra vires* review in this case broadens the scope of the Court's review and distinguishes it from 'the accepted standards of decentralized review of legality of Union acts. . . .'[181]

Another scholar criticized the OMT reference decision as 'the right thing done in the wrong way at the wrong time. The only thing it is not is a surrender, as some initial

174 Diss. Opinion Lübbe-Wolff, BVerfG, Case 2 BvR 2728/13 et al. *OMT*, order of 14 Jan. 2014, para. 2.

175 Wendel, *supra* note 1, at 265 (including extensive evaluation of the *OMT Judgment*.).

176 Asteris Pliakos & George Anagnostaras, 'Blind Date Between Familiar Strangers: The German Constitutional Court Goes Luxembourg', 15 German L.R. 369, 371 (2014).

177 Bast, *supra* note 17, at 168, referring to the BVerfG's *Honeywell Judgment*.

178 Id. 175-76.

179 Anna Viterbo, 'Oh My . . . OMT! Some Thoughts about the German Constitutional Court's Decision to Refer the Outright Monetary Transactions Programme to the Court of Justice of the European Union', SIDIBlog, 13 Feb. 2014, available at http://www.sidi-isil.org/sidiblog/?p=695.

180 Paul De Grauwe, 'Why the European Court of Justice should reject the German Constitutional Court's ruling on Outright Monetary Transactions', *EUROPP*, European Politics and Policy at LSE, available at http://blogs.lse.ac.uk/europpblog/2014/03/04/why-the-european-court-of-justice-should-reject-the-german-constitutional-courts-ruling-on-outright-monetary-transactions/ (last visited April 7, 2015.

181 Bast, *supra* note 17, at 179.

media comments suggested.'[182] Professor Franz Mayer endorsed Judge Lübbe-Wolff's dissenting criticism that the majority's opinion represents 'an anomaly of questionable democratic character,' tainted by inconsistencies and contradictions.[183] 'With two senior judges dissenting, the OMT reference of the German constitutional court is a weak decision of a divided court. This is regrettable . . . . The first preliminary reference of the German constitutional court to the ECJ should have been a better case.' [184] Mayer continued: the court's opinion 'represents a constitutional court moving in the wrong direction. It is a direction that has the potential for damaging the court's authority, its legacy and its achievements and to divert it from the realm of domestic fundamental rights protection that it should focus on.'[185]

Additional criticisms included: the BVerfG was reviewing actions of the ECB, an institution designed to be independent of control by either the EU or national governments;[186] the case itself raised a political question beyond the proper scope of the Court's powers and expertise (separation of powers?); and finally, that the BVerfG's cultural identity doctrine is anti-European and constitutes 'constitutional nationalism,' and that the BVerfG is merely trying to prevent itself becoming subordinate to the ECJ.[187] Subsequently, as one German news source expressed, 'Be it in Berlin or in Brussels, many politicians have little positive to say about the German Constitutional Court these days. The justices are being very publicly accused of overstepping the boundaries of their responsibilities and of placing themselves in the position of legislators.'[188]

VI. The ECJ Advocate General's opinion

Advocate General Cruz Villalón issued his elegantly and precisely written Opinion on January 14, 2015.[189] Commentators exhaled, relieving anxieties that the Advocate General's decision might exacerbate the conflict.[190]

The Advocate General opined that the OMT programme represents an unconventional monetary policy measure, though considering the extraordinary circumstances of the

182 Mayer, *supra* note 140, at 112 (2014).

183 Id. at 144.

184 Id.

185 Id. at 145.

186 See, Art. 130 TFEU and Art. 88(2) Grundgeseszt (GG).

187 'Drifting into Politics: Is Germany's Highest Court Anti-European?', *Spiegel Online International* 13 March 2014, available at http://www.spiegel.de/international/germany/the-eu-critical-course-of-the-german-high-court-a-958018.html.

188 Id.

189 Opinion of Advocate General, *supra* note 124.

190 'EU lawyer approves ECB bond-buying programme', *BBC News*, 14 January 2015 ('The sighs of relief from the ECB and the Eurozone finance ministries are almost audible.' Id.).

explosive sovereign bond market in the summer of 2012, it was within the broad discretion of the ECB in managing monetary policy, while at the same time necessarily within constraints in its implementation to conform to the ECB's mandate and the TFEU's prohibition against monetary financing of Member States.[191]

The Opinion insisted that the OMT programme, if implemented, must first retain its basic character as a monetary policy measure and must refrain from direct involvement in the financial assistance programmes provided to certain Eurozone Member States; second, that the ECB must adhere to the requirement of reasons, explaining its basis for engaging in such unconventional monetary policy measures, explicitly identifying the extraordinary circumstances that justify the action; third, that the OMT programme is suitable for achieving reductions in interest rates on distressed Member State government bonds, and could be both necessary and proportional, in that the programme does not require the ECB to assume a risk that makes it vulnerable to insolvency; and finally, these conditions for implementation must be strictly interpreted.[192]

The Advocate General observed that there may be 'a question of admissibility, which concerns the actionable nature of a decision only the basic features of which were set out in a press release,'[193] though 'the circumstances of the special role played by public communication in central bank activity, might be grounds for reaching a different conclusion.'[194] Admissibility may also be a question where a referring court suggests the possibility that it may 'depart from the answer given.'[195] Frankly expressing the point, the Advocate General wrote: 'Neither the significance nor the possible consequences of the aforementioned case-law of the BVerfG can be denied, as has long been made abundantly clear in a wide range of academic writing.'[196] It is difficult to disregard, he continued, the 'ambiguity' or the 'ambivalence' in a request for a preliminary ruling from a national court of last resort that has proclaimed a 'cooperative relationship' and an openness to European integration, while at the same time insisting on its own 'ultimate responsibility to state what the law is with regard to the constitutional conditions and limits of European integration so far as its own State is concerned.'[197] One scholar characterized the Advocate General's candor in direct terms: Cruz Villalon 'delivered a carefully argued Opinion that...acknowledged and unpacked the significance of the exchange for the dialogue between the German Constitutional Court and the Court of Justice. . . .'[198]

---

191 Opinion of Advocate General, *supra* note 124, at paras. 122 – 139, 158, 204, 262.

192 Id. at para. 263.

193 *Supra*, Opinion of the Advocate General, at para. 6.

194 Id.

195 Id. at para. 36.

196 Id. at para. 37.

197 Id. at para. 49.

198 Alicia Hinarejos, Downing College, University of Cambridge; author of 'The Euro Area Crisis in Constitutional Perspective' (forthcoming, OUP), *EU Law Analysis*, 17 Jan. 2015, available at http://eulawanalysis.blogspot.com/2015/01/is-ecbs-omt-programme-legal-advocate.html?m=1.

VII. Conclusion

On balance, it appears that the ECB in September 2012 did its job in the manner it had to, in exigent circumstances, for the maintenance of the Eurozone. Advocate General Cruz Villalón also reasonably defended this position. One expert concluded:

> Only the OMT programme managed to bring down financial fragmentation and thereby helped the ECB to reduce its current role as financial intermediary between banks in the fragmented financial system. The ECB took action that was effective and appropriate in solving a fundamental problem it faced, namely a dysfunctional monetary policy transmission mechanism. Its action was clearly within its mandate of ensuring the proper conduct of monetary policy.[199]

What will the two high Courts do, especially with their 'baggage' of virtuously intended, yet high powered, constitutional rhetoric? Only a few months will tell. Is the BVerfG trapped in its own statist, sovereignty ideology? Is the European Union trapped in its heavily invested doctrine? Or trapped by the BVerfG's doctrine? The optimistic view suggests that both Courts are led by jurists of formidable intellect, high sense of responsibility, and rich judgment. They will get through this trap. The pessimistic view would fear the enlarged confidence of jurists of formidable intellect, high positions of prestige, and rash judgment.

The prudent path forward seems to be for the two Courts, among the most powerful and influential courts worldwide, to continue their respectful and only softly-confrontational discursive collaboration, promoting a thorough examination of the complex issues involved in this case, as well as the hugely significant consequences that could result from some form of rupture.[200] The Eurozone constitutes an historic and thorny, complex step in European integration. Both the ECJ and subsequently the BVerfG would serve their fundamental purposes well to accept the reasoning of Advocate General Villalón, recognizing the exigency of the economic and monetary distress that prompted the OMT Decision. That Decision did promote and accomplish the stability of the explosive sovereign bond market in the summer of 2012. And if the OMT Decision is ever implemented, the narrow conditions first articulated by the BVerfG and subsequently interpreted by the Advocate General would guide future ECB conduct in a straightforward way.

The magnitude of the risk of conflict in the unprecedented case warrants the almost trite conclusion: concurrence, not conflict, presents the productive course. The ambiguities and complexities posed by such challenging economic times demand thoughtful, constructive collaboration among multiple sets of leaders facing the sometimes conflicting overlay of legal, economic, and political impulses. Evolving pluralism in Europe in multiple dimensions; the judicial conversation advances.

---

199 Guntram B. Wolf, 'The ECB's OMT Programme and German Constitutional Concerns' 26, 30, in *The G-20 and Central Banks in the New World of Unconventional Monetary Policy*, Bruegel, 29 Aug. 2013, available at http://www.bruegel.org/publications/publication-detail/publication/789-the-ecbs-omt-programme-and-german-constitutional-concerns/.

200 See, Várnay, note 43.

Better safe than sorry: the dangers of too much precaution revisited

JACQUELYN MACLENNAN

'The torment of precautions often exceeds the dangers to be avoided. It is sometimes better to abandon one's self to destiny.'[1]

I. Introduction

The precautionary principle is a highly topical, highly emotional subject. This is a principle which gives us comfort that we can rely on someone somewhere, some authority, to be watching out for our best interests; taking the measures necessary for us to sleep at night secure in the knowledge that we are safeguarded from what could otherwise endanger us. Knowing how hard it is to have absolute truth in this complex world, the principle reassures us that even in the absence of 'full scientific certainty', we will be protected.

The precautionary principle gives us confidence. Our best interests are in good hands. Better safe than sorry. An ounce of protection is worth a pound of cure. Better a thousand times careful than once dead. What is there not to like in this?

Yet siren voices claim the precautionary principle is a danger: this is deceptively soft and cuddly; it is regulation as a comfort blanket, because in fact it promotes measures without a coherent, hard core rationale. The State will protect you where there's risk

---

1 Statement attributed to Napoleon Bonaparte.

– irrespective of scientific evidence or cost or adequate alternatives.[2] This has deeply undesirable results: it stifles discovery and new developments. Far from being a force for good, universal precaution equals total paralysis.[3] While this view is not by any means a wholly US view, it remains associated with mainly US commentators.[4]

Ian Forrester considered this dilemma in a *festschrift* for Judge David Edwards, in many ways his mentor over the years.[5] His article reflected the interest he developed in the principle from representing Pfizer[6] in a case which was to establish boundaries to the application of the precautionary principle, still relevant today, and then Servier.[7] He defined the principle as 'an attempt to offer an intellectual and politically defensible framework for deciding controversies where the science is uncertain'.[8] I would like to return to it now, for a number of reasons: I worked with Ian on the *Pfizer Animal Health* litigation. He has been a colleague and a mentor in many ways over the years. The issues addressed in 'The Dangers of Too Much Precaution' remain current. So I offer him these thoughts as a gesture of friendship, and in tribute to the scope and variety of his professional life.

It is uncontroversial that in some cases, it is right to turn away from a technology or from a product which offers too many uncertainties, too few benefits, too much risk. The question is: how do we make that decision? Where is the line to be drawn?

This is a good time to take stock of the precautionary principle, its merits and de-merits, since it is at the heart of a passionate debate regarding the proposed Transatlantic Trade and Investment Partnership (TTIP). The EU and the US are currently embroiled in negotiations for this ground-breaking agreement. These began in July 2013, with the original – ambitious-- aim of concluding an agreement by now. The European Commission has again confirmed that the agreement is a high priority policy. However, serious concerns have been raised by stakeholders in the EU about potential negative effects of a TTIP Agreement on both existing EU regulations and future legislation, and whether this would endanger the high level of environmental and health standards achieved in the EU. Is there in reality an EU affinity for and US scepticism about the precautionary principle which could contribute to the wreckage of the TTIP ideal?

---

2 See eg. Henk van den Belt, 'Debating the Precautionary Principle: "Guilty until Proven Innocent" or "Innocent until Proven Guilty"?', *Plant Physiol* 2003; M. Petersen 'The Precautionary Principle is incoherent', *Journal of Risk Assessment,* 2006.

3 See eg. Cass R Sunstein, 'Beyond the Precautionary Principle', 2003, The Chicago Working Paper Series Index http://law uchicago.edu/lawecon/index.html, p. 5.

4 See Vogel, *The Politics of Precaution: Regulating Health Safety and Environmental Risks in Europe and the United States*, (2012) and for an EU view see eg. Ragmar Lofsted 'Risk Communication Guidelines for Europe: a modest proposition', *Journal of Risk Research* 13:1, 87-109.

5 Ian S. Forrester 'The Dangers of Too Much Precaution' p. 207. in *A True European: Essays for Judge David Edward*, Hoskins and Robinson (eds).

6 Judgment in *Pfizer Animal Health v. Commission,* T-13/99, EU:T:2002:209.

7 Judgment of 28 January 2003, *Les Laboratoires Servier v. Commission*, T-147/00, EU:T:2003:17 and on appeal Judgment in *Commission v. Laboratoires Servier,* C-156/03 P, not published.

8 Ian S. Forrester, 'The Dangers of Too Much Precaution' p. 207. In Hoskins and Robinson (eds) *A True European: Essays for Judge David Edward.*

II. The precautionary principle – a (very) brief history

The history of the precautionary principle has been well rehearsed.[9] The first sighting seems to be in the mid-18th century in Sweden.[10] The '*vorsorgeprinzip*' as such was established in Germany in the early 19th century -- calling for forests to be conserved so that future generations would be able to rely on wood -- and developed in Sweden from the late 1960s. It has been built into US law.[11] Some argue the precautionary principle has become a customary norm of international law,[12] and it is certainly ubiquitous in international documents.[13] Since 1993, the European Union Treaty has required EU environmental policy to be based on it[14]– but EU policy in a much broader sense has been founded on the principle, as confirmed explicitly in 2000 by the European Commission in a detailed Communication on the subject.[15] It is now an explicit and central element in EU regulation, and been confirmed by the European Court as a general principle of EU law.[16]

9 For further discussion see eg. Cass R Sunstein, 'Beyond the Precautionary Principle', 2003, *The Chicago Working Paper Series Index* http://law.uchicago.edu/lawecon/index.html.

10 Karlsson, 2006, cited in Ragnar Loftsted, 'The Use and Abuse of the Precautionary Principle in Europe', Presentation at White & Case/Burson Marstellar Seminar, Brussels, 25 November 2013.

11 Eg. *Ethyl Corporation v. EPA*, 541 F.2d 1 (D.C. Cir. 1976) (en banc); *American Trucking Association v EPA* F.3d (DC Circ 2002).

12 Though some disagree, see Zander, J. (2010) *The Application of the Precautionary Principle in Practice: Comparative Dimensions*, CUP.

13 International recognition seems to date from 1982, when the UN World Charter for Nature posited that when 'potential adverse effects are not fully understood, the activities should not proceed.' In 1990, recognition was express: 'In order to achieve sustainable development, policies must be based on the precautionary principle. Where there are threats of serious or irreversible damage, lack of full scientific certainty should not be used as a reason for postponing measures…' (Closing Ministerial Declaration from the UN Economic Conference for Europe). It is now in hundreds of documents.

14 The Maastricht Treaty 1992 introduced the precautionary principle, and this is now embodied in Article 191 of the Treaty on the Functioning of the European Union.

15 Communication on the Precautionary Principle, European Commission, February 2, 2000, Com (2000) 1 final.

16 Judgment of 26 November 2002, *Artedogan v Commission*,T-74/00, ECLI:EU:T:2002:283: 'although the precautionary principle is mentioned in the Treaty only in connection with environmental policy, it is broader in scope. It is intended to be applied in order to ensure a high level of protection of health, consumer safety and the environment in all the Community's spheres of activity…It follows that the precautionary principle can be defined as a general principle of Community law' (paras. 183 - 184).

III. Precaution compared - the US and the EU

There has been substantial focus in recent years on whether regulatory policy in the US is more or less precautionary than the EU.[17] Predictably, there are different conclusions on this. David Vogel argues[18] that although the US was more precautionary than Europe during the 1970s and 1980s, the EU today is more precautionary than the US in dealing with risks to human health and the environment. As examples of this, Vogel mentions tighter EU regulation of chemical substances, greenhouse gas emissions, agriculture, food, and consumer products.

Conversely, others consider that, while the EU has more explicitly embraced the precautionary principle, in fact it is not more precautionary than the US in its regulatory approach:[19] 'Europe and the United States have maintained rough parity across all risks over the past four decades,' though with different approaches to different areas, and no real consistency.[20] Wiener concludes that the US is now more precautionary than the EU in dealing with the risks of mad cow disease, diesel engine exhaust, particulate air pollution, environmental tobacco smoke, biodiversity loss, and terrorism. But the EU is now more precautionary in responding to the risks of growth hormones in beef, genetically modified foods, stratospheric ozone destruction, climate change, and chemical risks.[21]

While comparative scholars reach different overall conclusions on the degree of precaution involved in law making on both sides of the Atlantic, they appear to converge in one area – that the EU has a more stringent regulatory approach when it comes to chemical risks, and the EU is more precautionary in regulation of the chemical sector.[22]

However, the implicit acceptance that stringency of regulation is a conclusive indicator of precaution has been criticized as ignoring the central meaning of the precautionary principle. Professor Morag-Levine has made an interesting study of the historical roots of differences in patterns of risk regulation between common law countries (the United Kingdom and the US) and civil law countries. She states: 'Used prescriptively, the precautionary principle *urges* regulators to take stringent, risk-averse measures in

---

17 E.g., Robert V. Percival, 'Risk, Uncertainty and Precaution: Lessons from the History of U.S. Environmental Law', http://digitalcommons.law.umaryland.edu/cgi/viewcontent.cgi?article=2404&context=fac_pubs.

18 Vogel, *The Politics of Precaution: Regulating Health, Safety, and Environmental Risks in Europe and the United States* (2012).

19 Jonathan Wiener (ed) The Reality of Precaution (Wiener et al. 2011).

20 Wiener et al. 2011, p. 521.

21 See Percival 2014, p. 9.

22 I.e., REACH Regulation (EC) 1907/2006 concerning the Registration, Evaluation, Authorisation and Restriction of Chemicals, see http://echa.europa.eu/web/guest/regulations/reach/legislation; ROHS Directive 2011/65/EU on the Restriction of the use of certain hazardous substances in electrical and electronic equipment. See http://ec.europa.eu/environment/waste/rohs_eee/legis_en.htm; WEEE Directive 2012/19/EU on waste electrical and electronic equipment. See http//ec.europa.eu/environment/waste/weee/legis_en.htm.

response to scientifically uncertain risks. Used permissively, the principle authorizes the state to regulate even in the face of scientific uncertainty. In this fashion, the principle is said to act as both a sword and a shield. Understood as a permissive rather than prescriptive rule, the principle can be restated as a requirement of judicial deference towards regulatory measures irrespective of the strength of the evidence linking the regulated activities to distinct harms.'[23]

US-EU tensions over the use of the precautionary principle have tended to be focused on the scope of regulatory discretion, rather than on the obligation to regulate – i. e., on the permissive meaning of the principle. The EU approach before the WTO and the European Courts has concerned the authority to regulate in the face of scientific uncertainty. Morag-Levine draws a link with the different historical approaches to legal review under common law and civil law systems. Under the common law 'nuisance model', judges are given the final say on the reasonableness of administrative, public health interventions. Under the civil law 'police model', there is a presumption of autonomous regulatory discretion with correspondingly limited judicial oversight. The precautionary principle thus reflects the civil law 'police model' requiring judicial deference to the sovereign prerogative of the regulatory authority to regulate to protect public health and safety. Morag-Levine concludes that this explains the greater US scepticism towards the principle, and the fact that continental Europe historically has been more precautionary than the US.[24]

1. US position

Whatever the merits from a public policy perspective of recourse to the precautionary principle, one view common in the US is that it is fundamentally at odds with traditional requirements of proof. It is seldom raised in litigation, and when it is, it fares poorly:[25] 'While it has some prominence in the environmental literature, the precautionary principle's efficacy as a litigation argument has proven scant. A common strain through the opinions dismissive of it is the precautionary principle's inherent conflict with traditional framework of proof in litigation. So while the precautionary principle should be taken seriously when encountered, its persuasive value in court is not likely to be high.'

Vogel, who believes the shift in greater precaution in the EU is due to political changes in both the EU and the US, considers one factor for this to be greater emphasis on risk assessment and less deferential judicial review provided in the US, which has increased

23 See: http://www.regblog.org/2013/09/23/23-morag-levine-precaution/, Noga Morag-Levine, 'The History of Precaution', 23 Sep. 2013, Penn Program on Regulation Blog.

24 One interesting example given by Morag-Levine concerns England, a common law country; while precautionary regulation emerged in Britain with the adoption of the Alkali Act in 1863, she argues that this Act was directly inspired by French and other continental regulatory models developed under the civil law tradition.

25 See: http://www.law360.com/articles/501280/print?section=california, James Sabovich, 'The Paltry Power of the Precautionary Principle', 27 Jan. 2014, referring to *CTIA v City and County of San Francisco*, 827 F. Supp. éd 1054, 1062-1063 (N.D. California, 2011); *Sancho v US DOE*, 578 Supp. 2d 1258, 1260-61 (D. Haw. 2008), 392 Fed. Appx 610, 611 (9th Circ. Haw. 2010), ...

the level of scientific evidence necessary to justify new risk regulations.[26] The precautionary principle has been clearly recognized and judicially validated in the US. The 1976 decision in *Ethyl Corp v. EPA* is a landmark in US environmental law. It endorsed the precautionary principle long before it was accepted into global environmental policy. The decision established that precautionary regulation could be based 'on the inconclusive but suggestive results of numerous studies' indicating that exposure to a substance could endanger health even in the absence of conclusive proof that such adverse health effects actually had occurred. It also indicated that courts would be deferential in reviewing the judgment of the EPA Administrator in assessing the significance of scientific evidence.'[27]

However, the Supreme Court has also insisted on reliance on risk assessments and cost benefit analyses,[28] and been unsympathetic to maverick scientific arguments.[29] The US judiciary is much more likely to constrain attempts by law makers to regulate for the protection of health or the environment than their judicial brethren in the EU. This has unsurprisingly been welcomed by some and criticized by others depending on which side of the ideological debate they sit.[30]

Ultimately, it seems that although almost all US environmental statutes authorize regulation prior to definitive proof of harm, in part due to enormous political pressures, federal agencies usually wait for proof of harm before adopting regulations. Most of the chemicals that have been stringently regulated in the US became the focus of regulatory attention only after highly publicized incidents in which they caused visible and substantial harm.[31] US regulatory intervention has been largely reactionary more than precautionary.

2. EU position

In the EU, the same political impetus exists to give rise to regulation in different sectors, and particularly with regard to chemicals, but the response has been more accepting of a precautionary approach. One recent example of this can be seen in the regulation of Bisphenol A ('BPA'), a chemical with a great variety of uses including the lining of

26 See Percival p. 11. Vogel cites two other factors for the shift: first, '[d]uring the last two decades, Europeans have perceived more health, safety, and environmental risks caused by business to be both credible and politically unacceptable than have Americans'. Second, the politics of regulatory policy in the US has become more 'polarized along ideological and partisan lines' as politicians supported by business interests have sought to demonize regulation.

27 Percival, ibid. p.19.

28 See *Corrosion Proof Fittings v. EPA*, 947 F.2d 1201 (5th Cir. 1991), concerning asbestos. The court echoed critics of the precautionary principle who charge that precautionary regulation may create greater risks than it prevents, by chastising the EPA for failing to perform detailed analyses of the risks of any potential substitutes for asbestos. Surprisingly, however, the court upheld the government's ban on new uses of asbestos without requiring any cost-benefit analysis, noting that the 'EPA cannot possibly evaluate the costs and benefits of banning unknown, uninvented products.'

29 *Kumho Tire Company v Carmichael* 526 US 137 (1999) provides that expert evidence, including scientific evidence, can be excluded if it is not in the mainstream.

30 See Percival, ibid. p.25-26; Perlstein, 'a new breed of activist judges are waging a determined and largely successful war on federal regulatory agencies' through the use of 'legal sophistry, procedural hair-splitting and scientific conjecture'.

31 Percival, p. 22.

cans and in polycarbonate plastic used for baby feeding cups and bottles. It has been used for more than 40 years. BPA can migrate in small amounts into food and beverages stored in materials containing the substance. Concerns about BPA have been expressed world-wide – the question being whether it can disrupt hormone levels, particularly in foetuses and small children, and lead to developmental issues, cancer, behavioural problems, heart disease and other conditions. Hysterical claims tend to hit the headlines, and are then countered, such as 'Gender-bending chemical in soup claims overstated!'[32]

In the US, there are no restrictions on the use of BPA. The FDA notes that no risks have been established, and it is waiting for further research. However, it recommends in the meantime that 'reasonable steps' be taken to reduce human exposure to BPA in the food supply, and has ever expressed support for manufacturers who have stopped using BPA in products for babies and for companies working to develop alternatives to BPA in canned foods.

In the EU, BPA is authorized for materials which come into contact with food, subject to certain maximum levels, which are agreed to be much higher than actual levels of exposure.[33] The European Food Safety Authority (EFSA) has been studying BPA for the last ten years in order to identify whether more restrictive measures should be taken. In 2015, after a major review of all new data, it concluded that there was no consumer health risk from exposure to BPA:

'EFSA's comprehensive re-evaluation of bisphenol A (BPA) exposure and toxicity concludes that BPA poses no health risk to consumers of any age group (including unborn children, infants and adolescents) at current exposure levels. Exposure from the diet or from a combination of sources (diet, dust, cosmetics and thermal paper) is considerably under the safe level (the "tolerable daily intake" or TDI).'[34]

In recent years however there has been a domino effect of bans imposed on BPA. This began in March 2010 when Denmark decided to temporarily ban BPA for use in plastic materials in contact with food for children up to the age of three. Then in July 2010, France banned feeding bottles containing BPA. Both of these measures were notified to the Commission, which responded by adopting a Directive, in an almost unprecedentedly short time, banning the use of BPA in plastic baby bottles from June 2011.[35] This notes:

'The precautionary principle referred to in ... Regulation (EC) No 178/2002 .... laying down the general principles and requirements of food law, establishing the European Food Safety Authority and laying down procedures in matters of food safety allows

32 http://www.nhs.uk/news/2011/11november/pages/gender-bending-chemical-in-soup-claims.aspx.

33 Commission Directive 2002/72, now Regulation 10/2011 on Plastic Food Contact Materials, as amended, see ec.europa.eu/food/food/chemicalsafety/foodcontact/legisl_list_en.htm.

34 See EFSA press release: http://www.efsa.europa.eu/en/press/news/150121.htm. Based on new studies, the EFSA decided to lower the TDI for BPA, but it noted that the highest estimate of actual exposure levels to BPA are three to five times lower than the level established.

35 Commission Directive 2011/8/EU of 28 January 2011 amending Directive 2002/72/EC as regards the restriction of use of Bisphenol A in plastic infant feeding bottles, OJ L 26/11; 29/01/2011.

the Union to provisionally adopt measures on the basis of available pertinent information, pending an additional assessment of risk and a review of the measure within a reasonable period of time.'

The Commission Directive referred to uncertainties in the current state of the scientific research, considered the availability of alternate products and the economic impact of the ban, and concluded that in light of that, a ban was justified. The Directive does not appear to have been challenged in any court. France has now gone further and introduced a law which bans BPA in all receptacles intended to contain food.[36] This has been indirectly challenged before the French Supreme Administrative Court, the Council of State, and a referral has been made to the French Constitutional Court. A complaint has also been made to the European Commission[37] which may decide to bring France before the European Court. These proceedings should provide an opportunity for consideration of the legal propriety of recourse to the precautionary principle in a situation where the economic impact of a ban on a cross section of French industry is said to be severe; while alternative products may be available, there is agreement they have not been subject to anything like the testing applied to BPA; and where according to the EFSA -- a body specifically intended to provide independent, reliable in-put to the EU regulatory process -- the scientific evidence provides no basis for any ban.

The precautionary principle is thus the accepted foundation in the EU for regulatory activity, certainly as regards environmental protection and public safety. As a general principle of EU law, it cannot be changed, even by a Treaty modification. The only issue is how the principle is *implemented*.

At the end of the day, the decisive factor in regulation is the political judgment of the regulator (whether that is the European Institutions or a Member State) of the level of risk acceptable at any point in time. Science is always uncertain. Precautionary regulation has, over the years, been instrumental in some highly commendable legislation – for example in banning asbestos, or lead. But good governance requires that this political judgment should be based as much as possible on the sound science that exists. And that this judgment be subject to effective judicial review.

The European Commission has in fact requested the European Court to set limits on the abuse of the precautionary principle – for example, where a Member State bans a product based on the need for precaution, which then undermines the free movement of goods in the EU, and the Commission does not consider an EU ban is justified in the circumstances. In *Commission v France*, the CJEU stated at §93:

> 'Where it proves to be impossible to determine with certainty the existence or extent of the alleged risk because of the *insufficiency, inconclusiveness or imprecision of the results of studies conducted*, but the likelihood of *real harm*

---

36 Law No. 2012-1442 of 24 December 2012 suspending the manufacture, import, export and marketing of all receptacles intended to contain food containing bisphenol A, modifying law No. 2010-729 of 30 June 2010 suspending the sale of baby bottles containing bisphenol A.

37 http://www.foodqualitynews.com/Industry-news/French-ban-on-BPA-challenged-after-EFSA-opinion.

> to public health persists should the risk materialize, the precautionary principle justifies the adoption of restrictive measures, provided they are *non-discriminatory and objective'*.(emphasis added).

Importantly, the CJEU said, 'A correct application of the precautionary principle presupposes, first, identification of the potentially negative consequences for health . . . and, secondly, a *comprehensive assessment of the risk* to health based on the *most reliable scientific data available and the most recent results of international research*.'[38] (emphasis added)

Reliance on a generalized presumption of a risk to health was not held by the Court to be sufficient. At the very least, the CJEU says, a risk assessment meeting the requirements set out should be carried out, and then, in light of that, if there is uncertainty, a view can be taken on whether a restriction is justified by the need for precaution. This is in line with the approach of the Court in *Pfizer*. Any evidence of risk is enough to allow politicians to decide to ban a product based on their judgment of what level of risk is acceptable; but: 'a preventive measure *cannot properly be based on a purely hypothetical approach to the risk*, founded on mere conjecture which has not been scientifically verified' (para 143, emphasis added).

However, in *Afton Chemical*,[39] the CJEU appears to have compromised this basic position. The situation in that case was that no comprehensive risk assessment had actually been completed. The case concerned a political compromise which resulted in EU limits being introduced on the use of a fuel additive known as 'MMT', and the CJEU specifically noted that 'no public body or independent entity had undertaken a scientific assessment of the effects of MMT.' Nevertheless the CJEU considered the restriction was justified because 'the European Union's broad discretion, which implies *limited judicial* review of its exercise, applies not only to the nature and scope of the measures to be taken but also, to some extent, to the *finding of the basic facts*.' (para. 33 emphasis added) The CJEU then acknowledged that the Institutions took 'several scientific studies into account' during the legislative process 'in order to exercise their discretion properly.' Hopefully, an important qualification was added by the CJEU though, when it said that the precautionary principle could be relied on in these circumstances only because the measure adopted was temporary and 'capable of amendment according to thc result of developments which may be observed.'

It has been asked if the CJEU in *Afton* is effectively sanctioning an 'act now and assess later' approach, and if so, if that does not contravene international commitments.[40] Further, the approach mandated by the CJEU has been criticized (inter alia) for

---

38 Judgment in *Commission v France*, C-333/08, EU:C:2010:44, para. 92.

39 Judgment in *Afton Chemical*, C-343/09, EU:C:2010:419.

40 Fast, 'A Troubling Precedent: Implementing the Precautionary Principle to Limit the Role of Science in European Decisionmaking' 41 *Environmental Law Reporter* 10520-10526.

empowering the EU legislature to act on a 'highly selective and potentially biased subset of the available "science"'.[41]

Afton sets a very low bar for what is required as a scientific assessment, reflecting the approach of the Court in *Alpharma*[42]. It establishes that in the final analysis, the Institutions may be entitled to ignore the advice of scientific experts and enact a political agreement with little and/or opaque underlying evidence. The more recent *International Cadmium Association* case[43] perhaps gives cause for more optimism. It involved a restriction on the use of all cadmium compounds as colouring agents for plastics. The Commission tried to justify the ban based on reports that did not cover the cadmium pigments at issue (or did not cover all plastics), but it had essentially no evidence to support this. In the absence of at least some scientific evidence, the Court struck down the ban.

The problem with the European Court in Luxembourg remains that it is not prepared to, or suited to, engage in a full review of the basis for the decision taken by the regulator. It checks only for manifest error on the part of the legislator. It does not wish to assess the adequacy of the scientific assessment. Indeed[44], it is not a good forum for a 'battle of experts' on science – there is no cross examination to challenge the positions taken, there is no accepted procedure for the experts to find common ground and identify their differences so the Court may proceed from there, there is no expertise within the court, and –fundamentally – judges, like most lawyers, are risk averse. So if there is at least some recourse to some science in justification of a precautionary ban, and the ban is not some form of protectionism imposed by a Member State,[45] the chances are the ban will not be questioned by the European judges.

What could be done to remedy the situation? The Court could change its approach to the level of review to be given to these cases. Killick[46] has suggested that the European Institutions should adopt a 'hard law' setting out criteria on how to approach risk assessment and the implementation of the precautionary principle which the Court could then use to assess a measure and its adoption against. The fact that the Commission could be bound by its existing Communication, or even more detailed Guidelines that it might adopt, is insufficient, since as *Afton* has shown, the Commission's views can be effectively ignored by the legislature. Ragnar Lofstedt[47] has called for a clear definition of the precautionary principle, based expressly on an examination of the

---

41 Fast, ibid. p. 10525. See also: Roger, Apolline: 'Comment on case C-343/09 - Afton Chemical Limited v Secretary of State for Transport', 08.07.2010, *Journal for European Environmental & Planning Law* 2011 Vol. 8 n° 2 p.220-224.

42 Judgment of 11 September 2002, *Alpharma*, T-70/99, EU:T:2002:210.

43 Judgment of 14 November 2013, *International Cadmium Association*, Case T-456/11, EU:T:2013:594.

44 The situation is unchanged since this was discussed by Forrester in 'The Dangers of Too Much Precaution'.

45 e.g., *EFTA v Norway*, judgment of the EFTA Court of 5 April 2001; Judgment in *Commission v Denmark*, C-192/01 ECLI:EU:C:2003:492; Judgment in *Commission v France*, EU:C:2010:44.

46 James Killick, 'The Precautionary Problem - The European Courts and the Precautionary Principle', presentation at White & Case/Burson Marstellar Seminar, Brussels, 25 November 2013.

47 'The use and abuse of the precautionary principle in Europe', presentation at White & Case/Burson Marstellar Seminar, Brussels, 25 November 2013.

potential benefits and costs of action or lack of action, since these criteria are currently not being considered. To be effective however, such a definition would have to come from the CJEU.

Like Forrester in 'The Dangers of Too Much Precaution', I am not suggesting that the European Court should substitute its own views in place of legislative decisions which have been lawfully adopted. The Court should however be prepared to review decisions to assess and ensure that the regulator or legislator has been conscientious and impartial; that it has gathered together and fully taken account of available scientific opinion, particularly independent opinion; if evidence has been ignored – particularly from scientific committees or experts created as part of the regulatory process – there should be a cogent statement of reasons for that; if harm has been identified it should be quantified in terms of its seriousness; if restrictions are imposed there should be some consideration of their cost/benefit.

Generally in life it is better to do something rather than nothing.[48] The politicians may have got it right and history may validate a precautionary approach – but the possibility they have not must be recognized. A regulatory process which is transparent and accountable and rigorous, which identifies and quantifies harm, which assesses science where it exists, which does not unreasonably stifle innovation, is surely a desirable process for the EU. Three years ago, the European Commission introduced a new position: a Chief Scientific Officer, with the mandate to 'provide independent expert advice on any aspect of science, technology and innovation as requested by the President.' In controversial circumstances, this post was abolished by President Juncker when the new Commission was formed in 2014, and no replacement is in place.[49] This does not harbinger well for the approach the EU will adopt to implement precaution, and makes effective judicial oversight even more important.

IV. The (mis)perception of precaution - TTIP

Current EU public opinion, it seems clear, does not take the view that the US is just as precautionary as the EU, and is extremely distrustful about the difference in the US approach with regard to chemical risk. This distrust is evident in the reaction to the proposed TTIP Agreement under negotiation by the US and EU. The discussions are now squarely in the radar of environmental and consumer policy activists – and therefore public opinion - because the TTIP has a number of innovative and controversial aspects – in particular, the intention to seek regulatory convergence between the EU and US.

48 Taking no action where action is justified may result in avoidable harm. Fyodor Dostoyevsky's novel *Notes from the Underground* depicts the tragic consequences which ensue when a person has deliberately chosen to do nothing at all with his life.

49 See e.g., http://www.nature.com/news/european-commission-scraps-chief-scientific-adviser-post-1.16348; https://www.pressandjournal.co.uk/fp/news/politics/holyrood/457693/confusion-over-eu-chief-scientific-adviser-role/.

The European Commission's consultation exercise regarding the proposed TTIP[50] indicates there is a clear incongruity between EU industry, which is strongly in favour of TTIP, and the 'average EU citizen', who appears to believe EU regulatory standards are substantially higher than the US, and that a TTIP agreement would be an unacceptable weakening of these standards. According to the Commission:

> 'In the public debate, various stakeholders have raised concerns about possible negative effects of a TTIP Agreement on the implementation of existing EU regulations as well as on future legislative developments. The proposals concerning chemicals in TTIP have attracted particular attention from stakeholders, and some concerns have been expressed that the inclusion of chemicals related disciplines in a TTIP Agreement would endanger the high level of environmental and health standards achieved in the EU.' [51]

The European Commission has belatedly realized that it is not carrying 'hearts and minds' in its approach to TTIP (the question of what type of investor state dispute settlement mechanism should be included in the TTIP has resulted in an unprecedented 150,000 responses to the Commission's online consultation exercise[52]). Indeed, as I write this piece, an email has just been circulated:

> 'Please note that on Saturday the 18th of April [2015] there will be a street protest for TTIP Trans-Atlantic Trade Agreement in central Brussels from 14:00 to 17:00. The police asked us to make sure that the building stays closed and advised us not to come in that day, as there will be 10,000-15,000 protesters.'

Concern about the lack of transparency of the initiative, including a successful complaint to the European Ombudsman,[53] has now resulted in a somewhat remarkable degree of openness.[54] The initial legal texts under negotiation, and some Discussion Non-Papers and Memos, have been published. In particular, these texts include the EU position on the regulatory aspects of TTIP (but not negotiating positions on market access where the EU is still defining its stance, and not texts where there is no US agreement on publication). DG Trade has embraced social media, and accessible 'Fact Sheets' and a brochure called 'The Top 10 Myths about TTIP' are on the web.[55] The Commissioner's

---

50 See: http://ec.europa.eu/trade/policy/in-focus/ttip/.

51 See: http://trade.ec.europa.eu/doclib/docs/2014/november/tradoc_152914.pdf, European Commission Chemicals in TTIP – Publication of non-papers 'Draft outline for provisions on chemicals' and 'How to put ideas for cooperation under TTIP into practice – a few examples.'

52 See: http://ec.europa.eu/trade/policy/in-focus/ttip/have-your-say/.

53 See: http://www.ombudsman.europa.eu/en/press/release.faces/en/58669/html.bookmark, and http://www.ombudsman.europa.eu/en/cases/decision.faces/en/58668/html.bookmark. The Ombudsman's own consultation elicited 6,000 email responses. In addition, the new Commission, under President Junker, which took power in July 2014 has set out a policy of greater transparency generally.

54 Headline on http://ec.europa.eu/trade/policy/in-focus/ttip/: 9 April 2015, 'European Commission publishes TTIP legal texts as part of transparency initiative: The texts published today include textual proposals and position papers. Factsheets on each chapter help understand what is at stake in the EU US trade talks.' Despite the rhetoric, environmental activists continue to criticize the substance of what is made available by the EU.

55 For example: Myth – 'TTIP will weaken strict EU standards that protect people and the planet' vs. Fact - EU standards simply aren't up for negotiation. TTIP would uphold them all.

speeches are directly aimed at assuaging public concerns.[56] Clearly, the Commission is now fully engaged in making the case for TTIP, and trying to dispel the widespread rumour and anxiety which abounds. How successful that effort will be is difficult to predict. Irrespective of that, the increased level of transparency – even if not meeting the demands of all – is an interesting and necessary reflection of the difference in the character of the proposed TTIP, as a 'new generation preferential trade agreement' which goes beyond traditional market access and existing WTO commitments into the area of regulatory cooperation and mutual recognition or functional equivalence. When the exercise began, the former Trade Commissioner De Gucht described it as the first steps to the creation of a 'transatlantic internal market'.[57] The TTIP will thus be quasi-legislative in nature, and increased openness to consultation and debate in its negotiation is the proper democratic response to this.[58]

The ultimate goal of the proposed TTIP may be the harmonisation of standards – and to bring more countries into this exercise[59] – but the European Commission has also stated as a matter of principle:

> 'TTIP provisions shall not affect the ultimate sovereign right of either party to regulate in pursuit of its public policy objectives and shall not be used as a means of lowering the levels of protection provided by either party...'[60]

and specifically with regard to chemicals:

> 'The EU position is that TTIP should under no circumstances result in the lowering of existing EU environmental and health standards with regard to chemicals. TTIP will also have no chilling effect on the implementation of existing EU chemicals regulations, such as the REACH and the CLP (Classification, Labelling and Packaging of Substances and Mixtures) Regulations, which will continue to be implemented in full compliance with the existing rules and procedures and respecting the applicable deadlines as foreseen in the respective Regulations.'[61]

Evidently, these objectives – regulatory coherence and the ultimate right of each party to regulate for itself – are 'in stark contrast with each other'.[62] When it comes to the chemicals sector, the situation seems to be characterized by the 'the precautionary principle divide'.[63] This sector, according to economic analysis by the European

56 See: http://europa.eu/rapid/press-release_SPEECH-15-4182_en.htm.

57 See: *Financial Times*, 13 Feb., 2013.

58 See Cremona, 'Negotiating the Transatlantic Trade and Investment Partnership', CMLRev 52:351-362, 2015, p.353, 362.

59 See Vogel, p. 12, regarding the EU's efforts to globalize its regulations and 'act as the world's economic regulator'.

60 See Cremona, 'Negotiating the Transatlantic Trade and Investment Partnership', CMLRev 52:351-362, 2015, p.353, footnote 9.

61 See: http://trade.ec.europa.eu/doclib/docs/2014/november/tradoc_152914.pdf.

62 As noted for example in Buonsante, 'Regulatory coherence in the TTIP Agreement: the case of Chemicals,' 2/14 ELNI Review 39-43.

63 Buonsante, ibid., p. 42.

Commission, would be the second biggest beneficiary of TTIP liberalisation[64] -- and is the sector in which there is the greatest divergence in levels of protection between the two trading blocs.[65] The EU has moved to a hazard-based approach, which recognizes that there are benefits in avoiding or limiting exposure to certain substances even without having to prove in each specific case that there is an unreasonable risk, and in the EU this is explicitly based on the precautionary principle. The precautionary principle is not included in the formal TTIP debate however.

So is there any way regulatory cooperation between the EU and the US can be effective and lead to convergence? The European Commission has suggested that it can.[66] Others suggest that this would be 'very difficult as the two blocs works at a very different pace and the underlying regulations under which they operate are two separate planets'.[67] Much of the regulation of chemicals of concern in the US now is done at state level (in particular California) rather than federal level. No restriction of a chemical under TSCA has been approved for over 20 years, and there is no equivalent of the REACH approach to authorisation of chemicals. Depending on the perspective, involvement of the US federal authorities in EU regulatory initiatives could have a 'chilling effect' -- or bring in a welcome voice of reason, encouraging a more evidence-based, risk-focused approach.

In any event, since the EU has embraced the precautionary principle as a fundamental legal principle, embodying it in the Treaty, and the US regulatory agencies and Supreme Court have not eschewed it as a matter of principle (rather, it has been used less in federal law-making because of political impasse, and controlled more by judicial oversight), and since the EU has successfully exported its regulatory approach to a much greater extent than the US, it would seem in all likelihood that the US will be nudged in a more precautionary direction. If the TTIP is agreed, then the world could become a more precautionary place.

In truth, that does not have to be a bad thing. The precautionary principle, in itself, does not purport to dictate how precautionary regulatory policy should be. It simply says it is not acceptable to justify postponing action to prevent harm on a lack of full scientific certainty:

> 'Properly understood, the precautionary principle is neither incoherent, paralyzing, nor a prescription for overregulation.[68] Rather it cautions that regulatory policy should be proactive in responding to uncertainty concerning potentially serious

64 See http://trade.ec.europa.eu/doclib/docs/2013/march/tradoc_150737.pdf.

65 USTR, *2013 Report on Technical Barriers to Trade.*

66 See: http://trade.ec.europa.eu/doclib/docs/2014/november/tradoc_152914.pdf. The Commission proposes that whenever a chemical undergoes a regulatory process, the US government is given the possibility to comment on the plans, and to participate with experts in meetings reviewing data of the proposed regulatory action.

67 Buonsante, ibid., p. 43, comparing in particular TSCA: the US 1976 Toxic Substances Control Act and REACH: the EU's 2006 Regulation concerning Registration, Evaluation, Authorisation and restriction of Chemicals.

68 e.g., Cass Sunstein, 2005.

> threats to human health and the environment, mindful of the potential consequences for future generations.'[69]

But if the precautionary principle in its own terms does not deserve some of the criticism it has received, the question comes back to how should it be implemented looking forward, to avoid undoubted excesses. How serious or irreversible does the harm that has been identified have to be? What level of scientific proof is required? What level of action is justifiable, and how cost-effective should that action be? The costs of preventive actions are usually tangible, clearly allocated and often short term, whereas the costs of failing to act are less tangible, less clearly distributed and usually longer term, posing particular problems of governance. Weighing up the overall pros and cons of action, or inaction, is without doubt a difficult exercise, involving ethical as well as economic considerations.

That, ultimately, is a matter for the regulator – the legislature -- to determine, on the basis of the political environment at a particular time *and* the scientific evidence at hand. Full and effective judicial review is essential for the policy makers to understand and abide by sensible constraints on arbitrary decision making. It is hard to disagree with the European Environment Agency that:

> 'Decision-makers need not only to have more and better quality information but also to act wisely more often so as to achieve a better balance between the benefits of innovations and their hazards. Learning and applying these late lessons from the last century's early warnings could help all of us to achieve this better balance during this century.'[70]

V. Conclusion

'Out of this nettle, danger, we pluck this flower, safety'[71]

Life is a journey fraught with risk, with the unknown, with danger. The question is: what should be the limits on regulating with good intent for safety? That is the discussion which has come to the fore in the current EU/US TTIP negotiations. Like motherhood and apple pie, how can measures taken to protect our children in an uncertain world be anything other than good and right and justifiable? But sometimes, we can go too far. Good intention can run wild. When it comes to the precautionary principle, there is a fine line to be traced in ensuring good intention is backed with good evidence.

It seems apt that Ian Forrester has been involved in this debate. Ian has been a risk taker throughout his professional career – studying in New Orleans not New College Oxford; taking and passing the New York bar exam when it was a rarity for foreigners,

---

69 Percival, 2014, pp. 5, 7.

70 Introduction to *Late lessons from early warnings: the precautionary principle 1896–2000*, European Enviroment Agency, Environmental issue report 22/2001.

71 Shakespeare: *Henry IV*, Part 1, Act 2, Scene 3.

and litigating to be registered to practice as a non-US citizen; moving from the relative comfort of the Scottish bar ultimatly to Brussels to practice European law; starting his own practice with Chris Norall (see separate contribution); and now, in his leadership of White & Case's *pro bono* practice (see also separate contribution), he does not shy from controversy and risk. Ian Forrester certainly can't be accused of succumbing to Alfred Adler's warning that the chief danger in life is that you may take too many precautions.

In search of a status: where does the jobseeker fit in EU free movement law?

Niamh Nic Shuibhne

I. Introduction

Reflecting on the occasion of happy returns that this volume celebrates, two notable judgments of the Court of Justice turn 40 in 2015. In *Cristini,* the Court considered the nature and scope of the 'social advantages' to which migrant workers are entitled in a host State, within the meaning of (then) Article 7(2) of Regulation 1612/68.[1] It ruled that the concept of social advantages could not be interpreted restrictively; moreover, 'in view of the equality of treatment which the provision seeks to achieve, the substantive area of application must be delineated so as to include all social and tax advantages, whether or not attached to the contract of employment'.[2] In *Mr and Mrs F*, the Court addressed legislative rules on the coordination of social security benefits. In his Opinion, AG Trabucchi observed that the referring Belgian court 'displays a keen awareness of the injustice of the solution which might be reached by the internal law on the basis of the interpretation normally placed on the relevant provisions...and has not made the request to the Court purely in order to resolve doubt as to the interpretation of Community law, but asks something more of the Court: assistance in eliminating once and for all a situation which would conflict with its

1 Now repealed and replaced by Article 7(2) of Regulation 492/2011, 2011 OJ L141/1.

2 Judgment in *Cristini*, C-32/75, EU:C:1975:120, paras. 12-13.

conscience'. Framing a broader vision as much as an individual resolution of the case at hand, he continued:

> [I]f we want Community law to be more than a mere mechanical system of economics and to constitute instead a system commensurate with the society which it has to govern, if we wish it to be a legal system corresponding to the concept of social justice and European integration, not only of the economy but of the people, we cannot disappoint the [national] court's expectations, which are more than those of legal form.[3]

The judgment of the Court in *Cristini* and the analysis of AG Trabucchi in *Mr and Mrs F* were milestone points on the vital trajectory of free movement law that humanised both the status and needs of migrant workers. Equality of treatment remains a core guiding principle in that regard.[4] For Union citizens who are not economically active in a host State, the reach of EU equal treatment law is less clear-cut – and remains less certain.[5] But what is the legal position for jobseekers – Union citizens who are not economically active *yet* but who do move to another Member State deliberately to seek employment there?

Against that background, this contribution considers the extent to which EU law induces host State obligations to support jobseekers from other Member States. In Part 2, the origins of the jobseeker as a *legal* status in EU law are outlined. In path-breaking case law, the Court of Justice derived legal protection for jobseekers from Article 45 TFEU, which confers rights on migrant workers. However, since the creation of distinct free movement and residence rights as an element of Union citizenship, the jobseeker as a legal status is now tied to *both* Article 45 TFEU and Article 21 TFEU.[6] In Part 3, the implications of that conjunction are examined in two specific contexts. First, what are the contours of the jobseeker's right to *reside* in a host State? Second, what other rights can a (lawfully resident) jobseeker claim there? It will be demonstrated that these questions are only partly accommodated in EU legislation and therefore continue to reach the Court of Justice for more definitive resolution. Overall, it is argued that the jobseeker is concurrently a privileged yet also a neglected citizen in the framework of EU free movement law. Furthermore, while being legally overlooked, relatively speaking, may have worked to the jobseeker's advantage in the past, the position has become more precarious as even core principles of free movement law are being opened up in current political debates. In particular, it is difficult to see how more targeted EU legislation can be avoided in the future.

---

3 Opinion of AG Trabucchi in *Mr and Mrs F*, C-7/75, EU:C:1975:75.

4 E.g., confirming the continuing centrality of equal treatment in the context of social advantages for workers, Judgment in *N*, C-46/12, EU:C:2013:97, paras. 48-49.

5 See, in particular, Judgment in *Dano*, C-333/13, EU:C:2014:2358. For analysis, see Verschueren, 'Preventing "benefit tourism": a narrow or broad interpretation of the possibilities offered by the ECJ in *Dano*?' (2015) 52:2 *Common Market Law Review* 363; and Thym 'When Union citizens turn into illegal migrants: the *Dano* case' (2015) 40:2 *European Law Review* 249.

6 In particular, Article 21(1) TFEU, which provides that '[e]very citizen of the Union shall have the right to move and reside freely within the territory of the Member States, subject to the limitations and conditions laid down in the Treaties and by the measures adopted to give them effect'.

II. Origins: a new dimension of the free movement of workers

Article 45(1) TFEU provides that '[f]reedom of movement for workers shall be secured within the Union'. Article 45(2) states that '[s]uch freedom of movement shall entail the abolition of any discrimination based on nationality between workers of the Member States as regards employment, remuneration and other conditions of work and employment'. Reflecting the significance of these objectives, protection against discrimination on the grounds of nationality has been found to reach into the regulation of even private employment relationships, too.[7]

Core elements of the *search* for employment are addressed in secondary legislation. In particular, Articles 1-6 of Regulation 492/2011 outline the scope of equal treatment regarding the process and conditions of recruitment. Article 64(1) of Regulation 883/2004 provides that '[a] wholly unemployed person who satisfies the conditions of the legislation of the competent Member State for entitlement to benefits, and who goes to another Member State in order to seek work there, shall retain his entitlement to unemployment benefits' subject to specified conditions and limits.'[8] Additionally, Article 64(1)(c) states that 'entitlement to benefits shall be retained for a period of three months from the date when the unemployed person ceased to be available to the employment services of the Member State which he left, provided that the total duration for which the benefits are provided does not exceed the total duration of the period of his entitlement to benefits under the legislation of that Member State' but provides also that 'the competent services or institutions may extend the period of three months up to a maximum of six months'. However, no provisions of either this Regulation or Regulation 492/2011 – or of their predecessors[9] – explicitly addressed a critical prior question: do jobseekers have a right to *reside* in a Member State for the purposes of seeking employment there? Relatedly, on what legal basis would that right be constructed, and what conditions would limit it?

The Court of Justice first considered these questions in the *Antonissen* case, in which judgment was delivered not long before the creation of Union citizenship through the Maastricht Treaty.[10] The case concerned a Belgian national who had arrived in the United Kingdom in October 1984. In March 1987, he was convicted of drugs offences and sentenced to two terms of imprisonment. He was released on parole in December 1987, but a deportation order was then issued against him. Mr Antonissen argued that, as a Community national, he could only be deported from the UK within the terms of

7 Judgment in *Angonese*, C-281/98, EU:C:2000:296; Judgment in *Raccanelli*, C-94/07, EU:C:2008:425.

8 Regulation 883/2004/EC on the coordination of social security systems, 2004 OJ L166/1.

9 Regulation (EEC) No 1408/71 of the Council on the application of social security schemes to employed persons and their families moving within the Community, 1971 OJ L149/1; Regulation (EEC) No 1612/68 of the Council on freedom of movement for workers within the Community, 1968 OJ L257/2.

10 Judgment in *Antonissen*, C-292/89, EU:C:1991:80.

Directive 64/221, i.e., on the basis of a decision justified by reasons of public policy, public security or public health.[11] Article 1 of that Directive provided that the measure applied 'to any national of a Member State who resides in or travels to another Member State of the Community, either in order to pursue an activity as an employed or self-employed person, or as a recipient of services'. Mr Antonissen had not found work during his stay in the UK, ruling out a straightforward application of Directive 64/221; but his situation is presented in terms of having entered the UK to *seek* employment throughout the judgment.

Importantly, the relevant national rules established that a national of another Member State who entered the UK in order to seek employment could be required to leave the territory (subject to appeal) if he had not found employment there after six months. Assessing the compatibility of that condition with EU law, the Court emphasised that 'freedom of movement for workers forms one of the foundations of the Community and, consequently, the provisions laying down that freedom must be given a broad interpretation'.[12] Therefore, on the basis that a strict interpretation of Article 45 TFEU would 'jeopardize the actual chances that a national of a Member State who is seeking employment will find it in another Member State, and would, as a result, make that provision ineffective', the Court ruled that freedom of movement for workers '*also entails the right* for nationals of Member States to move freely within the territory of the other Member States and to stay there for the purposes of seeking employment'.[13]

Addressing the question of whether the Member States could place temporal limits on a jobseeker's right of residence, the Court considered that the effectiveness of Article 45 TFEU is nevertheless 'secured in so far as Community legislation or, *in its absence*, the legislation of a Member State gives persons concerned *a reasonable time* in which to apprise themselves, in the territory of the Member State concerned, of offers of employment corresponding to their occupational qualifications and to take, where appropriate, the necessary steps in order to be engaged'.[14] The Court then proceeded to rationalise and articulate a two-part test:

> *In the absence of a Community provision prescribing the period during which Community nationals seeking employment in a Member State may stay there*, a period of six months, such as that laid down in the national legislation at issue in the main proceedings, does not appear in principle to be insufficient to enable the persons concerned to apprise themselves, in the host Member State, of offers of employment corresponding to their occupational qualifications and to take,

11 Council Directive 64/221/EEC on the co-ordination of special measures concerning the movement and residence of foreign nationals which are justified on grounds of public policy, public security or public health, 1964 OJ L56/850; this measure has been repealed and replaced by Directive 2004/38, which is considered in more detail below.

12 Judgment in *Antonissen*, EU:C:1991:80, para. 11.

13 Ibid., paras. 12-13 (emphasis added). In para. 14, the Court added that the protections outlined in (now) Articles 1-6 of Regulation 492/2011 'presuppose that Community nationals are entitled to move in order to look for employment, and hence to stay, in another Member State'.

14 Ibid., para. 16 (emphasis added).

> where appropriate, the necessary steps in order to be engaged and, therefore, *does not jeopardize the effectiveness of the principle of free movement*. However, if after the expiry of that period the person concerned *provides evidence that he is continuing to seek employment and that he has genuine chances of being engaged*, he cannot be required to leave the territory of the host Member State.[15]

Interestingly, the Court declined to attach any interpretative significance to a declaration recorded in the Council minutes marking the adoption of both Regulation 1612/68 and of Council Directive 68/360/EEC, which stated that '[n]ationals of a Member State... who move to another Member State in order to seek work there shall be allowed a minimum period of three months for the purpose; in the event of their not having found employment by the end of that period, their residence on the territory of this second State may be brought to an end. However, if the abovementioned persons should be taken charge of by national assistance (social welfare) in the second State during the aforesaid period they may be invited to leave the territory of this second State'.[16]

The Court's two-part test, which eschews a fixed temporal limit approach, fits with its general preference for case-by-case assessments of each individual situation and thereby reflects the essential premises of proportionality analysis.[17] However, while the requirement of evidence that a jobseeker is continuing to seek employment is not problematic to realise in practice, the notion of *proving* a genuine chance of being engaged is a very different, more abstract expectation.[18] Commission guidance advises that jobseekers can prove the cumulative parts of the *Antonissen* test by providing 'copies of job applications, invitations to interviews or positive reactions to your applications'.[19] The latter example, in particular, would seem to speak to the requirement of proving a genuine chance of being engaged. But projects assessing the application and interpretation of EU legal tests at national level will make a crucial contribution to providing evidence of a different kind: on whether these tests actually *work* and really *do* contribute to the effectiveness of the EU rights that they are intended to facilitate. A well-placed fear is that awkward tools that seem unhelpfully to require somehow 'proving' the future could, in fact, be used to curtail the scope of those rights.[20]

More positively, the origins of specific EU rights for jobseekers fit within the EU institutions' consistently expressed understanding of freedom of movement for workers as a personal, individual right, which is conferred directly on all Member State nationals by the Treaty. For example, it was indicated in the preamble to Regulation 1612/68

15 Ibid., para. 21 (emphasis added).

16 Cited in *Antonissen*, EU:C:1991:80, para. 17.

17 See further, the Opinion of AG Darmon in *Antonissen*, EU:C:1990:387, para. 29.

18 AG Darmon had focused his analysis more on the first part of the Court's approach i.e., being 'actively, persistently and seriously engaged' in seeking employment (para. 36 of the Opinion).

19 European Commission, 'Frequently Asked Questions and Answers on citizens' EU rights', at http://europa.eu/youreurope/advice/docs/faq_en.pdf.

20 A current UK-based project has uncovered specific concerns in this regard: see O'Brien, 'The pillory, the precipice and the slippery slope: the profound effects of the UK's legal reform programme targeting EU migrants' (2015) *Journal of Social Welfare and Family Law* 111 at 118-119.

that 'freedom of movement constitutes a fundamental right of workers and their families' and considered that 'mobility of labour within the Community must be one of the means by which the worker is guaranteed the possibility of improving his living and working conditions and promoting his social advancement, while helping to satisfy the requirements of the economies of the Member States'. The depth of that characterisation has since been underlined by the inclusion of the right to 'to seek employment, to work, to exercise the right of establishment and to provide services in any Member State' in Article 15(2) of the Charter of Fundamental Rights.

However, notwithstanding *Antonissen*, the extent to which host Member States would be obliged to *support* jobseekers from other States was a materially different question.

III. Evolutions: (still) a status apart?

While residence rights for jobseekers, as well as the permitted limitations of those rights, were rooted originally in Article 45 TFEU, we saw in Part 2 that the decision of the Court in *Antonissen* also reflected the wider dynamic of 'humanisation' that had characterised the evolution of free movement law. Two legal evolutions harnessed that dynamic more formally: first, the creation of Union citizenship per se and, second, the subsequent adoption of Directive 2004/38/EC, a key purpose of which was to consolidate the multiplicity of context-specific EU measures that had previously regulated free movement and residence rights.[21] Regulation 1612/68 was one of the few pieces of secondary legislation that survived that process, although the new Directive absorbed the rights of the family members of a worker, which had been outlined in Articles 10 and 11 of the Regulation.

Transformative judgments in the field of citizenship were concerned initially with strengthening the impact of primary EU rights in situations involving Union citizens who were not economically active in a host State.[22] However, the complex interaction between Article 21(1) TFEU as a source of primary rights and the provisions of Directive 2004/38 – as the legislative spelling out of these rights *and* of their limits – would come to dominate later case law. In the sections that follow, the particular implications of this altered and often unstable legal environment for the *residence rights* of jobseekers are first outlined, followed by an exploration of what *other rights* a lawfully resident jobseeker might enjoy in the host State. It will be shown that, notwithstanding both the degree and the detail of legal change effected by the Directive, the legal status of the jobseeker remains complicated; moreover, the source(s) and substance of associated rights remain surprisingly uncertain.

---

21 Directive 2004/38/EC on the right of citizens of the Union and their family members to move and reside freely within the territory of the Member States, [2004] OJ L158/77.

22 Eg, Judgment in *Martínez Sala*, C-85/96, EU:C:1998:217, Judgment in *Grzelczyk*, C-184/99, EU:C:2001:458, Judgment in *Baumbast*, C-413/99, EU:C:2002:493, and Judgment in *Trojani*, C-456/02, EU:C:2004:488.

1. The right to reside

Four key points from the judgment in *Antonissen* can be briefly recalled here in order to frame the analysis that follows. First, the particular UK rule at issue in that case established that a jobseeker from another Member State could be required to leave the territory, subject to appeal, if he had not found employment there after six months. Second, the Court indicated that this national rule 'does not appear *in principle* to be insufficient to enable the persons concerned to apprise themselves...of offers of employment...and to take...the necessary steps in order to be engaged'. Third, the Court developed a less fixed text from that reasoning, ruling that a jobseeker's residence rights could not be withdrawn '*if after the expiry of that period* the person concerned provides evidence that he is continuing to seek employment and that he has genuine chances of being engaged'. Fourth, the Court had premised that determination on 'the absence of a [Union] provision prescribing the period during which [Union] nationals seeking employment in a Member State may stay there'. The central question addressed here therefore is: does Directive 2004/38 now provide the necessary '[Union] provision prescribing the period during which [Union] nationals seeking employment in a Member State may stay there' or do the residence rights of jobseekers continue to derive autonomously from primary Union law?

The Directive attaches legal significance to specific acts and also to specific temporal markers. Three particular time-points are important in the regulation of residence rights. First, according to Article 6 of the Directive, all Union citizens (as well as family members within the meaning of Article 2(2) where relevant) have the right to reside in another Member State for up to three months 'without any conditions or any formalities other than the requirement to hold a valid identity card or passport'. A corollary limit on host State obligations is found in Article 24(2) i.e., 'the host Member State shall not be obliged to confer entitlement to social assistance during the first three months of residence'. Second, under Article 7(1), for periods of residence of more than three months but less than five years, Union citizens must be economically active as a worker or self-employed person; or, 'have sufficient resources for themselves and their family members not to become a burden on the social assistance system of the host Member State during their period of residence and have comprehensive sickness insurance cover in the host Member State'; or, be 'enrolled at a private or public establishment, accredited or financed by the host Member State on the basis of its legislation or administrative practice, for the principal purpose of following a course of study' (again subject to conditions regarding sufficient resources and sickness insurance). In *Dano*, the Court ruled that the principle of equal treatment outlined in Article 24(1) of the Directive – which is a specific expression of the prohibition on nationality discrimination in Article 18 TFEU – only applies when the Article 7(1) conditions for lawful residence in a host State are met.[23] Other derogations from equal treatment are set out in Article 24(2), including, for example, restrictions on eligibility for maintenance aid for studies. Finally, third, after five years of continuous and lawful

---

23 Judgment in *Dano*, EU:C:2014:2358, paras. 68-73.

residence in a host State, Union citizens (and their family members) may acquire a right of permanent residence there in accordance with Article 16 – a critical consequence of which is absolution from the requirement to satisfy the conditions laid down in Article 7.

The particular reference to jobseekers in Article 24(2) of the Directive is picked up in subsection (b) below. But where do jobseekers fit within the Directive's system of rules more generally? Their residence rights were drawn originally from Article 45 TFEU so in that respect, jobseekers were aligned, broadly speaking, with migrant workers. However, jobseekers are not economically active *yet*. After the first three months of residence, do they therefore fall within the scope of Article 7(1)(a) of the Directive, as 'workers' who are not required to satisfy any further conditions; or within the scope of Article 7(1)(b), as citizens who can be required to demonstrate that they possess sufficient resources and comprehensive sickness insurance; or do their residence rights flow from somewhere else entirely? Surprisingly, neither the EU legislature nor the Court of Justice has yet considered this question directly.

The jobseeker was surprisingly absent from the process of adopting the Directive, making only a late and limited appearance in the documented discussions as part of a political compromise. The Commission had proposed an unconditional right of residence for up to six months for all Union citizens.[24] But '[a]fter careful consideration, the Council agreed to set the period at three months as in the existing *acquis*...However, a more favourable treatment is applicable to job-seekers as recognised by the case-law of the Court of Justice'.[25] But two alternative interpretations of what this 'more favourable treatment' applicable to jobseekers – a phrase also included in recital 9 of the preamble to the adopted Directive – might actually constitute are possible. First, the Commission appears to have adopted the view that jobseekers have a right to reside in other Member States for up to six months under no further conditions; to retain that right of residence thereafter, they need then, and only then, to demonstrate both parts of the *Antonissen* test.[26] That interpretation would appear to be premised on a generalisation to EU-wide level of the specific national rule contested in *Antonissen*. But that is not a convincing basis for the genesis of such a specific and temporally fixed residence right – all the more since the adoption of Directive 2004/38, a key objective of which was to ensure that free movement and residence rights for *all* Union citizens were systematised.[27] Instead, therefore, it is argued here that a second construction of 'more

---

24 COM(2001) 257, para. 1.4.

25 Common Position (EC) No 6/2004 of 5 December 2003 adopted by the Council, 2004 OJ C54E/12.

26 See eg, *Right of Union citizens and their family members to move and reside freely within the Union: Guide on how to get the best out of Directive 2004/38/EC*, Chapter 5, at http://ec.europa.eu/home-affairs/faq/freetravel/doc/guide_2004_38_ec_en.pdf: 'Union citizens benefit from the right to reside without any conditions and formalities for a period of six months and even longer, if they continue to seek employment in the host Member State and have a genuine chance of being engaged, as the European Court of Justice confirmed'.

27 See e.g., recital 3 of the preamble: 'Union citizenship should be the fundamental status of nationals of the Member States when they exercise their right of free movement and residence. It is therefore necessary to codify and review the existing Community instruments dealing separately with workers, self-employed persons, as well as students and other inactive persons in order to simplify and strengthen the right of free movement and residence of all Union citizens'. Recital 4 then proceeds on the basis of 'remedying this sector-by-sector, piecemeal approach to the right of free movement and residence and facilitating the exercise of this right'.

favourable treatment' is more logical, i.e., jobseekers, like all Union citizens, enjoy an unconditional right to reside in other Member States for up to three months; after that point, however, they retain their residence rights subject only to fulfilling the requirements of the *Antonissen* test.

One of the few explicit references to jobseekers in the Directive, in Article 14(4)(b), also fits with the second interpretation. That provision – supported by the intentions set out in recital 16 of the preamble[28] – states that only an expulsion measure based on grounds of public policy or public security may be issued against Union citizens who 'entered the territory of the host Member State in order to seek employment. In this case, the Union citizens and their family members may not be expelled *for as long as* the Union citizens can provide evidence that they are continuing to seek employment and that they have a genuine chance of being engaged'. Article 14(4)(b) signals that the general framework of the Directive applies to jobseekers in their basic capacity as Union citizens – here, the measure's provisions on expulsion. But the same principle could be extended to the provisions of the Directive that cover other basic rights – for example, the rights of family members since, once again, no *explicit* reference to the family members of jobseekers can be found anywhere in the relevant provisions. The same logic can be extended to the Directive's three-stage framework of residence rights, applying as the basic starting point the fact that jobseekers are Union citizens. No other group of Union citizens – including the fully economically active – need to look beyond the Directive in order to understand the basic right to reside in another State: why should that be the case for jobseekers?

Importantly, that conclusion does not rule out the possibility that the distinct case law conditions developed in order to test the *retention* of jobseekers' residence rights survived the adoption of the Directive. The less controversial aspect of this claim would require that we continue to accommodate the jobseeker as an offshoot of freedom of movement for workers under Article 45 TFEU.[29] The harder part of the argument is that the *conditions* for lawful residence outlined for different categories of citizen in Article 7 of the Directive are not, therefore, exhaustive – a point expanded upon below in the context of entitlement to social assistance from the host State. At this stage, however, it can be noted that examples of rights beyond the walls of Directive 2004/38 have been established in other strands of case law on the basis of both primary[30] and secondary[31] EU law. So while 'Directive 2004/38 codified existing Community instruments which, until then, had determined the legal position of certain categories

28 I.e., 'As long as the beneficiaries of the right of residence do not become an unreasonable burden on the social assistance system of the host Member State they should not be expelled. Therefore, an expulsion measure should not be the automatic consequence of recourse to the social assistance system...In no case should an expulsion measure be adopted against workers, self-employed persons *or job-seekers* as defined by the Court of Justice save on grounds of public policy or public security' (emphasis added).

29 A point confirmed post-citizenship in, e.g., *Martínez Sala*, para. 32.

30 E.g., on residence for pregnant workers beyond the circumstances for retention of the status of worker in Article 7(3) of the Directive, see Judgment in *Saint Prix*, C-507/12, EU:C:2014:2007.

31 E.g., on residence rights for the children of migrant workers who are in host State education on the basis of Regulation 492/2011, see Judgment in *Ibrahim*, C-310/08, EU:C:2010:80.

of person [and it] undeniably applies to all Union citizens and their family members... it does not contain comprehensive and definitive rules to govern every conceivable right of residence of those Union citizens and their family members'.[32] Accepting an unconditional residence right for jobseekers for up to three months and a right governed by the *Antonissen* test thereafter reflects both acknowledging the force of the provisions of the Directive where they are *specific* in temporal terms, while allowing for a degree of 'more favourable treatment' for jobseekers – signalled in Article 14(4)(b) as well as in the Directive's preamble – in terms of the retention of those rights after that initial three month period. In essence, the legislature's concern for some degree of more favourable treatment for jobseekers can perhaps be linked to the commitment to both integration in the host State and the realisation of fundamental Union objectives that the act of moving to another State to look for work is perceived to convey.[33]

2. Rights beyond residence

The adoption of Directive 2004/38 is also critical in trying to understand what other rights a lawfully resident jobseeker may claim from the host State in which he is seeking employment. Recalling the judgment in *Cristini*, we saw that the Court of Justice has applied a generous reading of the concept of social and tax advantages for the purpose of determining the scope of Regulation 1612/68. However, even though jobseekers were confirmed to fall under Article 45 TFEU as a work-relevant category of free mover, the Court ruled in *Lebon* – just before its decision on residence rights in *Antonissen* – that 'the right to equal treatment with regard to social and tax advantages applies only to workers. Those who move in search of employment qualify for equal treatment only as regards *access* to employment'.[34] The status of jobseeker was thus conceived as a limited one: mirroring the approach taken in case law that shaped free movement rights for students,[35] protection against non-discrimination was extended to certain aspects of the work-seeking experience, but the extent of possible financial implications for host States was significantly capped.

However, before Directive 2004/38 came into force, the reach of equal treatment for jobseekers was reconsidered against the requirements of the distinctive primary rights that stemmed from Union citizenship. In *Collins*, the referring court queried 'whether there is a provision or principle of [Union] law on the basis of which a national of a Member State who is genuinely seeking employment in another Member State may claim there a jobseeker's allowance'.[36] Again reflecting parallel developments in the case law on students,[37] the Court used the legal relevance of citizenship to reorient

---

32 AG Kokott in Judgment in *Teixeira*, C-480/08 EU:C:2009:642, para. 48 of the Opinion.

33 See e.g., AG Wathelet in *Dano*, EU:C:2014:341, para. 116 of the Opinion, distinguishing between the situation under EU law of jobseekers and that of citizens who never intend to engage in economic activity in the first place.

34 Judgment in *Lebon*, C-316/85, EU:C:1987:302, para. 26 (emphasis added).

35 Extending equal treatment in the context of enrolment and/or tuition fees (Judgment in *Gravier*, C-293/83, EU:C:1985:69) but stopping short of support for maintenance aid (Judgment in *Lair*, C-39/86 EU:C:1988:322, Judgment in *Brown*, C-197/86, EU:C:1988:323).

36 Judgment in *Collins*, C-138/02, EU:C:2004:172, para. 51.

37 See Judgment in *Bidar*, C-209/03, EU:C:2005:169, paras. 38-42.

established case law principles and stated: 'in view of the *establishment of citizenship of the Union* and the interpretation in the case-law of the right to equal treatment enjoyed by citizens of the Union, it is no longer possible to exclude *from the scope of Article [45(2) TFEU]*...a benefit of a financial nature intended to facilitate access to employment in the labour market of a Member State'.[38] That reasoning fuses elements of the citizen with elements of the worker, unpicking the barriers to more substantive – and *costly*, for host States – equal treatment that had been raised in pre-Maastricht case law. However, the Court did accept that proportionate residence restrictions could limit eligibility for such allowances, on the premise that it was 'legitimate for a Member State to grant such an allowance only after it has been possible to establish that a genuine link exists between the person seeking work and the employment market of that State. The existence of such a link may be determined, in particular, by establishing that the person concerned has, for a reasonable period, in fact genuinely sought work in the Member State in question'.[39]

The enactment of Directive 2004/38 appeared to curtail the ambition of the approach developed in *Collins*. Specifically, Article 24(2) of the Directive rules out a host State obligation to confer entitlement to social assistance for the 'longer period provided for in Article 14(4)(b)' -- i.e., in situations where Union citizens 'entered the territory of the host Member State in order to seek employment...*for as long as* the Union citizens can provide evidence that they are continuing to seek employment and that they have a genuine chance of being engaged'. The lawfulness of that exclusion from equal treatment against the requirements of Articles 18 and 21 TFEU was explicitly questioned in *Vatsouras and Koupatantze*. Resourcefully, after restating the citizen-worker fusion constructed in *Collins*, the Court ruled that '[b]enefits of a financial nature which, independently of their status under national law, are intended to facilitate access to the labour market *cannot be regarded as constituting "social assistance"* within the meaning of Article 24(2) of Directive 2004/38'[40] – meaning that migrant job-seekers *might* even be eligible to receive them during the first three months of residence in a host State and, indeed, for as long as they can provide evidence that they are continuing to seek employment and that they have a genuine chance of being engaged. Eligibility in reality depends on the specific conditions laid down in the host State's proportionate exclusionary framework, as approved of in *Collins*. But if States constrain that framework *beyond* what is necessary for the demonstration of genuine links to their labour markets, EU law intervenes to correct them – as demonstrated by the decision in *Prete*.[41]

---

38 Judgment in *Collins*, EU:C:2004:172, para. 63 (emphasis added).

39 Judgement in *Collins*, EU:C:2004:172, paras. 69-70. The real link premise had been developed in circumstances involving a claim against a Union citizen's home State; Judgment in *D'Hoop*, C-224/98, EU:C:2002:432. See generally, O'Brien 'Real links, abstract rights and false alarms: the relationship between the ECJ's "real link" case law and national solidarity' (2008) 33:4 *European Law Review* 643.

40 Judgment in *Vatsouras and Koupatantze*, joined Cases C-22/08 and C-23/08, EU:C:2009:344, para. 45 (emphasis added). For analysis, see the annotation of the judgment by Damjanovic, (2010) 47:4 *Common Market Law Review* 847; and Fahey, 'Interpretive legitimacy and the distinction between "social assistance" and "work seekers allowance"' (2009) 34:6 *European Law Review* 933.

41 Judgment in *Prete*, C-367/11, EU:C:2012:668; here, the Court ruled that a single condition – in this case, making eligibility for a 'tideover allowance for the benefit of young people looking for their first job conditional upon the person concerned having completed at least six years' studies in an educational establishment of the host Member State' (para. 14) – will fail an analysis of its necessity, 'insofar as that condition prevents other representative factors liable to establish the existence of a real link between the person claiming the allowance and the geographic labour market concerned being taken into account' (para. 52).

Linking back to the questions raised in subsection (a) above, the broader effect of what the Court has done is therefore, in effect, to remove migrants *seeking* work from the reach of the conditions laid down in Article 7(1)(b) of Directive 2004/38 – even though they are not yet workers in a literal sense for the purposes of Article 7(1)(a). We can affirm that conclusion inversely from the reasoning of AG Wathelet in *Dano*. He first recalled that Article 24(2) of the Directive permits Member States not to confer entitlement to social assistance to persons '"other than workers, self-employed persons, persons who retain such status and members of their families" during the first three months of residence or during the period of seeking employment extending beyond that initial period'.[42] However, since the applicant in that case had resided in the host State for more than three months, was not seeking employment there, and had not entered the country in order to find employment in the first place, the Advocate General concluded that 'she does not fall within the scope ratione personae of that provision. *On the other hand, her situation is covered by Article 7(1)(b)* of Directive 2004/38, relating to the requirement to have sufficient resources not to become a burden on the social assistance system of the host Member State'[43] – with the implication, then, that her situation would *not* be covered by Article 7(1)(b) if she had been able to demonstrate compliance with the *Antonissen* test. The rights of jobseekers as fused citizen-workers thus generate distinctly more than the sum of the individual parts – they are neither required to have sufficient resources to support themselves in a host State, nor subject to deportation from that State or removed entirely from the reach of its social provision while the *Antonissen* tests can be met – despite the attempt of the Member States, acting through the Council, to prescribe precisely that exclusion as one of the (few) categories of citizen mentioned explicitly in Article 24(2) of the Directive.

The critical final question then is what benefits, precisely, will be considered to constitute 'benefit[s] of a financial nature intended to facilitate access to employment in the labour market' per the test applied in *Collins* – meaning that a jobseeker may be entitled to them – as distinct from social assistance more generically – for which, following Article 24(2), jobseekers will not be eligible. For example, a housing benefit will certainly, in practical terms, 'facilitate' a jobseeker's access to the labour market. But is such a holistic understanding of that term what the Court had in mind in *Collins* and *Vatsouras and Koupatantze*? Or perhaps more accurately – and more pressingly – in the wider environment of austerity and related acute debates on what level of governance should manage control over public spending, would even an intended broad understanding now be protected?

At the time of writing, this issue was a central factor in the pending *Alimanovic* case. In his Opinion, AG Wathelet has followed the trail set by *Vatsouras and Koupatantze* in general terms, one important element of which is that 'it is for the competent national authorities and, where appropriate, the national courts…to assess the constituent elements of that benefit, in particular its purposes and the conditions subject to which

42 Opinion of AG Wathelet in *Dano*, EU:C:2014:341, para. 92.

43 Ibid (emphasis added).

it is granted'.[44] He also noted a second point confirmed in recent case law: that a benefit will amount to 'social assistance' when it constitutes 'part of an assistance scheme established by the public authorities, whether at national, regional or local level, to which recourse may be had by an individual who does not have resources sufficient to meet his own basic needs and the needs of his family'.[45] Crucially, then, if a benefit fits with that definition, it must be treated as social assistance, i.e., as falling *within* the exclusions set out in Article 24(2) of Directive 2004/38, which should have an impact directly on jobseekers.

The national rule at issue in the *Alimanovic* case itself 'provides that both benefits to cover subsistence costs and benefits for integration into the labour market may be claimed under the entitlement to basic provision for jobseekers'.[46] Importantly, AG Wathelet has advised that 'should the national court find that the benefits claimed pursue a twofold objective, of ensuring that basic needs are met, on the one hand, and of facilitating access to the labour market, on the other...the decision must be based on the predominant function of the benefits, which, in the present case, is, unquestionably, to cover the subsistence costs necessary to lead a life in keeping with human dignity'.[47] However, notwithstanding that signal and rather than progressing in consequence towards a literal reading of Article 24(2) of the Directive vis-à-vis the circumstances of the applicants in the case – who had previously worked in the host State, but were at the material time reclassified as jobseekers – AG Wathelet drew instead from case law that emphasises the importance of undertaking an individual assessment of each claimant's integration in the host State. He placed particular emphasis on the criteria established in *Prete* – even though the benefit at issue in that case fell unambiguously within the *Collins* test.[48] The Advocate General has proposed, therefore, that we should operate a distinction *among* jobseekers, extending greater protection to jobseekers who had previously worked in the host State. His reasoning opens a door for a more favourable outcome for this category of jobseekers than the Directive would suggest; but it has to be admitted that this citizen-worthy solution would have the effect of perpetuating tensions between the limiting legislative framework and the deeper principles of citizenship law that seem fated to evade more definitive reconciliation.

---

44 AG Wathelet in *Alimanovic*, C-67/14, EU:C:2015:210, para. 61 of the Opinion, citing para. 41 of *Vatsouras and Koupatantze*.

45 AG Wathelet in *Alimanovic*, EU:C:2015:210, paras. 65-66 of the Opinion, citing *Dano*, para. 61 and the judgement in *Dano*, C-333/13, EU:C:2014:2358, para. 63.

46 AG Wathelet in *Alimanovic*, EU:C:2015:210, para. 67 of the Opinion.

47 Ibid, para. 72.

48 Ibid, paras. 108-111.

IV. Conclusion

Jobseekers are a hybrid species of EU free movement law in several respects. Their legal claims rest partly in the rights conferred on workers, yet also in the more complicated and unsettled legal ecology of Union citizenship; partly in provisions of EU legislation, yet also in the foggier landings of the case law. Even the most basic understanding of their residence rights has not yet been definitively settled. Additionally, jobseekers are more privileged in equal treatment terms than citizens who demonstrate no connection (or inclination) to economic activity at all, yet less supported than citizens who do engage in work even if only to a limited degree.[49] We may even soon see the Court extracting new categories of jobseekers from *within* the category of jobseekers.

Jobseekers may therefore have a status in EU law, but they remain in search of its material content and of clarity on its limits. In 1975, AG Trabucchi presented the future direction of free movement law as a choice, clearly favouring a 'concept of social justice and European integration, not only of the economy but of the people'. In 2015, AG Wathelet framed that choice around the same fundamental concerns: '[t]he problem is sensitive in human and legal terms. It will necessarily lead to the Court ruling both on the protection offered by EU law to its citizens, as regards their financial situation and their dignity too, and on the current scope of the fundamental right to free movement, a founding principle on which the European Union is built'.[50] In *Brey,* AG Wahl cut even more keenly to the chase: '[t]he idea that a Union citizen could say "civis europeus sum" and invoke that status against hardships encountered in other Member States was famously pioneered 20 years ago. The present case raises the question whether that status can be relied upon today, against the economic difficulties of modern life'.[51]

The case law on jobseekers is navigating precisely these critical lines. But if it does not do so altogether successfully, it should not be forgotten that Directive 2004/38 – the intended 'one stop' frame of reference for the free movement and residence rights of all Union citizens – fails properly to accommodate the particular situation, and needs, of work-seeking citizens. The Union institutions and Member States alike have strongly prioritised increasing the level of employment right across the EU as an urgent policy objective.[52] More *coherent* as well as *substantive* support for Union citizens who choose – and even more so, have no choice but – to seek employment in another State clearly merits greater attention within that agenda.

---

49 The classic definition of work in EU law – i.e., the pursuit of 'effective and genuine activities which are not on such a small scale as to be regarded as purely marginal and ancillary' (*N*, para. 42) – remains unchanged. That workers who meet this definition may also be eligible for social assistance in the host State stems from Judgment in *Kempf,* C-139/85, EU:C:1986:223, para. 14.

50 AG Wathelet in *Alimanovic,* EU:C:2015:210, para. 2 of the Opinion.

51 AG Wahl in *Brey*, C-140/12 , EU:C:2013:337, para. 3 of the Opinion.

52 See e.g., on the European Commission's Jobs, Growth and Investment package, http://ec.europa.eu/priorities/jobs-growth-investment/index_en.htm.

The *Google Spain* judgment and the right to be forgotten

José Pérez Santos, Alfonso Gutierrez and Cecilia Álvarez

On 13 May 2014, the European Court of Justice ('ECJ')[1] published a judgment contrary to the previous conclusions proposed by the Advocate General, in response to a series of questions referred by the Spanish National High Court (*Audiencia Nacional)* regarding a dispute between the Spanish Data Protection Agency ('Spanish DPA') and Google on the controversial 'right to be forgotten' on the Internet.

Google and other search engines and websites have had to face the Spanish DPA in several 'right to be forgotten' cases. Regarding Google, all the Spanish DPA's resolutions were appealed to the Supreme Court and amounted to over 200 when the preliminary questions were posed to the ECJ.

The background to the preliminary questions is rather unique: the information referred to a seizure in 1998[2] which was published in a Spanish newspaper by operation of law (and not in exercise of the freedom of expression). Google Inc. (responsible for the search engine) and its Spanish subsidiary requested the annulment of a decision of the

---

1 http://curia.europa.eu/juris/document/document.jsf?docid=152065&doclang=ES.

2 The seizure information published referred to certain properties, to the owners thereof (identified by their full names) as well as to the minimum official price established for the sale of those properties.

Spanish DPA requiring it to de-index this information (i.e., to stop it appearing as a search result), although the claim against the newspaper had been previously dismissed.[3]

We will address what questions were posed and some closely-related legal background before analyzing the Advocate General's opinion and the ECJ's responses, which are not confined to recognizing the 'right to be forgotten' online, but also address the controversial issue of applying European data protection standards to entities, such as Google Inc., which operate from outside the European Union ('EU'). The first reactions by Google and other search engines as well as other stakeholders in Europe and beyond have come and reveal that the manifold consequences of this important ruling will have a considerable impact on the lives of citizens and all types of organizations.

I. Preliminary questions and some background

The Spanish National High Court referred nine questions in three blocks:[4]

(i) The territorial application of Directive 95/46/EC[5] ('Directive 95/46/EC') according to the criteria set out in Article 4, as implemented in Spain by Article 2(1) of Basic Law 15/1999 on the protection of personal data ('LOPD') and the impact of Article 8 of the EU Charter of Fundamental Rights ('Charter').

(ii) The role of the 'data controller' in respect of the activities of the search for the purposes of Directive 95/46/EC.

(iii) The scope of the right to cancel and/or object in relation to the right to be forgotten.

1. Territorial application

Leaving aside the so-called diplomatic case, which is not analyzed by the ECJ, the application of Directive 95/46/EC depends on whether the following requirements are met: (i) the existence of a processing 'within the context' of an establishment in a Member State (Article 4(1)a)); or (ii) the existence of means (other than for transit

---

3 As stated in the resolution of the Spanish DPA R/01680/2010 (TD/00650/2010):

(i) regarding La Vanguardia Ediciones, S.L.: 'it has been evidenced that this entity replied to the data subject's request and properly denied the cancellation of his personal data since the publication of these data was legally based on the publication of the real estate auctions by the Executive Collection Unit, in this case, the Provincial Directorate of the General Treasury of the Social Security in Barcelona, which professed aim is to give the maximum publicity to the auctions in order to get the highest turnout of bidders. By virtue of this, these rights enforcement proceedings against La Vanguardia Ediciones, S.L. are dismissed'; and

(ii) regarding Google: 'consider that the claim filed by Mr. AAA against GOOGLE SPAIN, S.L. and against GOOGLE INC. is properly grounded, urging this entity to take the necessary measures to remove the data from its index and make any future access to them impossible.'

4 http://curia.europa.eu/juris/document/document.jsf?docid=123131&doclang=ES.

5 Directive 95/46/EC of the European Parliament and of the Council of 24 October 1995 on the protection of individuals with regard to the processing of personal data and on the free movement of such data.

purposes) in a Member State where the data controller's establishment is outside the EU (Article 4(1)c)).

In this respect, the Spanish National High Court posed the following questions:

(a) must it be considered that an 'establishment', within the meaning of Article 4(1) (a) of Directive 95/46, exists when any one or more of the following circumstances arise:

- when the undertaking providing the search engine sets up in a Member State an office or subsidiary for the purpose of promoting and selling advertising space on the search engine, which orientates its activity towards the inhabitants of that State,

or

- when the parent company designates a subsidiary located in that Member State as its representative and controller for two specific filing systems which relate to the data of customers who have contracted for advertising with that undertaking,

or

- when the office or subsidiary established in a Member State forwards to the parent company, located outside the European Union, requests and requirements addressed to it both by data subjects and by the authorities with responsibility for ensuring observation of the right to data protection, even where such collaboration is engaged in voluntarily?

(b) Must Article 4(1)(c) of Directive 95/46 be interpreted as meaning that there is 'use of equipment ... situated on the territory of the said Member State':

- when a search engine uses crawlers or robots to locate and index information contained in web pages located on servers in that Member State,

or

- when it uses a domain name pertaining to a Member State and arranges for searches and the results thereof to be based on the language of that Member State?

(c) Is it possible to regard as a use of equipment, in the terms of Article 4(1)(c) of Directive 95/46, the temporary storage of the information indexed by internet search engines? If the answer to that question is affirmative, can it be considered that that connecting factor is present when the undertaking refuses to disclose the place where it stores those indexes, invoking reasons of competition?

Furthermore, as opposed to the Spanish DPA, the Spanish National High Court introduced in its questions a matter of paramount importance, namely, the impact of the Charter which recognizes, with the value of the EU Treaties, the right to data protection:[6]

(d) Regardless of the answers to the foregoing questions and particularly in the event that the Court . . . considers that the connecting factors referred to in Article 4 of [Directive 95/46] are not present:

must Directive 95/46 . . . be applied, in the light of Article 8 of the [Charter], in the Member State where the centre of gravity of the conflict is located and more effective protection of the rights of . . . Union citizens is possible?

This same question referred to the concept of 'centre of gravity of the conflict'. This concept has been analyzed by the ECJ in previous cases, such as in the judgment of 25 October 2011 (Joined Cases C -509/09 and C - 161/10), eDate GmbH and X and Olivier Martinez, Robert Martinez and MGN Limited,[7] to establish the applicable jurisdiction in events of infringement of personality rights on the Internet:

> The place where a person has the centre of his interests corresponds in general to his habitual residence. However, a person may also have the centre of his interests in a Member State in which he does not habitually reside, insofar as other factors, such as the pursuit of a professional activity, may establish the existence of a particularly close link with that State.

2. Data controller

Provided that Directive 95/46/EC is deemed applicable as a result of any of the above criteria, the role of the search engine must be assessed and, in particular, its role as 'data controller':

(a) in relation to the activity of [Google Search], as a provider of content, consisting in locating information published or included on the net by third parties, indexing it automatically, storing it temporarily and finally making it available to internet users according to a particular order of preference, when that information contains personal data of third parties: must an activity like the one described be interpreted as falling within the concept of 'processing of . . . data' used in Article 2(b) of Directive 95/46?

(b) If the answer to the foregoing question is affirmative, and once again in relation to an activity like the one described:

6 'Article 8 - Protection of personal data:

1. Everyone has the right to the protection of personal data concerning him or her.

2. Such data must be processed fairly for specified purposes and on the basis of the consent of the person concerned or some other legitimate basis laid down by law. Everyone has the right of access to data which has been collected concerning him or her, and the right to have it rectified.

3. Compliance with these rules shall be subject to control by an independent authority.'

7 Judgment in *eDate Advertising and Others*, joined cases C-509/09 and C-161/10, EU:C:2011:685.

must Article 2(d) of Directive 95/46 be interpreted as meaning that the undertaking managing [Google Search] is to be regarded as the 'controller' of the personal data contained in the web pages that it indexes?

(c) In the event that the answer to the foregoing question is affirmative:

may the [Spanish DPA], protecting the rights embodied in [Article] 12(b) and [subparagraph (a) of the first paragraph of Article 14] of Directive 95/46, directly impose on [Google Search] a requirement that it withdraw from its indexes an item of information published by third parties, without addressing itself in advance or simultaneously to the owner of the web page on which that information is located?

(d) In the event that the answer to the foregoing question is affirmative:

would the obligation of search engines to protect those rights be excluded when the information that contains the personal data has been lawfully published by third parties and is kept on the web page from which it originates?

The data controller is defined in Article 2(d) of Directive 95/46/EC[8] and in article 3d) of the LOPD) as the person who makes decisions about the means and purpose of the processing of personal data, the definitions of 'processing'[9] and 'personal data'[10] being likewise quite wide-ranging.

However, it is surprising that the National High Court did not pose any question to the ECJ on the impact on Directive 95/46/EC of the liability regime of the search engines (as intermediaries of the information society services) set out in Directive 2000/31/EC on electronic commerce ('Directive 2000/31/EC')[11], implemented in Spain by E-Commerce Law 34/2002 on information society services and electronic commerce ('E-Commerce Law 34/2002').

Indeed, this question should have been posed, in particular, taking into account that the Spanish Supreme Court – in its judgment 2245/2013 of 4 March[12] – found that the

---

8 'Controller' means 'the natural or legal person, public authority, agency or any other body which alone or jointly with others determines the purposes and means of the processing of personal data; where the purposes and means of processing are determined by national or Community laws or regulations, the controller or the specific criteria for his nomination may be designated by national or Community law' (Article 2 d) of Directive 95/46/EC).

9 'Processing' means 'any operation or set of operations which is performed upon personal data, whether or not by automatic means, such as collection, recording, organization, storage, adaptation or alteration, retrieval, consultation, use, disclosure by transmission, dissemination or otherwise making available, alignment or combination, blocking, erasure or destruction' (Article 2 b) of Directive 95/46/EC).

10 'Personal data' means 'any information relating to an identified or identifiable natural person ('data subject'); an identifiable person is one who can be identified, directly or indirectly, in particular by reference to an identification number or to one or more factors specific to his physical, physiological, mental, economic, cultural or social identity' (Article 2.a) of Directive 95/46/EC).

11 Directive 2000/31/EC of the European Parliament and of the Council of 8 June 2000 on certain legal aspects of information society services, in particular electronic commerce, in the Internal Market.

12 http://www.poderjudicial.es/search/doAction?action=contentpdf&databasematch=TS&reference=6713993&links=&optimize=20130522&publicinterface=true.

right of honour was not violated by the search engine based on its lack of 'actual knowledge' of the illegality of the information made available:[13]

> (...) this Court agrees with the factual and legal assessment of the appealed ruling, *as there is no breach of Article 17 of the LSSICE*, which has been properly applied since the plaintiff's liability has been excluded based on the lack of actual knowledge that the information was false.
>
> This same argument leads to the *dismissal* of the third ground of the appeal in which the appellant seeks the application of the Basic Law 1/1982 to declare Google's liability "based on the actual knowledge and the technical ability to control the information (...) because (. . .) it is perfectly aware of the illegality of the information." *The lack of actual knowledge of the unlawfulness of the information diminishes the arguments of the appellant*.[emphasis added]

In addition, the Spanish DPA used E-Commerce Law 34/2002 to apply the right to be forgotten.[14] Indeed, justifying the application of E-Commerce Law 34/2002 to a service provider established in the US is easier than justifying the application of the LOPD: the only requirement for E-Commerce Law 34/2002 to apply to a US services provider is that it addresses its services specifically to the Spanish territory (which is precisely the new criterion included in the Proposal for a Data Protection Regulation issued by the EU Commission on 25 January 2012 ('EC Proposal')).[15]

As it was clear that the territorial criteria of E-Commerce Law 34/2002 were met, the Spanish DPA, without making any reference to the liability regime of Article 17 of E-Commerce Law 34/2002[16], applied Article 8.1.c) which states that if a particular information society service is detrimental to the dignity of a person, the relevant

---

13 In this case, the information accessed through the browser referred to some news that linked the data subject to a very well-known corruption case in Spain. In addition, one of the media recognized in a court settlement that this news was false. However, the Court did not consider that there was 'actual knowledge' because the search engine was not provided with a copy of the court settlement.

14 For all of them, see DPA Resolution R/02679/2009 (TD/01000/2009) of 8 February 2010.

15 'Article 3'- Territorial scope

'1. This Regulation applies to the processing of personal data in the context of the activities of an establishment of a controller or a processor in the Union.

2. This Regulation applies to the processing of personal data of data subjects residing in the Union by a controller not established in the Union, where the processing activities are related to:

(a) the offering of goods or services to such data subjects in the Union; or

(b) the monitoring of their behaviour.

3. This Regulation applies to the processing of personal data by a controller not established in the Union, but in a place where the national law of a Member State applies by virtue of public international law.' [emphasis added]

16 Article 17 of the E-Commerce Law 34/2002 states the following:

'17. Liability of services providers which provide links to contents or search tools.

1. *The information society services providers which provide links to other contents or include in their directories or search tools shall not be liable for the information to which they address their recipients of their services, provided that:*

a) they do not have actual knowledge of the fact that the activity or the information to which they address or recommend are illegal or violate third parties' goods or rights that could be compensated, or

b) If they have such knowledge, they act expeditiously to remove or to disable access to the corresponding link. (...)' [emphasis added]

authorities must adopt the necessary measures to ensure that the performance of this service is interrupted or the infringing data removed. Moreover, the following paragraph of that article explicitly states that the adoption and enforcement of these measures must respect 'the safeguards, standards and procedures foreseen in the law in order to protect the rights to personal and family privacy, the protection of personal data, the freedom of expression or the freedom of information, when these might be affected'.

3. Scope of the 'right to be forgotten'

Finally, the last question concerned the scope of the right to be forgotten on the basis of the rights of 'erasure and blocking'[17] (called 'cancellation right' in the LOPD) and 'objection' under Directive 95/46/EC:

> must it be considered that the rights to erasure and blocking of data, provided for in Article 12(b), and the right to object, provided for by [subparagraph (a) of the first paragraph of Article 14] of Directive 95/46, extend to enabling the data subject to address himself to search engines in order to prevent indexing of the information relating to him personally, published on third parties' web pages, invoking his wish that such information should not be known to internet users when he considers that it might be prejudicial to him or he wishes it to be consigned to oblivion, even though the information in question has been lawfully published by third parties?

It is important to bear in mind that, when the National High Court posed these questions, there was already some debate about the existence of the 'right to be forgotten' and the Spanish DPA always argued that this right was just the application of the rights of cancellation and objection on the Internet. In addition, this debate intensified upon the publication of the EC Proposal because it contained a rather long 'right to be forgotten' provision[18] (renamed in the amendments made by Parliament on 12 March 2014 as the 'right of erasure').

---

17 Article 12b) regulates the cancellation right as follows: 'Member States shall guarantee to every data subject the right to obtain from the controller: (...) (b) as appropriate the rectification, erasure or blocking of data which processing does not comply with the provisions of this Directive, in particular because of the incomplete or inaccurate nature of the data'.

Article 14a) of Directive 95/46/EC regulates the right of objection as follows: 'Member States shall grant the data subject the right: (a) at least in the cases referred to in Article 7 (e) and (f), to object at any time on compelling legitimate grounds relating to his/her particular situation to the processing of data relating to him/her, except where otherwise provided by national legislation. Where there is a justified objection, the processing instigated by the controller may no longer involve those data'.

18 http://eur-lex.europa.eu/LexUriServ/LexUriServ.do?uri=COM:2012:0011:FIN:EN:PDF.

II. The Advocate General's opinion

On 25 June 2013, the Advocate General Niilo Jääskinen issued his opinion[19] providing the ECJ with a response to a significant number of the questions referred by the Spanish National High Court and which can be summarized as follows:

1. Search engines and providers of information society services

The Advocate General considered that the search engines on the Internet are not regulated in EU legislation and, in particular, in Directive 2000/31/EC: 'internet search engine service providers like Google who do not provide their service in return for remuneration from the internet users, appear to fall in that capacity outside the scope of application of ecommerce Directive 2000/31'.

However, the Advocate General did not take into account the activity of the search engines, which should be subject to the specific liability regime allocated to information services providers which act as 'intermediaries'. This is precisely the liability regime expressly regulated in E-Commerce Law 34/2002 that implemented Directive 2000/31/EC in Spain.

2. Functional concept of 'establishment'

The Advocate General stated that 'the Court should approach the question of territorial applicability from the perspective of the business model of internet search engine service providers. This, as I have mentioned, normally relies on keyword advertising which is the source of income and, as such, the economic *raison d'être* for the provision of a free information location tool in the form of a search engine. The entity in charge of keyword advertising (called 'referencing service provider' in the Court's case-law) is linked to the internet search engine. This entity needs presence on national advertising markets. For this reason Google has established subsidiaries in many Member States which clearly constitute establishments within the meaning of Article 4(1)(a) of the Directive. It also provides national web domains such as google.es or google.fi. (...) For these reasons I would adhere to the Article 29 Working Party's conclusion to the effect that the business model of an internet search engine service provider must be taken into account in the sense that its establishment plays a relevant role in the processing of personal data if it is linked to a service involved in selling targeted advertisement to inhabitants of that Member State.'

The Advocate General did not examine the other criteria of territorial application of Directive 95/46/EC, i.e., the existence of 'means' in a Member State.

19 Opinion of Advocate General Jääskinen in *Google Spain and Google*, C-131/12, EU:C:2014:317 http://curia.europa.eu/juris/document/document.jsf?text=&docid=138782&pageIndex=0&doclang=EN&mode=req&dir=&occ=first&part=1&cid=392631.

3. Indexing and personal data controllership

Although the Advocate General considered that indexing is a processing of personal data, he also considered that the search engine should not be considered a data controller of such processing for the purposes of Directive 95/46/EC since the search engine does not index personal data in third party sources 'with some intention which relates to their processing *as* personal data' i.e., the processing is not performed 'in some *semantically relevant way*' but rather as 'a mere computer code'.

4. Processing of personal data contained in indexed web pages means that the search engine is a data controller

The Advocate General considered that the search engine would be the data controller of the processing of personal data contained in an indexed website only if it does not respect the exclusion codes of this website or if it does not update a web page in its cache despite a request received from the website.

For the Advocate General, the criteria making the data processing legitimate is the search engine's legitimate interests regulated in Article 7(f) of Directive 95/46/EC, 'namely (i) making information more easily accessible for internet users; (ii) rendering dissemination of the information uploaded on the internet more effective; and (iii) enabling various information society services supplied by the internet search engine service provider that are ancillary to the search engine, such as the provision of keyword advertising.'

He therefore considered that 'a national data protection authority cannot require an internet search engine service provider to withdraw information from its index except for the cases where this service provider has not complied with the exclusion codes or where a request emanating from the website regarding update of cache memory has not been complied with. This scenario does not seem pertinent for the present preliminary reference. A possible 'notice and take down procedure' concerning links to source web pages with illegal or inappropriate contents is a matter of national law civil liability based on grounds other than the protection of personal data.'

5. The role of the search engine when the information is lawfully published

According to the Advocate General, Directive 95/46/EC does not grant a general 'right to be forgotten' against search engines:

- Directive 95/46/EC recognizes the right of rectification and deletion of data (in particular, when data are incomplete or inaccurate), which is not the case here because it relates to a mandatory statutory publication in Spain.
- Directive 95/46/EC also recognizes the right to object which requires the data subject to specify legitimate grounds relating to his/her particular situation. This relates to a mandatory statutory publication and a subjective preference alone would not be a legitimate ground. Therefore, to request the search engine to

remove information that has legally been made public constitutes an interference with the website's freedom of expression.

However, the Advocate General also stated that 'it is possible that the secondary liability of the search engine service providers under national law may lead to duties amounting to blocking access to thirdparty websites with illegal contents such as web pages infringing IP rights, or displaying libellous or criminal information'.

III. ECJ judgement

The ECJ judgment has been a surprise not only because it does not follow the Advocate General's opinion but also because it takes a firm position regarding the weight of the protection of personal data (in line with the ECJ's previous annulment of Directive 2006/24/EC on data retention[20]) in the development of the digital economy as already stated by the European Data Protection Supervisor (EDPS).[21]

1. The search engine is a data controller of the published 'personal' information

The ECJ considers that the processing activities performed by the search engine (collection, recording, organisation, storage and communication) are processing of 'personal data'. However, as opposed to the Advocate General, it also states that this processing is carried out by the search engine as a 'data controller' since it determines the purpose and means of the processing despite not exerting any control over the personal data published in third parties' websites.

2. The 'establishment': an economic concept

As we have seen, since Google Inc. is established in the US, the application of the EU data protection rules (in this case, Spanish data protection rules) depends on whether (i) an establishment in Spain was involved in the processing of the personal data or (ii) processing means were located in Spain.

In this case, the ECJ considers that there is an establishment in Spain since the activities of Google's Spanish subsidiary are inextricably linked to the promotion and sale in Spain of advertising space, which is an essential elements to the economic viability

20 Judgment in *Digital Rights Ireland and Seitlinger and Others*, joined cases C-293/12 and C-594/12, EU:C:2014:238. http://curia.europa.eu/juris/document/document.jsf?text=&docid=153045&pageIndex=0&doclang=es&mode=req&dir=&occ=first&part=1&cid=747765.

21 'The European Court of Justice is sending a strong message in this case', said Peter Hustinx, the European data protection supervisor. 'It's now up to the countries to provide consistency in how it's interpreted.' http://www.nytimes.com/2014/05/15/technology/one-court-ruling-on-privacy-in-europe-and-28-regulators.html.

of the search engine managed by Google Inc., following the opinion of 4 April 2008 of the Article 29 Working Party (WP 148).[22]

This broad interpretation of 'establishment' has a significant impact on many multinational groups with subsidiaries or representative offices in EU countries and developing ancillary activities, to the extent that they may be deemed 'inextricably' linked to the activity of the 'principal'. And, more specifically, the main issues arise for entities established in an EU country with establishments in other Member States which activities are linked. Indeed, they would apply several local rules implementing Directive 95/46/EC and this was not the purpose of article 4.1.a) (even if its potential impact on the harmonization of the internal market should be limited).[23] In our opinion, the ECJ has tried to correct the absence of criteria of territorial application such as that

---

22 'Article 4(1)(a) states that a Member State's data protection law should be applied, when certain operations of personal data processing by the controller are carried out 'in the context of the activities of an establishment' of that controller on the territory of a Member State. A particular processing operation of personal data should be taken as the starting point. *When applied to a particular search engine whose headquarters are located outside of the EEA, the question needs to be answered whether the processing of user data involves establishments on the territory of a Member State.*

As the Working Party has already pointed out in its previous Working document 13, *the existence of an "establishment" implies the effective and real exercise of activity through stable arrangements* and has to be determined in conformity with the case law of the Court of Justice of the European Communities. *The legal form of the establishment – a local office, a subsidiary with legal personality or a third party agency – is not decisive.*

However, a further requirement is that the processing operation is carried out 'in the context of the activities' of the establishment. This means that the establishment should also play a relevant role in the particular processing operation. This is clearly the case, if: - an establishment is responsible for relations with users of the search engine in a particular jurisdiction;

- a search engine provider establishes an office in a Member State (EEA) that is involved in the selling of targeted advertisements to the inhabitants of that state;

- the establishment of a search engine provider complies with court orders and/or law enforcement requests by the competent authorities of a Member State with regard to user data.' [emphasis added]

23 The Article 29 Working Party has explained the ratio of the criteria for the territorial application of Directive 95/46/EC as follows (Working document on determining the international application of EU data protection law to personal data processing on the Internet by non-EU based web sites (WP 56), of 30 May 2002): 'The directive distinguishes in general terms between, on the one hand, situations where the cross-frontier elements are confined to EU Member States or with territories outside the geographical borders of the European Union, but where the law of a Member State applies by virtue of international public law (the "diplomatic case") and, on the other hand, situations where the processing involves elements going beyond the borders of the European Union.

Concerning the situations within the Community, the objective of the directive is twofold: it aims at avoiding gaps (no data protection law would apply) and at avoiding multiple/double application of national laws. As the directive addresses the issue of applicable law and establishes a criterion for determining the law on substance that should provide the solution to a case, the directive itself fulfils the role of a so-called "rule of conflict" and no recourse to other existing criteria of international private law is necessary.

In order to find an answer, the directive uses the criterion or "connection factor" of the "place of establishment of the controller" or, in other words, the country of origin principle typically applied in the Internal Market. (...)

The application of the country of origin principle is justified in an Internal Market where national data protection laws afford equivalent protection thanks to the harmonisation of the data protection rights of individuals and obligations of industry and other controllers of processing of personal data. In such a way the country of origin principle, which is in some way a restriction of the scope of application of the data protection laws of the Member States, does not have adverse effects on the rights and interests of its residents or industry. In effect, even if the Member States laws are not applicable to all processing involving a national data subject or taking place on the national territory, the fact that the law of another Member State alone is applicable, has a very limited impact, given that both laws are harmonised by the directive and thus equivalent. (...)

The situation is different as regards processing operations, which involve a controller in a third country. The national laws of these third countries are not harmonised, the directive is not applicable in these countries and the protection of individuals with regard to the processing of their personal data may therefore be missing or weak. *The country of origin principle, which is linked to the establishment of the controller, can no longer serve the purpose of determining the applicable law. It is necessary to switch to another connection factor.* The European Parliament and the Council decided to come back to one of the classic connection factors in international law,

in Directive 2000/31/EC and Article 3(2) of the EC Proposal and have expanded in a somewhat artificial way the concept of establishment. In other words, it has tried to apply the simple principle of 'who operates and makes a profit in a market must be governed by the rules of that market'.

Having determined the existence of an establishment in the EU, the Court does not examine the other territorial criteria, in particular, the existence of 'processing means', which still requires some interpretation, in particular, in view of the controversial criteria adopted by the Article 29 Working Party regarding 'cookies',[24] extensively used by the Spanish DPA in order to apply the LOPD to Google US.[25] Finally, the ECJ did not take the time to develop, as it should have done, the impact of the Charter to ensure effective protection in the EU in view of the shortcomings of the territorial criteria of application of Directive 95/46/EC.

3. The 'right to be forgotten' and the liability of the search engines

Unlike the Advocate General, the ECJ recognizes (as the Spanish DPA did) the 'right to be forgotten' as a specific expression on the Internet of the cancellation and objection rights recognized by Directive 95/46/EC. And it does so by separating the processing by the source of information from the processing of the search engine. This disconnection partially explains the lively debate regarding the impact of the 'right to be forgotten' on the scope of freedom of expression and information, the legitimacy of the processing of sensitive data by the search engine, the expectations of other individuals whose information is mixed with that of the person who wishes to be 'forgotten' and the liability regime of information society providers which are acting as mere intermediaries.

It is surprising to see that the ECJ did not carefully address any of these issues in its judgment since these issues (and many others) were raised and extensively discussed when the new provision on the 'right to be forgotten' of the EC Proposal was published in 2012.

---

which is the physical link between the action and a legal system. The EU legislator chose the country of the territorial location of equipment used. The directive therefore applies when the controller is not established on Community territory, but decides to process personal data for specific purposes and makes use of equipment, automated or otherwise, situated on the territory of a Member State.

The objective of this provision in Article 4 paragraph 1 lit. c) of Directive 95/46/EC is that an individual should not be without protection as regards processing taking place within his country, solely because the controller is not established on Community territory. This could be simply, because the controller has, in principle, nothing to do with the Community. But it is also imaginable that controllers locate their establishment outside the EU in order to bypass the application of EU law'.(http://ec.europa.eu/justice/policies/privacy/docs/wpdocs/2002/wp56_en.pdf)

24 'As explained above, the user's PC can be viewed as equipment in the sense of Article 4 (1) c of Directive 95/46/EC. It is located on the territory of a Member State. The controller decided to use this equipment for the purpose of processing personal data and, as it has been explained in the previous paragraphs, several technical operations take place without the control of the data subject. The controller disposes over the user's equipment and this equipment is not used only for purposes of transit through Community territory.

The Working Party is therefore of the opinion that the national law of the Member State where this user's personal computer is located applies to the question under what conditions his personal data may be collected by placing cookies on his hard disk.' (http://ec.europa.eu/justice/policies/privacy/docs/wpdocs/2002/wp56_en.pdf)

25 See, for example, DPA resolutions R/02679/2009 (TD/01000/2009), of 8 February 2010 or R/01545/2001 (TD/00249/2011), of 12 July 2011.

Since the search engine gives any Internet user a structured view of information about anyone which potentially affects a variety of aspects of his/her private life, the ECJ concludes that, after applying the balance test of the 'legitimate interest ground' of Article 7(f) of Directive 95/46/EC,[26] the data protection right of cancellation 'override[s], as a rule, not only the economic interest of the operator of the search engine but also the interest of the general public in finding that information upon a search relating to the data subject's name'.

The ECJ has been accused of not providing any criteria to carry out this balance of the interests at stake and of establishing a presumption of prevalence of data protection rights. This criticism is not entirely true if the ruling is read carefully: it clearly mentions that the nature of the information at hand, its age, its sensitive nature and the public interest in question must be analyzed on a case-by-case basis. It also states that the role played by the data subject in public life may prevail over data protection rights.

The grounds for this balancing act exist but do not consist of rules that can be implemented through algorithms (at least in the current state of artificial intelligence). In addition, not in every case does the right to be forgotten oppose the freedom of expression (actually, this was not the issue in the Google case). However, the clash between the rights of privacy or honour and the freedom of expression and information is not new and has been examined by the European Court of Human Rights and by national constitutional courts. However, it is also true that this clash is evolving in a globalized and digital world, as already highlighted in the recommendations of the Council of Europe CM/Rec(2012)3 on the protection of human rights with regard to search engines[27] and CM/Rec(2011)7 on a new notion of the media.[28]

---

26 The ECJ seems to forget that the processing of sensitive data, such as those regulated under Article 8 of Directive 95/46/EC, cannot be considered legitimate on this ground.

27 '4. The action of search engines can affect freedom of expression and, given their role in facilitating access to information, can bear even more on the right to seek, receive and impart information; similarly, their action has an impact on the right to private life and the protection of personal data. Such challenges may stem, inter alia from the design of algorithms, de-indexing and/or partial treatment or biased results, market concentration and lack of transparency about both the selection process and ranking of results.

5. The impact on private life may result from the pervasiveness of search engines or their ability to penetrate and index content which, although in the public space, was not intended for mass communication (or mass communication in aggregate), and from data processing generally and data retention periods. Moreover, search engines generate new kinds of personal data, such as individual search histories and behaviour profiles.

6. There is a need to protect and promote access, diversity, impartial treatment, security and transparency in the context of search engines. Media literacy and the development of skills that enable users to have informed access to the greatest possible variety of information, content and services should be promoted having regard to Recommendation CM/Rec(2011)7 on a new notion of media.' (http://www.coe.int/t/dghl/standardsetting/dataprotection/TPD_documents/CM%20Rec(2012)3%20E%20-%20Search%20engins.pdf)

28 '95. Harassment, bullying, intimidation and stalking can be facilitated in the new media ecosystem by collective online shared spaces, tracking applications or even search engines and profiling technology. Women are frequent victims of these forms of abuse, which can lead to physical (including sexual) abuse and violence which are unacceptable expressions of inequality. Attention should also be paid to the possible abusive use of technology in respect of members of minorities.

96. In the above-mentioned cases, the response will depend on the circumstances, including the nature and scope of the activity or service in question, as well as the actor's own editorial processes. A graduated approach should consider the possibilities of the actors concerned (for example those operating collective online shared spaces or offering search engine, tracking or profiling applications and technology) to address or mitigate the risks in question. Relevant stakeholders could be encouraged to explore together the feasibility of removing or deleting content in appropriate cases, to the extent that it is not inconsistent with the fundamental right to freedom of expression,

In this case, the publication of the information in the newspaper was justified because it was imposed by law and was a result of the exercise of the freedom of expression. However, the information referred to an individual who was not a public figure and the facts dated back over 16 years. Based on this, and although no removal at source was required (because it was legally published), the ECJ considered that the browser should remove the links to that information (resulting from a search of the data subject's name) since the information 'is, at this point in time, incompatible (...) because that information appears, having regard to all the circumstances of the case, to be inadequate, irrelevant or no longer relevant, or excessive in relation to the purposes of the processing at issue carried out by the operator of the search engine'.

Leaving aside the existence of criteria to balance the interests at stake, it is startling that the search engine is made responsible for carrying out this balancing act and that it has to be carried out regardless of the legitimacy of the data processing in the original source. And this is so surprising because the search engine is in the worst possible position to make this judgment and this is not consistent with the liability regime of the intermediaries of the information society services based on the 'actual knowledge' concept. 'Actual knowledge' is linked to the unlawfulness of the data and must be declared by a supervisory authority or a court.

IV. First consequences

Besides superficial debates about the alleged demise of freedom of expression and information in the EU, the first consequences of the ECJ decision have not taken long to materialize. The first reaction came from the search engines and data protection authorities in the EU, followed by the first civil actions requesting compensation for damages in Spain and by the application of the ECJ criteria by courts for the first time both in the EU and beyond.

1. The search engines

Google reacted almost immediately to the ECJ judgment making available to Internet users a form allowing them to request the removal of search results (https://support.google.com/legal/contact/lr_eudpa?product=websearch). Microsoft also made available its own form for this purpose (https://www.bing.com/webmaster/tools/eu-privacy-request).

Google has also created an Advisory Board to help manage the avalanche of requests that they are receiving (https://www.google.com/advisorycouncil/). A transparency

including its traces (logs, records and processing), within a reasonably short period of time. Greater technical capabilities bring with them greater responsibility. Self-regulation could usefully be complemented by capacity building (for example enhancing intercultural competencies) and by sharing best or corrective practices developed within sectors of activity in the new media ecosystem.'

(https://wcd.coe.int/ViewDoc.jsp?id=1835645&Site=CM&BackColorInternet=C3C3C3&BackColorIntranet=EDB021&BackColorLogged=F5D383)

report on petitions received and processed released by Google[29] showed that over half a million applications were filed in September 2014. The final report of the Advisory Board has also been recently issued based on different inputs, including the suggestions of experts around Europe received during a seven-city tour.[30]

Furthermore, Google also published a notice for users in order to stress the significance of the ECJ ruling (which, as shown below, has been criticized by the Article 29 Working Party).

The ECJ decision has generated other reactions. Indeed, the BBC said in October 2014 that it intended to publish a list of all items that were deleted from the list of Google Search results as a result of the 'right to be forgotten' requests, in order to alert the public of its existence and help locate the source.[31]

Another controversial issue has been the territorial scope of the ECJ decision since the search engines have tried to limit the application of the judgment to the EU territorial domains and not beyond, such as www.google.com. However, the *Tribunal de Grande Instance de Paris*, applying the ECJ ruling,[32] on 16 September 2014 ordered Google

---

29 The transparency report (accessible at http://www.google.com/transparencyreport/removals/europeprivacy/?hl=es) highlights the number of applications received in March 2015.

Likewise, the report provides for examples of requests received and the decisions adopted by Google, such as:

Example	Decision
A woman requested that we remove a decades-old article about her husband's murder, which included her name.	We have removed the page from search results for her name.
A victim of rape asked us to remove a link to a newspaper article about the crime.	We have removed the page from search results for the individual's name.
We received multiple requests from a single individual who asked us to remove 20 links to recent articles about his arrest for financial crimes committed in a professional capacity.	We did not remove the pages from search results.
A media professional requested that we remove 4 links to articles reporting on embarrassing content he posted to the Internet.	We did not remove the pages from search results.
We received a request from a crime victim to remove 3 links that discuss the crime, which occurred decades ago.	We have removed the pages from search results for her name.
An individual asked us to remove links to articles on the internet that reference his dismissal for sexual crimes committed on the job.	We did not remove the pages from search results.
We received a request from an individual to remove over 50 links to articles and blog posts reporting on public outcry over accusations that he was abusing welfare services.	We did not remove the pages from search results.
An individual asked us to remove a link to a page that had taken a self-published image and reposted it.	The page has been removed from search results for her name.

30 https://drive.google.com/a/google.com/file/d/0B1UgZshetMd4cEI3SjlvV0hNbDA/view?pli=1

31 http://www.bbc.com/news/technology-29658085; http://www.kitguru.net/channel/generaltech/matthew-wilson/bbc-to-publish-list-of-removed-right-to-be-forgotten-articles/

32 'Attendu que pour contester aux demandeurs le droit de rechercher sa responsabilité, Google France fait valoir qu'elle n'a qu'une activité de fourniture de prestations de marketing et de démonstration auprès d'une clientèle utilisant des services publicitaires et est étrangère à toute activité éditoriale ou d'exploitation de sites internet, que l'éditeur et l'exploitant du moteur de recherche et du site «google.fr» est la société Google Inc, laquelle, en tant que responsable du traitement des données, doit être saisie de toute demande à ce sujet ; qu'elle invoque subsidiairement un formulaire en ligne récemment mis en place par Google Inc permettant à tout requérant de demander la

France to de-index all domains worldwide and not to limit to google.fr the defamatory content (the term defamation having been defined by another court decision) identified by the applicant of the right to be forgotten. This position has been later endorsed by all EU data protection supervisory authorities (see 4.2 below).

2. EU authorities

On the same day the judgment was published, the DPA issued a press release with this heading: 'The ECJ endorses the DPA's position in relation to the search engines and the right to be forgotten in the Internet'.[33] The Spanish DPA and the other EU DPAs have promptly realized that they need to adopt a position in common in relation to the right to be forgotten requests regarding both the search engines and the websites of origin.

In this regard, in June 2014, the EU data protection supervisory authorities analyzed, within the Article 29 Working Party,[34] the consequences of the ECJ judgment and tried to identify relevant issues to develop a position in common. To this end, they met with the major search engines in July 2014[35] and, subsequently, with the media. They also created a specific network to record the decisions taken by them to identify similar cases or particularly complex ones.

- Finally, on 26 November 2014, the Article 29 Working Party published some guidelines which are summarized below:[36]
- Search engines are considered data controllers.

suppression de résultats de recherche contenant des données personnelles ; Mais attendu que si la société Google Inc est certes l'exploitant du moteur de recherche, Google France, qui en est une filiale à 100%, a pour activité la promotion et la vente d'espaces publicitaires liés à des termes recherchés au moyen du moteur édité par Google Inc, et assure ainsi, par l'activité qu'elle déploie, le financement de ce moteur de recherche ; que la Cour de Justice de l'Union européenne a ainsi, le 13 mai 2014, considéré que l'établissement ou la filiale implantée par Google Inc dans un Etat membre de la Communauté européenne en est son représentant dans l'Etat concerné et que «les activités de l'exploitant du moteur de recherche et celles de son établissement situé dans l'Etat membre concerné sont indissociablement liées», après avoir rappelé l'exigence posée par la Directive 95/46, posée en vue d'assurer une protection efficace et complète des libertés et des droits fondamentaux des personnes physiques, notamment du droit à la vie privée, que le traitement de données à caractère personnel soit effectué non pas par l'établissement concerné lui-même mais uniquement dans le cadre des activités de celui-ci ; qu'il en résulte que les requérants sont recevables en leur demande dirigée contre Google France, tendant à ce qu'elle effectue les diligences nécessaires pour mettre fin aux atteintes qu'ils dénoncent ; (...)

Que c'est vainement que Google France sollicite à titre infiniment subsidiaire que l'injonction soit limitée aux seuls liens avec Google.fr, alors qu'il n'établit pas l'impossibilité de se connecter depuis le territoire français en utilisant les autres terminaisons du moteur de recherche google ;' (http://www.legalis.net/spip.php?page=jurisprudence-decision&id_article=4291)

33 https://www.agpd.es/portalwebAGPD/revista_prensa/revista_prensa/2014/notas_prensa/common/may_14/NP_STJUE_derecho_olvido.pdf

34 http://ec.europa.eu/justice/data-protection/article-29/press-material/press-release/art29_press_material/20140523_wp29_press_release_ecj_google.pdf.

35 http://ec.europa.eu/justice/data-protection/article-29/press-material/press-release/art29_press_material/20140725_wp29_press_release_right_to_be_forgotten.pdf; http://ec.europa.eu/justice/data-protection/article-29/press-material/press-release/art29_press_material/20140918_wp29_press_release_97th_plenary_cjeu_google_judgment__17sept_adopted.pdf

36 http://ec.europa.eu/justice/data-protection/article-29/documentation/opinion-recommendation/files/2014/wp225_en.pdf

- There must be fair balance between fundamental rights and interests which outcome will mainly depend on the nature and sensitivity of the processed data and on the interest of the public having access to that particular information.
- There is a limited impact of de-listing on the access to information (mainly, when individuals' rights to freedom of expression and access to information must prevail).
- No information is deleted from the original source.
- Individuals are not obliged to contact the original website to exercise their rights towards the search engines.
- DPAs will focus on claims with a clear link between the data subject and the EU.
- Territorial effect of a de-listing decision: 'de-listing decisions must be implemented in such a way that they guarantee the effective and complete protection of data subjects' rights and that EU law cannot be circumvented. In that sense, limiting de-listing to EU domains on the grounds that users tend to access search engines via their national domains cannot be considered a sufficient mean to satisfactorily guarantee the rights of data subjects according to the ruling. In practice, this means that in any case de-listing should also be effective on all relevant domains, including .com.'
- The information to the public on the de-listing of specific links is based on no legal requirement under data protection rules ('Such a practice would only be acceptable if the information is presented in such a way that users cannot, in any case, conclude that one particular individual has asked for de-listing of results concerning him or her').
- Communication to website editors on the de-listing of specific links should not be carried out as a general practice.

The European Commission also welcomed the ECJ decision which has been construed as an endorsement of the EC Proposal to regulate the right to be forgotten.[37] It highlighted that the ECJ judgment was not creating a 'super right' which overrides others and, in particular, the freedom of expression.[38] It also mentioned an issue that was also present in the dispute between the search engine and the Spanish DPA, i.e., the fact that search engine has implemented procedures for 'forgetting' in order to meet US legal requirements concerning certain types of sensitive personal data in such

37 http://ec.europa.eu/justice/data-protection/files/factsheets/factsheet_data_protection_en.pdf

38 'The Court also clarified, that a case-by-case assessment will be needed. Neither the right to the protection of personal data nor and the right to freedom of expression are absolute rights. A fair balance should be sought between the legitimate interest of internet users and the person's fundamental rights. Freedom of expression carries with it responsibilities and has limits both in the online and offline world.

This balance may depend on the nature of the information in question, its sensitivity for the person's private life and on the public interest in having that information. It may also depend on the personality in question: the right to be forgotten is certainly not about making prominent people less prominent or making criminals less criminal'.

jurisdiction and copyright infringements[39] (which does not seem to be consistent with Google's position regarding data protection).

3. First indemnity for damages awarded in Spain

In July 2014, the Barcelona Court of Appeal ordered Google to pay EUR 8,000 in compensation for moral damages in a 'right to be forgotten' claim.[40]

The data subject exercised his 'right to be forgotten' with a number of search engines, which included Yahoo Iberia, S.L. and Google Spain, S.A. regarding a pardon granted by the Spanish Government in relation to a public health offence committed in 1981 and published (by operation of law) in Spain's Official Gazette.

Yahoo and Google did not satisfy the data subject's request and he filed an administrative claim with the Spanish DPA which was upheld. Yahoo fulfilled the DPA's resolution but Google challenged it before the Spanish National High Court.

Despite Google's appeal being pending, the data subject claimed over EUR 5 million in damages before the Barcelona Court of Appeal (civil jurisdiction) as a result of the alleged infringement of his rights to personal data protection, privacy and honour.

The following aspects of the Court's reasoning in the case are worth highlighting:

- *Liability of search engine service providers*. Pursuant to E-Commerce Law 34/2002, search engines may be held liable if they have actual knowledge that the relevant content is illicit and they do not act diligently to suppress or remove it. Since Google did not fulfil the DPA's resolution ordering the de-indexation, the court found that it could be held liable for the alleged infringements as from that moment.

---

39 'How is Google expected to comply with this ruling? Will it not be very costly for search engines to comply? It is not yet possible to determine how the ruling of the Court on the Right to be Forgotten will impact the number of people who ask to have their data deleted from Google.

In any event, *Google already has a system in place to handle deletion requests, such as national identification numbers (like U.S. Social Security Numbers), bank account numbers, credit card numbers and images of signatures. It also has set up a parallel system for dealing with take-down requests for copyright violations.*' [emphasis added]

40 'Consideramos que es la decisión de la AEPD (R/02694/2009, del procedimiento TD/00921/2009) de 19 de enero de 2010, que estimó la reclamación del actor contra Google Spain y que instó a esta entidad a que adoptara las medidas necesarias para retirar los datos de su índice e imposibilitar el acceso futuro a los mismos -o más exactamente, la notificación de esa resolución- la que marca el momento en que el mantenimiento del resultado controvertido en el índice del buscador deviene incumplimiento culpable de las normas legales de protección de datos. Con la lectura de la resolución motivada de la Spanish DPA, Google Spain debía conocer la antijuricidad de su actuación. La copia de la decisión remitida a don Domingo tiene fecha de salida de 21 de enero de 2010 (f. 305). Por tanto, en defecto de más precisiones por las partes, se toma como fecha de notificación a Google Spain la de 22 de enero de 2010. (…) Ya hemos repetido que la decisión final sobre el control administrativo de la protección de datos no opera como requisito de la acción civil de indemnización por daños. La decisión de la Spanish DPA solo tiene relevancia en este juicio como determinante, por su contenido, del momento en el cual Google Spain tuvo que conocer razonablemente que el buscador afectaba el derecho fundamental de protección de datos personales del Sr. Domingo.

(…) Los criterios expuestos (así, la afectación de la dignidad del demandante por la naturaleza de la información divulgada, relativa a un antiguo delito; la publicación como resultado del poderoso buscador Google; el quebranto derivado de las dificultades para conseguir su supresión, la duración del daño atribuible a la demandada), así como la comparación con las sumas establecidas por los tribunales -en la propia STS de 22 de enero de 2014 -, nos llevan a fijar prudencialmente en 8.000 euros la indemnización que Google Spain, S.L. debe pagar al demandante por el daño causado.'

- *Privacy considerations*. Based on the ECJ decision in the Google Spain Case, the Court considered that the publication in the list of results of a pardon that referred to facts (which took place in 1981) regarding an individual who is not a public figure was contrary to the data protection principles.
- *Damages*. The Court only took into account the period of ten months between the DPA's resolution and the date on which Google de-indexed the pardon information. It dismissed the claim for economic damages. The indemnity was granted on the basis of the existence of moral damages in view of the nature of the data that was made public and of how old they were (the facts dated back to 1981), the vast scope of diffusion in a 'powerful' search engine, the claimant's difficulties in obtaining a remedy from Google and the time that it took Google to adopt the requested measures.

4. First rulings of the Spanish National High Court applying the ECJ decision

The Spanish National High Court recently issued several rulings regarding 18 appeals lodged by Google Spain challenging the Spanish DPA's rulings that were suspended until the ECJ issued its decision. These are the first rulings issued by the National High Court following the publication of the ECJ decision. Fourteen of the appeals lodged by Google Spain have been dismissed, recognising the data subjects' 'right to be forgotten'. However, the National High Court upheld the other four appeals lodged by Google Spain.

Mainly, and following the doctrine of the ECJ decision, the National High Court concluded that:

(i) the search engines' activity – that is, briefly, retrieving information published on the Internet by third parties, indexing it in an automated manner, storing it temporarily and making it accessible to Internet users – implies the processing of personal data;

(ii) the territorial scope of European legislation on data protection also applies when the search engine manager creates, in a Member State (such as Spain), a branch office or an affiliate aimed at ensuring the commercial and advertising activities of the search engine's advertising spaces addressed to those who reside in that Member State;

(iii) the lack of standing exception alleged by Google Spain should be dismissed because its activity is considered indispensable for the functioning of the search engine as the commercial and advertising activities of the search engine's advertising spaces ensure its profitability and subsistence, constituting a business unit with Google, Inc.; and

(iv) a case-by-case assessment of the interests involved must be carried out, that is, on the one hand, the right to the protection of personal data and, on the other, the right to freedom of expression and information; the assessment must take into account that, generally, the right to data protection prevails over the search engine manager's interest in the activities undertaken; although this primacy is not absolute and, in any case, the specific situation of the data subject must be taken into account.

In most cases, after assessing the rights, the National High Court did not uphold the appeal lodged by Google Spain. The claims were only upheld in four cases: (i) those in which the data provided by the claimant did not sufficiently determine the sensitive nature of the information for his/her private life; or (ii) those in which the websites, the content or the characteristics of the controversial information were not specified or, where the links were specified, the content of the information affecting the data subject was not specified.

5. Other jurisdictions

In addition to the French judgment cited above, the ECJ decision has had an impact on other non-EU jurisdictions:

(i) *Japan*.[41] On 22 October 2014, the Tokyo District Court ordered Google to withdraw search data relating to a Japanese citizen. It was requested to withdraw 120 of 237 results of the search which linked the data subject to a crime committed years before.

(ii) *Argentina*.[42] On 28 October 2014, the Supreme Court of Justice of the Nation (CSNJ), after analysing the role of search engines in the development of freedom of expression[43] and the scope of the right of honour,[44] dismissed a claim against

41 http://www.rpp.com.pe/2014-10-22-google-borra-los-datos-de-un-japones-por-orden-de-un-tribunal-nipon-noticia_735811.html

42 http://www.informaticalegal.com.ar/2014/10/28/sentencia-de-la-corte-suprema-de-justicia-de-la-nacion-csnj-rodriguez-maria-belen-c-google-inc-s-danos-y-perjuicios/

43 '10) Que la libertad de expresión comprende el derecho a transmitir ideas, hechos y opiniones difundidos a través de Internet. Así ha sido reconocido por el legislador nacional al establecer en el artículo 1° de la ley 26.032 que "[la búsqueda, recepción y difusión de información e ideas de toda índole, a través del servicio de Internet, se considera comprendido dentro de la garantía constitucional que ampara la libertad de expresión". (...) Por su parte, la importancia del rol que desempeñan los motores de búsqueda en el funcionamiento de Internet resulta indudable. Así lo ha señalado el Tribunal de Justicia de la Unión Europea al señalar que "la actividad de los motores de búsqueda desempeña un papel decisivo en la difusión global de dichos datos en la medida en que facilita su acceso a todo internauta que lleva a cabo una búsqueda a partir del nombre del interesado, incluidos los internautas que, de no ser así, no habrían encontrado la página web en la que se publican estos mismos datos" (conf. 'Google Spain S.L. Google Inc. v. Agencia Española de Protección de Datos, Mario Costeja González', sentencia del 13 de mayo de 2014).

11) Que desde este punto de vista, el derecho de expresarse a través de Internet fomenta la libertad de expresión tanto desde su dimensión individual como colectiva. Así, a través de Internet se puede concretizar el derecho personal que tiene todo individuo a hacer público, a transmitir, a difundir y a exteriorizar -o no hacerlo- sus ideas, opiniones, creencias, críticas, etc. Desde el aspecto colectivo, Internet constituye un instrumento para garantizar la libertad de información y la formación de la opinión pública.

Es por ello que se ha subrayado el carácter transformador de Internet, como medio que permite que miles de millones de personas en todo el mundo expresen sus opiniones, a la vez que incrementa significativamente su capacidad de acceder a la información y fomenta el pluralismo y la divulgación de información (conf. 'Declaración Conjunta sobre Libertad de Expresión e Internet', citada ut supra, del 1° de junio de 2011). El acceso a Internet, debido a su naturaleza multidireccional e interactiva, su velocidad y alcance global a un relativo bajo costo y sus principios de diseño descentralizado y abierto, posee un potencial inédito para la realización efectiva del derecho a buscar, recibir y difundir información en su doble dimensión, individual y colectiva (Comisión Interamericana de Derechos Humanos, "Libertad de Expresión e Internet", citado anteriormente, párrafo 36).'

44 '13) Que el derecho al honor se refiere a la participación que tiene el individuo dentro de la comunidad amparando a la persona frente a expresiones o mensajes que lo hagan desmerecedor en la consideración ajena al ir en su descrédito (Fallos: 331:1530, voto de la jueza Highton de Nolasco). Por su parte, el derecho a la imagen integra el derecho a la privacidad protegido por el artículo 19 de la Constitución Nacional. Al respecto, esta Corte ha dejado claramente establecido que dicha norma otorga al individuo un ámbito de libertad en el cual éste puede adoptar libremente las decisiones fundamentales acerca de su persona, sin interferencia alguna por parte del Estado o de los particulares, en tanto dichas decisiones no violen derechos de terceros.

Google and Yahoo because the results showed the image of a model in sites linked to sexual, erotic or pornographic content. The Court considered that the search engines were not liable for the contents of the results of their searches to the extent that they had no actual knowledge of their illegality.[45]

(iii) *Mexico*. The Mexican data protection supervisory authority, the *Instituto Federal de Acceso a la Información y Protección de Datos* (IFAI) has initiated sanctioning proceedings against Google México, S. de R.L. de C.V. based on alleged infringements of Mexican data protection regulations in a right to be forgotten case, following a reasoning similar to that set out by the ECJ.[46]

V. Final thoughts

The ECJ judgment shows that data protection rights are not just a theoretical or ancillary issue in the EU: these rights have an important role to play in our global and digital society. This message is clear and has two main dimensions.

Firstly, it establishes a rule aimed at achieving fair competition in the EU market, applying the EU standards to non-EU entities operating in the EU market. These standards are no longer confined to pursuing an economic harmonization (this was the main goal of Directive 95/46/EC) but they project the EU conception of human dignity under the Charter.

Knowing that the criteria used for the territorial application of Directive 95/46/EC are unsuited to achieve protection in today's world, the ECJ has artificially expanded the

---

Así, en Fallos: 306: 1892 el Tribunal estableció que el citado artículo 19 "protege jurídicamente un ámbito de autonomía individual constituida por los sentimientos, hábitos y costumbres, las relaciones familiares, la situación económica, las creencias religiosas, la salud mental y física y, en suma, las acciones, hechos o datos que, teniendo en cuenta las formas de vida aceptadas por la comunidad están reservadas al propio individuo y cuyo conocimiento y divulgación por los extraños significa un peligro real o potencial para la intimidad. En rigor, el derecho a la privacidad comprende no sólo la esfera doméstica, el círculo familiar y de amistad, sino a otros aspectos de la personalidad espiritual o física de las personas tales como la integridad corporal o la imagen y nadie puede inmiscuirse en la vida privada de una persona ni violar áreas de su actividad no destinadas a ser difundidas, sin su consentimiento o el de sus familiares autorizados para ello y sólo por ley podrá justificarse la intromisión, siempre que medie un interés superior en resguardo de la libertad de los otros, la defensa de la sociedad, las buenas costumbres o la persecución del crimen" (en igual sentido, Fallos: 335:799).'

45 'Son manifiestas las ilicitudes respecto de contenidos dañosos, como pornografía infantil, datos que faciliten la comisión de delitos, que instruyan acerca de éstos, que pongan en peligro la vida o la integridad física de alguna o muchas personas, que hagan apología del genocidio, del racismo o de otra discriminación con manifiesta perversidad o incitación a la violencia, que desbaraten o adviertan acerca de investigaciones judiciales en curso y que deban quedar secretas, como también los que importen lesiones contumeliosas al honor, montajes de imágenes notoriamente falsos o que, en forma clara e indiscutible, importen violaciones graves a la privacidad exhibiendo imágenes de actos que por su naturaleza deben ser incuestionablemente privados, aunque no sean necesariamente de contenido sexual. La naturaleza ilícita -civil o penal- de estos contenidos es palmaria y resulta directamente de consultar la página señalada en una comunicación fehaciente del damnificado o, según el caso, de cualquier persona, sin requerir ninguna otra valoración ni esclarecimiento.

Por el contrario, en los casos en que el contenido dañoso que importe eventuales lesiones al honor o de otra naturaleza, pero que exijan un esclarecimiento que deba debatirse o precisarse en sede judicial o administrativa para su efectiva determinación, cabe entender que no puede exigirse al "buscador" que supla la función de la autoridad competente ni menos aún la de los jueces. Por tales razones, en estos casos corresponde exigir la notificación judicial o administrativa competente, no bastando la simple comunicación del particular que se considere perjudicado y menos la de cualquier persona interesada.'

46 http://inicio.ifai.org.mx/Comunicados/Comunicado%20IFAI-009-15.pdf

concept of establishment which is now an economic and functional concept. However, the resulting dysfunctions created for controllers established in several EU Member States are likely to be diluted if the EC Proposal is approved (both under the original EC Proposal and the Parliament's approved version).

On the other hand, personal data protection has been given a prominent place to provide a (flawed) solution to the impact on personality rights (especially, of the general public) of technology (which surpasses the barriers of time and space) and the dissemination of information through the new media.

Such prominent place is neither absolute nor static, in the same way that the freedom of expression and information are not. We have a long tradition of coexistence of these rights and freedoms and, in addition to the criteria mentioned by the ECJ in this judgment, there are already many criteria in our legal tradition that should guide us when facing new challenges. However, it is true that these criteria were prepared for those who create the contents and those who take the active decision to disseminate them in a certain channel.

We now have an excellent opportunity to think about these two dimensions in the EC Proposal which is likely to be adopted in the near future (perhaps in 2016). In particular, we probably need to reconsider the role to be played by search engines. It is clear that they are part of the problem and should be part of the solution. What needs to be discussed further is whether search engines must assume all the obligations of a 'data controller' regarding content that it does not create (but that it merely indexes) and a balance test that does not work (to date) for sensitive data and requires applying a specific cultural and legal context which is better known by the creators of the contents and original 'broadcasters' (in addition to the data subjects). We definitively need to think again about the kind of justice we need and that which we should expect to benefit from in the digital world.

The contribution of religion to the building of the European Union

KONRAD SCHIEMANN*

The mere heading of this essay will occasion surprise. A historical fallacy has become the received orthodoxy, perhaps particularly in the United Kingdom. It is asserted that the EU was primarily created in order to enable each of us to obtain a larger share of worldly riches. Who now, apart from a minority widely regarded as having a bias towards propagating a religious view of life, reflects on the contribution of religion to the creation and development of the European Union? The main textbooks on European integration hardly touch on the subject. Those wishing to make their way in politics or the academy seem in general to consider silence to be the wisest course.[1]

An examination of the history, laws and constitutions of Member States of the EU reveals the well-known fact that they have been hugely influenced over the past thousand years by moral values with a religious origin. Some, while acknowledging the moral values prevalent in the monotheistic religions and declaring human rights to be inalienable, do not base this inalienability upon any religious concept. Others do. The Polish Constitution[2] is very open about this duality:

---

* Save where otherwise indicated, the translations from French and German are the author's.

1 See however Joseph Weiler, *Unilerweve cristiana,* Rizzoli 2003 and Lorenzo Zucca, *A secular Europe: Law and Religion in the European Constitutional Landscape*. Oxford University Press 2012.

2 www.sejm.gov.pl/prawo/konst/angielski/kon1.htm.

We, the Polish Nation - all citizens of the Republic,

Both those who believe in God as the source of truth, justice, good and beauty,

As well as those not sharing such faith but respecting those universal values as arising from other sources,

...

Recognizing our responsibility before God or our own consciences,

...

I do not propose in these lines - dedicated to one who, apart from being an eminent lawyer, is an elder of the Church of Scotland - to dwell on the historical responsibility of Christianity for values now widely accepted in Europe, but rather to consider briefly something of the Christian motivation behind the creation of the European Community during the last century and to note the gradual move into the background of any acknowledgement of this history as the Community was changed into a Union and as the proportion of the population confessing a religious basis to their lives has declined.

I shall refer, by way of example of the recent religious contribution, to the thinking of the Kreisau Circle in Germany during the Second World War, then to Robert Schuman at the time of the creation of the European Coal and Steel Community, and then to the contribution of recent popes at the time of the collapse of the Soviet Union and the enlargement of the Community to take in the ex-communist states. All of these contributed to the development of the new European polity which is the European Union of today and were motivated by religious considerations. There were of course many others similarly motivated but these examples will suffice to make the point.

After examining those contributions, I end by referring to the gradual abandonment of the approach of the Founding Fathers of Europe and the return to the 19th century, state-centred, concert of Europe approach which, so the founding fathers thought, had to be set aside in order to avoid the horrors of war and dictatorship.

I. The Kreisau Circle

The Kreisau circle, formed in 1942, was led by Helmuth James, Graft von Moltke[3]. It consisted initially of Protestants but was widened to include Roman Catholics and non-religious opponents of Nazism. They discussed among themselves what Germany and Europe should look like after the eventual defeat of Nazism. This activity was discovered and in due course most of them, including Moltke, were hanged or shot by the régime. A few, including Eugen Gerstenmaier, later President of the German Bundestag, survived to play a political role in the construction of Europe after the war.

3 Born 11.3.1907. Hanged 23.1.1945.

The centre of their endeavour was to resist the idea that the totalitarian state was entitled to overrule the individual's duties to God. In a farewell letter to his wife written after his sentence, Moltke writes that the judge who presided over his trial had accurately commented 'Only in one respect are we [sc. the Nazi régime] and Christianity alike: we demand the whole man.'[4]

The flavour of Moltke's thinking can be gleaned from the following documents gathered together after the war:[5]

> I am quite clear what our aim should be: the reawakening in the individual of the feeling that he is bound by values which do not arise out of this world which alone will restore freedom to him. Through this the individual will once more be conscious of his responsibility which in turn will lead to a blossoming of true Community.[6]
>
> The great dangers by which we are threatened on the demise of National-Socialism compel us to envisage how Europe will look after the war. The only prospect of persuading our people finally to overturn this rule of terror is to put before them a picture of what can be brought into being after the fall of the regime. A picture of something to which to aspire, something for which to work, something in which one can believe which a disappointed people will find it worthwhile to embark upon. For us, Europe after the war is not so much a question of borders and soldiers, of complicated organisations or great plans. The question for Europe after the war is the following: How can we restore the picture of a human being in the hearts of our fellow citizens. That is a question of religion, upbringing, obligations to work and family, and the proper relationships between responsibility and rights.[7]

Adam von Trott[8] put the matter thus:

> The establishment of a government which would return to the standards of civilised Europe is only conceivable if it is linked up outside Germany with the final overcoming of German nationalism particularly its military expression . . . The forces in Germany striving for this are inspired by the ideas and the circles of the Christian opposition which has crystallised in years of struggle against national-socialism. Militant Christianism in its widest sense is the only unbroken core of resistance within the Nazi state, and it has now formed powerful contacts with groups hitherto indifferent to church and religion. The key to their common effort is a desperate attempt to rescue the substance of personal human integrity, equally

---

4 Helmuth James von Moltke, *Letters to Freya 1939-1945*. Translation Beate Ruhm von Oppen. Collins Harvill, 1991, p. 409.

5 Brakelmann, G.409ls, *Der Kreisauer Kreis,* LIT Verlag MMrlag , 2004.

6 Ibid. Document 17 memorandum by Moltke.

7 Ibid. Document 22 letter from Moltke to Lionel Curtis 18.4.1942 (My loose translation. I suspect the original was in English but I have not traced it).

8 Another member of the Kreisau circle. Born 9.8.1909. Hanged 26.8.1944.

> threatened by Nazism and anarchic Bolshevism. Restitution of the inalienable right, divine and natural, of the human person forms their basic aim. The political and constitutional reconstruction for which they are working is conceived in terms of a practical application of the Christian European tradition to modern human needs in the social, political, economic, and international sphere.[9]

A joint document prepared by members of the Kreisauer circle in 1942 takes these thoughts forward:

> After the dissolution of the current forms of international order in Europe and now that it has become obvious that Europe is too small for states setting the limits of their own absolute sovereignties the only way that the West can retain its own strength and individuality in the midst of a world of great powers and continental alliances is through *a new European joint political enterprise. But for every political organisation what matters is the spiritual basis upon which it is founded.* A new European enterprise can only come into being as a real basis for joint endeavour by Europeby Europerprise can only come into being as a real basis for joint endeavour by Europe the spiritual basis upon which it is foundes-tates setting the limits oy a Christian one which takes account of the historical reality that Europe was formed under the Cross and only on this basis can it be formed into a cultural unity.
>
> ...
>
> The consequence of this way of looking at things is the construction of a European Union endowed with a single permanent Union government with the necessary powers for the common endeavour. It seems pointless to begin with the old ideas of federation or confederation. Rather one should put before these constitutional organs concrete and specific necessities from which the organs can develop.
>
> ...
>
> It is fundamental that if the European Union is to have in its political leadership the possibility of stability and quick decisions then decisions can not be made dependent upon the decisions of 20-24 national parliaments. Therefore all important decisions and main political directions must be reserved for a new body.[10]

The document makes various proposals reflecting the Christian concerns of its authors as regards the composition and organisation of this body - for instance the inclusion of a Protestant and a Catholic bishop and the taking of religious oaths.

Another document, drafted by a Catholic member of the Circle, Father Delp SJ,[11] came into existence a year later. This stresses the need to reawaken people's consciousness

---

9 Ibid. Document 23 April 1942, Memorandum for the British government. English original.

10 Ibid. Document 30.

11 Born 1907. Hanged 1.2.1945.

of rules laid down by God which are not to be altered by man and from which spring the concept of unalterable human rights. It emphasises the unacceptability of an approach that what is useful for the state constitutes law. It makes the point that the State is not its own purpose but has as its obligation the protection of life in society.[12]

II. Robert Schuman

Schuman, who was France's foreign minister between 1948 and 1953, having spent part of the war in prison for political reasons, was moving in the same direction as the Kreisau Circle. He played a part in the founding of the Council of Europe in 1949 and at that time referred to Europe in these terms:

> The European spirit signifies being conscious of belonging to a cultural family and to have a willingness to serve that *community* in the spirit of total mutuality, without any hidden motives of hegemony or the selfish exploitation of others. The 19th century saw feudal ideas being opposed and, with the rise of a national spirit, nationalities asserting themselves. Our century, that has witnessed the catastrophes resulting in the unending clash of nationalities and nationalisms, must attempt and succeed in *reconciling nations in a supranational association*. This would safeguard the diversities and aspirations of each nation while coordinating them in the same manner as the regions are coordinated within the unity of the nation.

In the next year the European Convention on Human Rights was concluded and Schuman made the famous Schuman declaration which was the basis of the European Coal and Steel Community. What was common to many was a consciousness of the horror of what had been done in the name of Nazism and Communism, of the total wreckage to which Europe had been reduced, and a desire to create something which would help prevent any recurrence. This is clear from the following recital to the ECSC Treaty:

> Convinced that that the contribution which an organised and vital Europe can bring to civilisation is indispensable to the maintenance of peaceful relations;
>
> Conscious of the fact that Europe can be built only by concrete actions creating a real solidarity and by the establishment of common bases for economic development;
>
> Resolved to substitute for historic rivalries a fusion of their essential interests to establish by creating an economic community, the foundation of a broad and independent community among peoples long divided by bloody conflicts;
>
> and to lay the bases of institutions capable of giving direction to their future destiny.

---

12 Ibid. Doc 37, Delp 1943.

While it is noticeable that in the public declarations made or drafted by Schuman when he was foreign minister there is no reference to religion, this is what one would expect: after all, the French Republic is notoriously influenced by the desire to separate Church and State.

It is however well known that Schuman himself was an avowed Christian and impregnated by much the same religious ideas as those which motivated Moltke. This is apparent from his book, *Pour l'Europe,* written after he was out of office. He wrote this:[13]

> Democracy owes its existence to Christianity. It was born on the day that man was called to realise in his temporal life the dignity of the human person, in his individual liberty, in the respect of each person person as those which motivated , this is what one would expect: after all, the French Republic is notoriously influenced by the desire Christianity both doctrinally and chronologically. It took flesh with Christianity in stages, via tentative steps sometimes taking erroneous ones and relapsing into barbarism.
>
> Christianity taught the natural equality of men: children of the same God, redeemed by the same Christ, without distinction of race, colour, class or profession. It bestowed dignity on work and the obligation on all to work. It recognised the primacy of interior values which alone ennoble man. The universal law of love has made every man our neighbour and in consequence in the Christian world all rests on this foundation. This teaching and its practical consequences have turned the world upside down.
>
> ...
>
> One must distinguish between the domain of Caesar and the domain of God. Each of these powers has its own responsibilities. The church must guard the natural law and revealed truths. ... The task of the politician is to reconcile, in a sometimes tricky synthesis, spiritual and profane considerations.
>
> Theocracy rejects the principle of the separation of these two domains. It imposes upon the idea of religion responsibilities which do not belong there. Under such a regime political differences are in danger of escalating to religious fanaticism.
>
> From the start, Christ was opposed to fanaticism; he agreed to be its most august victim. His kingdom is not of this world. This implies that Christian civilisation ought not to be the product of violent revolution with immediate results but of a progressive transformation resulting from the great principles of love, sacrifice and humility which are at the basis of the new society.

It was in this era that Robert Schuman, Konrad Adenauer, the German Chancellor, and Alcide de Gaspari, the Italian prime minister, all practicing Christians, had major input

13 R.Schuman (2005) *Pour l'Europe, Ecrits politiques,* quatrième edition, Paris: Editions Nagel Briquet, pp. 56-66.

into the foundation of the Community. It is this which led Vincent Auriol[14] to refer disparagingly to the Church having created 'the triple alliance Adenauer-Schuman-Gasperi, three tonsures under the same skull cap.'[15]

Pierre Pflimlin, sometime prime minister of France and president of the European Parliament summed the matter up as follows:

> Although the approach of Schuman was essentially realistic he nevertheless thought that the Christian spirit, in which non-believers can share, allowed people to pass beyond nationalism in order to submit themselves to a law of a noble but humble fraternity. This was the meeting point between Schuman from Lorraine and Adenauer from the other side of the Rhine, who were both convinced that the demons of the French and the Germans could be overcome by spiritual values which alone could ennoble man.[16]

III. The papal contribution

Schuman's thesis that Christian civilisation ought not to be the product of violent revolution with immediate results but of a progressive transformation resulting from the great principles of love, sacrifice, and humility, which are at the basis of the new society, is one which was put into practice in the years preceding the fall of Communism.

Pope John Paul II began the process by which communist rule collapsed in Poland, Czechoslovakia, Germany, Hungary and everywhere else in the Soviet bloc. He encouraged the creators of the free Polish Trade Union Solidarnosc which, in part the result of the guidance of Jósef Tischner[17] its first chaplain and a close friend of Pope John-Paul II, achieved its ends without major violence. Tischner taught that:

> A revolution, that is, an event in the spiritual sphere, is authentic to the degree that it is bloodless. The spirit rules through persuasion and not through fear. This is why a truly
>
> great revolution is, at the same time, a holiday of the liberation of a human being from
>
> the fear of other human beings.[18]

In his address to the European Parliament in October 1988, before the fall of the Berlin Wall, the Polish Pope John-Paul II expressed the hope that 'Europe, endowed with

---

14 President of France, 1947-1954.

15 Vincent Auriol, *Mon septennat,* ed. Gallimard, 1970, cited in René Lejeune, *Robert Schuman: Une âme pour l'Europe,* Editions Saint-Paul (1986). p. 207.

16 René Lejeune, *Robert Schuman: Une âme pour l'Europe,* Editions Saint-Paul (1986), p. 201.

17 1931-2000.

18 J931- Tischner, *The Spirit of Solidarity,* Harper & Row, 1984, at p. 51. Translated from the Polish.

sovereign and free institutions, will one day reach the full dimensions that geography, and even more, history have given it.[19]

The example of Solidarnosc and the Pope's firmness in the face of Communism coupled with his devotion to peaceful means of reforming the communist states contributed to the demise of the Soviet Union and the subsequent adhesion of many ex-communist states to the European Union. It is clear that the enlarged Union is in considerable part the result of his peaceful persuasion.

John Paul II's successor, the German Pope Benedict XVI, in an address to the German parliament in 2011, echoed themes explored by the Kreisau circle. He said:

> At this point Europe's cultural heritage ought to come to our assistance. The conviction that there is a Creator God is what gave rise to the idea of human rights, the idea of the equality of all people before the law, the recognition of the inviolability of human dignity in every single person and the awareness of people's responsibility for their actions. Our cultural memory is shaped by these rational insights. To ignore it or dismiss it as a thing of the past would be to dismember our culture totally and to rob it of its completeness. The culture of Europe arose from the encounter between Jerusalem, Athens and Rome ople before the law, the recognitio's monotheism, the philosophical reason of the Greeks and Roman law. This three-way encounter has shaped the inner identity of Europe. In the awareness of man's responsibility before God and in the acknowledgment of the inviolable dignity of every single human person, it has established criteria of law: it is these criteria that we are called to defend at this moment in our history.

Recently, the Argentinian Pope Francis, in his address to the European Parliament in November 2014, gave

> a message of encouragement to return to the firm conviction of the founders of the European Union, who envisioned a future based on the capacity to work together in bridging divisions and in fostering peace and fellowship between all the peoples of this continent. At the heart of this ambitious political project was confidence in man, not so much as a citizen or an economic agent, but in man, in men and women as persons endowed with transcendent dignity.
>
> I feel bound to stress the close bond between these two words: 'dignity' and 'transcendent'. 'Dignity' was a pivotal concept in the process of rebuilding which followed the Second World War. Our recent past has been marked by the concern to protect human dignity, in contrast to the manifold instances of violence and discrimination which, even in Europe, took place in the course of the centuries. Recognition of the importance of human rights came about as the result of a lengthy process, entailing much suffering and sacrifice, which helped shape an awareness of the unique worth of each individual human person. This awareness was grounded not only in historical events, but above all in European thought,

19 John Paul II, *Address to the European Parliament* (11 October 1988), 5.

> characterised as it is by an enriching encounter whose 'distant springs are many, coming from Greece and Rome, from Celtic, Germanic and Slavic sources, and from Christianity which profoundly shaped them',[20] thus forging the very concept of the 'person'.
>
> Today, the promotion of human rights is central to the commitment of the European Union to advance the dignity of the person, both within the Union and in its relations with other countries.
>
> ...
>
> Promoting the dignity of the person means recognising that he or she possesses inalienable rights which no one may take away arbitrarily, much less for the sake of economic interests.
>
> ...
>
> A Europe which is no longer open to the transcendent dimension of life is a Europe which risks slowly losing its own soul and that 'humanistic spirit' which it still loves and defends.
>
> Taking as a starting point this opening to the transcendent, I would like to reaffirm the centrality of the human person, which otherwise is at the mercy of the whims and the powers of the moment. I consider to be fundamental not only the legacy that Christianity has offered in the past to the social and cultural formation of the continent, but above all the contribution which it desires to offer today, and in the future, to Europe's growth.

IV. The absence of religious references in the Treaties and the Charter

As was evident in the discussions concerning the proposed European Constitution, there is a strong current of opinion which does not accept a reference to religious premises in such a document. In consequence, the Preamble to the Treaty on European Union contents itself with:

> Drawing inspiration from the cultural, religious, and humanist inheritance of Europe, from which have developed the universal values of the inviolable and inalienable rights of the human person, freedom, democracy, equality and the rule of law.

The Preamble to the Charter of Fundamental Rights of the European Union, cautiously omits any reference to religion and states:

20 John Paul II, *Address to the European Parliament* (11 October 1988), 5.

> Conscious of its spiritual and moral heritage, the Union is founded on the indivisible, universal values of human dignity, freedom, equality and solidarity; it is based on the principles of democracy and the rule of law. It places the individual at the heart of its activities by establishing the citizenship of the Union and the creating of an area of freedom, security and justice.

Weiler and Zucca, in their books cited at note 2 above, adopt somewhat differing views as to the desirability of the omission in these documents of an express reference to Christianity. Weiler, a Jew, considers that the deliberate omission to cite the Christian contribution to the values esteemed in Europe is a perverse sign of what he terms Christophobia. Zucca argues[21] that religion is not the prime problem of the secular state. Religion, in his view, is there to remind the state that it constantly needs to articulate its normative premises. The secular state itself is in search of a better foundation which he terms secular law. He concludes[22] that secular law is the tool which deals with the conflicts between people and ideas. Conflicts between religious and non-religious people cannot be solved, avoided or defined away. Secular law pursues the overarching goal of social peace, which is not posited from outside as an ideal goal, but is instead intrinsic to the very formation of communities: secular law aims at a unitary framework which is not transcendent, but immanent. The framework provided by secular law, he argues, is a default arrangement within which diversity thrives. Religion has to be fitted within this framework and not outside of it.

Various human rights are frequently declared in Member States to be inalienable. By virtue of what principle they are considered to be inalienable is often left unstated - no doubt because different people arrive at the same conclusion by different paths. In contradistinction to earlier centuries, an overtly religious outlook on life is not currently manifestly shared by the European populace at large. There is a tendency in religious writings to suggest that if the theocentric basis of the concept of inviolable human rights is discarded then in due course the same fate will overtake the concept itself. This may be right; we do not know. Zucca's position is that it is perfectly possible for some people to adopt a religious basis for human rights, and equally possible for other people to adopt other bases, and that the function of a constitution is to allow freedom to both religious people and to humanists to argue for the implantation of their values for the reasons which they can articulate.

---

21 Zucca, *op.cit.* p. 39.

22 Ibid. chapters 9 and 10.

V. From community to Union

Frans Alting von Geusau[23] well describes the original assumptions and objectives behind the creation of the European Coal and Steel Community.

- Real solidarity within the limited scope of heavy industry and organised by common institutions under common rules was assumed to generate a threefold dynamics of unification:
- It would *widen* the scope of real solidarity to economic policies at large (and eventually defence and foreign affairs);
- it would *deepen* solidarity through the transfer of real legislative, executive and judicial powers to common institutions;
- it would *enlarge* membership of the Community as other European States wanted to join.

Alongside the abandonment of the religious approach of the founding fathers by the European Union, and some would say because of this, there has been another development. The Union - much influenced by General de Gaulle and successive British governments - has moved away from the idea of a true Community for whose common good measures should be taken by Community authorities. Instead there has been a move towards a Union of States headed by a European Council consisting largely of heads of government, each pursuing at best what they see as their national interest, at worst pursuing some narrower interest.[24] That European Council is charged with providing the Union with the necessary impetus for its development and defining the general political directions and priorities thereof[25] and is not subject to judicial oversight. By contrast, the early emphasis of the founders of the European Community was on the creation of a true community with its own institutions, including a court of justice, acting for the common good of a community. This movement away from the political convictions of the founding fathers is well traced by von Geusau in his book cited at note 23.

He regrets it. So do I.

---

23 Von Geusau, *European Unification into the Twenty First Century,* second edition (2012), Wolf Legal Publishers, p. 140.

24 This development is well traced by von Geusau in the book cited in the previous note.

25 TEU Article 15.

Israel's occupation of Palestine and the EU reaction: towards a common European policy

MICHEL WAELBROECK

I. Background

On 29 November 1948 the General Assembly of the United Nations adopted Resolution 181 on 'The Future Government of Palestine'. The resolution took note of the intention of the government of the United Kingdom to put an end to the mandate it had exercised over Palestine since 1922 in accordance with Article 22 of the League of Nations Covenant. It further provided that the territory of Palestine would be partitioned into two units, one of which (comprising roughly 55 % of the total) would be allotted to a future independent Jewish State whereas the remainder (composed basically of two units: the West Bank and the Gaza Strip) would constitute an independent Arab State. Both States were to come into existence no later than 1st October 1948. The City of Jerusalem would be subject to a special international regime and an economic union would be established between the units.

Subsequent events rendered that plan moot: it was rejected by the Arab nations; fighting broke out between Palestinian forces and Israeli militias; atrocities were committed on both parts. When the UK pulled out in mid-May, Israel unilaterally proclaimed independence. It was attacked the following day by the armies of Egypt, Saudi Arabia, Syria, Lebanon, Iraq and Transjordan. When hostilities ended in March 1949 the territory controlled by Israel was considerably larger than planned under the UN 1947 resolution. The part initially allotted to the Palestinian State was occupied by Jordan[1], thus preventing Palestine from coming to existence.

The situation remained unchanged until the Six Day War[2] of 5 to 10 June 1967 when Israel succeeded in driving Jordan[3] out of and occupied the West Bank, the Gaza Strip and East Jerusalem[4]. The Palestinian State foreseen in 1947 remained in limbo.

Twenty years after the Yom Kippur war of October 1973, during which the Arab States made an ultimate attempt to annihilate Israel, the so-called Oslo process finally set the stage for a peaceful settlement. A Declaration of Principles on interim self-government arrangements (Oslo I) was signed on 13 September 1993 in which the leader of the Palestinian Liberation Organization Yasser Arafat formally recognized the right of Israel to exist. Two years later, the Oslo II agreement[5] set up a process providing for the end of the occupation and the birth of a Palestinian State as the result of a negotiated process to be completed before the end of 1999. A Palestinian Council would be established. The West Bank would be divided into three areas: A, B and C. The Palestinian Council would enjoy limited autonomy over areas A and B (composed mainly of cities); Israel would continue to exercise military and civil control over area C during eighteen months from the inauguration of the Council. All three areas remained subject to Israeli occupation: Israel retained the right unilaterally to conduct military incursions in Areas A and B for security reasons.

After the assassination of President Yitzhak Rabin on 4 November 1995 by an Israeli extremist and the victory of Benjamin Netanyahu's 'anti-Oslo' Likud party at the elections on 22 May 1996, the Oslo process gradually unravelled. Several attempts to re-launch it were made under US Presidents Clinton, George W. Bush and Obama. All failed. Palestine remains occupied to this day.

---

1 And, as regards the Gaza Strip, by Egypt.

2 5 – 10 June 1967.

3 And, as regards the Gaza Strip, Egypt.

4 Although the Sinai Peninsula was also occupied by Israel as a result of the Six Day War, it was returned to Egypt in September of 1978 as a result of the US-brokered Camp David Agreement between the Egyptian president Anwar Es Sadat and the Israeli prime minister, Menachem Begin. Israel did not give up control over the Gaza Strip.

5 Interim Agreement on the West Bank and the Gaza Strip, signed on 24 September 1995.

II. Applicable legal principles

The international community has developed an extensive set of rules designed to protect civilian populations in occupied territories. Foremost among these are the so-called 'Hague Regulations'[6] and the 'Fourth Geneva Convention'.[7]

Whereas Israel does not dispute that the provisions of the Hague Regulations have become part of international customary law and are therefore binding upon it, it denies the applicability of the Fourth Geneva Convention to the occupied Palestinian territory, citing 'the lack of recognition of the territory as sovereign prior to its annexation by Jordan and Egypt' and inferring that it is 'not a territory of a High Contracting Party as required by Article 2(2) the Convention.' [8]

This argument is specious. It was rejected by the International Court of Justice in the Wall Opinion.[9] After pointing out that the Fourth Convention had been ratified by Israel as well as by Egypt and Jordan, the Court noted that, according its Article 2(1), the Convention is applicable whenever there exists an armed conflict between two of the contracting parties. Any territory occupied in the course of such a conflict is 'occupied' within the meaning of the Convention. The object of Article 2(2), on which the Israeli government relied, is not to restrict the scope of the Convention but to make clear that, even if the occupation meets with no armed resistance, the Convention is applicable.[10]

For its part, the UN Security Council has stated on numerous occasions that the Fourth Geneva Convention applies to Israel's occupation of the occupied Palestinian territory (OPT).[11]

The relevance of the Wall Opinion is sometimes called into question on the ground that it is 'advisory' and therefore not legally binding. Those who maintain that view lose sight of the fact that an advisory opinion of the International Court of Justice constitutes an authoritative statement of the law by the UN's principal legal organ. Moreover, the Wall Opinion was adopted by a majority of 14 out of 15 judges; on the core issue of illegality of settlements the Court's opinion was unanimous; it was

---

6 Regulations Respecting the Laws and Customs of War on Land, annexed to the Fourth Convention Respecting the Laws of War on Land signed in The Hague on 18 October 1907.

7 Fourth Convention Relative to the Protection of Civilian Persons in Time of War signed in Geneva on 12 August 1949.

8 Text of Article 2(2) : 'The Convention shall also apply to all cases of partial or total occupation of the territory of a High Contracting Party, even if the said occupation meets with no armed resistance'.

9 Advisory Opinion of 9 July 2004 on the Legal Consequences of the Construction of a Wall in the Occupied Palestinian Territory ('Wall Opinion'), ICJ Reports, 2004, p. 136, spec. §§ 89-101.

10 *Wall Opinion*, para. 95.

11 UNSC Resolutions 237 (1967) ; 446 (1979, 681 (1990), 799 (1992) and 904 (1994).

approved by the UN General Assembly[12] by a majority of 150 States, with only six negative votes[13] and 10 abstentions. It is therefore fully justified to consider that it reflects the current state of international law.

III. Israel's violations of its obligations as an occupying power

1. The continued occupation of the OPT

Occupation does not vest the occupying power with sovereignty over the occupied territory. The occupant is entrusted with the management of public order and civil life in the territory under control. It must exercise its powers in the interest of the inhabitants of that territory. [14]

It follows that occupation is necessarily a temporary occurrence. Were it otherwise, the distinction between occupation – in which the occupant acquires only limited prerogatives – and annexation – in which the annexing State acquires full sovereignty over the annexed territory – would disappear.

It is apparent from the actions taken by Israel since 1967 that Israel no longer considers the occupation of Palestine as temporary. Indeed, an increasing number of voices within the Israeli governmental polity advocate the outright annexation of the West Bank. Israel's actions over the years, including the construction of settlements protected by a separation barrier and connected to Israel by reserved roads, the appropriation of Palestinian land, of natural resources (including water), the destruction of Palestinian villages and the application of Israeli legislation to Palestinians and their territory, indicate that Israel considers the occupation as being of a lasting nature. With respect to East Jerusalem and the Golan Heights, Israel has already crossed the line and officially annexed these areas.

Several UN Security Council resolutions have called upon Israel to evacuate the OPT. The most famous is Resolution 242 of 22 November 1967 which called for the 'withdrawal of Israel armed forces from territories occupied in the recent conflict'.[15] Israel's argument that the resolution did not require the withdrawal from *all* occupied territories but only from some of them, to be determined by negotiation between the parties within the context of a global peace agreement, cannot be accepted. The equally authentic French version of the resolution states expressly that Israel must withdraw

---

12 UNGA Resolution ES 10/15 of 20 July 2004.

13 Israel, the United States, Canada and 3 Pacific Island States.

14 Article 43 of the Hague Regulations : 'The authority of the legitimate power having in fact passed into the hands of the occupant, the latter shall take all measures in his power to restore and ensure, as far as possible, public order and safety, while respecting, unless absolutely prevented, the laws in force in the country.'

15 Further resolutions calling for the end of the Israeli occupation of the OPT were adopted by the Security Council on 22 October 1973 (resolution 338) and 30 January 1980 (resolution 476).

'*des territoires occupés*'. This clearly indicates that *all* the territories concerned should be evacuated.

It can therefore be concluded that Israel's continued occupation, for more than 48 years, of the OPT constitutes in itself a breach of international law.

2. The occupant's obligation to exercise its powers for the benefit of the occupied area

According to Article 43 of the Hague Regulations, as generally interpreted - and notably by the Israeli Supreme Court - an occupying State has the duty to exercise its powers under all circumstances for the benefit of the occupied area and to refrain from taking into consideration its national economic and social interests inasmuch as these interests have no effect on its security or the interest of the local population.[16]

Israel's conduct has been the exact opposite of this. Since the very beginning of the occupation it has introduced a wide variety of policies and measures that, taken together, thwart the socio-economic and industrial development of the OPT. By a combination of incentives in favour of its own nationals and restrictions on Palestinian firms and individuals, it has created an uneven playing field in which Palestinians are systematically maintained in a subordinate role, unable to compete on an even footing with their Israeli counterparts. This has been documented in numerous reports of international governmental and non-governmental agencies, including the World Bank, the UN Human Rights Council and the EU Heads of Mission in Jerusalem.[17]

The construction of a separation barrier going deep into Palestinian territory has led to the establishment of a closed area between the barrier and the 1967 border, cutting off the population living in that area from the remainder of Palestine, imposing substantial restrictions on their freedom of movement and leading to increasing difficulties regarding access to health services, educational establishments and primary sources of water.[18]

3. Israel has brought changes to existing legislation in violation of international law

Article 43 of the Hague Regulations obliges the occupying power to respect, unless absolutely prevented, the laws in force in the country.

This obligation has been deliberately ignored by Israel. Israel has introduced planning legislation requiring Palestinians in Area C to obtain the prior authorization of the occupation authorities for any new construction. Less than one percent of Area C,

---

16 HCJ 393/82, *Jamit Askaan v. The Commander of the IDF Forces in the Area*; HCJ 2056/04, *The Beit Surik Village Council v. The Government of Israel* cited *supra*, fn. 14.

17 The World Bank's 2013 Report is particularly instructive in this connection. See: 'West Bank and Gaza – Area C and the Future of the Palestinian Economy', Document of the World Bank, October 2, 2013 (cited hereafter 'World Bank 2013 Report').

18 Wall Opinion, para. 133.

which is already built up, is designated for Palestinian use; 68% is reserved for Israeli settlements, 21% for closed military zones and 9% for nature reserves.[19] Needless to say, under such circumstances building permits are only exceptionally delivered to Palestinians.

Nor can it be argued that under the Oslo II agreement Israel was given control over planning and zoning in Area C.[20] The relevant provisions of the Oslo II agreement[21] provided that the 'powers and responsibilities' in planning and zoning (except for the issues to be discussed in the final status negotiations[22]) would be transferred to Palestinian jurisdiction within eighteen months of the inauguration of the Palestinian Council, i.e., before 7 September 1997. Israel's control was therefore of a strictly residual nature. Moreover, under Article 47 of the Fourth Geneva Convention, Palestinians may not be deprived of the benefit of the Convention by any agreement concluded between the authorities of the occupied territories and the occupying power. Thus the restrictions on construction introduced by Israel may not validly deprive Palestinians of rights they enjoyed under the previous regime.

4. Israel's settlement policy

Article 49(6) of the Fourth Geneva Convention states that:

'The Occupying Power shall not deport or transfer parts of its own civilian population into the territory it occupies.'

Since 1968 the Israeli government has engaged in a policy of settlement building in and around Jerusalem and throughout Area C. The settlements are connected with each other and with the territory of Israel by a network of roads specially reserved to the inhabitants of Israel and to settlers. The settlements themselves are protected by the Israeli military. Settlers benefit from tax and social advantages. They have preferential access to water resources. Although the built-in settlement areas only covered 3.25% of the West Bank in 2010, the territory they actually control far exceeds this, and according to Israeli sources amounts to fully 68% of Area C. Israeli Ministry of Defence reports stated in 2012 that an additional 10% of Area C had been earmarked for settlement expansion.[23] By their sheer number and location the settlements put in danger the survival of the Palestinian State.

---

19 World Bank 2013 Report, para. 9.

20 Article XI.2.2 and 3.

21 Article XI, paragraph 2, sub-paragraph 5 of the Oslo II agreement and Article 27 of Appendix 1 to Article IV of Annex III (Protocol Concerning Civil Affairs) to the Oslo II agreement.

22 These were: Jerusalem, settlements, specified military locations, Palestinian refugees, borders, foreign relations and Israelis: see Art. XVII, para. 1, sub-para. 1 of the Oslo II agreement.

23 World Bank 2013 Report, para. 10.

Israel's settlement policy constitutes a clear violation of the Fourth Geneva Convention. It has been condemned practically universally. In its *Wall Opinion* the ICJ unanimously[24] condemned it, noting that the Fourth Hague Convention 'prohibits not only deportations and forced transfers of population such as those carried out during the Second World War, but also any measures taken by an occupying power to organize or encourage transfers of parts of its own population into the occupied territory'.

The argument is sometimes made on the Israeli side that Article 49 was drafted after the Second World War during which millions of people were deported, displaced and massacred, and that it does not apply to voluntary transfers.[25] There is nothing in the text of the Convention to support such a narrow construction. As the words 'deport or transfer' make clear, the prohibition was meant to apply whether the movement of persons is voluntary or forcible. The mere fact of transferring on occupying State's population into occupied territory is likely to entrench the occupation and worsen the economic situation of the local population, endangering its long-term existence as a nation.

Settlements in East Jerusalem are also illegal. Indeed East Jerusalem's unilateral annexation by Israel was never internationally recognized.[26]

5. The Wall

In April 2002 the Israeli government decided to build a security fence or wall ('the Wall') with the stated purpose of preventing infiltration of Palestinian terrorists into the territory of Israel. The Wall does not follow the 1967 border; it is built on Palestinian territory and frequently deviates from that border, sometimes by several kilometres, in such a way that it encompasses several settlements while encircling Palestinian areas.[27] The effect of these deviations is to cut off 16,6 % of the territory of the West Bank to include it in a 'Closed Area' where Palestinian residents may no longer stay unless they hold an identity card or a permit issued by the Israeli authorities. Access to and exit from the Closed Area by Palestinians residing outside can only be effected

---

24 It is worthy of note that even the American judge, who was the only member of the Court to dissent from the main findings of the opinion, agreed that the Fourth Geneva Convention and international human rights law were applicable to the OPT (see para. 2 of the Declaration of Judge Buergenthal) and that the settlements violate Article 49(6) of the Fourth Geneva Convention (see para. 9 of the Declaration).

25 See inter alia: Rachel Avraham, 'Why Israel Is Not Violating the Fourth Geneva Convention', http://unitedwithisrael.org/why-israel-is-not-violating-fourth-geneva-convention/.

26 UN Security Council resolutions 252 of 21 May 1968 and 298 of 25 September 1971 decree that Israel's attempts to change the status of the Holy City are 'invalid' and 'cannot affect that status'. Resolution 298 of 25 September 1971 added that the legislative and administrative actions taken by Israel aiming at the incorporation of the occupied section of Jerusalem are 'totally invalid' and urged Israel to rescind all previous measures and to take no further steps in attempting to change the status of the city.

In defiance of this resolution, on 30 July 1980 the Knesset enacted a 'basic law' formally annexing East Jerusalem. The Security Council's reaction was quick : on 20 August 1980 it adopted resolution 478 affirming that the enactment of the basic law 'does not affect the continued application' of the Fourth Geneva Convention in the occupied Arab territories 'including Jerusalem' ; the law was 'null and void' and had to be rescinded forthwith. It also called upon third States to withdraw their diplomatic missions from the Holy City.

27 This is notable in the area around the Palestinian city of Qalqiliya.

through special gates which are few in number and whose opening hours are few and unpredictably applied.

In the *Wall Opinion*, the ICJ held that construction of the Wall on Palestinian territory was contrary to international law. Indeed, it impedes the exercise by the Palestinian people of its right to self-determination, it creates a '*fait accompli*' on the ground that could become permanent, its route consolidates Israel's illegal settlements, and its construction led to the destruction or requisition of properties under conditions that contravene Articles 46 and 52 of the 1907 Hague Regulations and Article 53 of the Fourth Geneva Convention. The Court further noted that the Wall imposes substantial restrictions on the freedom of movement of Palestinians inhabiting the West Bank and entails serious repercussions for agricultural production, access to health services, educational establishments and sources of water by Palestinian residents of the Closed Area.[28]

The Court called upon Israel to cease building the Wall, to dismantle those parts that had been built and to make reparation for the damage caused. It also called upon all States not to recognize the illegal situation resulting from construction of the Wall and not to render aid or assistance in maintaining the situation created thereby, adding that all States parties to the Fourth Geneva Convention had the obligation to ensure compliance by Israel with international humanitarian law as embodied by that convention.

Israel has not taken a single step to comply with these demands.

6. Destruction of real and personal property

Article 53 of the Fourth Geneva Convention states:

'Any destruction by the Occupying Power of real or personal property belonging individually or collectively to private persons, or to the State, or to other public authorities, or to social or cooperative organizations, is prohibited, except where such destruction is rendered absolutely necessary by military operations.'

In the course of its occupation, Israel has destroyed and continues to destroy property belonging to Palestinians without military justification.

One reason is punishment: it is common for the IDF, when arresting Palestinians accused of engaging in violent action against the occupation, to destroy the house in which they lived, thus depriving not only them but also their families, of a home. In such cases, the destruction contravenes not only Article 53 but also Article 33(1) of the Fourth Geneva Convention.[29]

Another frequently invoked motive is the absence of the required construction permit from the Israeli Civil Administration. However it is well-known that this administration

---

28 Wall Opinion, paras. 117-122 and 132-137.

29 Article 33(1) of the Fourth Geneva Convention: 'No protected person may be punished for an offense he or she has not personally committed'.

hardly ever delivers permits to Palestinians living in Area C.[30] This contrasts with its attitude regarding illegal outposts established by Israeli nationals, which seldom give rise to repressive measures.

Other motives for demolition orders are the needs of the construction of the Wall, the intention to establish a natural or archaeological site, the desire to reserve space for the possible extension of a nearby Israeli settlement, plans to create a firing range for use by the army, etc. All these actions are violations of Article 53 of the Fourth Geneva Convention, since they cannot be justified as being 'rendered absolutely necessary by military operations'.

7. Confiscation of private property

Article 46(2) of the Hague Regulations states:

'Private property cannot be confiscated'.

Since the 1967 war, Israel has seized over a million dunums[31] of Palestinian land through seizure for military needs, application of absentee property laws and declarations of State land. Seized land is placed within the jurisdictional boundaries of local and regional settlement councils and is used not only for urbanization but also as a buffer zone surrounding settlements or turned into recreational and nature areas which cannot be accessed by Palestinians. [32]

In practice it is virtually impossible for Palestinians to obtain construction permits.[33] Palestinians who, for want of alternative, build homes without permits on nearby land owned by them, live under the constant threat of demolition. Moreover the shortage of space for construction has resulted in a steep rise in the price of land.

Here too Israel acts in disregard of its international obligations.

8. Exploitation/destruction of natural resources (including water)

Article 55 of the 1907 of the Hague Regulations provides that an occupying State shall be regarded as an 'administrator or usufructuary' of the property situated in the occupied country. According to generally recognized principles of civil law, an usufructuary has the right to use and enjoy the fruits of another's property for a period without damaging or diminishing its substance. In the case of non-renewable resources such as mines and quarries, there is authority for the view that an occupying power may, as usufruc-

---

30 The Civil administration does not prepare master plans for Area C communities and uses this failure as justification for prohibiting the construction of virtually all Area C construction. See World Bank 2013 Report, paras. 35-39. See also *supra:* '(b)Israel deliberately ignores its basic obligation to exercise its powers for the benefit of the occupied area'.

31 One dunum = 1000 m2.

32 Report of the UN Human Rights Council's Independent Fact Finding Commission to Investigate the Implications of the Israeli Settlements on the Rights of the Palestinian People, paras. 63-64.

33 W*orld Bank 2013 Report, paras. 9 and 34-36.*

tuary, continue exploitation of existing sites but may not create new sites or extend existing ones.

Moreover Article 43 of the Hague Regulations has generally been interpreted, including by the Israeli Supreme Court,[34] as obliging the occupying State to exercise its powers for the benefit of the occupied area. It follows that the occupying power must use the proceeds of its usufruct exclusively to satisfy the needs of the local population.

The principle of permanent sovereignty of peoples and nations over their natural resources[35] is one of the main pillars of contemporary international law. Like other peoples and nations, Palestinians are entitled to have it respected. This was recognized by the UN General Assembly resolution of 29 March 2012 on the permanent sovereignty of the Palestinian people over their natural resources'.[36]

Israeli actions have repeatedly violated the above rules. by up-rooting fruit-bearing trees, destroying farms, greenhouses and vital infrastructure such as water pipelines and sewage networks, diverting water resources for the benefit of its settlements, denying permits for Palestinians to dig wells and build water conveyance and wastewater treatment infrastructure, etc. It has been calculated that in 2007 the Palestinian population had access to only about one quarter of the ration of their Israeli counterparts.[37] An Israeli company[38] has been granted the right to extract valuable mineral deposits from the Dead Sea, others have been allowed to operate stone quarries in the West Bank (although no new permits have been issued to Palestinian firms since 1994) .[39]

9. Condoning settler violence

Article 43 of the Hague Regulations obliges an occupying power 'to take all the measures in his power to restore, and ensure as far as possible, public order and safety'.

Israeli settlers regularly engage in violence and intimidation with the aim of forcing Palestinians off their land. The occupation authorities seldom intervene to put an end to these actions. Even though the identities of the perpetrators are well-known and they could easily be identified, few have been prosecuted.[40]

---

34 See *Jamit Askaan* case cited above, note 16.

35 Resolution 1803 (XVII) of 14 December 1962.

36 The resolution was adopted by a majority of 167 affirmative votes, 6 abstentions and 7 votes against: the United States, Canada, Israel, and 4 Pacific Island States.

37 World Bank 2013 Report, para. 18.

38 Ahava Dead Sea Laboratories.

39 World Bank 2013 Report, para. 30. In a case where the authorities' decision was challenged by a Palestinian association, the Supreme Court rejected the complaint on the dubious ground that the occupation of Palestine was 'unique' in that it had lasted for such a long time that this required 'an adjustment of the law to the reality on the ground' – thus justifying Israel's failure to comply with international law by its own breach of that law. The Court also noted with approval that the royalties paid for the operation of the quarries were used to finance the operations of the Israeli military (sic!) administration (*Yesh Din v. The Commander of the IDF Forces in the West Bank and 11 others*, December 2011).

40 Report of the UN Independent Fact-Finding Commission (cited *supra,* fn. 32, paras. 50, 56).

10. Appropriation of cultural property

According to Article 5(1) of the Hague Convention for the Protection of Cultural Property in the Event of Armed Conflict of 14 May 1954:

Any Contracting Party in occupation of the whole or part of the territory of another High Contracting Party shall as far as possible support the competent national authorities of the occupied country in safeguarding and preserving its cultural property.

Both Israel and Palestine are parties to that convention. As a result, Israel as an occupying power is not entitled to conduct archaeological excavations in Palestine without the collaboration of the Palestinian authorities and to appropriate the results of these excavations and exhibit them in its own museums as it does today.

11. Administrative detention

In order to discharge its responsibility under Article 43 of the Hague Regulations to maintain public order and safety, an occupying power may adopt various measures, of which internment is the most severe.[41] Internment may be imposed only if the security of the detaining power makes it 'absolutely necessary'.[42] Anyone who is arrested must be informed, at the time of arrest, of the reasons therefor and the charges against him.[43] Any internment decision must be reviewed periodically and at least twice a year.[44] A right of appeal must be provided for. Any appeal must be decided with the least possible delay. If the decision is upheld, it must be subject to periodic review, if possible every six months.[45]

In practice, Israel routinely uses administrative detention. This by itself constitutes a violation of Article 78(1) of the Fourth Geneva Convention which makes it clear that detention constitutes a last remedy, to be resorted to only if required for imperative reasons of security if less extreme methods fail. Moreover, arrests are often based on secret information to which neither the detainee nor his lawyer have access, thus violating the detainee's right of due process. There is no limit on the maximum detention period.

---

41 Article 41 of the Fourth Geneva Convention: 'Should the Power in whose hands the protected person may be consider the measures of control mentioned in this Convention to be inadequate, it may not have resort to any measure of control more severe than that of assigned residence or internment, in accordance with the provisions of Articles 42 and 43.'

Article 78(1) of the Fourth Geneva Convention: 'If the Occupying Power considers it necessary, for imperative reasons of security, to take safety measures concerning protected persons, it may, at the most, subject them to assigned residence or to internment'.

42 Article 42 of the Fourth Geneva Convention.

43 Article 9(2) of the International Covenant on Civil and Political Rights of 19 December 1966. Israel ratified the Covenant. In the *Wall Opinion* the ICJ opined that the protection offered by the Covenant does not cease in case of armed conflict and that it extends wherever the State exercises its jurisdiction, even if that is in foreign territory (*Wall Opinion*, paras. 106 and 109).

44 Article 43 of the Fourth Geneva Convention.

45 Article 78(2) of the Fourth Geneva Convention.

Moreover Article 76 of the Fourth Geneva Convention states that 'protected persons accused of offences shall be detained in the occupied country, and if convicted they shall serve their sentences therein.'

Since the very beginning of the occupation, Israel has infringed this provision. Indeed *all but one* of the localities in which Palestinians are detained are situated inside its borders and not within the OPT.

12. The Gaza closure

After the take-over of the Palestinian government in Gaza by Hamas in June 2007, Israel closed off the border crossings between its territory and the Gaza Strip. The great difficulties arising from this closure for the local population and the reactions of the international community caused Israel to alleviate these restrictions slightly so as to allow the import of limited quantities of essential goods including medical products, fuel and food. Israel strictly limits the import of cement and construction materials on the pretext that these could be used for military purposes. It also makes limited supplies of electricity. However these are notoriously insufficient. The lack of sufficient fuel to sustain electricity production prevents water and sewage facilities from operating normally.

Israel uses its control over Gaza's borders as a means of reprisal against rocket attacks from jihadist forces based in Gaza. It closes the crossings following each such incident and punishes the entire Gaza population for acts committed by a few.

This closure causes undue delay to the reconstruction of the Strip after the recent 'Protective Edge' operation.[46]

The fact that Egypt has also closed its border crossing with the Gaza Strip in no way diminishes Israel's responsibility. As an occupying power Israel is under an obligation to ensure the welfare of the Gaza population; Egypt is not.

Israel also prohibits the export of goods from the Gaza Strip towards the West Bank and Israel. Again, this restriction is not based on security considerations since Israel allows goods from Gaza to transit through its territory en route to other destinations. Rather, it reflects Israel's policy of separating the Gaza Strip from the West Bank, disregarding the fact that both were to form a single territorial unit under the Oslo II agreement.[47]

Israel also limits travel by individuals between the West Bank and the Gaza Strip. Thus students in Gaza are denied the right to study in the West Bank. Here also it is difficult to see a connection between the restrictions and the security of Israel. Israeli authorities acknowledge that the purpose of the restrictions is to enforce Israel's 'separation policy' between the two areas.

---

46 The operation started on 8 July and ended on 26 August 2014. It resulted in over 2200 casualties on the Palestinian side, of which nearly 1500 Palestinian civilians, and 72 on the Israeli side, of which 6 civilians.

47 See Article XI, paragraph 1 of the Oslo II Agreement: 'The two sides view the West Bank and the Gaza Strip as a single territorial unit, the integrity and status of which will be preserved during the interim period.'

Article 50 of the Hague Regulations provides that:

'No general penalty, pecuniary or otherwise, shall be inflicted on the population on account of acts of individuals for which they cannot be regarded as jointly and severally responsible.'

Article 33(2) of the Fourth Geneva Convention states:

'Collective penalties and likewise all measures of intimidation or of terrorism are prohibited.'

By imposing a near total closure of its borders with the Gaza Strip the Israeli government is imposing a collective punishment on the Gaza population in violation of these two provisions of international humanitarian law.

13. Non-compliance with UN Security Council resolutions

Article 25 of the UN Charter provides:

'The Members of the United Nations agree to accept and carry out the decisions of the Security Council in accordance with the present Charter.'

Israel is a member of the UN. In failing to accept and carry out the decisions of the Security Council Israel is not living up to the obligations imposed upon it by the Charter.

IV. The EU reaction

1. Forging the instruments

Initially, the EU did not react to these many breaches of international law. Indeed, the EEC (as it then was) did not have any competences in matters of foreign policy. Not before the 1970's did the Member States start coordinating their foreign policies on an informal basis. The Single European Act[48] institutionalized this cooperation, providing that it would take place during twice yearly meetings of the Heads of State and Governments. It was further developed in the Maastricht Treaty.[49] The Amsterdam Treaty[50] entrusted the Secretary General of the Council with the role of High Representative for the Common Foreign and Security Policy. Under the Lisbon Treaty,[51] that role was given to a Commission Vice-President who would also preside over the sessions of the Foreign Affairs Council. Today, the High Representative is charged with conducting the Union's common foreign and security policy, making proposals to develop that policy and carrying them out as mandated by the Council.[52]

---

48 Signed on 17/28 February 1986.

49 Signed on 7 February 1992.

50 Signed on 2 Octobre 1997.

51 Signed on 13 December 2007.

52 Article 18 (2) of the European Union Treaty.

In parallel, Article 3(5) of the EU Treaty, as revised at Lisbon,[53] now provides that the Union must contribute to 'the strict observance of international law', and in particular 'the principles of the UN Charter'. The European Court of Justice has since made clear that acts of an institution may be declared invalid if they do not comply with international law in its entirety, including customary international law.[54] This has increased the importance of international law in the shaping of the EU's policies, simultaneously enhancing the High Representative's role within the EU decision-making process.

2. The EU's 'engagement' policy

As a result of these changes, a common EU attitude has slowly started to emerge. Initially it consisted in a policy of engagement. The close economic, political, cultural and (often) personal links between politicians, businessmen and other opinion-makers on both sides made a harsh reaction unrealistic. The terrorist policies pursued under the leadership of Yasser Arafat also initially obfuscated the gravity of the breaches committed on the part of Israel. Nevertheless, in the 1980 Venice Declaration the EU recognised 'the need to fulfil the legitimate expectations of the Palestinian people'. In the 1999 Berlin Declaration it declared its commitment to the creation of a Palestinian State. However, until recently, engagement with Israel was considered to be the best way to achieve these results. Thus, in 1995, an association agreement was signed with Israel; Article 2 stated that the relations between the parties, as well as the agreement itself, were to be based on respect for human rights and democratic principles 'which guides their internal and international policy'.[55]

With the failure of the Camp David summit in early 2000, the situation became more critical. The outbreak of the second Intifada, the take-over of the Gaza Strip by Hamas after the Israeli pull-out of 2005, the increase in terrorist incidents within Israel, the construction of the separation barrier between the West Bank and Israel and the acceleration of Israel's settlement policy caused the EU to express its concerns in a more focused manner.

At first it did so in a purely rhetorical fashion. Successive Council resolutions expressed the EU's 'deep concern' about the construction and expansion of settlements, 'regretted' eviction and demolition orders, 'condemned' the construction of the separation barrier, 'refused to recognize' the changes made to Israel's pre-1967 borders and called for the 'immediate, sustained and unconditional opening of crossings to and from Gaza'. Although ritually repeated over the years, none of these statements was accompanied by corresponding action. Nor did they cause Israel to modify its policies. Their main purpose seemed to be to allow the EU it to pursue its policy of 'business as usual' with

---

53 Treaty on the European Union signed in Lisbon on 13 December 2007, entered into force on 1st December 2009.

54 Judgment in *Air Transport Association of America*, C-366/10, EU:C:2011:864.

55 Euro-Mediterranean Agreement establishing an Association between the European Communities and their Member States, of the one part, and the State of Israel, of the other part, O.J. L 147/3, 21.06.2000.

Israel with a clear conscience. This became particularly evident in late 2008 when the Council decided to 'upgrade' its relations with Israel.[56]

Shortly thereafter, Israel launched operation 'Cast Lead' against Gaza;[57] a few months later the Gaza flotilla incident[58] focused attention on the brutality of the Israeli reaction. The result was a loud public outcry which caused the European Parliament to defer its assent to a recently negotiated agreement that would have allowed Israel to participate in future Community programmes.[59] The Council had no choice but to freeze the 'upgrade'. [60]

The failure of the EU's engagement policy had become evident. More concrete measures were required if the EU was to honour its international obligations.

3. Towards a more effective policy

The first sign that the EU might be roused from its apathy came with the European Court's Brita ruling of 2010[61] in which a German court asked whether products made by a company in an Israeli settlement[62] were entitled to preferential treatment under the 1995 EU-Israel Association Agreement. In paragraph 54, the Court made crystal clear that the territorial scope of the EU-Israel Association Agreement did not include territories placed under Israeli administration since 1967. Preferential treatment was therefore not available.

This judgment pushed the Commission to take more effective action to facilitate detection by national customs authorities of cases where preferential treatment was wrongfully claimed.[63] This was done by requiring importers, as a condition for obtaining preferential treatment, to mention the place of production and its postal code in the import documents; the Commission also published on its website an up-to date list of ineligible locations (i.e., Israeli settlements) and their postal codes.[64] This facilitated the task of the Member States' customs authorities in detecting unjustified claims of preferential treatment.

---

56 Council Conclusions, Strengthening of the EU's Bilateral Relations with its Mediterranean Partners, Brussels, 8 and 9 December 2008.

57 27 December 2008.

58 31 May 2010.

59 Protocol on the general principles governing the State of Israel's participation in Community programmes, O.J. L 129/39, 17.05.2008.

60 Statement of the European Union on the occasion of the 9th meeting of the EU-Israel Association Council, Luxembourg, 15 June 2009, points 2 and 3.

61 Judgment in *Firma Brita/Hauptzollamt Hamburg Hafen*, C-386/08, EU:C:2010:91, spec. para. 54.

62 The products involved were drink-makers for sparkling water, as well as accessories and syrups. They were produced by Soda Club Ltd in Mishor Adumin in the West Bank, east of Jerusalem.

63 Hitherto the Commission had already informed importers in three official notices of its opinion that settlement goods were not entitled to preferential treatment under the Association Agreement and advised them to exercise caution in respect of import documents issued by the Israeli authorities: Notice to importers: Importations from Israel into the Community, O.J. C 338/13, 8.11.97, O.J. C 328/6, 23.11.2001 and O.J. C 20/2, 25.01.2005. However these notices remained largely ineffective.

64 Notice to importers – Imports from Israel into the EU, O. J. C 232/5, 3.8.2012.

On the political level, the Foreign Affairs Council drew its conclusions from the Court's judgment on 10 December 2012. For once, it did not satisfy itself with platonic declarations but committed 'to ensure that – in line with international law – all agreements between the State of Israel and the European Union unequivocally and explicitly indicate their inapplicability to the territories occupied by Israel in 1967' [65].

A few months later, the Commission published the so-called 'Grants Guidelines'.[66] These make clear that the Commission will not grant financial assistance under EU programmes to Israeli entities having their legal address in occupied Palestine (including Israeli settlements) or who, whilst established within Israel proper, carry out activities there. The guidelines aroused considerable emotion within Israel and the Israeli government exerted vehement but ultimately unsuccessful pressures to delay their application.

Later in the same year, the EU Parliament and the Council adopted a package of regulations to establish a new framework programme for research and innovation for the years 2014-2020. The Commission's initial proposals, made in 2012, did not provide a safeguard against the possibility that entities engaged in Israeli settlements might participate in and receive funding under the programme. Thanks to an amendment proposed by the European Parliament, this possibility was eliminated.[67]

Further significant policy changes in line with the Council December 2012 conclusions occurred in 2014. Thus, the Commission stopped recognizing veterinary certificates issued for farm produce by Israeli governmental services where the products come from outside Israel's pre-1967 borders.[68] Where no system exists to allow distinguishing products from settlements in the West Bank from those originating in Israel proper, this has the effect to block the import of all Israeli products.

A fair number of Member States now discourage investment by their businesses in projects connected with the occupation of Palestine. Initially, they intervened only in individual cases;[69] now they have published notices warning their firms of the risks of dealing in settlements or with firms involved there.[70] The text of these notices, which had been coordinated within the EU, stresses the legal and economic risks, as well as

65 Press Release of the Council meeting in Brussels on 10 December 2012, para. 4.

66 Guidelines on the Eligibility of Israeli Entities and their Activities in the Territories Occupied by Israel Since June 1967 for Grants, Prizes and Financial Instruments Funded by the EU from 2014 Onwards, O.J. C 205/9, 19.07.2013.

67 Regulation N° 1290/2013 of 11 December 2013 laying down the rules for participation and dissemination in 'Horizon 2020 – the Framework Programme for Research and Innovation 2014-2020' and repealing Regulation (EC) N° 1906, O.J. L 347, 20.12.2013, p. 81; the amendment concerned recital 9 of the Preamble.

68 See, with respect to poultry meat: Commission Implementing Regulation N° 166.2014 (O.J. L 54/2, 22.02.2014, amending Regulation (EC) n° 798/2008.

69 Thus in 2011 the German government persuaded Deutsche Bahn to refrain from participating in the construction of an Israeli railway that would pass through Palestinian territory, and in June 2013 the Dutch government obtained the withdrawal of the engineering firm Royal Haskoning DHV from a sewage treatment project in occupied East Jerusalem. The French government recently intervened to stop the French firm Safege's involvement in a cable car project in Jerusalem (Haaretz, 25 March 2015).

70 The United Kingdom took the lead in publishing a notice in December 2013; it was followed in the summer by France, Spain, Italy, Portugal, Austria, Ireland, Finland, Denmark, Belgium and Croatia.

potential reputational damage, that financial transactions, investments, purchases, procurements and other economic activities (including tourism) related to the settlements could entail due to the fact that the settlements are built on occupied land and are not recognized as a legitimate part of Israel's territory.

Closely related to the question of preferential treatment (at issue in the *Brita* case) is the problem of labelling settlement products. In a variety of sectors EU law requires retailers to indicate the origin of the goods they offer for sale.[71] More generally, the Unfair Commercial Practices Directive of 11 May 2005[72] prohibits misleading indications of origin when they cause or are likely to cause a consumer to take a transactional decision he would not have taken otherwise.[73] Nevertheless, most EU retailers label settlement products as coming from 'Israel', thereby concealing their true origin.

Here too, at EU prompting, Member States are beginning to react. Some have enacted guidelines requiring the correct labelling of settlement goods.[74] Thirteen Member States[75] are reported to be in favour of firm enforcement of EU legislation regarding the labelling of settlement products[76] (although many still have to publish guidelines to that effect). The Commission has prepared its own guidelines but provisionally delayed their publication so as not to interfere with the US-sponsored peace negotiations that were proceeding at the time. With the breakdown of these negotiations in April 2014 and the elections in Israel on 17 January 2015 likely to lead to a right-wing government intent in pursuing the occupation and the settlement enterprise, it is probable that the guidelines will be published by the EU in the near future.

On a more general level, attitudes towards recognition of the Palestinian State are changing. For a long time the EU shied away from immediate recognition, considering that this had to be the result of negotiations with Israel. When the interim period foreseen in the Oslo process came to an end in 1999 without agreement having been reached and the president of the Palestinian Authority Yasser Arafat announced his intention to declare statehood without further delay, the EU pressured him not to act unilaterally, while promising that it would consider recognition 'in due course'.[77]

Thirteen years later the issue was brought before the UN General Assembly, which decided on 29 November 2012 by a crushing majority to grant 'non-member observer

---

71 This applies in the following sectors: fruits and vegetables, wine, olive oil, honey, fish, chicken and eggs, and cosmetics.

72 Directive 2005/29/EC of 11 May 2005 concerning unfair business-to-consumer practices in the internal market, OJ L 149/22, 11.06.2005.

73 Article 6(1)(b) of the Unfair Trade Practices Directive.

74 Denmark, the United Kingdom, Belgium.

75 These include the United Kingdom, France, Spain and the Netherlands.

76 Akiva Eldar, 'EU Countries to Label Products from Israeli Settlements', *Al-Monitor*, http://jfjfp.com/?p=42260.

77 EU Council Berlin Declaration, 26 March 1999.

State status' to Palestine.[78] The Czech Republic was the only EU Member State to vote against. All the others either voted in favour[79] or abstained.[80]

Eight Member States had recognized Palestine before becoming EU members.[81] Although the favourable votes of the others implied that they considered Palestine as a State, this did not amount to recognition under international law. Many stuck to the view subordinating formal recognition to the successful outcome of negotiations with Israel. However, after the breakdown of the negotiations in April 2014 and the cause of the breakdown generally being considered to lie with Israel,[82] this position was no longer tenable. Indeed it gave Israel a veto right over recognition by third States.

On 30th April, the Swedish government drew its conclusions and decided to recognize Palestine officially. The governments of the other Member States adopted a more cautious attitude despite growing pressure from their Parliaments and civil society. Between October 2014 and February 2015 the legislatures of six Member States adopted resolutions urging their governments to recognize Palestine.[83] On 17 December 2014, the European Parliament adopted a resolution supporting in principle the recognition of Palestinian statehood and the two State solution. In view of these pressures it is becoming increasingly likely that more Member States will officially recognize the Palestinian State in the future.

V. Conclusion

The picture emerging from this analysis is of a slow but steady coming together of Member States' attitudes towards the Israeli-Palestinian conflict. True, significant differences still exist: the German approach is still largely fashioned by that nation's feeling of responsibility for the horrors of the holocaust; the former communist countries are still influenced by the United States' strongly pro-Israel bias; the Western Member States adopt a more detached attitude. Nevertheless, whereas a couple of years ago many ministers were afraid of being singled out as being too critical of Israel if they spoke their minds, [84] there is a greater willingness today to confront Israel head-on where this is dictated by the need to defend certain principles such as the illegality of the occupation and of the settlements, or to provide humanitarian assistance to the Palestinian population.

---

78 There were 138 votes in favour, 9 against and 41 abstentions.

79 Austria, Bulgaria, Cyprus, Denmark, Finland, Greece, Ireland, Italy, Luxembourg, Malta, Portugal, Spain, Sweden.

80 Bulgaria, Croatia, Estonia, Germany, Hungary, Latvia, Lithuania, the Netherlands, Poland.

81 Malta, Cyprus, the Czech Republic, Slovakia, Hungary, Romania, Bulgaria, Poland.

82 Israel reneged on the promise it had made at the start of the negotiations to release a certain number of Palestinians by that date.

83 Ireland, Spain, France, Portugal, Luxembourg, Belgium.

84 As was the case at the time the 'upgrade' was being discussed: see *The Guardian*, 'EU move to upgrade relations with Israel', 23 July 2012, http://www.theguardian.com/world/2012/jul/23/israel-eu.

There is also a greater appreciation of the need to adopt, where necessary, an independent line rather than defer to the US. This was evident at the time of the Grants Guidelines: US State Secretary Kerry failed in his effort to get the EU ministers to delay publication of the guidelines when he met them in Vilnius on 6 September 2013.[85] Similarly, when Palestinian President Mahmud Abbas announced that he would adhere to the Statute of the International Criminal Court (ICC), the US declared itself 'deeply troubled' by this 'badly damaging move'[86] whereas the EU considered that the Palestinian initiative was in line with its own policy of supporting the ICC.

There is no doubt that the action led by the two High Representatives who have been in charge of the Common Foreign and Security Policy up to now, with the assistance of a highly competent and dedicated External Action Service staff, has been instrumental in providing the initiative and continuity necessary for the pursuit of a consistent independent foreign policy. The fact that Article 3(5) of the EU Treaty now expressly mentions the EU's duty to contribute to the strict observance of international law, and in particular the principles of the UN Charter, has been a major factor in the development of this rule-based approach. It remains to be seen whether the same can happen in other sectors.

---

85 Reuters: 'Kerry urges EU to postpone funding ban in Israeli-occupied territories', http://www.reuters.com/article/2013/09/07/us-palestinians-israel-usa-europe-idUSBRE98609U20130907.

86 Statement of State Department spokeswoman Jen Psaki, 6 January 2015, http://www.i24news.tv/en/news/israel/diplomacy-defense/56812-150106-obama-administration-mulls-cutting-annual-aid-to-palestinians.

Part III

Human Rights
Intellectual Property
Other

Interim orders against healthcare professionals in disciplinary proceedings (in the United Kingdom)

BARRY BAINES

I. Birth of the interim order

In January 2001, Dame Janet Smith, a Lord Justice of Appeal, commenced chairing an inquiry into the circumstances surrounding the conviction of Dr Shipman, who was convicted of murdering 15 of his patients between 1995 and 1998.

At the conclusion of the trial it came to light that in 1976 Dr Shipman had been convicted of offences of forgery, unlawful possession of pethidine and obtaining pethidine by deception, and questions were raised as to how he had been able to return to unsupervised general practice in 1977, just over one year later.

The first of a series of reports was published by the inquiry by 2003, and Dame Janet Smith found that between 1975 and 1998 Dr Shipman had killed at least 215 patients.

A major issue which arose was the inability of the regulator, the General Medical Council (GMC), when Dr Shipman was under investigation for murder, and even after his arrest, to take any steps to suspend him from practice. Under the arrangements which were then in force, the GMC was powerless to take action until Dr Shipman had been convicted of murder, and that was over a year later; in the meantime, he was at liberty to practise unrestricted.

The Interim Orders Committee of the General Medical Council (later to be replaced by the Interim Orders Panel) was created in 2000. It was tasked with deciding whether it was necessary to suspend a doctor's registration or to impose conditional registration pending a final determination of the case.

Since then each of the other healthcare regulators[1] has introduced similar provisions into its own statutes and regulations, varying a little from each other in some respects, but each with the same intention: to provide emergency protection to patients and public whilst safeguarding the reputation of the profession and, where appropriate, the registrant's own interests.

Between the arrest of Dr Shipman and the inquiry, many changes took place within the National Health Service together with a number of bodies to oversee healthcare in its various aspects.

Since 2012, doctors have been required to undertake revalidation every five years, which is based on annual appraisals against the GMC's core guidance. At the end of 2014, the Nursing & Midwifery Council announced that it, too, would be introducing a system of revalidation for nurses and midwives.

Dame Janet Smith concluded that the General Medical Council focused too much on the interests of doctors and insufficiently on the public interest and the need for patients to be protected from drug abusing doctors. Since then the landscape has changed dramatically. Health regulation now is patient centred.

Much more recently, a non-governmental departmental body was created to promote the health, safety and well-being of users of health and social care services and the public, although it enthusiastically refutes the style 'super regulator'. Now titled the Professional Standards Authority for Health and Social Care ('PSA'), and formerly known as the Council for Healthcare Regulatory Excellence ('CHRE'), it has undergone some shifts of focus and several name changes.

During 2014 the Medical Practitioners' Tribunals Service[2] held over 1,000 initial interim orders and review hearings in respect of performance, conduct and health of doctors, whilst the General Dental Council held over 300, and the Nursing & Midwifery Council heard something of the order of 950 new applications for interim orders.

Why then are there so many interim orders applications to restrict or suspend the practice of health professionals (registrants)? Is it that health regulation in the past was so lax that it concentrated too heavily on the wellbeing of those it was designed to regulate at the expense of patients? Or has the pendulum swung too far in the other direction at the expense of the professionals?

---

1 The nine healthcare regulators: General Chiropractic Council; General Dental Council; General Medical Council; General Optical Council; General Pharmaceutical Council; Health and Care Professions Council; Nursing and Midwifery Council; Pharmaceutical Society of Northern Ireland.

2 The Medical Practitioners' Tribunals Service ('MPTS') is now the adjudication service for doctors in the United Kingdom.

Most health regulators have a triage system of some sort for filtering the receipt of new cases. They first establish if the individual complained of is one of their registrants and whether the information received is capable of amounting to an allegation within its fitness to practise rules or whether, for example, it is a complaint about the amount charged for services or is a domestic or business dispute.

Once a case is received into the system, good practice requires that it be immediately risk assessed. At each stage of the investigation, the regulator considers whether interim action is required on one or more of three grounds: (i) for the protection of the public; (ii) in the public interest; (iii) in the registrant's own interests.

Each regulator follows its own guidance but, in practice, there is little difference between them. The regulator may consider whether there has been a series of failures to provide a proper standard of care or one particularly serious failure; a serious lack of basic professional knowledge or skills; serious criminal allegations, particularly those involving allegations of sexual or violent offences or serious dishonesty offences; situations where a registrant has breached conditions previously imposed or undertakings previously given.

If the case is identified as falling into one of those categories, a caseworker refers it to the next stage for investigation and urgent consideration. Depending upon the particular rules, it may be that the Registrar (usually via a designated senior manager or a case examiner appointed for the purpose) has power to send the case directly to an interim orders panel, in which case the application for interim measures is usually listed for hearing within three weeks or so, but sometimes quicker. Other regulators may refer by a more cumbersome and lengthy process of requiring the case to come first before an investigation committee which makes the decision for onward referral to an interim orders panel.

At each stage of the process, the regulator will be aware that the PSA is, so to speak, looking over its shoulder. At its annual review it will be asked to explain failures to consider referral, and the quality of decisions not to refer may be challenged, so there is a temptation to refer and accept failure to obtain an order rather than risk adverse criticism and the political consequences which may follow.

An interim orders panel may impose an order for suspension or conditional registration, in either case for a period not exceeding eighteen months, or make no order at all. Any order must be reviewed after each period of not more than six months, when it may be discharged, an order for conditions amended to one of suspension, or an order of suspension reduced to one of conditions. Either party may seek an earlier review if it is merited by the circumstances.

The registrant must have the right to appear before the committee and give evidence if he wishes. Because the hearing does not determine facts, that evidence should generally be confined to showing why it would be disproportionate to make an order against the registrant. There may conceivably be circumstances where an interim orders panel could be persuaded that such charges as were being put forward are of no real substance and therefore do not merit any interim measures, but normally where the case has progressed beyond the screening stage it will be assumed that they are charges which may be proved in due course.[3]

In a case based upon a criminal prosecution, it was held that refusal to consider evidence to demonstrate the weakness of the Crown Prosecution Service's case was correct. To consider that evidence, and thereby to attempt to second guess the CPS, was not a valid exercise. Consideration of only parts of the evidence in relation to parts of the Crown's case would have given no true indication of the strength or weakness of the case as a whole.[4]

II. Emergency application

Delay may be fatal to the regulator's application which is made because speedy and urgent action is required to protect the public or the public interest. It is an emergency rather than an administrative procedure.

Where a regulator was informed of the dismissal of a social worker for serious professional negligence, misconduct and wilful failure to carry out the normal duties of the post, it did nothing with the information for six months when it informed the registrant that it was reviewing the information. The following month an order for interim suspension was applied for, and after a further month an interim orders panel made the order.[5] Allowing the appeal to discharge the order, the appellate tribunal observed that the irony of the case was that the regulator was guilty of the very failures that the registrant had been suspended for: failure to act upon and apply appropriate procedures.

The panel hearing a case is invited to make a risk assessment without determining the facts. It is the current risk that is important and must be weighed against current circumstances and recent improvements. The panel does not engage in a fact finding role or resolve conflicts of evidence, although it will weigh the information before it. The rules are silent as to the threshold test, and the interim orders committee may make an order when it has not yet reached a decision that there is a case to answer.[6] A panel should expect the allegation to have been made or confirmed in writing, even if it has not yet been reduced to a formal witness statement. It is necessary to consider the source of the allegation and its potential seriousness. One that is trivial or clearly misconceived should not be given weight.[7]

---

3 *R (Stephen James Walker) v. General Medical Council* [2003] EWHC 2308 (Admin).

4 *Fallon v. Horseracing Regulatory Authority* [2006] EWHC 2030 (QB).

5 *Bradshaw v. General Social Care Council* [2010] UKFTT 3 (HESC) (04 January 2010).

6 *Perry v. The Nursing & Midwifery Council* [2013] EWCA Civ 145.

7 *General Medical Council v. Dr Michael John Sheill* [2006] EWHC 3025 (Admin).

III. Extension of order

If the case is not ready for final determination after eighteen months and the regulator wishes to extend an order, the usual position is that application must be made to the Administrative Court, which may extend the order on any one occasion for not more than twelve months, after which time a further application must be made. In this respect, the exercise in decision making is to be performed by the court as the primary decision maker.

The criteria of public protection, the public interest or the practitioner's own interests remain the same as for the original order. The court is entitled to take into consideration the gravity of the allegations, the nature of the evidence, the seriousness of the risk of harm to patients, the reasons why the case has not been concluded, and the prejudice to the practitioner if an interim order is continued.

The onus of satisfying the court that the criteria are met falls upon the regulator as the applicant for the extension and, these being civil proceedings, the standard is the civil one, a balance of probabilities. Any witness statement in support of the application should explain, as a self-standing document, the regulator's reasons for making the application, and the judge should examine those reasons with care.

In respect of its other functions on review, the powers of the Court are limited to confirming the order made by the regulator's interim orders panel, to substituting a different period, or terminating the order forthwith; it may not vary conditions or change an order of suspension into one of conditions. It appears that Parliament took the view that the organs of the respective regulators are better placed than the courts to investigate and evaluate those matters.

It is not the function of the judge to make findings of primary fact about events leading to suspension or other sanction, or to consider the merits of the case in that respect. Neither is there a threshold test to be satisfied before the court can exercise its power, such as a condition that the court should be satisfied that there is evidence to show a case to answer. Conversely, if the judge can clearly see that the case has little merit, he may take that into account in weighing his decision on the application. This is, however, to be undertaken as part of the ordinary task of making a judicial decision, and a case where a statutory body makes an application on obviously unsupportable grounds is likely to be rare.

Evidence on the application includes evidence of the regulator's opinion and the interim orders panel as to the need for an interim order. It will be for the court to decide what weight to give that opinion. The court should give that opinion such weight as in the circumstances of the case it thinks fit; no more is required. Weighing up the opinion of a body that has special statutory responsibilities and relevant experience and expertise is once again part of the ordinary task of judicial decision making.

The court does not express any view on the merits of the case against the practitioner. Its function is to ascertain whether the allegations made against the practitioner, rather than their truth or falsity, justify the prolongation of the suspension. In general, it need not look beyond the allegations. If the practitioner contends that the allegations are unfounded, the practitioner should challenge the original order for suspension or conditions by judicial review.

The approach of the court to an opinion of an interim orders panel is one of attaching appropriate weight to the evidence in the ordinary way. There is no automaticity about the attaching of weight to evidence. Weight does not attach to a person's evidence by virtue only of his experience or status. The giving of weight to opinion evidence entails a holistic evaluation of the persuasiveness of the evidence on the relevant issue, having regard to all the circumstances including its content as well as the viewpoint of the author of the opinion.[8]

The Court of Appeal's guidance is that the court has power to determine that there should be no extension, the extension asked for by the regulator, or some lesser extension.

The courts have become more cautious and adversely critical about granting the maximum additional extension periods of 12 months on expiry of the initial period of the order, so routinely applied for by regulators, without careful scrutiny; so much so, that anecdotal evidence suggests that on occasions some regulators do not ask for extensions rather than risk the wrath of the court and attendant publicity over the dilatory way they have progressed their investigations.

It is for the regulator to satisfy the court that public protection or public interest requires the conditions now in place to be extended. Where the original order had already been extended by six months, and the regulator applied for a further extension of eight months but the initial allegation of rape had not been pursued by the police (although the aggrieved thereafter complained to the regulator), the application was refused.[9] Not all the delay that had occurred could be explained by reference to vulnerability of the aggrieved. On the contrary, large parts of it were merely because of inactivity on the part of the regulator for long periods.

Conditions that may be considered proportionate when an order is first imposed may become disproportionate with the passage of time, so delay is a material consideration in deciding whether it would be proportionate to continue an interim order of conditions or suspension, or relax it in whole or in part. It was no longer clear in *Dr E's*[10] case that the imposed conditions were necessary for the protection of the public, and the regulator's witness statement had failed to address the necessary considerations. Because there had been a total failure by the regulator to address the matters upon which a court must be satisfied if it were to grant an extension, the regulator's application was refused.

---

8 *General Medical Council v. Dr Stephen Chee Cheung Hiew* [2007] EWCA Civ 369.

9 *General Medical Council v. Dr E* [2014] EWHC 1620 (Admin).

10 Ibid.

Changes of circumstances during the progress of an investigation will be critical. Where the first interim order in a case had been made in 2010, the application before the court would expire over four-and-a-half years after it was first made if it were to be granted.[11] The fitness to practise hearing, which was estimated to last 30 days, had been adjourned and was part heard. There was an unsatisfactory history. The role of material no longer relied upon should have been explained and acknowledged in the supporting evidence for the application. It should be a freestanding accurate and objective summary of the material relied upon. It is not appropriate for a regulator to invite a court to extend suspension on the basis of allegations or evidence that is no longer relied upon by that regulator.

IV. The grounds - public protection

The interim orders panel decides whether there is such a serious and immediate risk to public safety that it is necessary to make an interim order of conditions or suspension now: that is to say, before there has been a final hearing on the merits.

An interim orders panel of the General Medical Council was faced with an application for an interim order after a doctor was charged with money laundering.[12] The doctor's husband, who was an accountant, had been charged with an advance fee fraud and sentenced to a term of two years and nine months' imprisonment. The doctor denied the charges and pleaded not guilty. The allegation appears to have been that moneys discovered in the doctor's bank account may have come from a fraudulent source connected with her husband. Undoubtedly, the case came before the interim orders panel because the doctor had been charged and was due to appear before the Crown Court.

After the doctor's arrest, but before charge, the doctor applied to a training scheme for general practitioners but did not disclose her arrest at that stage. When, later, she was charged, the doctor did not herself volunteer those facts to the GMC and said she assumed the police would have done so.

Suspending the doctor for 18 months, the committee indicated that this may indicate a lack of probity, and said: 'Having taken into account all the information available, the panel is satisfied that there may be impairment of your fitness to practise which poses a real risk to members of the public or may adversely affect the public interest or your own interests and, after balancing your interests and the interests of the public, an interim order is necessary to guard against the risk.'

We will return later to discuss the public interest and the interests of the registrant, but for the moment will concentrate on public protection. Undoubtedly, if the doctor were subsequently convicted at trial or, after a full hearing on the merits, a professional

11 *General Medical Council v. Sondhi* [2013] EWHC 4233 (Admin).

12 *Sosanya v. General Medical Council* [2009] EWHC 2814 (Admin).

conduct committee found the allegations proved, it may wish to take action upon the doctor's registration. But how, exactly, did the public need to be protected from this doctor in the interim?

The charges had nothing to do with the registrant's ability as a doctor. Her patients were not in any way jeopardised by her conduct (if it subsequently turned out to be proved). The panel did not indicate why it thought the doctor was a danger to the public.

When the case came before the Administrative Court on an application to terminate the suspension, Davis J felt that an interim orders panel should at least be asking itself as part of the thought process: will it be acceptable for us not to suspend in a case of this kind if at the end of the day the charges are proved and the guilt of the applicant is established? Another part of the thought process should be: will it be acceptable for us to suspend an applicant in a case of this kind if, at the end of the day, the applicant may be acquitted of all charges?

Although the charges were serious, they were not of the most serious kind and they were denied. The doctor had not been convicted of anything. The panel did not identify in its reasons any risk in the doctor continuing to practise. So why was it necessary to suspend her?

A statement attributed to Sedley LJ is that that suspension cannot be taken as a neutral act. Of course, it involves no ultimately binding finding of fact: but it does have an immediate and dramatic impact upon the reputation and potential career of any professional person.

Since the case of *Sosanya,* panels have generally been more careful to identify the precise legal ground upon which the order is being made but, as we will see below, health professionals face considerable obstacles when allegations are made on other grounds as well.

It follows that if it is considered necessary to take interim action against a registrant on the ground of public protection, it must also be in the public interest. When public protection does not arise as a specific issue or the panel considers that the case does not meet the statutory criterion of necessity in respect of public protection, it moves on to consider whether to make an order in the public interest only.

V. The grounds - public interest

An order sought in the public interest is for the protection of public confidence in the relevant profession and to uphold and maintain proper professional standards pending a determination of the proceedings as a whole.

How was it in the public interest to suspend Dr Sosanya in the circumstances described above? The Medical Director at the employing trust submitted a letter strongly supportive of the doctor's clinical abilities and confirmed that there was no adverse criticism of her.

The panel observed that its function was not to resolve conflicts of evidence or disputes of fact, and that it was not satisfied that the imposition of conditions would be appropriate in this case given its seriousness. It added: 'The panel has taken account of the issue of proportionality in that the panel must act in a way which is fair and reasonable. Whilst it notes that its order has removed your ability to practise medicine, the panel has determined that the suspension of your registration is a necessary and proportionate response to the risks posed.'

Nonetheless, the panel did not indicate how it was proportionate, fair or reasonable to suspend this doctor, or how it was in the public interest to deprive the public of the services of the doctor. The conclusion was announced without any proper analysis.

There was no suggestion that if the doctor continued in practice she would be given access to money or might then become tempted into activities of the kind with which she was charged. The panel did not even state that maintenance of public confidence in the medical profession required suspension.

Terminating the order, the judge could find no public interest grounds for imposing the suspension. Neither could it be said to be in the doctor's own interests.

In another case,[13] it was necessary for the Court to consider whether the word 'necessary' in the phrase 'necessary for the protection of the public or is otherwise in the public interest' was to be construed conjunctively with 'public interest'. The Court found that as a matter of strict language, no grammatical interpolation of the word 'necessary' fell to be applied to the phrase 'or is otherwise in the public interest'. The judge added that if the public interest was to be invoked in this context under the statute it at least carried some implication of necessity, and certainly at least the implication of desirability. He adopted the words of defence counsel that the bar was set high and, in the ordinary case at least, necessity was an appropriate yardstick.

Davis J said that was the case because of reasons of proportionality: 'It is a very serious thing indeed for a dentist or a doctor to be suspended. It is serious in many cases just because of the impact on that person's right to earn a living. It is serious in all cases because of the detriment to him in reputational terms. Accordingly, it is in my view, likely to be a relatively rare case where a suspension order will be made on an interim basis on the ground that it is in the public interest.' It is right, of course, that each case has to be decided on its own facts.

Not all judges of the Administrative Court are entirely *ad idem* with this interpretation. Nicol J[14] agreed that a registrant could not be the subject of interim suspension unless it was at least desirable in the public interest. Furthermore, the panel must consider very carefully the proportionality of their measure by weighing the significance of any

---

13 *Shiekh v. General Dental Council* [2007] EWHC 2972 (Admin).

14 *Sandler v. General Medical Council* [2010] EWHC 1029 (Admin).

harm to the public interest in not suspending the registrant against the personal damage by preventing him from practising. The judge added: '… but I do, with respect, think that the Court must be cautious about superimposing additional tests over and above those which Parliament has set.'

Dr Sandler[15] was subject to an NHS Trust disciplinary hearing in relation to forms he had completed under the Cremation Act 1902. Forms which he had signed required the doctor to confirm, amongst other things, that he had seen the body of the deceased, examined the body externally and that he had seen and questioned the medical practitioner who had attended the deceased during his last illness.

The hearing found that the doctor had done none of those things and, in addition, received a total payment from the trust of around £4,500 for carrying out those duties. He was given a final written warning, referred to his regulator and the police were notified. He was charged with a total of seven offences under the Cremation Act 1902, one of which alleged that he wilfully signed 110 false certificates between 31 December 2005 and 1 June 2008.

Relying on *Shiekh*[16] the doctor sought, unsuccessfully, to terminate an order of suspension when an interim order was imposed solely on public interest grounds. On the information before the panel, the allegations spanned something of the order of seven years. The alleged lack of probity took place in a clinical setting, for the statute relied on the honest statements of a senior doctor to ensure that bodies were not cremated unless correct procedures had been followed. Although it was not for the interim orders panel to consider the truth of the allegations, the doctor had admitted some of them before the disciplinary hearing so it was not open to him to allege that they were baseless.

The court considered that interim suspension was appropriate and there was a distinction to be drawn between *Sandler*, where such conduct occurred during the course of the doctor's clinical duties, and *Shiekh,* which also involved dishonesty on a large scale.

Shiekh was a dentist who retained a number of self-employed dentists in his practice. Over a period of time a number of those dentists made false expense claims and ultimately a charge of conspiracy to defraud was laid against the registrant.

During a lengthy Crown Court trial, the registrant offered a plea of guilty to the charges. Part of the basis of the plea was that he had failed to police adequately the travel claims of the other dentists, although it was accepted that he received a percentage of those claims. Passing a suspended sentence of imprisonment, the judge commented that there was nonetheless sustained dishonesty but considered it unlikely that the dentist would indulge in making dishonest claims in the future.

The period of the alleged conspiracy was between 1994 and 2000. The case first came before an interim orders panel in 2006. It was accepted that the registrant posed no

15 Ibid.

16 *Shiekh* (n 13).

direct risk to the safety of the public. There had been no complaints in the intervening period, and since his conviction the registrant had made full reparation and been entrusted by the local Trust with a large multi-million pound contract.

The cases of *Sosanya* and *Shiekh,* on the one hand, where orders on public interest grounds were not upheld, and *Sandler,* on the other, where the order was upheld, indicate the general approach the court will take to decisions of interim orders panels taken on public interest grounds.

The Court terminated an order for suspension where the interim orders panel did not expressly identify the risk or focus on the question of likelihood of *serious* damage to the public interest and how that outweighed the doctor's interests.[17]

There were multiple allegations, including treatment of colleagues – which resulted in his dismissal -- and the provision of inaccurate information to patients, but central to the complaint was forging documents (and passing them off as authentic) for Employment Tribunal proceedings alleging unfair dismissal, race and religious discrimination. All matters were denied by the doctor although the Employment Tribunal described him as a liar who deliberately attempted to mislead the Tribunal. Again, the case did not relate to the doctor's clinical competence.

A much more recent case, but a rare one, where suspension in the public interest was upheld, related to multiple areas of concern identified on inspections by the Care Quality Commission.[18] The doctor and owner of premises delegated responsibilities to others. But there were also allegations of misleading a previous Fitness to Practise Panel, amending patient records falsely and dishonestly obtaining insurance cover. It was said that there was a high level of forging and fabrication of documents taking place at the clinic under the direct instructions of the registrant.

The difficult balancing exercise between the interests of the registrant and those of the public, together with the registrant's Article 8 rights, were further considered in the case of a 73-year-old doctor[19] who was charged with conspiracy to defraud in respect of unauthorized payments said to total £1.8 million.

The registrant was the governor of a school who had allegedly authorized substantial payments to members of staff between 2003 and 2009 when they were not entitled to them. In support of an application to terminate an interim order of suspension, it was submitted that the registrant was a person of exemplary and unblemished character and that the order was neither necessary nor proportionate. Furthermore, it breached his Article 8 rights because suspension interfered with his right to make a living, the welfare of his patients, and his reputation.

The regulator accepted that the interim orders panel was required to act proportionately and to balance the public interest against that of the registrant, but contended that the

17 *Shirazad Houshian v. General Medical Council* [2012] EWHC 3458 (QB).

18 *Bhatnagar v. General Medical Council* [2013] EWHC 3412 (Admin).

19 *Dr Indravadan Patel v. General Medical Council* [2012] EWHC 3688 (Admin).

reach of Article 8 should not be overstated. It referred to Baroness Hale's remarks: 'There will be some people for whom the impact upon personal relationships is so great as to constitute an interference with the right to respect for private life and others for whom it may not.'[20]

What was critical in *Patel* was the nature of the wrongdoing. The court observed that it would not be right to suspend purely because of the sum involved if otherwise, in principle, it would not be appropriate.

It had to ask itself what a reasonable onlooker would think, in the event of the registrant's ultimate conviction on the conspiracy charge, about his being allowed to go on practising in the meantime. Would confidence in the profession be undermined? Such a reasonable onlooker would need to have attributed to him knowledge of the relevant facts. Otherwise, there would be a danger of proceeding on a superficial analysis or even mere prejudice.

In this case the court adjudged that no reasonable and properly informed member of the public would be offended or surprised to learn, even following a hypothetical conviction at some later period, that the registrant had been permitted to go on serving his patients in the interim. There was no evidence of any threat to their welfare. Such a decision would not undermine confidence in the medical profession. Most citizens would understand the notion that a person is to be treated as innocent until proved guilty, and its practical implications. In such a case the balancing exercise came down clearly in favour of the registrant. Accordingly, the order was terminated.

VI. The grounds - registrant's own interests

It seems to be impossible to find a case in the reports where interim measures have been imposed solely on the grounds of the registrant's own interests. Inevitably, when a panel makes such a finding it will be because of the registrant's ill health. A panel will be looking at the risk of significant harm in the future if no restriction is imposed on registration. Frequently, it will be used as a ground when the registrant suffers from drug or alcohol addiction, but it is also used as support for a further finding on public protection and/or public interest grounds.

In *Sosanya,* where the panel purported to make an order based on all three grounds but failed to give supporting reasons, Davis J felt it hard to understand why the panel concluded that suspension would be in the registrant's own interests. She had resisted suspension. This was her only employment. Her husband could not earn because he was in prison, she had two young children to care for and, above all, she had her reputation to consider.

20 *R (Wright) v. Secretary of State for Health* [2009] 1 AC 739 paras 33-36.

It may be there are very rare occasions when a registrant is so overcome by an addiction or illness that he has no insight and is a danger to himself. Perhaps it is appropriate then to find suspension is in that registrant's interests. But it is also at least in the public interest and it may well be that the public also needs to be protected from him.

So it is respectfully submitted that interim measures taken purely in the registrant's own interests are not in themselves sustainable. Such a measure must be underpinned by one of the other limbs. To do otherwise would be to fail to give adequate consideration to the test of proportionality and balance the registrant's other interests such as his ability to support himself and his family and to maintain his professional reputation. It follows, therefore, that this limb as a ground for interim suspension or conditions could be dispensed with; it is otiose.

VII. Length of interim order

The regulator is expected to get on with the process of its investigation and to indicate when applying for an interim order how long it needs for that process. It is no longer acceptable for panels to suspend for the maximum period without giving further thought to the time needed.

Lindblom J observed[21] that the effect of an interim suspension order on a registrant's livelihood and reputation will always be grave. He may find himself as the sole principal in his practice and unable to carry on his profession, and without any funding available to him to maintain and care for his patients until the decision on his fitness to practise is made.

It is insufficient for a panel to impose the maximum period because of, for example, the 'uncertainty of the time needed to resolve all the issues in the case.' The panel should enquire of the regulator why, exercising a due sense of urgency and without jeopardising the fairness of the proceedings, the investigation cannot be concluded in a lesser period.

There is always a judgmental or balancing exercise to be carried out in deciding the period of a suspension, just as there is in ordering the suspension itself. In view of the considerable deprivation which a registrant is likely to suffer as a result of suspension, it follows that there is a real need to identify what the next steps are, how long they are going to take, and minimise the period of any suspension.[22]

VIII. Article 6 – the right to a fair trial

It appears that Article 6, which creates the right to a fair trial under the European Convention of Human Rights, is engaged by the interim orders process of regulatory authorities. The House of Lords observed[23] that there is no general principle of

21 *Abdullah v. General Medical Council* [2012] EWHC 2506 (Admin).

22 *Hayat v. General Medical Council* [2014] EWHC 1477 (Admin).

23 *Sadler v. General Medical Council* [2003] 1 WLR 2259, para 77 per Lord Walker.

Convention jurisprudence which prevents professional self-regulation: see also *Albert and Le Compte v Belgium*.[24]

Article 47 of the Charter of Fundamental Rights of the European Union guarantees the right to a fair trial. Unlike Article 6 of the European Convention on Human Rights, the Charter's provision does not confine this right to disputes relating to civil rights and obligations or to any criminal charge, and does not refer to determination of those rights. The European Court of Justice has held that provisional measures given *ex parte* without hearing the defendant could not be recognised according to its case law, which implies that such safeguards should apply also outside the context of final decisions.[25]

Recognising this, in its more recent decision on the applicability of Article 6 to interim orders[26] the Grand Chamber reviewed its previous decisions and decided that a new approach was required. The exclusion of interim measures from the ambit of Article 6 had so far been justified by the fact that they did not in principle determine civil rights and obligations. However, in circumstances where many contracting States faced considerable backlogs in their overburdened justice systems leading to excessively long proceedings, a judge's decision on an injunction would often be tantamount to a decision on the merits for a substantial period of time or, in exceptional cases, even permanently.

The right to continue in professional practice is a civil right[27] and Article 6(1) has been applied to disciplinary proceedings involving a variety of professionals including temporarily suspending a doctor from practice[28] or preventing a doctor from running a clinic.[29] It will not apply, however, if the professional does not face risk of being prevented from practising[30] or if the nature of the proceedings is confined to the assessment of professional liability.[31]

The applicability of Article 6 would depend on whether certain conditions were fulfilled. First, the right at stake in both the main and injunction proceedings should be civil within the autonomous meaning of that notion under Article 6 of the Convention. Second, the nature of the interim measure, its object and purpose as well as its effects on the right in question, should be scrutinised. Whenever an interim measure can be considered effectively to determine the civil right or obligation at stake, notwithstanding the length of time it is in force, Article 6 will be applicable.

---

24 (1983) 5 EHRR 533, pp 541-542, para 29.

25 Judgment in *Denilauler v. SNC Couchet Frere*, C-125/79, EU:C:1980:130.

26 *Miscallef v. Malta* (Application No. 17056/06) (2010) 50 EHRR 37.

27 *Le Compte, Van Leuven and De Meyere v Belgium* (1981) 4 EHRR 1 para 48.

28 *Albert and Le Compte* (n 24).

29 *König v. Germany* (1978) 2 EHRR 170.

30 *X v. United Kingdom* (1983) 6 EHRR 583.

31 *Van Marle v. Netherlands* (1986) 8 EHRR 483.

In *Hiew v General Medical Council*[32] Arden LJ observed that a question had arisen in earlier cases[33] as to whether an interim orders panel in the exercise of its powers is subject not only to the common law requirements of acting fairly and reasonably but is also subject to proportionality under Article 6. It was held that the proportionality required by Article 6 applied when the right of access to court was in some way qualified, but considered that there may be little, if any, difference between proportionality in this context and the requirements of the common law.

The Court in *Miscallef*[34] accepted, however, that in exceptional cases where, for example, the effectiveness of the measure sought depended upon a rapid decision-making process, it may not be possible immediately to comply with all of the requirements of Article 6. In specific cases, while the independence and impartiality of the tribunal or the judge concerned was an indispensable and inalienable safeguard in such proceedings, other procedural safeguards may apply only to the extent compatible with the nature and purpose of the interim proceedings at issue. In any subsequent proceedings before the Court, it would fall to the government to establish that, in view of the purpose of the proceedings at issue in a given case, one or more specific procedural safeguards could not be applied without unduly prejudicing the attainment of the objective sought by the interim measure in question.

In *Perry*[35] the court did not find it easy to determine the test to be applied in order to determine whether interim proceedings resulted in an order that was determinative of the civil right. The right to work in one's chosen profession was certainly a civil right within the meaning of the Convention, and an order temporarily preventing the exercise of that right may determine that right. Nonetheless, the court was content to proceed on the basis that Article 6 was engaged at the hearing before the interim orders committee.

The only question for the Court of Appeal in this case was whether fairness required the registrant to have the opportunity to give evidence and for the committee to consider the truth of the allegations made against him. He had been denied that opportunity.

The court reminded itself that the statutory right of the registrant in this case was to give relevant evidence. That required the committee to decide whether it was satisfied that an order was necessary for the protection of the public, or otherwise in the public interest or in the interests of the registrant. The committee was required to permit both parties to make their submissions on the need for an interim order and, if one were made, its nature and terms. It was entitled to discount evidence that was inconsistent with objective or undisputed evidence or which was manifestly unreliable. The

32 *Hiew* (n 8).

33 *Madan v General Medical Council* [2001] Lloyd's Rep 539; *Chaudhury v General Medical Council* [2004] Lloyd's Rep Med 251 where the Privy Council expressed the view that there was little or no difference between the requirement of the common law that an interim orders panel must act in a way which is fair and reasonable, and the Convention.

34 *Miscallef* (n 26).

35 *Perry* (n 6).

committee may receive and assess evidence on the effect of an interim order on the registrant, and the registrant was entitled to give evidence on this. The registrant may also give evidence, if he could, to establish that the allegation was manifestly unfounded or manifestly exaggerated; but the committee was not otherwise required to hear his evidence as to whether or not the substantive allegation against him was or was not well-founded: that was not the issue on the application for an interim order.

What the committee could not, and should not, do was to seek to decide the credibility or merits of a disputed allegation: that was a matter for the substantive hearing of the allegation in due course. The interim orders panel, or committee, on the other hand, may make an interim order when it had not yet reached a decision that there was a case to answer.

IX. Conclusion

There is little doubt that regulators need the draconian power to impose conditional registration or suspension upon a registrant where it is necessary for public protection, but it is questionable whether such powers are desirable purely in the public interest or in the interests of the registrant.

In a 2012 consultation paper[36] the Law Commission floated the idea of a single test for imposing an order: '... that it is necessary to protect, promote and maintain the health, safety and well being of the public (and maintain confidence in the profession).' That appears to have been too much of a mouthful for consultees to swallow because when the final report and draft bill[37](which has yet to find parliamentary time) was published, section 152(5) reflected the law as it currently stands: 'A panel may make an interim order only if it is satisfied that an order (a) is necessary for the protection of the public; (b) is otherwise in the public interest; (c) is in the interests of the registered professional.'

Recent decisions of the Administrative Court in particular demonstrate that the Court will do its best to ensure that interim orders decisions which are brought before it go no further than are necessary for public protection or in the public interest. Of even greater concern, however, are the not insignificant number of healthcare professionals who suffer injustice at the hands of interim orders panels, but cannot afford the advantage of legal representation and the opportunity for their cases to be considered judicially.

---

36 Regulation of Healthcare Professionals: Law Commission Consultation Paper 2012.

37 Regulation of Healthcare Professions Etc Bill, published 2014.

Flogging a dead horse: the appropriate human rights policy for judicial treatment of competition fines

PAUL MAHONEY*

I. Preface

In the land of academic comment the topic of the intensity of judicial review that is required for competition fines imposed by an administrative regulatory body such as the European Commission is a well-trodden path, along which Ian Forrester himself has walked on several occasions.[1] At various times in the past it has been argued by many, including Ian, that the arrangements existing within the legal order of the European Union ('the EU'), and in particular the kind of review carried out by the EU courts in Luxembourg (the General Court at first instance and the Court of Justice on appeal), in regard to competition fines imposed by the European Commission did not measure up to the 'superior law' embodied in the standards of fair trial as guaranteed by human rights instruments, notably the European Convention on Human Rights ('the

* Thanks are due to the author's son, Stefan Mahoney, a lawyer on the staff of the EFTA Surveillance Authority and who formerly worked under Ian Forrester at White and Case, for suggestions and research, although the content is the sole responsibility of the author. As usual, any views expressed are personal.

1 See, e.g., Ian Forrester, 'A Bush in Need of Pruning: The Luxuriant Growth of "Light Judicial Review"', in C.-D. Ehlermann and M. Marquis (eds.) *European Competition Law Annual 2009: Evaluation of Evidence and its Judicial Review in Competition Cases* (Oxford, Hart Publishing, 2009); and Ian Forrester, 'A Challenge for Europe's Judges: The Review of Fines in Competition Cases', *European Law Review*, Issue 2, 2011, pp. 185-207.

ECHR') (Article 6) and the Charter of Fundamental Rights of the European Union ('the EU Charter') (Article 47§2).[2]

The reaction of many will doubtless be that that particular debate has now more or less been closed by a series of judgments delivered between 2011 and 2013 by the three European Courts – that is to say, by the Court of Justice of the European Union ('the CJEU') (in *Schindler, KME* and *Chalkor* – the latter company being represented before the CJEU by one I. Forrester Q.C.),[3] the European Court of Human Rights ('the ECtHR') (in *Menarini*)[4] and the Court of the European Free Trade Association ('the EFTA Court') (in *Posten Norge*).[5] To the informed reader the present choice of topic may therefore appear to be flogging a dead or at least dying horse; but, if that is so, the hope is to sow a little doubt in the reader's mind that maybe the horse should not be killed off too early. The object is not to attempt a comprehensive analysis of the requisite scope of judicial control of competition fines under European law. No attempt is made, for example, to explore any difference or interaction between the standard of review of legality required under Article 263§1 of the Treaty on the Functioning of the European Union ('TFEU') in relation to decisions of the European Commission finding and sanctioning cartel infringements, and the standard of judicial review attaching to the 'inherent jurisdiction' in financial disputes as conferred by Article 261 TFEU on the EU courts in relation to competition fines. The more modest aim is to demonstrate the utility of standing back from a due-process focus on the rights of defence of companies suspected of participation in cartels, in favour of a broader look through human rights spectacles at the general phenomenon of cartels and at possible legal mechanisms for dealing with that phenomenon in the overall interest of the community. What will be urged is that, rather than tracing case law development over time as the primary indicator for the (now accomplished?) resolution of the conundrum of the appropriate judicial treatment to be reserved for the imposition of competition fines on companies by virtue of the ECHR (and presumably also by virtue of the EU Charter), one should start by trying to identify the acceptable underlying human rights policy or policies in modern democratic society for regulating the mischief represented to the community and its individual members by cartels operated by companies. The conclusion arrived at is that, on such a wider-vision approach, a so-called 'deferential' style of judicial review, at least to a certain degree, is not necessarily as reprehensible in human rights terms as it has hitherto been made out to be.

Competition fines now reach astronomical levels. Ian Forrester has been known to jokingly introduce himself as the world's least successful competition lawyer, since he represented the two companies, Microsoft and Intel, condemned to the largest

---

2 To give one recent example, see Eric Barbier de la Serre, 'Standard of Review in Competition Law Cases: *Posten Norge* and Beyond', in *The EEA and the EFTA Court - Decentred Integration*, edited by the EFTA Court, pp. 417-433 (Oxford, Hart Publishing, 2014).

3 Judgment in *Schindler Holding Ltd. and Others v. Commission,* C-501/11 P, EU:C:2013:522; Judgment in *KME Germany AG and Others v. Commission*, C-389/10, EU:C:2011:816; and Judgment in *Chalkor AE Epexergasias Metallon v. Commission*, C-386/10 P, EU:C:2011:815.

4 *A. Menarini Diagnostics S.R.L. v. Italy*, no. 43509/08, 27 September 2011, unreported – text exists only in French.

5 Case E-15/10, *Posten Norge AS v. EFTA Surveillance Authority*, 18 April 2012.

competition fines ever imposed –fines of 899 million euros and 1.06 billion euros imposed in 2008 and 2009 by the European Commission. Since the present author knows that Ian not only has a sense of fun but also is in fact regarded as one of the brightest and best of the world's competition lawyers, it is hoped that the following, albeit provocative and none too academic, account of a topic close to his heart might appeal to him.

II. Introductory propositions

In order to set the scene, it may be useful to start with a number of simple, introductory propositions which are uncontroversial or which can be taken to be accepted by most, though not all, commentators:

1. The right to a fair trial under Article 6 ECHR is guaranteed to 'everyone', including legal persons such as commercial companies, and it embraces for natural and legal persons a right of access to court in order to obtain a determination either of their 'civil rights and obligations' or of 'any criminal charge' brought against them. Very early on in its life, in 1976, in the case of *Engel and Others v. Netherlands*,[6] the ECtHR established that a 'criminal charge', since it has an autonomous meaning under the ECHR, may exist in a legal domain outside the formal framework of the national criminal law, depending on the nature of the offence or illegal activity held against the person concerned[7] and on the nature and severity of the penalty liable to be incurred.[8] By virtue of the *Engel* doctrine, what counts for the applicability of Article 6 ECHR under its 'criminal' head is the substance of what is at stake for the person concerned, not the formality of the legal label (criminal, civil, administrative, regulatory, etc.) put on the impugned procedure by the national law.

2. For the purposes of EU law, competition fines are expressly classified as not being 'criminal', in that Article 23§5 of Regulation 1/2003 on the implementation of the rules on competition specifies that the European Commission's decisions imposing antitrust fines 'shall not be of a criminal nature'. But in the *Engel* doctrine that clearly is far from being decisive for the purposes of the ECHR.[9] Despite the absence of any direct authority in the jurisprudence of the ECtHR regarding EU competition proceedings, in itself the potential severity of the fines liable to be imposed by the European Commission brings a distinctly 'criminal' colouring to the whole process. As one – directly interested – commentator, Wouter Wils, one of the European Commission's Competition Hearing Officers, has put it: 'That the application of [the] *Engel* criteria to the European Commission's [competition] fining procedures leads to the conclusion

6 8 June 1976, Series A no. 22, §82.

7 See, e.g., Öztürk *v. Germany*, 21 February 1984, Series A no. 73, §53, where the illegal activity held against the applicant consisted in 'regulatory' motoring offences punishable by fine, including causing a traffic accident.

8 See, e.g., *Ezeh and Connors v. United Kingdom*, nos. 39665/98 and 40086/98, ECHR 2003-X, §§120-124, where a disciplinary punishment of additional imprisonment imposed on prisoners by the prison governor was held to constitute a 'criminal' penalty.

9 See, e.g., Özturk, n. 7 above, §52.

that the procedures are "criminal" within the autonomous meaning of Article 6 ECHR is no longer news today. Indeed, it has been recognised by the EU courts for some years now.'[10]

3. The applicability of Article 6 ECHR under its 'criminal' head to competition proceedings does not carry the consequence that the competition infringement must be found, and the ensuing fine must be imposed, by a court at the close of adversarial judicial proceedings. A two-tier system involving an initial procedure before an administrative body with regulatory power (to investigate, prosecute, fact-find and then impose a financial penalty/fine), followed by the opportunity for the company concerned to bring judicial proceedings before a court in order to contest any adverse decision, including any fine imposed, will not as such give rise to a violation of the company's human right under Article 6 to a fair trial 'in the determination of any criminal charge against [it]'.[11] Before percolating through into the autonomous 'criminal' sphere, the compatibility of such two-tier, regulatory-judicial systems with Article 6 was first established in the 1980s in relation to fair trial in 'civil' matters. In a Belgian case concerning disciplinary sanctions imposed on doctors by their governing professional association, the ECtHR ruled that even where an adjudicatory body determining disputes over 'civil rights and obligations' does not comply with Article 6 in some respects, no violation can be found if the proceedings before that body are subject to subsequent control by a judicial body that has 'full jurisdiction' ('*pleine juridiction*' in French) and does provide the guarantees embodied in Article 6 ECHR, such as independence, impartiality and a proper judicial procedure.[12] Compliance with Article 6 ECHR will depend on the safeguards attending both the regulatory and the judicial stage of the proceedings.

On this introductory proposition, it has to be said that we already part ways with the more militant proponents of justice for cartel companies (that is, companies accused of participation in a cartel), notably Ian Forrester, for whom 'the imposition of severe fines' – including for him EU competition fines – 'other than by an independent and impartial tribunal is a breach of the [EU] Charter and the [ECHR]'.[13]

---

10 Wouter P.J. Wils, 'The Increased Level of EU Antitrust Fines, Judicial Review and the European Convention on Human Rights', *World Competition* 33, no. 1 (2010): 5. See also Wouter P.J. Wils, 'EU Antitrust Enforcement Powers and Procedural Rights and Guarantees: The Interplay between EU Law, National Law, the Charter of Fundamental Rights of the EU and the European Convention on Human Rights', *World Competition* 34, no. 2 (2011): 189.

11 *Menarini*, no. 4 above, §59, cited and approved by the CJEU in *Schindler*, EU:C:2013:522.

12 *Albert and Le Compte v. Belgium*, 10 February 1983, Series A no. 58, §29.

13 Forrester, *Review of Competition Fines*, no. 2 above, p. 185 (abstract). See also the comment in Christopher Bellamy, 'ECHR and Competition Law Post-Menarini: An Overview of EU Law and National Case-Law', *e-Competitions*, No. 47946, 5 July 2012: 'Arguably the extension of that [EU] jurisprudence [emphasizing the deference to be accorded to the European Commission in matters of complex economic and technical assessments] to the penal sphere is in any event contrary to principle, on the grounds that "criminal" liability created on the basis of administrative action without full judicial oversight is itself an affront to fundamental rights.'

III. ECtHR 'full jurisdiction' and competition fines

Those working within the European Commission[14] have not surprisingly put the case for arguing that the existing protective standards for companies in the regulatory procedures before the European Commission are, at their level, satisfactory. Members of the competition defence bar can be expected to be less convinced. The following discussion does not dwell so much on that aspect of the debate, although the presence or lack of protective safeguards available in the regulatory phase will have an incidence on what is to be expected of the court in the subsequent judicial-review phase. The main bone of contention addressed in this paper is whether, after the recent wave of European judicial pronouncements, the kind of judicial review required under the ECHR for the fair trial of a 'criminal charge' is provided by the second tier of the EU competition procedure before the General Court of the EU, it being common ground that the requisite guarantees of independence, impartiality and proper judicial procedure are assured. Here the nub of the problem is what is meant in ECHR jurisprudence by 'full jurisdiction'/'*pleine juridiction*' in the context of judicial review of the 'criminal' sanctions imposed by regulatory competition bodies.

Although the point is not pursued in detail here, there is presumably common ground between the ECHR notion and both the *recours de pleine juridiction* under French administrative law and the 'unlimited jurisdiction'/'*compétence de pleine juridiction*' given to the EU courts by the EU Treaties. In other words, given its presumable origin in French administrative law, the expression 'full jurisdiction'/'*pleine juridiction*' is most likely a term of art and one should be wary of attributing to it an intended literal meaning of unrestricted jurisdiction over the entirety of the factual as well as legal merits.

The ECHR authority most in point is the judgment delivered in September 2011 in the Italian case of *Menarini*, where the applicant company challenged the conformity of the Italian two-tier competition system under Article 6 ECHR.[15] A chamber of the ECtHR held that the fine (of 6 million euros) imposed on the applicant company by the Italian Competition Authority was 'criminal' in character on the basis of the *Engel* criteria by reason of a combination of its punitive and deterrent character and the severity of the sanction imposed, but that the contested decision of the Italian Competition Authority had been subject to review by judicial bodies vested with 'full jurisdiction' as required by Article 6§1 ECHR. In particular, the judgment noted, the administrative courts had been able not only to control whether the Competition Authority had properly exercised its powers, but also 'to examine the merits and the proportionality of the choices made by the Competition Authority and even to verify

14 Notably *Wils*, n. 10 above.

15 *Menarini*, n. 4 above.

its technical assessments'.[16] It is thereby suggested, but not expressly stated, that 'full jurisdiction' requires on the part of the reviewing court at least a power to examine both the merits and the proportionality of the decision taken by the regulatory authority, if not even a power to 'verify the technical assessments'. This, however, as we shall see, is a proposition which, if taken in an unqualified manner, does not appear to be wholly borne out by preceding ECtHR case law, carefully not alluded to in *Menarini*. All in all, the *Menarini* judgment could be taxed with being none too clear on the point of interpretative principle raised, a shortcoming exacerbated by brevity of reasoning and the lack of explanatory justification.

IV. EU 'effective legal protection' and competition fines

Be that as it may, in a couple of judgments (in the cases of *KME* and *Chalkor*)[17] handed down just two months after *Menarini*, the CJEU, taking an approach similar to that suggested between the lines in *Menarini*, laid down quite a robust test for what is required of the EU General Court in order to satisfy the requirements of the fundamental general principle of effective legal protection as now expressed in Article 47 of the EU Charter when reviewing competition decisions taken by the European Commission. The applicant companies in *KME* and *Chalkor* were appealing to the CJEU against the dismissal by the General Court of their claim for a reduction in the fines imposed on them by the European Commission by way of sanction for participation in a cartel (involving copper industrial tubes). The CJEU rejected the notion that what is sometimes called 'light' judicial review of legality is appropriate whenever, as in competition cases, the European Commission is undertaking complex technical assessments:

> [W]hilst, in areas giving rise to complex economic assessments, the Commission has a margin of discretion with regard to economic matters, that does not mean that the courts of the European Union must refrain from reviewing the Commission's interpretation of information of an economic nature. Not only must those courts establish, among other things, whether the evidence relied on is factually accurate, reliable and consistent but also whether that evidence contains all the information which must be taken into account in order to assess a complex situation and whether it is capable of substantiating the conclusions drawn from it . . . .[18]

Although the European Commission has set out in (2006) Fining Guidelines the numerous relevant factors that it will take into consideration in assessing the gravity of antitrust conduct prior to fixing any penalty, as well as the relative importance and incidence of those factors on the amount of any fine, this auto-limitation of its discre-

16 Ibid., §64 (unofficial translation from the French original by the present author).

17 Judgment in *KME*, EU:C:2011:816; Judgment in *Chalkor*, EU:C:2011:815.

18 Judgment in *KME*, EU:C:2011:816, §94.

tionary power by the regulatory authority does not circumscribe the scope of the judicial scrutiny incumbent on the EU courts – in that the requisite scrutiny does not stop at a verification that the Commission has correctly applied its own Guidelines. When carrying out their review, so the CJEU explained, the EU courts 'cannot use the Commission's margin of discretion - either as regards the choice of factors taken into account in the application of the criteria mentioned in the Guidelines or as regards the assessment of those factors - as a basis for dispensing with the conduct of an in-depth review of the law and of the facts'.[19] The CJEU noted that the remedy provided to cartel companies in EU law furnished a review of both the law and the facts and that, in particular, it empowered the EU courts to assess the evidence, to annul the contested decision and to alter the amount of any fine imposed. Its conclusion was that the review of legality provided for under the EU Treaties, supplemented by the 'unlimited jurisdiction' in respect of the fine, was not contrary to the requirements of effective judicial protection as guaranteed by Article 47 of the EU Charter.[20]

Arguably the *KME* and *Chalkor* judgments of 2011 signal a move away from the CJEU's previously criticised 'deferential' approach in competition cases, in going beyond the classic test of 'manifest error of appreciation' on the part of the European Commission. Certainly the tone changed, in particular regarding the degree of deference to be shown by the EU courts towards the European Commission's assessment of complex economic issues. The more stringent test formulated in these two judgments, which would appear to have been transposed from CJEU case law on mergers, notably in the *Tetra Laval* case,[21] was confirmed two years later in *Schindler*,[22] where several companies were contesting the fines imposed on them by the European Commission for participation in cartels for the sale and maintenance of elevators and escalators.

The final chapter in this abbreviated story is provided by the 2012 judgment of the EFTA Court in the *Posten Norge* case, which concerned the imposition of a fine of almost 13 million euros on Norway Post by the EFTA Surveillance Authority ('ESA') for abuse of a dominant position.[23] In its judgment the EFTA Court, unlike the CJEU, framed a good part of its analysis explicitly in terms of the requirements of Article 6 ECHR, with direct reference to the ECtHR's judgment in *Menarini*. While one may suspect that in *KME* and *Chalkor* in 2011, the CJEU, without acknowledging so, may have been prompted by the ECtHR *Menarini* line of jurisprudence to make the scope of judicial control by EU courts in competition cases less 'deferential', the EFTA Court had no *états d'âme* in overtly throwing open its own legal system to review for

19 Judgment in *KME*, EU:C:2011:816, §102.

20 Judgment in *Chalkor*, EU:C:2011:815, §67.

21 Judgement in *Commission v Tetra Laval*, C-12/03 P, EU:C:2005:87, §39.

22 Judgement in *Schindler*, EU:C:2013:522.

23 *Posten Norge*, n. 5 above. See the very positive commentary on this judgment in John Temple Lang, 'Judicial Review of Competition Decisions under the European Convention on Human Rights and the Importance of the EFTA Court: The Norway Post Judgment', E.L. Rev. 2012, 37(4), 464-480B. *Barbier de la Serre*, n. 3 above, talks of *Posten Norge* being a 'milestone' judgment.

compliance with ECHR standards of fair trial. The differing attitudes of the two courts are striking in this regard.[24]

The EFTA Court held, on the basis of the reasoning found in the ECtHR jurisprudence, that the guarantees of a fair trial under the 'criminal' head of Article 6 ECHR applied. It took the 'criminal charge' at hand to be a serious one, remarking in passing that 'the stigma attached to being held accountable for an abuse of a dominant position is not negligible'. It ruled that 'when imposing fines for infringement of the competition rules, ESA cannot be regarded to have any margin of discretion in the assessment of complex economic matters which goes beyond the leeway that necessarily flows from the limitations inherent in the system of legality review'. It added that in a criminal case 'the question whether the evidence is capable of substantiating the conclusions drawn from it by the competition authority must be answered having regard to the presumption of innocence'. And it emphatically concluded, with a frankness absent in the CJEU's rulings, that 'the submission that the Court may intervene only if it considers a complex economic assessment to be manifestly wrong must be rejected'.[25]

V. The implications of ECtHR, EU and EFTA case-law

Are the ECtHR *Menarini* judgment, the CJEU *KME*, *Chalkor* and *Schindler* judgments and the EFTA *Posten Norge* judgment to be read as establishing that, in competition cases where the company concerned is challenging an adverse decision (such as a fine) taken by an administrative regulatory authority, the courts – EU and national – should always carry out a full *merits* review going to the facts as well as the law? And, if so, is that necessarily such a good thing for the community? The present author is not so sure. If the surface is scratched, it can be seen, he believes, that lurking beneath is a social mischief that is far from best being dealt with according to the orthodox methods of the criminal law, with courts deciding on the full – factual and legal – merits of the alleged infringement and any penalty to be imposed.

What are the arguments for such a vision, which would at first sight appear to go against the purity of a human rights analysis, namely that of protecting vulnerable individuals from the potentially overbearing power of public administrations?

---

24 According to *Barbier de la Serre*, n. 2 above, p. 421, 'one of the reasons that makes *Posten Norge* so remarkable [is that] in this judgment the EFTA Court had the audacity of directly confronting the issue avoided by its sister courts', the CJEU and the ECtHR.

25 *Posten Norge*, n. 5 above, §§89-102.

VI. ECtHR 'full jurisdiction' and regulatory procedures

To begin with, as intimated above, looking outside the narrow confines of competition procedures, the 'full jurisdiction' that was read into the concept of a fair trial in Article 6§1 ECHR by the 1983 Belgian doctors' case about professional disciplinary sanctions does not always have to extend to the merits of a contested regulatory decision or to revisiting findings of fact made by a regulatory authority. The following qualifying explanation of the implications of 'full jurisdiction' in relation to administrative law and legal challenges of decisions taken by regulatory authorities can be found in a judgment delivered in 2011 a few months before *Menarini* in a Cypriot case called *Sigma Radio and Television*:

> [It has been acknowledged in ECtHR] case-law that the requirement that a court or tribunal should have 'full jurisdiction' will be satisfied where it is found that the judicial body in question has exercised 'sufficient jurisdiction' or provided 'sufficient review' in the proceedings before it …
>
> In adopting this approach the [ECtHR] organs have had regard to the fact that it is often the case in relation to administrative-law appeals in the Member States of the Council of Europe, that the scope of judicial review over the facts of a case is limited and that it is the nature of review proceedings that the reviewing authority reviews the previous proceedings, rather than taking factual decisions. It can be derived from the relevant case-law that it is not the role of Article 6 [ECHR] to give access to a level of jurisdiction which can substitute its opinion for that of the administrative authorities. In this regard, particular emphasis has been placed on the respect which must be accorded to decisions taken by the administrative authorities on grounds of 'expediency' and which often involve specialised areas of law (for example, planning …; environmental protection …; regulation of gaming …).
>
> In assessing the sufficiency of a judicial review available to an applicant, the Court will have regard to the powers of the judicial body in question …, and to such factors as (a) the subject-matter of the decision appealed against, in particular, whether or not it concerned a specialised issue requiring professional knowledge or experience and whether it involved the exercise of administrative discretion and if, so, to what extent; (b) the manner in which that decision was arrived at, in particular, the procedural guarantees available in the proceedings before the adjudicatory body; and (c) the content of the dispute, including the desired and actual grounds of appeal …[26]

The case concerned judicial review proceedings brought by a broadcasting company in order to challenge decisions taken by the Cyprus Radio and Television Authority

26 *Sigma Radio Television Ltd. v. Cyprus*, nos. 32181/04 and 35122/05, 21 July 2011, §§152-154.

by virtue of which the company was fined for various infringements of the domestic law on broadcasting. Although the applicant company's grievance was examined under the 'civil', rather than the 'criminal', head of Article 6§1, the ECtHR, in dismissing the complaint of a violation of the right to a fair trial as manifestly ill-founded, did not appear to have considered that that made any difference to its analysis of the scope of judicial review that was required.[27] For the present writer, there is no reason why the long-standing analysis reiterated in this Cypriot case should not apply to the 'criminal' limb of Article 6§1 when the 'criminal charge' attracting the application of the judicial fair-trial guarantees likewise has its origins in administrative law procedures and not the mainstream procedure of prosecution under the criminal justice system of the country.

VII. ECHR fair trial outside the 'hard core' of criminal law

The second – linked – argument derives from the consequence which the attribution of an 'autonomous' character to 'criminal charges' on the basis of the *Engel* criteria has in extending Article 6's safeguards of a fair trial in criminal matters into legal areas outside the traditional framework of the criminal justice system, including in particular into the field of administrative law. Given this consequence, the ECtHR has, not surprisingly, been led to the common-sense conclusion that the full strictness of a classic criminal trial is not in principle called for in situations of such extended 'criminal' application of Article 6. This was spelt out in 2006 by the Grand Chamber of the ECtHR in the Finnish case of *Jussila*:

> Notwithstanding the consideration that a certain gravity attaches to criminal proceedings, which are concerned with the allocation of criminal responsibility and the imposition of a punitive and deterrent sanction, it is self-evident that there are criminal cases which do not carry any significant degree of stigma. There are clearly 'criminal charges' of differing weight. What is more, the autonomous interpretation adopted by the [ECtHR] institutions of the notion of a 'criminal charge' by applying the *Engel* criteria have underpinned a gradual broadening of the criminal head to cases not strictly belonging to the traditional categories of the criminal law, for example administrative penalties ..., prison disciplinary proceedings ..., customs law ..., competition law ..., and penalties imposed by a court with jurisdiction in financial matters ... . Tax surcharges differ from the hard core of criminal law; consequently, the criminal-head guarantees will not necessarily apply with their full stringency (see [cases] where it was found

27 Loc. cit., §§126-127, where the ECtHR stated that it did not find it necessary to examine whether the 'criminal' limb of Article 6§1 was applicable to the facts of the case, since neither of the parties disputed applicability of the 'civil' limb – thereby implying that the relevant requirements were the same under both limbs.

> compatible with Article 6 § 1 for criminal penalties to be imposed, in the first instance, by an administrative or non-judicial body ...).[28]

In *Jussila,* tax surcharges imposed by the tax authorities in an administrative procedure were held to constitute 'criminal' penalties attracting the application of Article 6. Nonetheless, the absence of an oral hearing in the subsequent appeal proceedings brought by the applicant before the Finnish administrative courts was not found to give rise to a violation of the right to a fair trial.[29]

The *Menarini* chamber judgment in 2011 passes over in silence this distinction established in *Jussila* beween the 'hard core of criminal law' and other infringements falling under the autonomous 'criminal' head of Article 6 but attracting less stringent procedural requirements, despite competition law being specifically mentioned as one of the sources of administrative penalties falling outside the hard core. Instead the *Menarini* judgment offers a much more diluted proposition, citing the lesser authority of an Italian inadmissibility decision called *Varico*:[30]

> ... the nature of administrative proceedings may differ in several respects from that of criminal proceedings in the strict sense of the term. Whilst such differences are not such as to dispense the Contracting States from their obligation to respect all the guarantees offered by the criminal limb of Article 6, they may nonetheless influence the manner of their implementation ...[31]

In thereby simply ignoring a binding Grand Chamber judgment which was inconvenient for the desired line of reasoning, the authority of the *Menarini* judgment for laying down any unqualified rule as to the need for a review going to the merits of the regulatory competition decision challenged or to technical assessments relied on by the competent regulatory authority is considerably weakened.

VIII. Underlying human rights policies

The main conclusions that have been drawn from the two preceding arguments may be summarized, in reverse, as being:

(1) in proceedings outside the 'hard core' of criminal law for the purposes of the applicability of Article 6 – such as administrative law proceedings -, 'the criminal-law guarantees will not necessarily apply with their full stringency' (*Jussila*); and

(2) the subject-matter of the decision contested and the content of the dispute are relevant factors to be taken into account in assessing the sufficiency of the judicial

28 *Jussila v. Finland*, no. 73053/01, ECHR 2006-XIV, §43.

29 *Jussila*, n. 28 above, §§29-49.

30 *Valico S.r.l. v. Italy* (dec.), no. 70074/01, ECHR 2006-III.

31 *Menarini*, n. 4 above, §62 - unofficial translation from the original French text by the present author.

review available to the person, natural or legal, concerned by the regulatory sanction imposed (*Sigma Radio and Television*).

If these conclusions are correct, the applicable legal framework, including the safeguards offered to the persons concerned at the regulatory stage, should be examined as a whole in order to decide whether the procedure provided for 'the determination' of the autonomous 'criminal charge' is compliant with Article 6 and, as part of this overall assessment, whether the review available at the judicial stage is wide enough in scope. The starting point for any such overall assessment must be the aim that the State is pursuing in operating the regulatory system in question – and this will vary from context to context. The type of aim pursued may place practical constraints, concerning both substance and procedure, on the manner in which laws susceptible of achieving those aims can be framed. Such practical constraints, while clearly never decisive, should not be ignored in any human rights assessment. Again the aim may well have implications for the kind and the contours of human rights protection to be afforded in the context. In simple terms one should first look at the reality of the human rights basics at issue before being sucked into more sophisticated legal analysis. In this connection, the human rights of companies may well have to be balanced against or distinguished from those of individuals.

On this latter point, the present author tends to the view that the prevailing human rights thinking regarding competition fines may be too simplistic in some respects. Although reading the respective ECHR and EU clauses as guaranteeing in competition proceedings full judicial re-examination of the facts and the law would strengthen the legal protection of cartel companies, whether it would be beneficial for the community as a whole and for the 'ordinary Joe' who is a consumer is far from certain.

As far as practicalities are concerned, adopting the suggestion that, for instance, the courts – national or EU – should have to redo all the detailed process of taking and appraisal of the evidence would entail escalating costs for the taxpayer, delays for the consumer, overloading of the courts and so on. What is the point of going to the trouble and public expense of setting up an expert regulatory authority to do the work if the courts are subsequently going to be required to redo all the same work again in a full appeal on the merits?

On the other side of the coin, apart from the claim to be entitled to more or less the same judicial treatment as an individual human being charged with a 'hard core' offence punishable by a severe fine, what in the present two-tier systems with judicial review of legality can be said to involve an injustice, in the ordinary sense of the word, for the cartel companies? The appellant company in *Schindler*, echoing Ian Forrester's sentiments,[32] had argued that EU competition proceedings do indeed form part of 'the hard core of criminal law'.[33] It isdifficult, however, to see how objectively this can be so. Arguments stressing the social opprobrium and stigma attaching to competition

32 *Forrester-Review of Competition Fines*, n. 1 above, pp. 202, 204.

33 Judgment in *Schindler*, EU:C:2013:522.

probes, office searches, infringement proceedings and heavy fines running into millions of euros come across as somewhat strained and hardly convincing in this regard, at least to the present author. As long as there is no prosecution of individuals and no threat of personalised criminal sanctions such as fine or imprisonment, do competition proceedings culminating in a heavy fine represent much more than an essentially financial business risk for the company to be taken into account along with other risks when deciding on business strategy? That is not to say, however, that only a very light judicial scrutiny is to be applied to the conduct and the outcome of administrative infringement proceedings in competition cases which are brought within the scope of the right to a fair trial under Article 6 ECHR by virtue of the 'autonomous' meaning of a 'criminal charge'.

What the lawyers who represent these large cartel companies before the European Commission want is to sideline the classic administrative law concept of judicial review of the legality of administrative action and to replace it with something more like an appeal on the merits. In other words, the objective is to convert the General Court's jurisdiction in competition cases more into an appellate one, as far as possible empowering the judges to substitute their own assessment of the entirety of the factual and legal merits, including on technical issues, for that of the European Commission – 'a full merits appeal' involving 'a full examination of the underlying merits', as Ian Forrester has put it.[34] They want this result because it would give their clients a second full bite of the cherry. The specialist cartel-company lawyers presumably feel that they would stand a greater chance of convincing the (on the whole) non-specialist judges on the General Court, who do not possess the expertise and the institutional back-up of the European Commission.

The question to be asked, though, is whether there are any other legitimate human rights interests in the picture which should influence the kind of 'fair trial' called for. In this connection it is nowadays generally recognized that threats to individual liberty and fundamental rights of the individual human being come not only from public authorities but also from concentrations of private power, such as large multi-national commercial and industrial enterprises. The positive duty of the State in human rights terms is to use its power (legislative, executive and judicial) so as to protect the individual from the mischiefs perpetrated by such concentrations of private power. It could be that in relation to combating cartels this positive human rights duty is better served by entrusting an expert authority with the responsibility, in the public interest, for finding and assessing the necessarily technical facts so as to decide, in a procedure that ensures natural justice and adequate procedural safeguards for the company concerned, whether the finding of an infringement and the imposition of a fine are appropriate, while leaving it to the less well technically qualified judges to control the legality and overall justice of that preceding regulatory procedure.

There is also the general issue of the separation of powers in democratic society between the courts and the other arms of government. Not all the democratic societies making

34 Forrester, *Review of Competition Fines*, n. 1 above, pp. 185 (abstract), 206, 207.

up the ECHR community of States and the EU are convinced of the wisdom of endowing judges with more and more responsibility for making the ultimate choices important for the running of society (the fear of government by judges). In the particular context of competition procedures, this conception of the legitimate role of the courts in political democracies finds expression in a reluctance to give judges the power to substitute their own assessment of the actual merits for the assessment of an expert regulatory authority acting solely in the public interest to protect individual citizens from exploitation by powerful commercial enterprises. The split of responsibility in this regard could be regarded as an essentially political choice for each legal order to take according to normal democratic processes.

The temptation for public officials working for regulatory authorities to behave in an overbearing manner when wielding their regulatory power (and the risks that that entails for the rights of the defence, natural justice and so on) should not be underestimated, and adequate legal protection should be provided to counter such risks and to afford redress in appropriate instances. It is debatable, however, whether the legitimate concern to rein in the excesses of administrative or regulatory action – what Ian Forrester once described to the present author as 'unchecked civil service licence' – should lead to the consequence of going to another extreme, that of, in effect, putting (generalist) judges ultimately in charge of the merits of competition decisions (that is, finding whether an infringement has been committed and imposing a fine).

IX. Conclusion

What prompted the present paper was the concern that has been expressed over the years, and even now after the recent series of judgments from the three European courts, whether the review standard applied by the EU courts in competition cases is not too deferential to the regulatory body, namely the European Commission, particularly in the light of the ECtHR case law on the right to a fair trial before a court in criminal matters. The CJEU has ruled in *Schindler*, in the wake of *KME* and *Chalkor*, that the applicable EU legal framework and the practice of the General Court do ensure cartel companies 'effective legal protection' under Article 47 of the EU Charter. The guiding intent of the present paper was not to offer any specific conclusion on the residual question of the interaction between the EU competition procedure and the ECtHR standards and case law. Rather, it was to urge a departure from accepted human rights analyses concentrating almost exclusively on the rights of defence of cartel companies, by suggesting that a wider societal vision should be taken of the human rights argument before reading into Article 6 ECHR under its criminal head any unqualified right to *full* judicial examination of both facts and law in relation to fines imposed by competition regulators.

It may well be that the ECHR's 'fair trial' and the EU Charter's 'effective judicial protection' at the judicial stage in competition proceedings – before the national as well as EU courts – both require that there should be judicial examination of all matters of fact and law, in the sense that the 'margin of appreciation' or the 'deference' to be shown to the independent regulatory authority acting in the public interest should not exclude or unduly restrict review of the factual, as opposed to strictly legal, aspects of the case. The question is how deep, how intense should be the examination of the facts and the merits, in particular. In the present author's view, while a probing, rigorous examination – an 'in-depth' one, as the CJEU put it in *Chalkor* and *KME* – is doubtless required, covering such matters as whether there is a sufficient factual basis for findings made, the appropriateness of the considerations and of the method relied on for making assessments and the proportionality and overall fairness of the penalty, a *de novo* trial on the merits of the claim, a re-run of the proceedings conducted before the regulatory authority, a completely fresh re-assessment of the penalty in the light of the particular facts, are not.

It may well be that the recent series of European judgments has effectively sounded the death knell on the limitation of judicial review of legality by the EU courts to 'manifest errors of appreciation' in competition cases. Whether the demise of the 'manifest-error' standard should be accompanied by the complete elimination of the notion of a margin of assessment or appreciation in this context[35] is, however, a more radical leap in logic – doubtless supported by members of the competition defence bar – that would not appear justified. Although the EFTA Court, after holding the fair-trial requirements of Article 6 ECHR under its criminal head to be applicable, resolutely rejected a 'deferential' review in favour of a rigorous review – affirming, for example, that it 'must ... be convinced that the conclusions drawn by ESA are supported by the facts' –, that court nonetheless acknowledged that it could not simply replace the regulatory authority's assessment with its own. In *Posten Norge*, the EFTA Court recognised that there did indeed exist 'a leeway' – that is, a margin of discretion – 'that necessarily flows from the limitations inherent in the system of legality review'.[36] In other words, we are talking about a narrow(er), or less wide, margin of appreciation in competition cases, not a total absence of any margin of appreciation.

One last plea, looking to national legal orders and not solely the EU or EFTA context: whether in regard to competition or other regulatory procedures, the notion of judicial review of legality by administrative courts, as it has been developed in democratic European legal systems, should not be emptied of its meaning and replaced by a full re-hearing on the merits as a ricochet of the extension of Article 6 ECHR outside the 'hard core' of criminal justice into the field of administrative law. As it is, the administrative courts in Europe are now expected to develop two kinds of judicial review of administrative action – one for normal cases and a separate, special one for cases judged to fall within the ambit of Article 6 ECHR under its autonomous 'civil' or 'criminal' heads. Are they now to be expected to develop yet a third model for competition cases where a heavy fine is liable to be imposed?

35 As urged by *Barbier de la Serre*, n. 2 above, p. 432.

36 See, generally, *Posten Norge*, n. 5 above, §§96, 98, 100-101.

The wider-vision approach of human rights policy urged in the foregoing brief overview of judicial review of competition fines marks something of a departure from the accepted wisdom as deployed in the accumulated case law and academic writings; and, in arriving at his conclusions, the present author is swimming against the current of juristic opinion, including Ian Forrester's at the forefront. Having been recently – and deservedly – appointed as the UK judge on the General Court in succession to Nicholas Forwood, Ian Forrester may now be in a position to definitively kill off the horse that the present paper has valiantly been trying to keep alive…

Who should own patentable inventions and copyrightable works created during employment?

Isao Noishiki*

This Article examines the ownership of the right to employees' creative works. The Article looks to the underlying goals of the patent system and the intrinsic nature of employment contracts to evaluate the party that should be entitled to own intellectual property rights associated with the employees' inventions and other work products created during the course of employment. The Article concludes that employers should possess such intellectual property rights. The Article further points out that the decision to reward employees' inventive activities should be made by each employer, since an employment contract is made between an employee and its employer. For example, employers may decide to pay a significant bonus to employees who conceive an invention that leads to an immensely valuable patent. The decision should be a business decision. It should not be a decision coerced by a judicial finding or a statutory doctrine grounded in the legal system.

The Article also provides an observation on the copyright of computer programs created at the workplace. The Article points out that, historically, the fundamental legislative goal of protecting computer programs was to prevent the electronic copying of computer programs.

The Article thus contributes to the current literature by presenting arguments that serve as profoundly useful principles for resolving unprecedented intellectual property issues that emerge in the future.

* The author welcomes comments. The author may be contacted at noishiki@r2.ucom.ne.jp.

I. Implications of an employment contract on information generated by employees

Generally speaking, an enterprise engages in a multitude of projects and operations including research, designing, manufacturing, process control, distribution, marketing, and administrative affairs. The enterprise hires employees to perform these numerous tasks. The relationship between an employer and its employees is normally governed by an employment contract. An employment contract embodies an agreement between an employer and its employees that the employer will pay the employees, and in turn, the employees will provide all necessary labour to the employers.

Under this employment contract, the employer owns all work product created by its employees under the employer's supervision. Employment contracts are often abstract, and necessarily include implicit agreements as well as explicit agreements. Implicit agreements often reflect social norms. Implicit agreements are incorporated into the employment contract for two reasons. First, the period of the employment is expected to continue for a long time or, in some cases, indefinitely. Second, it is difficult to stipulate all types of labour that the employees are expected to proffer for an extended period of time.

There is no doubt that the product of physical labour is owned by the employer. Employment contracts cover not only these physical tasks but also the employees' mental tasks. Examples of employees' mental tasks include obtaining new information, discovering new facts, analyzing information, creating new information, storing information, and processing information in various other ways. The processing of information is characteristic of mental tasks, and is often not required for performing physical tasks.

Mental tasks are performed, for instance, by research and development divisions as well as sales divisions. In these divisions, employees are required to create knowledge and process a vast array of information. Such knowledge and information are reported to the employees' supervisors. This information is then systematically managed and controlled by the employer. Information is crucial for maintaining an active business organization that operates effectively. Since inventions conceived by employees also constitute technical information generated by the employees, employers control these inventions. Thus, inventions made by employees are attributed to the employer as a result of the contractual relationship between the employer and the employees.

In further detail, focus is now placed on information provided by employees to their employer in the course of employment. Such information can be categorized into three types depending on its source: (1) information obtained from outside the organization, (2) information generated inside the organization, and (3) ideas created by an employee. New ideas, discoveries, and inventions can be categorized as information (3) created by an employee. Regardless of the categories, employers are entitled to manage and control any information provided by their employees. The content of an invention consisting of technical information is not special in the sense that it comes under employers' management as any other information.

Having creativity is important for an entrepreneur to survive competition. Employers often require and encourage their employees to be creative in their daily work. Inventions are not the only products of creative activities. In the employer's field of business, employees engage in various ingenious efforts and generate innovative work product other than inventions. In general, all information obtained and generated by an employee during the course of his or her employment must be reported to the employer or other management personnel. The employer exercises control over such information and may decide that the information ought to be shared and used among employees to make the organization more effective and productive.

The tertiary sector primarily provides services as opposed to tangible products.[1] This means that mental tasks performed by employees in the tertiary sector carry significantly greater weight than physical labour. Mental tasks are almost always accompanied by creativity.

Employees are generally obligated to report all information that they generate while performing their job duties to their employers or management personnel. Such information includes inventions. Therefore, pursuant to the employment contract between the employer and its employees, the inventive concept, specifications, embodiments, and any technical details of inventions made by employees in the course of their employment are pieces of information that all come under the employer's ownership and control from the instant that the employees conceive the invention. Accordingly, the technical information of an employee's invention also becomes the property of the employer.

Inventions made during employment might be patented in the future. In particular, novel and inventive technology pertaining to the invention are likely to become the subject of a patent application. Other information provided from employees to an employer will likely not be patented, especially if the information is neither novel nor inventive. Thus, technical information generated by employees often has the potential to result in patents of considerable value. If a patent application covering the technical information produced by the employee is granted, the technical information would be protected by a patent. Who is entitled to such patents -- the employee who invented the technology or the inventor's employer? The entitlement to a patent is grounded upon the institutional framework established by the patent system. Therefore, the answer to our inquiry, 'Who is entitled to patents covering an employee's invention?'

---

1 Allan Fisher (1895-1976), Colin Clark (1905-1989), and Jean Fourastié (1907-1990) developed an economic theory in which the industry is divided into three sectors. The primary sector consists of the agricultural and 'extractive' industry, the secondary sector consists of the 'processing' industry, and the tertiary sector consists of the 'services' industry. See Cioban, Gabriela-Liliana, 'The Progress of Economic Thoughtfulness Concerning the Services' at 82, *The Annals of the University of Oradea Economic Sciences*, Tom XXIII, 1st Issue (2014), http://steconomiceuoradea.ro/anale/volume/2014/n1/008.pdf.

must be found in the patent system. From this standpoint, the following section analyzes the patent system.

II. The goal of the patent system

An invention that is kept confidential is bound to become public sooner or later.[2] The sooner an invention becomes part of the public domain, the better, because the novel and inventive technical information embodied by the invention could greatly improve a current state of technology and ultimately benefit the general public.

The primary objective of the patent system is to promote the disclosure and publication, in the best mode of explanation, of inventions in detail that otherwise could remain hidden for a long time. All the publications are made in governmental gazettes which are published, and, in recent years, constitute huge databases which are useful and freely accessible. That primary objective is essential to and most rational for the patent system as discussed below. Other than this primary objective, there are multiple justifications for the patent system. For instance, Article 1 of the Japanese Patent Act provides that '[t]he purpose of this Act is, through promoting the protection and the utilization of inventions, to encourage inventions, and thereby to contribute to the development of industry.'[3] Thus, the Japanese Patent Act stipulates that 'encourag[ing] inventions' is also an objective of patent law, in addition to 'contribut[ing] to the development of industry.' Yet, the encouragement of inventions is made possible by the disclosure of inventions that have already been made. An inventor's ability to conduct even further groundbreaking research and to conceive even more beneficial inventions is enhanced by the availability of information on past inventions. Hence, promoting disclosure is the primary goal essential to the patent system.

To encourage early disclosure of inventions, a strong and attractive incentive is necessary to prompt the person having possession of the secret invention to disclose it to the general public. This incentive must be so attractive that, for the inventor or the possessor of the secret invention, disclosing the invention would be much more profitable and advantageous than concealing the invention. The benefits of obtaining patent rights serve as one such incentive. Therefore, the protection conferred by a patent must be strong enough to encourage the disclosure of secret inventions. As long as secret inventions can be disclosed in this way, the anticompetitive effects of patent rights should be acceptable. If patent rights are stronger than what is necessary to serve as an incentive for disclosure of secret inventions, the overly strong patent rights start to become harmful to the economy. This would give rise to an unacceptable

---

2 Inventions generally include both methods and devices. Methods that are kept confidential within a corporation are likely to become public over time, as other employees learn of the methods by coincidence, and leave the corporation for various reasons. Inventions that are devices are likely to become public as well. For instance, such devices may be sold in the market, and purchasers of the devices may reverse-engineer. As a result, the components and workings of the devices may eventually become public.

3 Japanese Patent Act, Act No. 121 of 1959, 'Patent Act' is displayed on 'Japanese Law Translation' on the following website: http://www.japaneselawtranslation.go.jp/?re=02.

degree of anticompetitive effects, which an ideal patent system cannot tolerate. On the other hand, if patent rights are so weak that they do not serve as any incentive to disclose secret inventions, the inventor or the possessor of secret inventions would not have enough motivation to publish or disclose the inventions.

Keeping this objective in mind is essential in designing an effective and meaningful patent system. The objective of providing enough incentive to encourage early disclosure of secret inventions serves as a guiding principle in solving every problem of the patent system.

The concentration of investment in the production and sales of patented products is a resulting effect of the patent system and is by no means an essential objective of the patent system. Such investment in specific goods could be stimulated by taxation or government subsidies.

The patent system could be seen as bringing gains to an inventor. The patent system could also be viewed as giving the inventor or a potential inventor an incentive to invent. It is true that these favourable effects are due to the designs of the patent system. However, as discussed above, providing inventors with profits and prompting individuals and entities to invent are not the main goals of the patent system. Even if a patent system brings about strong patents covering a broad scope and having a long patent term, there is no guarantee that such a system would encourage inventive activities and contribute to an increase in the number of inventions. This is because inventions are conceived primarily by talent and curiosity, secondly by adequate ingredients, materials, and equipment, and thirdly by other support such as capable assistants or a work environment that is accommodating and convenient for inventive activities.

Meanwhile, prompt publication and disclosure of inventions cannot be realized without a proper incentive structure established by a sound patent system. Inventors are original holders controlling inventions in fact. Therefore, providing the incentives for the holders of inventions to bring inventions swiftly into the public domain is the primary and foremost objective of the patent system.

In the patent system, the disclosure of inventions begins with an application from the holders of inventions for a patent. In most instances, an inventor is qualified to apply for a patent because he or she has kept the invention confidential.

The first-to-invent regime is a patent system that lays emphasis on inventors' conception of inventions. Meanwhile, the first-to-file regime values early filing and disclosure of inventions. This first-to-file system has been adopted worldwide, including the United States of America.[4] This harmonization of the patent system indicates that the prompt

4 The patent prosecution system in the United States had operated under the first-to-invent system while most other countries in the world operated under the first-to-file system. However, on 16 September 2011, the United States enacted the Leahy-Smith America Invents Act. Section 3 of the America Invents Act created a 'first-inventor-to-file' regime to replace the former first-to-invent system. See Leahy-Smith America Invents Act, Pub. L. No. 112-29, 125 STAT. 284, Section 3 (2011). This change has been widely regarded as a step to harmonize the patent prosecution system worldwide.

disclosures of inventions, i.e., the early filing of a patent application disclosing an invention, is the true objective of the patent system and that the protection of inventors is not the primary objective of the patent system. Under the current patent system, the earlier the filing of patent applications is made, the better chances an inventor has for obtaining patent protection over his or her inventions.

Active disclosure of inventions may be achieved only by protecting the invention, not the inventor. The granting of patent rights is one way that state power provides protection to inventions. In so far as an inventor holds inventions in secret, such protection is beneficial to an inventor because the state will protect the invention on behalf of the inventor. Since inventors no longer need to keep the invention secret by themselves, protection by the state brings reassurance and peace of mind to these inventors. Consequently, inventors are prompted to disclose their inventions. It is important to note that protecting an invention is different from protecting an inventor.

Inventions are technical information and impersonal. An invention is transferable as an intangible asset by keeping the invention secret. An inventor who assumes a secrecy obligation for the assignee may assign all the technical information concerning the invention to the assignee so that the assignee can manage the technical information in its entirety. Consequently, the assignee of the technical information becomes the legitimate holder of the invention, who is entitled to decide whether to make the invention public. In this situation, it is clear that the patent system should protect an invention, but not an inventor.

As regards inventors, the honour of being an inventor is inherent to the inventor. The honour is a kind of moral right and is not transferrable. The Paris Convention provides that the inventor has the right to be mentioned as the inventor in the patent.[5]

As regards the patent system, its prime and essential objective is the earliest publication of inventions, whether held by the inventor or any assignee.

III. Inventions created by employees

When an invention by an employee is made while on duty during the course of employment, all technical information concerning the invention belongs automatically to the employer and comes under the custody and management of the employer, since an explicit and implicit employment agreement is effectively in place. As a result, the employee-inventor is not legally entitled to the technical information regarding the invention. The employee-inventor certainly has extensive knowledge of the content and details of the invention, since the employee-inventor himself or herself has invented it. However, the employee-inventor has no power to control the information. The employee-inventor is obligated under the employment contract to abide by the managerial decisions of the employer. If the employee-inventor discloses the confidential content of the invention to any outsiders without the employer's consent, he

5 The Paris Convention for the Protection of Industrial Property of 1883, revised at Stockholm in 1967, Article 4ter.

or she breaches a trust under the employment contract. If the employee-inventor applies for a patent based on the confidential invention without the employer's consent, as the application may proceed to publication, he or she may breach a trust under the employment contract.

Considering that the disclosure of inventions is the primary and genuine objective of the patent system, the employer who controls all the technical information of its employees' invention is in the most rational position to apply for a patent concerning the employees' inventions.

The Japanese Patent Act provides the right for an inventor to be entitled to obtain a patent,[6] and the right is transferable. This right does not confer power to manage or control the content of inventions. When the right to obtain a patent is transferred, the content of inventions does not accompany the right as a matter of law. The transfer of the content of inventions is to be made on agreement by both parties. The assignee needs the inventor's agreement of confidentiality.

This right is vested in the employee-inventor as an inventor. Meanwhile, the employer controls all the information concerning the employee's invention. Accordingly, an employee-inventor's right to obtain a patent for inventions made while on duty is nominal like the shell of a cicada. Logically speaking, the right to obtain a patent is inherent in a confidential invention. The right to obtain a patent should accompany inventions which are transferable, and should not accompany inventors. This logical result shows that the relevant statutory provisions of the Japanese Patent Act diverge from the rational formula in two respects. First, the right to obtain a patent is vested only in an inventor, and no right is vested in the legitimate holder, such as an employer, keeping inventions in secret. Second, the right to obtain a patent is thought of as a proprietary right of an employee-inventor, while the right is merely to require an administrative procedure for a patent.

As long as an invention is made by an employee while performing his or her job responsibilities, the law allows the employer to take over the employee-inventor's right on a regulatory or contractual basis, provided that the employer pays the employee a 'reasonable value' for the transfer of the right.[7]

---

6 Article 29 of Japanese Patent Act provides as follows:

(1) An inventor of an invention that is industrially applicable may be entitled to obtain a patent for the said invention, except for the following:
inventions that were publicly known in Japan or a foreign country, prior to the filing of the patent application;
inventions that were publicly worked on in Japan or a foreign country, prior to the filing of the patent application; or
inventions that were described in a distributed publication, or inventions that were made publicly available through an electric telecommunication line in Japan or a foreign country, prior to the filing of the patent application.

(2) is omitted. See Japanese Law Translation, *supra* at footnote 3.

7 Article 35 of the Japanese Patent Act provides as follows: (1), (2) and (4) are omitted.

Where the employee, etc., in accordance with any agreement, employment regulation or any other stipulation, vests the right to obtain a patent or the patent right for an employee invention in the employer, etc., or grants an exclusive licence therefor to the employer, etc., the said employee, etc. shall have the right to receive reasonable value.

In most cases in Japan, patent applications on employees' inventions made in the course of their employment are filed and prosecuted by their employer, who has taken over the inventions. The annual official patent statistics in Japan indicate that, in every year between 2004 and 2013, approximately 97% of patent applications were filed by corporate bodies.[8] The inventions covered by these applications are presumably created by employees during the course of their employment.

What should be the appropriate price for the right to obtain a patent over employees' inventions? This issue has been intensely debated in the past two decades in Japan. Before then, the prevailing common practice was that employers paid employee-inventors a small and fixed amount of money at the time of a report coming from the employee of the invention or at the time of application for a patent. Additional payment was made pursuant to each employer's regulation following achievements such as a patent registration and an annual evaluation of patented inventions being used. In particular, a Japanese Supreme Court decision in 2003[9] has become an authority to be relied upon when an employee-plaintiff claims that his or her former employer should make additional payments to the employee-plaintiff until the paid amount reaches the 'reasonable value' of the employee-plaintiff's right to obtain a patent for his or her invention. This controversy motivated the legislator to amend the provisions of the Japanese Patent Act on what the reasonable value should be that an employee-inventor is entitled to receive from the employer.

As discussed above, the ultimate justification of the patent system is to hasten the publication of inventions. Hence, the legitimate applicant for a patent is an employer, and not the employee-inventor. If any monetary payment is made to an employee-inventor from its employer, such payment does not relate to the patent system. Rather, the payment is the result of an entrepreneurial decision made by the employer.

On 13 March 2015, the Japanese Ministry of Economy, Trade and Industry announced that it would revamp the patent system concerning employee inventions. In particular, the amendments to the provisions of the Japanese Patent Act proposed by the Japanese government add more criteria on how an employer regulates the 'reasonable value' to be paid to an employee-inventor for the right to obtain a patent over an invention conceived by an employee. The proposed amendment is based on the belief that the 'reasonable value' for an employee-inventor is a critical concept for the patent system.

---

(5) Where no provision setting forth the value as provided in the preceding paragraph exists, or where it is recognized under the preceding paragraph that the amount of the value to be paid in accordance with the relevant provision(s) is unreasonable, the amount of the value under paragraph (3) shall be determined by taking into consideration the amount of profit to be received by the employer, etc. from the invention, the employer, etc.'s burden, contribution, and treatment of the employee, etc. and any other circumstances relating to the invention. See Japanese Law Translation, *supra* at footnote 3.

8 For example, according to the *Japan Patent Office Annual Report 2014*, there were 9,464 patent applications filed by individuals, 318,944 patent applications filed by corporate entities, and 28 patent applications filed by the government. Thus, in 2013, 97.1% of the patent applications were filed by corporate entities.

9 See *Olympus Optical Co., Ltd. v. Shumpei Tanaka* (Japanese Sup. Ct., 22 April 2003), Hanrei Jiho (Case Report) No. 1822, at 39.

IV. Copyrightable works created by employees

Copyright law protects expression. However, copyright law does not protect the idea that is expressed. Thus, there is a dichotomy between the expression and the idea of a copyrightable work. According to this dichotomy, the information or content of a work falls within the scope of an idea, and is therefore never protected by copyright law.

The idea expressed in a work bears social responsibility. In this sense, the idea expressed in a work is more important than the expression itself.

A very large number of works are created by employees while fulfilling their job duties. These works can be divided into two categories according to the content of their works. In the first category, an employer takes responsibility for the content of the works. In the second category, an individual employee takes responsibility for the content of the works. The works in both categories are created by employees during the course of employment. Copyright issues are generally discussed in terms of the expression of works. However, the content of the work is more important to society.

Employees are not allowed to change the content of the first category of works because the employer is responsible for the content. Accordingly, the expression of these works in the first category must be constrained by the content of the works. Even if the employer gives instructions only on the content of these works and gives no instructions on the expression of the content, the employee would recognize that the employer has the right to modify or reject any expression that the employees make. Employees are therefore expected to speculate how the employer intended to express the content of the works. Therefore, even though the expression itself may be made by the employee, the employer's personality is more or less reflected in both the content and the expression of the works to the extent the employer wishes. On the other hand, the employee could not fully reflect his or her personality into the expression of works made while on duty. Even though these works are created by an employee, the author of these works is the employer, who is solely responsible for the content, and the name of the employer is shown on these works as their author. The employee is not responsible for the content of the works, and would not wish to have his or her name listed as the author. This is because employees having self-esteem would not present themselves as the author of the work when they are not allowed to freely express their personality in both the content and the expression of the works. Characteristics of human nature such as self-esteem, pride, or individual dignity are a fundamental source of law.[10] All responsibility for such works shall be assumed by the employer.

---

10 Copyrightable works reflect authors' human individuality, while inventions don't. An inventor's name is to be mentioned in a patent.

Examples of such works include business reports for shareholders, annual securities reports, and instruction manuals for products. These works are impersonal both in content and expression. Meanwhile, employers' announcements of inauguration or retirement, employers' speeches, or articles under the name of the employer might all be written by employees while they are on job duty. These works are personal. However, the employer is the author of these works because the employer is socially responsible for them, and because the expression reflects the personality of the employer, as discussed above.

In the business of advertisement and design, an employee needs to use his or her expertise in design while performing job duties. A piece of advertisement or design may appear to be created freely by the employee, or there seems to be joint authorship between the employee and the employer. Ultimately, however, the employer's intent regarding the expression of the advertisement and design supersedes the intent of the employee. There can be no 'freely created' work by any employee. This is logically derived from the same theory that an employer is responsible with respect to its customers in both content and expression.

Employees report daily to their supervisors, make suggestions, and regularly communicate during their job duties. The contents of these reports, suggestions, and communications are information pertaining to the business of the employer. An employer has control over such information because the employer owns its business. Otherwise, the business organization consisting of the employer and the employee cannot function properly, as discussed earlier.

The expressions of these reports, suggestions, and communications are made by individual employees. The employee is responsible for the content, and therefore, is the author of these works. His or her name is posted on these works as the author. The employer must be interested in the information conveyed by such works made by their employees, and would not care much about how these reports, suggestions, and communications are expressed. When the employer has an interest in the information conveyed by such works, the employer may use the information freely, which is the content of these works. However, if the employer intends to use these expressions by making copies for distribution, the employee's permission is necessary. Yet, the employee ought to have expected that the expression would be used for business purposes. Implied permission from employees is presumed to have been obtained under the employment agreement. Explicit permission from the employee is required when the use of the expressions infringes on the moral rights of the employee.

In 1994, global society agreed to protect computer programs as copyrightable works.[11] Historically, national legislators had responded to a very urgent and strong demand from industrial leaders in the 1970's through 1980's to prohibit unauthorized copying of computer programs with copyright law. Indeed, tremendous labour and cost are

11 Agreement (1994) on TRIPs, Article 10, Computer Programs and Compilations of Data, at 1. Computer programs, whether in source or object code, shall be protected as literary works under the Berne Convention (1971). 2. is omitted.

expended to create computer programs. They can be copied instantly with negligible cost.[12] Copying computer programs is far easier than manufacturing copies of devices. At that time, it was easier and faster for the legislators to use copyright law to prohibit unauthorized copying of computer programs as literary works. Coding of computer programs conveys a person's idea to other individuals, and therefore, is a literary work. Computer programs are therefore protected as a copy of such literary work.

Computer programs are different from conventional works in that the final purpose of computer programs is to operate computers directly, based on how the computer programs are expressed. The expressions in computer programs are extremely important and extremely impersonal. In a preparatory stage of making computer programs, the purpose and design of function is always presented accurately and definitely, and a system to achieve the purpose of the computer programs is structured in rational logic. Accordingly, computer programs are made adhering to the logical design of the system as well as the logical rules of algorithms. The constraints on how to express computer programs are extremely rigid. Even if there is a single, extra comma in the computer program, the computer will not function. The content of a literal expression as a conventional copyrightable work can be understood even if there is a single, extra comma in the expression of the work. In these ways, computer programs have a unique nature that is entirely different from how conventional literal works are expressed. The scope of copyright over computer programs is very narrow because of the constraints concerning functionality.

The example of photographs is referenced to understand the copyrightable nature of computer programs. Photos are copyrightable by accumulating the creativities of layout, nuance of color, perspective, tone of light, and many other factors, each of which falls in the field of idea. Room for creative expression in photos is very narrow. Drawing a similar or even the same picture to the photo by looking at the photo does not infringe copyright of the photo. Taking a photo of the same object at the same place, under the same meteorological conditions, and with the same camera, does not infringe copyright of the target photo. The same or similar expressions common to the new photo and the target photo are not protected by copyright due to lack of creativity. The method and manner of taking a photo are not protected by copyright.

An original purpose of industrial leaders who promoted the legislation must have been to prohibit the direct electrical copying of computer programs. Once a decision was made to apply the law of copyright, the copyright holders of computer programs have been apt to invoke copyright to the full extent.

In the case of literal works, the purpose of copyright is to protect expression by letters, including symbols, as literal expression. However, as the purpose cannot be achieved by protecting literal expression alone, the copyright extends its protection to the

12 This was the point most focussed upon. The recital (2) of the EU Directive 2009/24/EC provides as follows: ... Whereas:...(2) The development of computer programs requires the investment of considerable human, technical and financial resources while computer programs can be copied at a fraction of the cost needed to develop them independently.

non-literal expression behind the literal expression. In that case, copyright protects adaptations which do not necessarily use the literal expression, but use non-literal expression of the target work.

Regarding computer programs, non-literal expressions are not to be protected by copyright, because the area of non-literal expressions is dictated by logic.[13] The Japanese Copyright Act specifically provides that algorithms, computer programming languages and computer programming rules are outside the scope of protection.[14]

A small portion of literal expression of computer programming cannot be protected by copyright due to lack of creativity of expression. Just like photos described above, the accumulation of slight creativity on many various factors or portions of expression allows a considerably large-sized computer program to be copyrightable. If copyrightable, copying of the entire literal expression is prohibited by copyright. In reality, direct electric copying alone is prohibited.

Since employees' jobs in making computer programs are directed by the employer, the authors of those computer programs are the employers. The employer's authorship of computer programs is supported by the fact that any defect in the expression of computer programs leads directly to a malfunction of a product for which the employer must be responsible to buyers as the seller. It would be a pity for an employee to be involved in damages claims incurred by any malfunction of a device, merely because he or she was the author of the computer program equipped inside the device. The Japanese Copyright Act provides that an employer shall be the author of computer programs made by an employee in the course of employment.[15]

---

13 The author did not reach the point in 1993. Isao Noishiki, *The Scope of the Copyright Holder's Right to Adapt Computer Programs*, IIC Vol. 24 No. 2/1993, p. 200.

14 Article 10 (Illustrations of works) of Japanese Copyright Act, Act No. 48 of 1970, revised by Act No. 121 of 2008, provides as follows:

(1) As used in this Act, examples of 'works' include, in particular, the following:

(ix) computer program works.

(2) is omitted.

(3) The protection granted by this Act to works provided in paragraph (1), item (ix) shall not extend to any computer programming language, rule or algorithm used for creating such work. For the purpose of this provision, the following terms shall have the meanings hereby assigned to them, respectively, in each of the items below:

(i) 'computer programming language' means letters and other symbols, as well as the systems for their use, as a means of expressing a computer program;

(ii) '[computer programming] rule' means a special rule with respect to how to use a particular computer program's computer programming language (as defined in the preceding item);

(iii) '[computer programming] algorithm' means the method of combining, in a computer program, the instructions given to a computer. The 'Copyright Act' is displayed on 'Japanese Law Translation' on the following website: http://www.japaneselawtranslation.go.jp/?re=02.

15 Article 15 (Authorship of a work made by an employee in the course of his duties) of Japanese Copyright Act provides as follows:

(1) ...a juridical person or other employer (hereinafter in this Article referred to as 'juridical person, etc.')....

(2) The authorship of a computer program which, on the initiative of a juridical person, etc., is made by an employee in the course of his duties in connection with the juridical person, etc.'s business, shall be attributed to such juridical person, etc., unless otherwise stipulated by contract, work regulations or the like at the time of the making of the work. See Japanese Law Translation, *supra* at footnote 15.

If an employee who wrote a computer program while on duty quits and gets a new job at another employer, he or she can write a new computer program for the same purpose without being afraid of infringing the former employer's copyright of the computer program that the employee previously made under the former employer.[16] This is because the literal expressions of the new computer program must be different from the former one, and the same literal expressions must come from the same function of the computer program.

V. Conclusion

Inventions and works are both produced by employees. Both are intellectual property. The common nature of these inventions and works is conspicuous in that both are created intellectually, and that both are valuable, intangible resources. However, the purpose and mechanism of protecting inventions are quite different from those of protecting works. Every problem concerning the protection of intellectual property must be examined respectively under the purpose and the mechanism of the intellectual property system. Inventions and copyrightable works created during employment are examined under this framework.

Practically speaking, intellectual property may appear to be protected in a similar manner to a certain extent. However, the nature of intellectual property protection varies depending on the characteristics of each type of intellectual property. To solve each issue, the basic nature of intellectual property protection serves as the guiding principle. The fundamental nature of the system and the nature of intellectual property rights must be taken into consideration and should be reflected as we solve various problems.

In addition to intellectual property issues on computer programs, intellectual property protection over databases and large volumes of data are drawing more and more attention nowadays. The concepts and analyses presented here are equally applicable to unprecedented intellectual property issues that emerge from state-of-the-art technology.

---

16 A court case from Japan as below is to be referred to. A consignee, entrusted to make an improved version of the consignor's computer programs, makes, after fulfilling the entrusted duty, a set of new computer programs to be equipped in the consignee's products for sales competing with the consignor's, the purpose and the functions of which are almost all the same as the computer programs entrusted and improved by the consignee. Some portions of literal expressions seem to be the same between them. The High Court of Intellectual Property of Japan determined that the consignee's making of the new computer programs does not infringe the copyright of the improved version, because the similarity of literal expressions comes from the function or commonness for the public, and the similarity of the structure of the computer programs comes from function or logic. See *Shinkowa Software K. K. v. Nippontekuno Lab K. K.*, Decided on 12 March 2014, Hanrei Jiho (Case Report) No. 2229, at 85. By replacing the consignee above with an employee and following the reasoning of the judgment, it is sustained that computer programs made by the employee employed by a future employer after leaving the former employer, the purpose, the functions and some portion of literal expressions of which are the same as the computer programs made for the former employer, without electric direct whole copying, do not infringe copyright of the computer programs of the former employer.

Copyright and human rights

DEAN SPIELMANN

I. Copyright in a 'human rights context'

1. Introductory remarks

Ian, to whom I am pleased to dedicate this contribution, loves music, literature and art, and he has always been deeply committed to justice and respect for fundamental freedoms. Copyright is at the intersection of culture and law. I am convinced, therefore, that the legal questions related to copyright must be a topic that has been, and remains, of interest to him. Copyright (or '*droits d'auteur*') and human rights might appear as somewhat uneasy bedfellows. At first sight, it might seem that linking copyright to human rights is quite an artificial exercise. However, that would be but a superficial impression. Human rights do affect copyright and the opposite is also true. As I seek to show in this contribution, copyright is a complex tool used to protect various interests. And as copyright protection also requires robust criminal and civil law remedies, the guarantees of a fair trial need to be respected. Moreover, the legal aspects of artistic freedom may well denote conflicts between equally protected rights. Limitation clauses in human rights provisions are often invoked to resolve such conflicts. But the outcome of the balancing exercise is not always easy to predict. As one author has put it, '... such balancing of human rights against each other requires a very careful analysis of the values protected and involved. It is nearly impossible to predict the results of balancing of legitimate interests on the level of the judiciary...'.[1] In this contribution I attempt to explore the legal framework concerning copyright in the context of human rights and then focus on the Strasbourg case law. Recent developments show that the question of victim status is relevant, but that, as to substance, the European Court of Human Rights mainly weighs in the balance freedom of expression against other rights and interests.

2. The legal framework

Article 10 of the European Convention on Human Rights protects freedom of expression, but no explicit reference to artistic freedom is to be found in the text.[2] However, under the relevant Strasbourg case law, artistic freedom is certainly covered by Article 10. In *Müller and Others v Switzerland*,[3] a judgment dating back to 1988, the Court thus stated:

> Those who create, perform, distribute or exhibit works of art contribute to the exchange of ideas and opinions which is essential for a democratic society. Hence the obligation on the State not to encroach unduly on their freedom of expression.[4]

The Court went on to say in that judgment:

> Artists and those who promote their work are certainly not immune from the possibility of limitations as provided for in paragraph 2 of Article 10. Whoever exercises his freedom of expression undertakes, in accordance with the express terms of that paragraph, 'duties and responsibilities'; their scope will depend on his situation and the means he uses...[5]

The exchange of ideas and opinions is of paramount importance, but artistic freedom is not an absolute right.[6] What then would the limitations be in the context of copyright?

One of the limitations to artistic freedom and freedom to play or consume music is of course the possibility of copyright proceedings which might be used to protect 'the

---

1 G. Jokhadze, 'The Big Ones of the Music Industry: Copyright and Human Rights Aspects of the Music Business', in I. Ziemele (ed.), *Expanding the Horizons of Human Rights Law, New Authors, New Themes*, Leiden/Boston: Martinus Nijhoff Publishers, 2005, pp. 237-287 at p. 272.

2 In contrast to Article 5(3) of the German Basic Law. The EU Charter of Fundamental Rights distinguishes between freedom of expression and information on one hand (Article 11) and freedom of arts and sciences (Article 13) on the other.

3 *Müller and Others v. Switzerland*, 24 May 1988, Series A no. 133.

4 Ibid., para 33.

5 Ibid., para 34.

6 In contrast with Article 5 (3) of the German Basic Law (artistic freedom), which can be subject to limitations only if it enters into conflict with another provision of this Law. See on this point my joint dissenting opinion (with Judge Jebens) in *Vereinigung Bildender Künstler v. Austria*, no. 68354/01, 25 January 2007 (footnote 3): '... It should be noted that in German Constitutional Law, freedom of the arts (*Kunstfreiheit*) is *specifically* protected by Article 5 (3) of the Basic Law. "The exercise of this freedom is not limited, as is freedom of expression, by the provisions of general laws or the right to reputation, but it must be considered in conjunction with other constitutional rights, notably the right to the free development of personality and human dignity." E. Barendt, *Freedom of Speech*, 2nd ed., Oxford: Oxford University Press, 2005, p. 229 ...'

rights of others', under Article 10 § 2 of the European Convention.[7] 'Prevention of crime' can be another legitimate aim. I have elaborated on 'copyright limitations' to artistic freedom in my contribution to the collection of essays in honour of my predecessor, Sir Nicolas Bratza.[8] I emphasized that a balancing exercise would inevitably be called for. Artistic freedom, as part and parcel of freedom of expression, including the right to quote from a work or freedom to receive information, may conflict with the property or personality rights of the original composer or performer, protected mainly through copyright actions.

The relationship between copyright, on the one hand, and freedom of expression, personality rights, rights of property, etc., on the other, have remained somewhat unexplored.[9] Moreover, in contrast to other international treaties and documents, there is no explicit reference to copyright or intellectual property in the European Convention on Human Rights.[10] Copyright protection is, for example, enshrined in Article 27(2) of the Universal Declaration, which reads as follows:

> Everyone has the right to the protection of the moral and material interests resulting from any scientific, literary or artistic production of which he is the author.

In a similar vein, Article 15(1)(c) of the International Covenant on Economic, Social and Cultural Rights ('CESCR') provides that '[t]he States Parties to the present Covenant recognize the right to everyone . . . [t]o benefit from the protection of the moral and material interests resulting from any scientific, literary or artistic production of which he is the author.'

It is disputed in legal literature whether copyright addresses as such the *idea* underlying the work that needs protection of free speech.[11] But it seems undisputed that the *expressions* of an author's ideas are not left entirely without copyright protection.[12] The *economic* protection of copyright is clearly covered by the right to property and the *underlying idea* seems to be covered by the *moral* rights of the author. Articles 10 (freedom of expression) and 8 (right to private life) of the Convention, as well as Article 1 of Protocol No. 1 to the Convention (protection of property) may be mobilised

---

7 For a particularly broad reading of the meaning of 'rights of others', see *Groppera Radio AG and Others v. Switzerland*, 28 March 1990, Series A no. 173. In this judgment, the Court seems to have included the public interest at large (fostering pluralism on the airwaves) within the notion of 'rights of others'.

8 See D. Spielmann, 'Variations on an original theme: Music and Human Rights, Variation II (*Contrapunctus*): Music, human rights and copyright', in J. Casadevall, E. Myjer, M. O'Boyle and A. Austin (eds.), *Freedom of Expression, Essays in honour of Nicolas Bratza*, Oisterwijk: Wolf Legal Publishers, 2012, pp. 363-381, at pp. 366-369.

9 As Christoph Beat Graber points out, '[i]f one looks at textbooks and monographs on human rights issues, one notices that reflections on conflicts of free speech and copyright hitherto are almost completely absent'. See C. B. Graber, 'Copyright and Access – a Human Rights Perspective', in C. Govoni, M. Girsberger and M. Nenova (eds.), *Digital Rights Management – the End of Collecting Societies?*, Berne: Stämpfli Publishers, New York: Juris Publishers, Brussels: Bruylant, Athens: Ant. N. Sakkoulas, 2005, pp. 1-42 at p. 5.

10 P. Bernt Hugenholtz, 'Copyright and freedom of expression in Europe', in R. Cooper Dreyfuss, H. First and D. Leenheer Zimmerman (eds.) *Expanding the Boundaries of Intellectual Property*, Oxford: Oxford University Press, 2001, at p. 3. See also, P.L.C. Torremans (ed.), *Copyright and Human Rights*, The Hague, London, New York: Kluwer Law International, 2004.

11 For an interesting discussion, also in the American context, see G. Jokhadze, *op. cit.*, at p. 285.

12 Ibid.

to solve potential problems. As I have argued in my essay presented to Sir Nicolas Bratza, it would not be unreasonable to include copyright as such within the realm of the freedom of expression guaranteed under Article 10 or even under Article 8, protecting private life. I find the latter provision particularly relevant in connection with the moral rights (*droit moral*) of the author. After all, if it is accepted that the 'moral right to "object to any distortion, mutilation or other modification of, or other derogatory action in relation to, the said work" can possibly encompass the freedom of speech',[13] I would argue that, even more so, the moral aspect of copyright might be encompassed by protection of private life. It has been emphasized that '[t]he Court seems willing to accept that Article 8 is to be understood as containing various guarantees to personal autonomy, personal privacy, personal identity, personal integrity, personal development, personal identification and similar concepts linked to the individual notion of personhood. Article 8, therefore, protects much more than a straightforward "right to privacy".'[14] In this context it may be of interest to cite, as an interpretative guide concerning the scope of Article 8, the Berne Convention for the Protection of Literary and Artistic Works, which under Article 6*bis* provides:

> (1) Independently of the author's economic rights, and even after the transfer of the said rights, the author shall have the right to claim authorship of the work and to object to any distortion, mutilation or other modification of, or other derogatory action in relation to, the said work, which would be prejudicial to his honour and reputation.

As Jokhadze has emphasized, 'it would be premature to state, beyond purely theoretical assumptions, that an author's moral rights do constitute a part of human rights per se; such a thesis is yet to be rendered valid through express pronouncement to this effect by relevant judicial authorities.'[15] Be that as it may in the copyright context, it should be noted that the European Court of Human Rights has developed in recent years a considerable body of case law related to the protection of honour and reputation under Article 8 of the Convention.[16]

It is therefore my submission that positive obligations under both Articles 10 and 8 of the Convention may be of relevance to the protection of the artist's copyright. Property

---

13 G. Jokhadze, *op. cit.*, at p. 285; at p. 286 the author even refers to the 'dignity of the author, by entailing [him] to maintain some of his non-commercial rights over musical works and, in particular, to object to censorship (as a form of derogatory treatment of the work, which is prejudicial to the honour of the author)'.

14 See A.W. Heringa and L. Zwaak, 'Right to respect for privacy (Article 8)', in P. van Dijk, F. van Hoof, A. van Rijn and L. Zwaak, *Theory and Practice of the European Convention on Human Rights*, 4th edition, Antwerp, Oxford: Intersentia, 2006, at p. 665.

15 G. Jokhadze, *op. cit.*, at p. 247.

16 For an overview see D. Spielmann and L. Cariolou, 'The right to protection of reputation under the European Convention on Human Rights', in D. Spielmann, M. Tsirli and P. Voyatzis (eds.) *The European Convention on Human Rights, a living instrument. Essays in Honour of Christos L. Rozakis*, Brussels: Bruylant, 2011, pp. 571-596 and by the same authors, 'The Right to Protection of Reputation under the European Convention on Human Rights', in *Law in the Changing Europe. Liber Amicorum Pranas Kūris*, Mykolo Romerio universitetas, 2008, pp. 401-424.

rights under Article 1 of Protocol No. 1 are, of course, also relevant.[17] Under the European Convention, complex scenarios involving delicate balancing may thus be imagined. The artist's freedom of expression, protected under the positive obligations of Article 10, may conflict with freedom of information, more precisely the freedom of the art consumer to gather information by listening to music, or more generally by copying or storing works of art, equally protected under Article 10. In this context, access to cultural information should not be forgotten. This right is provided for by Article 27 of the Universal Declaration of Human Rights, which guarantees the right to participate in cultural life. This latter freedom may in turn conflict with Article 8 of the Convention (moral rights) or the pecuniary rights of the artist. However, any precipitated conclusions should be avoided. After all, as one author has put it '... constitutional rights and in particular freedom of expression, cannot be properly applied as a match winning argument in conflicts among undertakings, which confront themselves at arm's length in economic controversies that can easily be resolved through typical private law instruments (i.e., contract).'[18]

II. Early Strasbourg case law

The creative ideas of authors are protected under the case law of the European Court of Human Rights, mainly by reference to economic aspects.[19] As already shown, the basis of copyright in Europe, as a 'natural' right combining personality and property interests, lies either in provisions protecting personality or in those protecting property. Intellectual property thus benefits from the protection afforded by Article 1 of Protocol No. 1 to the Convention[20] and in this context the fair trial guarantees are of great importance. For example, in *Dima v. Romania*,[21] the Court found a violation of Article 6 of the Convention in that the proceedings to assess the existence of copyright were unfair. Dima, a graphic designer and the creator of a design for a new national emblem

---

17 See, L. R. Helfer, 'The New Innovation Frontier? Intellectual Property and the European Court of Human Rights', (2008) 49 *Harvard International Law Journal*, pp. 1-52. The author's article concludes that 'the rule of law paradigm, which targets arbitrary government conduct, presents the strongest justification for the [European Court of Human Rights] to find in favour of intellectual property owners'. (at p. 51).

18 V. Zeno-Zencovich, 'Copyright and Freedom of Expression: An Ambiguous Relationship', [2007] *European Business Law Review*, pp. 351-362, at p. 357.

19 See L. R. Helfer, *op. cit.*

20 See the Court's case law examining whether copyright and patents are 'possessions': among others, *British-American Tobacco Company Ltd v. the Netherlands*, 20 November 1995, Series A no. 331 (an application for a patent that has been rejected by the competent national authority is not a protected possession); *Dima v. Romania* (dec.), no. 58472/00, 26 May 2005 (copyright is a possession); *Melnychuk v. Ukraine*, no. 28743/03, 5 July 2005 (dec.), ECHR 2005-IX (copyright is a possession); *Anheuser-Busch Inc. v. Portugal* [GC], no. 73049/01, ECHR 2007-I (concerning trademarks); and *Balan v. Moldova*, no. 19247/03, 29 January 2008 (copyright is a possession). See also the European Commission of Human Rights case law on patents: *Smith Kline and French Laboratories v. the Netherlands*, Decision of 4 October 1990, no. 12633/87, Decisions and Reports 66, p.70 (a patent is a possession); and *Lenzing AG v. United Kingdom*, Decision of 9 September 1998, no. 38817/97, Decisions and Reports no. 94-B, p. 136 (a patent from the European Patent Office (EPO) is a possession). See also A. Strowel, 'Pondération entre liberté d'expression et droit d'auteur sur internet: de la réserve des juges de Strasbourg à une concordance pratique par les juges de Luxembourg', (2014) 25 *Revue trimestrielle des droits de l'homme*, pp. 889-911, at p. 901, footnote 30.

21 *Dima v. Romania*, no. 58472/00, 16 November 2006.

and seal, had presented a challenge to a report produced by an expert witness for one of the defendants in domestic copyright infringement procedures. The European Court of Human Rights concluded that Romania had violated Article 6 of the Convention when the Romanian Supreme Court dismissed his appeal without addressing Dima's challenge to the expert's report.[22]

But the Court has not yet protected freedom of expression through copyright. Copyright has only been considered as a legitimate limitation to freedom of expression. This is surprising.

Copyright cases have reached Strasbourg only on rare occasions.[23] In the case of *De Geïllustreerde Pers N.V. v. the Netherlands*,[24] the now defunct European Commission of Human Rights decided that the broadcasters' copyright did not restrict freedom of expression and information, and concluded that there had been no interference with any of the rights protected by Article 10 of the European Convention. The applicant company had complained inter alia that it had been prevented by the relevant Netherlands broadcasting legislation (subjecting to copyright any reproduction or publication of programme lists other than on behalf or with the consent of the Netherlands Broadcasting Foundation) from publishing in its weekly magazines the complete schedule of television and radio programmes, and that this constituted an unjustified interference with the right freely to receive and impart information as guaranteed by Article 10 of the Convention. The Commission considered that the protection of the commercial interests of particular newspapers or groups of newspapers was not as such contemplated by the terms of Article 10.[25] The Commission also examined the complaint under Article 14 of the Convention. It came to the conclusion that there had been a difference in treatment as regards the communication of information on radio and television programmes, (a) between magazines published by broadcasting organisations and other periodicals, (b) between daily papers or newspapers appearing three times a week on the one hand, and weekly magazines on the other, and (c) between magazines published in the country concerned and those published abroad. However,

---

22 In an earlier inadmissibility decision (*Dima v. Romania* (dec.), no. 58472/00, 26 May 2005), the European Court of Human Rights examined Dima's claim under Protocol No. 1. As Helfer (*op.cit.*, at 16) explains in a detailed analysis, the applicant could not point to 'a judgment in his favour, nor could he rely on any favourable case law concerning the ability to copyright models of the State emblem and seal. In addition, the Supreme Court of Justice ultimately rejected Dima's proposed interpretation of [domestic law].' The Court declared this part of the application incompatible *ratione materiae* with the Convention, as 'Dima could not claim to have any "legitimate expectation" of acquiring a possession, since such an expectation cannot arise where there is "dispute" as to the interpretation and application of national law, and … the applicant's submissions [are] subsequently rejected by the national courts.' (Helfer, *ibid.*). The Court added that its scope of review was limited as to alleged errors of fact and of domestic law. On the limited scope of review concerning errors of fact and domestic law, see D. Spielmann, 'Le fait, le juge et la connaissance : aux confins de la compétence interprétative de la Cour européenne des droits de l'homme', in P. d'Argent, B. Bonafè, J. Combacau (coord), *The limits of international law - Essays in honour of Joe Verhoeven*, Brussels: Bruylant, 2014, pp. 519-535.

23 See *Copyright and human rights,* Report prepared by the Group of Specialists on Human Rights in the Information Society (MC-S-IS), September 2008, Directorate General of Human Rights and Legal Affairs, Strasbourg: Council of Europe, 2009. In recent years there have been a number of cases at domestic level involving the blocking or filtering of websites which are alleged to facilitate copyright infringement. See also Judgement in *Scarlet Extended SA v. Société belge des auteurs, compositeurs et éditeurs de musique (SABAM)*, C-70/10, EU:C:2011:771, and the opinion of Advocate General Pedro Cruz Villalón in *Scarlet Extended,* EU:C:2011:255, specifically at paras 85-86.

24 Report of the Commission of 6 July 1976, Decisions and Reports 8 (1977), p. 5.

25 The decision that there had been no interference has been heavily criticized. See C. B. Graber, *op. cit.*, at 16.

it held that the measures concerned could not in any way be regarded as discriminating against the applicant company.

However an interference with freedom of expression was found in the case of *France 2 v. France*.[26] This case concerned the issue of the quoting of copyright-protected material. The Commission declared the application inadmissible, holding that the ordering of the television channel France 2 to compensate the right holders amounted to an 'interference' prescribed by law and pursuing a 'legitimate aim', since it protected the 'rights of others' within the meaning of Article 10 § 2. The Commission added that it was not the task of the Convention organs to decide on conflicts between the freedom to impart information and the rights of the authors of the imparted information. This latter statement has been criticized.[27] As will be shown below, the balancing exercise has become a characteristic feature of recent case law.

In *Aral, Tekin and Aral v. Turkey*,[28] concerning the assignment of copyright by authors of cartoon stories to a publisher, the applicants complained under both Article 10 of the Convention and Article 1 of Protocol No.1 to the Convention. Thus, on the face of the application, there was no explicit conflict between two equally protected rights. The Commission declared the application inadmissible,[29] holding that any possible interference with the authors' freedom of expression was legitimized by the exception in favour of others. The Commission noted that the complaint concerned a dispute between the applicants and a third person with regard to commercial rights in respect of some artistic materials which had been designed by the first and second applicants in a given period. The domestic court expressly noted that the applicants were not prohibited from continuing to design and publish other artistic materials. Even assuming that there had been an interference with their right to freedom of expression and thought, to the extent that they were prevented from using the materials which had been created during the period of their contract, the Commission considered that the interference at issue could reasonably be considered necessary in a democratic society for the protection of the rights of others, in particular one of the parties to a contract, within the meaning of Article 10 § 2 of the Convention. But the applicants also complained of a violation of their right to property in that all the financial rights to the artistic materials had been assigned to the other party by the domestic courts. In this respect, the Commission reiterated its case law to the effect that intellectual property was covered by Article 1 of Protocol No. 1, but noted that the case concerned a commercial dispute between private parties. The State's intervention in the case had occurred only through its courts. The Commission reiterated that there was no interference with the right to peaceful enjoyment of possessions when, pursuant to the domestic law and a contract governing the relationship between the parties, a judge ordered one party to that contract to surrender a possession to another, unless it arbitrarily and unjustly

26 App. no. 30262/96, Report of the Commission of 15 January 1997, mentioned by C. B. Graber, *op. cit.*, at p. 17.

27 See P. Bernt Hugenholtz, *op. cit.*, at p. 359 et seq. See also C. B. Graber, *op. cit.*, at p. 17.

28 *Aral, Tekin and Aral v. Turkey*, no. 24563/94, Commission decision of 14 January 1998.

29 Ibid., quoted by C. B. Graber, *op. cit.*, at p. 17.

deprived that person of property in favour of another. In the present case, the domestic courts had interpreted the domestic law in the light of the contract and they had decided that the owner of the artistic materials, in particular, the pictures, cartoons, films, etc., which had been published or which remained unpublished but were held in the archives of the magazines 'Girgir' and 'Firt', was the other party. Furthermore, the courts decided that the applicants could continue to draw the same characters which they had drawn and published in the two magazines during the period of their contract, but in association with other subjects and stories, in other magazines or newspapers. The Commission therefore found no element in the case which allowed it to conclude that the courts had acted in an arbitrary or unreasonable manner. Accordingly, there was no shortcoming attributable to the State in that connection either.

III. Recent developments

1. Who can claim to be a victim?

Since 2013 the Court has had the opportunity to develop its case law concerning copyright issues.[30] The scope of Article 10 in relation to conflict between access to information and copyright has been clarified in the context of victim status under Article 34 of the Convention. Indeed, the European Court of Human Rights has recently delivered a noteworthy judgment on the right of access to information in the case of *Yaman Akdeniz v. Turkey*.[31]

The case concerned the blocking of access, at the request of a professional union of phonogram producers, to the websites 'myspace.com' and 'last.fm', the latter site being dedicated to music. This domestic decision was based on the protection of copyright. The applicant, a user of the said sites, relying on Article 10 of the Convention, requested before domestic authorities the annulment of the decision, arguing inter alia that it did not comply with the proportionality requirement.

In its inadmissibility decision of 11 March 2014, the Court denied the applicant victim status and hence came to the conclusion that he lacked *locus standi* before it. It declared the application incompatible *ratione personae* with the Convention. However, it came to this conclusion on the basis of detailed reasoning, tailored to the specific subject matter of access to information. The Court thus observed that the rights of Internet users nowadays constituted a matter of primary importance for individuals, since access to the Internet had become an essential tool for the exercise of freedom of expression. It pointed out that it had already emphasized the role of websites which, as a result of their accessibility and their capacity to store and disseminate vast quantities of data, greatly contributed to improving public access to news and, generally speaking, facilitated the imparting of information. However, in the Court's view, the mere fact that the applicant – like the other Turkish users of the websites in question – had been

30 A. Strowel, *op. cit.*, pp. 889-911.

31 *Yaman Akdeniz v. Turkey* (dec.), no. 20877/10, 11 March 2014.

indirectly affected by a blocking measure against two music-sharing websites could not suffice for him to be regarded as a 'victim' for the purposes of Article 34 of the Convention.[32] That being said, the Court noted that the sites affected by the impugned blocking measure were music sharing websites and they had been blocked because they did not comply with copyright legislation. As a user of these sites, the applicant had made use of their services and had been deprived of only one means of listening to music among many others. The Court found that he could thus without difficulty have had access to a range of musical works by numerous means without this entailing a breach of copyright rules. The applicant had not in fact denied that, at the time of the decision in question, he could have received the same or similar programmes by means other than the websites in question.[33] Moreover, the applicant had not been deprived of a major source of communication or prevented from taking part in a debate on a topic of general interest.[34] The applicant had acted as a simple user of two web sites dedicated to music.[35] Concerning the issue of collateral censorship, the Court had previously examined the collateral effects of decisions to block websites in the case of *Ahmet Yıldırım*,[36] where it found that any measure blocking access to a website had to be part of a particularly strict legal framework ensuring both tight control over the scope of the ban and effective judicial review to prevent possible abuse, because it could have significant effects of 'collateral censorship'. Moreover, it reiterated that, while Article 10 § 2 of the Convention did not allow much leeway for restrictions of freedom of expression in political matters, for example, States had a broad margin of appreciation in the regulation of speech in commercial matters,[37] bearing in mind that the breadth of that margin had to be qualified where it was not strictly speaking the 'commercial' expression of an individual that was at stake but his participation in a debate on a matter of general interest.[38] In this connection, as regards the balancing of possibly competing interests, such as the 'right to freedom to receive information' and the 'protection of copyright', the domestic authorities were afforded a particularly wide margin of appreciation.[39] In the light of that case law, the Court was not convinced that the present case raised a major question of general interest.[40]

32 Ibid., para. 24.

33 Ibid., para. 25.

34 Ibid., para. 26.

35 Ibid., para. 27.

36 *Ahmet Yıldırım v. Turkey*, no. 3111/10, 18 December 2012.

37 See *Mouvement raëlien suisse v. Switzerland* [GC], no. 16354/06, 13 July 2012, § 61.

38 See *Hertel v. Switzerland*, 25 August 1998, § 47, *Reports of Judgments and Decisions* 1998-VI.

39 *Ashby Donald and Others v. France*, no. 36769/08, 10 January 2013, § 41. On this case, see point 3.2 below.

40 *Ahmet Yıldırım*, para. 28.

2. Weighing freedom of expression against other rights and interests

In two other cases, the Strasbourg Court examined the merits of the complaints and engaged in a balancing exercise, weighing freedom of expression against the economic rights of the author.

(a) Ashby Donald and the fashion world

The first case (*Ashby Donald*) concerned the conviction of photographers for copyright infringement through publication on the Internet of photographs of a fashion show. The applicants were fashion photographers. Accredited by a fashion designers' federation, the *Fédération française de la couture*, for different fashion publications, they had been invited by various fashion houses to the women's winter 2003/2004 collection fashion shows in March 2003. They had not signed any exclusive agreements. Photographs they took at the fashion shows were sent to a company that published them online, a few hours after the shows, on a specialized website offering photos and videos of such shows on a free or pay-to-view basis and for sale. The designers' federation and several fashion houses lodged a complaint with the Central Industrial and Artistic Copyright Infringement Brigade. Ultimately the applicants were found guilty of copyright infringement.

In its judgment of 10 January 2013[41] the Court rejected as manifestly ill-founded the claim brought under Article 7 of the Convention to the effect that the domestic courts had interpreted domestic criminal legislation too broadly.[42] As to the claim under Article 10, the Court had no difficulty in finding that there had been interference with the applicants' legally protected right to freedom of expression, as they had been convicted of copyright infringement for disseminating or representing intellectual works in breach of the authors' rights under the Intellectual Property Code as interpreted by the domestic courts.[43] The interference pursued the legitimate aim of protecting the rights of others, namely the authors' rights of the fashion houses whose creations were featured in the disputed photographs.[44] The latter had been published on the website of a company

41 *Ashby Donald and Others,* cited above.

42 Ibid., paras 21-23. The applicants had argued that having regard to the fact that 'the exception contemplated by Article L. 122-5 9° of the Intellectual Property Code [had been] declared inapplicable to creations of the seasonal industries of clothing and apparel, the Court of Cassation [had] adopted a restrictive interpretation of that provision and had extended the scope of the offence of infringement, in breach of the principle of strict interpretation of criminal legislation.' (para. 20). Finding that the applicants' claim concerned, in reality, a challenge to the Court of Cassation's interpretation of French law, the Court pointed out that, while the applicants had argued that Article L. 122-5 9° of the Intellectual Property Code had to apply in their case – the provision in question stated that the author could not prohibit the reproduction or representation of 'works of graphic, visual or architectural art' for the sole purpose of immediate information and in direct connection with such work, provided the author's name was indicated – the Court of Cassation had dismissed their argument as the conditions stipulated in that provision were not satisfied. The Court found, firstly, that it was primarily for the national authorities, and in particular the courts, to interpret and apply domestic law. The Court's role was confined to ascertaining whether the effects of such interpretation were compatible with the Convention. Secondly, it was not for the Court to examine any errors of fact or law allegedly committed by a court, unless and to the extent that they might have impaired Convention rights and freedoms. The Court of Cassation had ruled on the scope of an exception to the rule protecting authors' legitimate rights. The Court did not find in its interpretation anything to suggest that it had acted in breach of the principles in Article 7 of the Convention.

43 Ibid., para. 34.

44 Ibid., para. 36.

run by the first two applicants, with the aim of selling them or charging a fee to view them. The applicants' approach had essentially been a commercial one. Although there was no denying the public appeal of fashion in general and designer fashion in particular, it could not be said that the applicants had taken part in a debate on a topic of general interest by simply publishing photographs of fashion shows.[45] The domestic authorities had a particularly wide margin of appreciation in this case considering the aim of the interference and the fact that, as Article 1 of Protocol No. 1 applied to intellectual property, the interference was also aimed at protecting rights safeguarded by the Convention or its Protocols.[46]

The applicants had argued that their conviction for copyright infringement was not 'necessary' as they had been invited to the fashion shows in question, in their capacity as photographers, to take photographs with a view to their publication, and as such publication outside the framework of their accreditation had given rise to no additional risk of copyright infringement because the same pictures had been published at the same time by accredited magazines. Moreover, the 'press commitment' practice whereby photographers were required to sign exclusive agreements with the magazines that accredited them was no longer really followed. The court of appeal had nevertheless found that the applicants had knowingly disseminated the photographs in issue without the authorization of the rights holders, that the argument that 'press commitment' agreements were unsuitable or no longer standard practice did not absolve them of their liability, and that they were accordingly guilty of copyright infringement. The domestic court had therefore not overstepped its margin of appreciation in privileging respect for the fashion designers' property over the applicants' right to freedom of expression.[47]

The applicants also contended that the sentences imposed on them had been disproportionately harsh. They had been sentenced not only to large criminal fines but also to pay substantial damages. They adduced no evidence, however, as to the consequences of these penalties on their financial situation. In any event, the domestic court had fixed the sums following adversarial proceedings, the fairness of which was not in dispute, and had given adequate reasons for its decision, explaining the circumstances which it regarded as warranting such penalties.[48] In these circumstances and regard being had to the particularly wide margin of appreciation open to the domestic authorities, the nature and gravity of the penalties imposed on the applicants were not such that the Court could find that the interference in issue was disproportionate to the aim pursued.[49]

---

45 Ibid., para. 39.

46 Ibid., paras. 40-41.

47 Ibid., para. 42.

48 Ibid., para. 43.

49 Ibid., para. 44.

(b) The 'Pirate Bay case' and file sharing services

The second case (*Neij and Kolmisoppi*) concerned the so-called 'Pirate Bay' case. The application was declared inadmissible in a decision of 19 February 2013,[50] following a similar line of reasoning as that in *Ashby Donald*. The circumstances of the case related to copyright-protected music, films and computer games. The applicants had been involved in 'The Pirate Bay' (TPB), one of the world's largest file-sharing services on the Internet. They had been charged with complicity to commit offences in violation of the Copyright Act and subsequently convicted.

Before the Court, they complained under Article 10 of the Convention that their right to receive and impart information had been violated when they were convicted for other persons' use of TPB. They argued that Article 10 enshrined the right to offer an automated service for the transfer of unprotected material between users, according to basic principles of Internet communication and within the information society. In their view, Article 10 protected the right to arrange a service on the Internet which could be used for both legal and illegal purposes, without the persons responsible for the service being convicted for acts committed by the people using it. In this connection, they referred to international frameworks, pointing to a far-reaching right to receive and provide information for the benefit of Internet users.

In its decision of 19 February 2013, the Court had no difficulty in deciding that there had been an interference with Article 10, as prescribed by law. The interference pursued the legitimate aim of protecting the initial claimants' copyright to the material in question and was covered by the aims referred to under Article 10 § 2, i.e., 'protection of the rights of others' and 'prevention of crime'. Alain Strowel[51] notes that 'prevention of crime' was added in the 'Pirate Bay' case in contrast to *Ashby Donald*, where the Court referred only to the protection of the rights of others, namely the authors' rights of the fashion houses whose creations were featured in the disputed photographs.

In *Neij and Kolmisoppi* the Court also held that the interference was necessary in a democratic society to attain such aims. The Court reiterated that the test of 'necessity in a democratic society' required it to determine whether the interference complained of corresponded to a 'pressing social need'. That test could not be applied in absolute terms. On the contrary, the Court held that it had to take into account various factors, such as the nature of the competing interests involved and the degree to which those interests required protection in the circumstances of the case. The Court was called upon to weigh up, on the one hand, the interest of the applicants in facilitating the sharing of the information in question and, on the other, the authorities' interest in protecting the rights of the copyright holders. As to the weight afforded to the latter interest, the Court reiterated that intellectual property enjoyed the protection afforded by Article 1 of Protocol No. 1 to the Convention. It also reiterated the principle that genuine, effective exercise of the rights protected by that provision did not depend

---

50 *Neij and Sunde Kolmisoppi v. Sweden* (dec.), no. 40397/12, 19 February 2013; published in (2013) 33 *Human Rights Law Journal*, pp.151-155.

51 A. Strowel, *op. cit.*, at p. 898.

merely on the State's duty not to interfere, but might require positive measures of protection. The respondent State thus had to weigh up two competing interests which were both protected by the Convention. In such a case, the State was afforded a wide margin of appreciation. The Court also underlined that the width of the margin of appreciation afforded to States varied depending on a number of factors, among which the type of information was of particular importance. In the present case, although protected by Article 10, the safeguards afforded to the distributed material in respect of which the applicants were convicted could not reach the same level as that afforded to political expression and debate. It followed that the nature of the information in question and the balancing of interests mentioned above were both such as to afford the State a wide margin of appreciation which, when combined as in the present case, rendered that margin particularly wide.

Since the Swedish authorities were under an obligation to protect the claimants' property rights in accordance with the Copyright Act and the Convention, the Court found that there were weighty reasons for the restriction of the applicants' freedom of expression. Moreover, the Swedish courts advanced relevant and sufficient reasons to consider that the applicants' activities within the commercially run TPB amounted to criminal conduct requiring appropriate punishment. The Court pointed out that the applicants had been convicted only for materials which were copyright-protected. Lastly, it observed that the nature and severity of the penalties imposed were factors to be taken into account when assessing the proportionality of interference with the freedom of expression guaranteed by Article 10. It considered that the prison sentence and award of damages could not be regarded as disproportionate. In reaching this conclusion, the Court had regard to the fact that the domestic courts had found that the applicants had not taken any action to remove the torrent files in question, despite having been urged to do so. Instead they had been indifferent to the fact that copyright-protected works had been the subject of file-sharing activities via TPB. In conclusion, having regard to all the circumstances of the present case, in particular the nature of the information contained in the shared material and the weighty reasons for the interference with the applicants' freedom of expression, the Court found that the interference was 'necessary in a democratic society' within the meaning of Article 10 § 2 of the Convention.

3. Copyright protection and criminal proceedings

As indicated in my introduction, robust copyright protection also requires criminal and civil law remedies. An interesting recent case (*Volkov and Adamskiy v. Russia*) involved two applicants who were targeted in undercover operations launched to expose individuals who distributed counterfeit computer software. The applicants had advertised their computer repair services to the general public. Police officers called them, as any other client would, and asked them to install some computer programs. The applicants both knowingly and freely obtained counterfeit copies of software and installed it. Before the Court, the applicants both complained that the police had incited them to commit the offence of copyright infringement and that as a result their conviction had been in breach of their right to a fair trial under Article 6 of the

Convention. In a judgment of 26 March 2015[52] the Court rejected the applicants' *agent provocateur* complaint as manifestly ill-founded.

It held that Mr Volkov and Mr Adamskiy had been engaged in lawful business activity. They had knowingly and publicly advertised their computer-repair services, providing their respective telephone numbers. They thereby solicited customers in need of computer repairs and offered their technical expertise to the general public.[53] Meanwhile, the police had received incriminating information about the applicants and, as such, were under an obligation to verify a criminal complaint. They had called the applicants on their respective numbers and asked them to install some computer programs. The applicants did not complain to the domestic courts that the police officers had specifically asked for unlicensed software or that they had exerted any pressure on the applicants at the time of the call or tried to pressure them into committing illegal acts. Moreover, from the records of the conversation between the applicants and the police officers in the course of the computer repairs, it was clear that the applicants had brought unlicensed software for installation on their own initiative, without any prior agreement with the undercover agents.[54]

The Court therefore considered that the undercover police officers' requests appeared to be regular orders of the kind usually placed by customers in response to online or newspaper advertisements for services. The actions of the police did not go beyond the ordinary conduct normally expected of clients in the course of lawful commercial activity. It was up to the applicants to respond to such requests in a lawful manner and to install licensed software.[55] However, Mr Volkov had admitted in court that after the order had been placed he had bought compact discs with counterfeit software on them for installation. Mr Adamskiy had acknowledged that soon after the call he had downloaded counterfeit copies of the required programs. The applicants thus both promptly found unlicensed software and installed it the next day. Neither of the applicants had indicated in the domestic proceedings that V and M had specifically asked them to install unlicensed software on their computers. Mr Adamskiy had also claimed that he had acted unlawfully because he had been in need of money at the time. However, nothing in the case materials suggested that the police had been aware of Mr Adamskiy's financial situation or that they had used it to incite him to commit a crime. Moreover, in the course of the computer repairs both applicants had openly informed the undercover agents that the software was counterfeit and that it would have been much more expensive to install licensed software.[56]

The Court thus held that it was the applicants' own deliberate and illegal conduct and not the actions of the police that had become the determining factor in the commission

52 *Volkov and Adamskiy v. Russia*, nos. 7614/09 and 30863/10, 26 March 2015 (not yet final).

53 Ibid., para. 40.

54 Ibid., para. 41.

55 Ibid., para. 42.

56 Ibid., para. 43.

of their offences. Mr Volkov and Mr Adamskiy appeared to have shown pre-existing criminal intent and had themselves contributed to the commission of the criminal offences without active intervention by the police.[57] In those circumstances, the police's conduct did not appear to have been unlawful or arbitrary given their obligation to verify criminal complaints, whereas the applicants had chosen of their own free will to act illegally.[58]

IV. An appraisal

The European Court of Human Rights protects the author's creative idea mainly by reference to its economic aspects. Copyright, protected under criminal and civil remedies, has generally been considered as a legitimate limitation to freedom of expression and the Court has upheld domestic decisions, granting a wide margin of appreciation to domestic courts. In particular, taking into consideration the nature of the information on the one hand, and the other interests to be weighed in the balance, on the other, the Court is willing to afford the State a margin of appreciation which is particularly wide.[59]

The rights of others and in particular the need to protect their creative work have been examined, albeit on rare occasions, by the European Court of Human Rights. However, surprisingly enough, the Court has not yet protected *freedom of expression* through copyright. Nor has it protected artistic honour, dignity or reputation through copyright. The economic aspects seem predominant in the scant case law. But the Court is bound by the framing of the application and it may very well transpire that one day copyright protection will be directly achieved under Article 10 or even Article 8 of the Convention. In any event, the human rights approach to copyright protection is very valuable from the standpoint of the administration of justice, since it provides a careful and balanced approach to the interests at stake.[60] After all, courts are best placed to achieve correct and concrete balancing by using their carefully calibrated margin of appreciation.

---

57 Ibid., para. 44.

58 Ibid., para. 45.

59 For a thorough discussion concerning balancing in the context of copyright, see A. Strowel, *op. cit.*, at p. 899. On the margin of appreciation doctrine, see D. Spielmann, 'Allowing the Right Margin: The European Court of Human Rights and The National Margin of Appreciation Doctrine: Waiver or Subsidiarity of European Review', (2011-2012) 14 *Cambridge Yearbook of European Legal Studies*, pp. 381-418; and 'Whither the Margin of Appreciation?', (2014) 67 *Current Legal Problems*, pp. 49-65.

60 G. Jokhadze, *op. cit.*, at p. 264.

For the love of God: the value of advocati pauperum

From poor tenants of the lands of Grenok to overturning 'don't ask, don't tell'

JO WEISS*

I. Even this road leads to Scotland

King James V of Scotland was not happy. 'We are daily infestit be the complant of divers our pur [poor] legis perserverand for justice,' he wrote to the nascent Scottish bar in 1535, 'quhilkis [which] an postponit tharfra in default of advocatis to procur for thame.'[1] Struggling with a system rooted in the medieval king's duty to dispense justice but operating in a much larger society, the King had reached the limits of his patience for dealing with unrepresented litigants and the challenges they posed for the legal system and themselves.[2]

---

* Opinions are wholly mine. With gratitude to Jacquelyn MacLennan & Assimakis Komninos for the opportunity, to Pauline Tart for her typically astute comments, to Larissa Liburd for research on pro bono in the US, to the White & Case pro bono team for their comments and support, and most of all to Ian for never making me feel like not being a lawyer was at all relevant to my ability to do this job. And for having the patience to teach me what I needed to know when it did matter.

1 C. Stoddart, *The Law and Practice of Legal Aid in Scotland*, 1979, p. 2.

2 I was led to the story of Scottish *advocatus pauperum* by Michael Millemann's 'Mandatory *Pro Bono* in Civil Cases: a Partial Answer to the Right Question: For,' *Maryland Law Review*, Volume 49, Issue 1, 1990.

He could not simply ignore the problem, for he had not only a moral duty but also a legal duty to address it. During the reign of David I in the 12th century, an act of the Scottish Parliament had established that 'all destitute of help from all others are in the care and protection of the King.'[3] The fittingly named David 'acted as a judge of first instance in the minor and summary complaints of poor people, sitting at his palace gate, or on circuit, and prescribed procedure in such cases.'[4] This legislation and kingly role originated in the Roman tradition of the wealthy patron (called *patronus* in court) acting free of charge for his dependents (called *clients*) and ultimately for people not in his household (giving rise to how we use the term 'client' today).[5] These Roman roots were extremely strong: at least one scholar has noted that during the Republic and early Empire 'we find no serious complaints that advocates' fees prevented the small man from litigating.'[6]

This value was transmitted through centuries of ecclesiastical legal practice, which included appointing clerical advocates to serve the poor.[7] The French get credit for being the first to jump from the ecclesiastical to the secular courts. In perhaps the first instance of state-funded legal aid, the French Parliament acted in 1400 and 1414 to provide legal counsel for the poor.[8]

The Scottish Parliament of 1424 then acted in a similar vein, perhaps unsurprisingly in light of the Auld Alliance. The Act of 1424 offered James a way forward, with what may be the first legislation calling for mandatory pro bono from a lawyer appointed by the court.

> If there be any poor person, for want of sophistication or expenses, that cannot or may not follow his cause, the King for the love of God shall order the judge, before whom the cause shall be determined, to obtain and get a loyal and a wise advocate, to follow such poor person's causes; and if such causes are successful, the wrong doer shall compensate both the party wronged, and the advocate's costs and travel.[9]

James took this and ran with it straight to the infant bar. He asked the bar to choose 'ane man of gud conscience [who] sall be callit *advocatus pauperum*, [whom] ye sall cause sweir that he sall administer to all our liegis cumand to him for help that will

3 Maxwell, 'Civil Procedure,' in *An Introduction to Scottish Legal History*, 1958, p. 413.

4 Ibid.

5 R. Pound, *The Lawyer From Antiquity to Modern Times*, 1953, pp. 44-45.

6 J. Kelly, *Roman Litigation*, 1966, p. 84.

7 H. Cohen, *History of the English Bar*, 1967, pp. 24-29.

8 Stoddart, p. 1.

9 Acts of the Parliament of Scotland 1424, ch. 45. In its original form, the statute read: 'Gif there bee onie pure creature, for faulte of cunning or expenses, that cannot, nor may not follow his cause, the King for the love of GOD, sall ordain the judge, before quhom the cause suld be determined, to purwey and get a leill and a wise Advocate, to follow sik pure creatures causes; And gif sik causes be obtained, the wranger sall assyith baith the partie skaithed, and the Advocatis coastes and travel.'

mak faith thai have nocht to persew justice with all of that awn.'[10] The bar conscripted two 'volunteers,' each of whom was given ten pounds a year as an honorarium and the risk that he could be 'deprived of his right to plead before the court if he failed to discharge his duty.'[11]

Scotland's *advocati pauperum* served clients (usually tenants who were sometimes close to serfs, and therefore in a more or less direct line from the clients of the Roman patrons) with a wide range of legal needs, but theft appears to have been a particularly common complaint.[12] The 'poor tenants of the lands of Grenok' sought justice after their goods were 'spuilzied' (stolen), a 'poor tenant of the lands of Campsfield' suffered from the theft of his oxen, and the 'poor tenants in the lands of Haystoun' claimed they were wrongly denied reimbursement for stolen goods. In a trickier case with an unfortunate outcome for the poor tenants, a dispute between the Abbot of Arbroath and the relevant Archbishop over the rights to the tithed crops of the Abbey's tenant farmers led to a countersuit by the farmers who availed themselves of pro bono legal assistance. The case ended up before the Scottish House of Lords, sitting as Lords of Session, who succumbed to ecclesiastical power politics over common sense and ordered the tenants to tithe to both the Abbot and the Archbishop.

By 1784, the Act of 1424 had been amended to provide for six fresh *advocati pauperum* to be appointed each year, as well as four agents and four solicitors, who held the poetic title of 'Writers to the Signet.'[13] By this time there was an uproar that too many people were being admitted to the Poor's Roll and therefore becoming eligible for legal aid. In an unsurprising move in its search for wise men to define what has become the modern practice of income qualification, Parliament turned to the church and vested the 'minister and two elders of the parish in which [the applicant] resided' with the power to judge whether the poor were truly poor. Parliament also gave the applicant's adversary the right to object to his opponent's classification as truly poor and formalized the test for determining the *probabilis causa litigandi* that was the second requirement of eligibility.[14]

Events developed similarly in medieval England, given impetus by the provision in Magna Carta's Article 40 to 'neither sell, nor deny, nor delay, to any person, equity or justice.' In 1495, Parliament enacted 11 Henry 7, ch. 12: 'An Acte to admyte such psons as are poore to sue in forma paupis.' It called for 'the justices to appoint attorney and attornies for the same poor person and persons…,which shall do their duties without any reward for their counsels help.' The 1495 Act stood until 1883, when it was repealed upon the enactment of the Statute Law Revision and Civil Procedure Act, which

10 Stoddart, p. 2.

11 King James V enacted a process for implementing this policy into law by the Act of Sederunt on 27 April 1535, cited in Stoddart, p. 2.

12 All examples cited in this paragraph are from 1532-33 as documented in *Selected Cases from Acta Dominorum Concilii Et Sessionis 1532-1533*, Stair Society, 1951.

13 Stoddart, p. 6. The title is still in use today for Scottish solicitors, including White & Case partner and contributor to this Liber Amicorum, Jacquelyn MacLennan.

14 Stoddart, pp. 6-7.

introduced a more comprehensive legal aid regime. Today, despite much prudent concern about the impact of recent and proposed cuts in the legal aid budgets of England, Wales, Scotland and Northern Ireland, there remains substantial financial support from government and deep pro bono engagement by the private bar. Alternative funding for public interest lawyers at nongovernmental organizations is being sought, as civil society adjusts to the cuts in legal aid. The courts are also piloting reforms that will make their procedures and the law itself more transparent and more easily navigated by litigants in person. There is still a gap in representation, but responsibility is shared across sectors for ensuring that everyone who needs but cannot afford a lawyer can obtain one.

In the 17th century, the tradition of a professional duty for lawyers in private practice to provide pro bono legal assistance and the concept of a court-appointed (and paid) advocate crossed the Atlantic to the American colonies. As of today, the American situation could scarcely be less like that of its British cousins. In what most accept as a knockout victory, history has declared the duty of private lawyers - and public interest lawyers at nonprofits funded by charitable donations, often from lawyers and law firms - to provide pro bono legal services for civil matters and criminal appeals the clear winner over government-funded legal aid. So how do we judge the value of pro bono for those of limited means in the United States? And is there any hope to resuscitate the argument for government to do more?

II. Pro bono in America: justice for one vs. justice for many

As Ian Forrester tells the story, it sounds a great deal like the opening scene of the Broadway musical *Chicago*. During a lover's spat in New York State in 1965, Louis Henry Burns and the red-headed vixen Doris Anderson struggle to the death with a revolver that goes off either accidentally or intentionally, a whiskey bottle allegedly used as a club over the head, and a possibly poisoned pastry. The head was Louis's, the death was Doris's, and the pastry was fed to Louis by the police and not, as it turns out if one reads the actual case,[15] poisoned. But it is the pastry upon which the case turns. The appeal, that is, not the murder trial. Burns did kill Doris and was convicted. He led the police to where he had buried the body. But he said nothing to indicate it was anything other than a horrible accident until he had endured more than 30 hours without food—except one or two pastries, and even this much food is disputed—and more than 18 hours of 'uninterrupted custodial interrogation.'[16]

15 United States Court of Appeals, Second Circuit. *United States of America ex rel. Louis Henry Burns v. J. Edwin Lavallee*, No. 238, Docket 34246, Argued 18 Nov. 1970. Decided 21 Dec. 1970.

16 Ibid.

Burns got the dream team for his appeal. The pro bono team from Davis Polk & Wardwell was led by the distinguished partner Robert B. Fiske, Jr.[17] and included a newly minted associate named Ian Forrester. That he was uppity for his age needs no research to confirm. That he feels enormous gratitude for the privilege of serving on this case with Fiske, whom he still admires greatly, is beyond doubt. Armed with his personal copy of *Legal Representation of the Poor: The New York City Experience*,[18] and in a scene reminiscent of the 1948 Hollywood Christmas movie *The Bishop's Wife* complete with Cary Grant as the Angel, Ian and team sprung their man from prison on Christmas Eve of 1970.[19] The court accepted their argument that Burns' self-incriminating testimony had been coerced, when—after 18 hours of questioning—Burns suddenly announced he had shot her intentionally. The case is still cited as an example of how the police are not supposed to treat suspects. As such it has had a much wider effect than just getting Burns out of jail, as valuable as that was to him and as happy as it made his legal team. Sadly, it is very relevant to today's headlines, as the US justice system struggles with too many examples of police behaviour ranging from inappropriate treatment of suspects or prisoners to tragically fatal brutality.

As Global Pro Bono Practice Leader at White & Case, Ian has been persistent, persuasive, eloquent, exasperated, compelling and convincing that representing people with serious legal needs who cannot afford a lawyer is what he calls the 'gold standard' of pro bono. People have sometimes been surprised when they learn that Ian plays this role, because he has had such a distinguished career as a commercially combative antitrust litigator, with an impact the many contributors to this book rightly honour. Two long-time friends and collaborators of his from academia have said independently to me, 'Ian as a human rights lawyer? Are you serious?' Some readers may have that same thought. In 2010, when Hugh Verrier, Chairman of White & Case, asked me and a few others to nominate partners whom he might consider for this new role, we knew we needed someone for the task of creating the new field of global pro bono who was not an American, but who also understood the legal landscape in the United States. When we looked around the world, no one stood out as Ian did. Not only had he studied and practiced law in the United States (and had sued the government for the right to do the latter, but that's a different article), he had handled pro bono matters of almost every stripe throughout his entire career, including two before the European Court of Human Rights. He accepted Hugh's invitation and has used the role to change the world in more ways than can be recited here.

---

17 Robert B. Fiske, Jr. was born in Brooklyn in 1930. He served as the United States Attorney for the Southern District of New York from 1976 to 1980 after serving as an assistant in the office from 1957 to 1961. He joined Davis Polk as an associate in 1955, was a partner from 1964 to 2010 (interrupted by his service as US attorney), and has been Senior Counsel from 2010 until the time of this writing. Notable cases include the Whitewater controversy, the death of White House Counsel Vincent Foster, and the defense of Exxon following the oil spill in Arthur Kill, New Jersey. Wikipedia: The Free Encyclopedia http://en.wikipedia.org/wiki/Robert_B._Fiske; accessed 29 January 2015. Also http://www.davispolk.com/lawyers/robert-fiske-jr/; accessed 18 May 2015.

18 *Legal Representation of the Poor: The New York City Experience*, Practicing Law Institute, 1970. This book was presumably provided to all associates by Davis Polk, or at least those who attended the continuing legal education course on pro bono.

19 According to Ian; according to the case citation, on December 21.

What role to play in addressing the 'access-to-justice gap' is a central issue for any law firm serious about pro bono work. In the United States, the gap is huge and growing.[20] There is no right to legal aid for civil cases at all and no public defenders available for criminal appeals. According to the 2011 World Justice Project Index, the civil justice system in the US is 'independent and free of undue influence,' but it remains 'inaccessible to disadvantaged groups,' ranking 21st out of 66 countries examined.[21] Even worse, the US ranked an embarrassing 52nd out of 66 countries on the relative cost and availability of civil legal assistance.[22] Studies have found that 80% of the civil legal needs of low-income people in the US go unmet.[23]

This deluge of need is a torrent, not a leak, in the dyke, and it cannot be plugged without a comprehensive programme of government-funded legal aid. Certainly the gap cannot be closed by pro bono activity by lawyers in private practice. Nor should private law firms be expected to carry more of the hugely substantial financial cost they already pay to support public interest law firms and the pro bono legal services sector, especially not in light of such extreme abdication of any sense of shared responsibility by government. There are solid theoretical justifications for a government to provide its citizens with access to the system it requires them to use if they cannot afford it on their own, but these fall mostly on deaf ears in the United States. The political climate does not offer any hope at all on the national level, but there are glimmers of possibility for dialogue at the state and local level in a few jurisdictions. One such glimmer is in San Francisco, where the Right to Counsel movement, driven by a coalition including pro bono lawyers from Morrison & Foerster,[24] led to that city becoming the first 'Right to Civil Counsel City.' It provides representation at city expense to low-income litigants in civil matters involving basic human needs.

If private law firms add their voices even more strongly to the longstanding calls for legal aid arising from civil society, it might be possible to start to show that the emperor has no clothes. Global law firms might draw attention to how the outrage over cuts in still-substantial civil legal aid in Britain contrasts with the total absence of debate about the nonexistence of civil legal aid in the United States. We are starting to move down this path, but it will be a long hard battle with no certainty of success.

Nevertheless, pro bono legal services have an important role to play. I wholeheartedly endorse Ian's view that individual representation is the gold standard of pro bono, and I suggest that it is true for two reasons. Despite the fact that pro bono lawyers cannot make a dent in the need in the United States, each life saved or made better is a precious

---

20 Legal Services Corporation, 'Report of the *Pro Bono* Task Force,' October 2012.

21 World Justice Project Index. http://worldjusticeproject.org/sites/default/files/wjproli2011_0.pdf, at p. 23.

22 ABA Journal, (1 June 2012), http://www.abajournal.com/magazine/article/unequal_justice_u.s._trails_high-income_nations_in_serving_civil_legal_need/, citing http://worldjusticeproject.org/rule-of-law-index/.

23 Laura K. Abel & David Pedulla, *Reform Federal Civil Justice Policy to Meet the High-Stakes Legal Needs of Low-Income People*, Brennan Ctr. for Justice at the NYU Sch. of Law Blog, (5 Jan. 2007), http://www.brennancenter.org/blog/archives/reform_federal_civil_justice_policy_to_meet_the_high_stakes_legal_needs_of/.

24 Morrison & Foerster. http://www.mofo.com/resources/news/2014/02/mofo-honored-with-2013-emsuper-lawyersem-pro-bono-award. Accessed 29 January 2015.

and priceless 'good,' as economists would say. Ian feels this keenly. But I believe it is also true that the body of work by pro bono lawyers has had a greater impact than simply the sum of their individual representations.

An astounding number of seminal cases in the United States that have advanced the cause of equal rights, decreased discrimination and protected other human rights have been argued and won by pro bono lawyers. It is not surprising that many such cases are handled by public interest lawyers working in nonprofit legal service organizations (or by legal aid-funded lawyers in other countries), but it would be an interesting paper for a JD/MBA candidate to analyze what proportion of a comprehensively defined universe of such cases has been done by lawyers in private practice working pro bono. That is beyond the scope of my efforts here, but I suggest the following examples illustrate that pro bono activity in the United States has been a powerful force both to drive social change and keep the law in step with social change that advances human rights.

In 1770, John Adams, future President of the United States and a lawyer by trade, represented pro bono the eight British soldiers accused, after firing into a crowd that was taunting a sentry, of killing five men and injuring six others in what became known as the 'Boston Massacre.' He won the acquittal of six, with the remaining two convicted of manslaughter, punished by having their hands branded. He wrote in his diary:

> The Part I took in Defence of Cptn. Preston and the Soldiers, procured me Anxiety, and Obloquy enough. It was, however, one of the most gallant, generous, manly and disinterested Actions of my whole Life, and one of the best Pieces of Service I ever rendered my Country. Judgment of Death against those Soldiers would have been as foul a Stain upon this Country as the Executions of the Quakers or Witches, anciently. As the Evidence was, the Verdict of the Jury was exactly right. This however is no Reason why the Town should not call the Action of that Night a Massacre, nor is it any Argument in favour of the Governor or Minister, who caused them to be sent here. But it is the strongest Proofs of the Danger of Standing Armies.'[25]

In a case immortalized by a play-turned-Hollywood-movie,[26] prominent criminal defence attorney Clarence Darrow, serving pro bono for the American Civil Liberties Union, represented John Thomas Scopes, the teacher accused of teaching evolution, in the circus-like but nonetheless influential 1925 'Scopes Monkey Trial' case.[27]

Other examples include the seminal abortion rights case of *Roe v. Wade*,[28] and the 'Miranda rights' case of *Miranda v. Arizona*,[29] which provided for the presence of

---

25 John Adams, Butterfield, L. H., ed. *Diary and Autobiography of John Adams, vol. 2*. Cambridge, MA: The Belknap Press of Harvard University Press, 1962, p. 79.

26 Jerome and Lee Lawrence, Robert Edwin. *Inherit the Wind,* 1955. (The 1960 film version starred Spencer Tracy.)

27 Bruce J. Ennis, 'ACLU: 60 Years of Volunteer Lawyering', *ABA Journal*, Vol. 66, 1980, pp. 1080-81.

28 *Roe v. Wade*, 410 US 335 (1973).

29 *Miranda v. Arizona*, 384 US 436 (1966).

counsel during police interrogation and led to the constitutional right for a defendant to be informed of his or her constitutional rights.

Like Davis Polk, many leading law firms have long traditions of pro bono work that changed law in the US. Arnold & Porter, led by distinguished partner Abe Fortas, has had multiple influential court cases including *Gideon v. Wainwright*,[30] in which the US Supreme Court ruled that states are required under the 14th Amendment to the US Constitution to provide counsel in all criminal cases where defendants cannot afford one themselves. A lawsuit filed by lawyers from the Los Angeles-based firm of Klee, Tuchin, Bogdanoff, & Stern on behalf of two consumer debtors whose lawful same-sex marriage was not recognized under federal law led to the holding of the Defense of Marriage Act as unconstitutional and resulted in a national change in the government's position in opposing same-sex jointly filed bankruptcies.[31] And the year Ian became Global Pro Bono Practice Leader, a team of lawyers from White & Case in New York and Los Angeles won a landmark victory[32] for the Log Cabin Republicans in its legal challenge to overturn the US government's 'Don't Ask Don't Tell' policy, which prohibited gay, lesbian and bisexual individuals from openly serving in the military.

Deploying the resources and finely honed advocacy skills of private firms on major cases that test issues affecting many in need of justice is a powerful multiplier for the value of pro bono work. Such cases are often lengthy and demanding. Law firms should be encouraged explicitly to take them on by modern-day leaders in all sectors who, like King James V of Scotland and his spiritual successor and countryman Ian Forrester, are fed up with having our courts 'infestit be the complant of divers our pur legis perserverand for justice.' Law firms who take on cases that make our laws more humane bring special value to the lives of those who require a change in the law itself to be treated equally by it.

The torrent of unrepresented litigants in the United States needs to be stopped, but pro bono work alone cannot do that. The quality and humanity of our laws in every country of the world can still be greatly improved and likely will always need improvement. Pro bono work is a powerful way to do that.

---

30 *Gideon v. Wainwright*, 372 US 335 (1963).

31 Klee, Tuchin, Bogdanoff, & Stern, http://www.ktbslaw.com/practices-17.html, accessed 29 January 2015.

32 *Log Cabin Republicans v. United States of America, et al.*, CV 04-08324-VAP (Ex), (C.D. Cal. 2010).

Contributors' Bios

Cecilia Álvarez Rigaudias
European Privacy Officer Lead at Pfizer. She formerly worked at Uría Menéndez, leading the data protection, IT and ecommerce areas of practice as well as the LATAM Data Protection Working Group. Cecilia is Vice-president of APEP (Spanish Privacy Professional Association), Spanish member of CEDPO (Confederation of European Data Protection Organisations) and member of the Steering Committees of The Sedona Conference.

Josef Azizi
Professor at University of Vienna Law Faculty, Lecturer at other universities. Formerly Coordinator responsible for the adaptation of Austrian federal law to Community law; Judge at the General Court from January 1995 to September 2013.

Barry Baines
Solicitor Advocate. Solicitor of the Supreme Court of England & Wales. Attorney-at-law for the State of New York. Experienced consultant in regulatory healthcare.

Jacques Bourgeois
Senior Advisor at Sidley Austin LLP. Professor at the College of Europe (Bruges) and Guest Professor at the University of Ghent (Jean Monnet Centre of Excellence).

Merijn Chamon
Academic Assistant at the Department of European, Public and International Law, University of Ghent (Jean Monnet Centre of Excellence).

Sir David Edward
Professor Emeritus of the University of Edinburgh. Judge of the European Court of First instance (1989-92) and of the Court of Justice (1992-2004). He practised as an advocate in Scotland and was Ian Forrester's 'devil-master' (pupil-master).

Claus-Dieter Ehlermann
Senior Counsel at Wilmer Cutler Pickering Hale & Dorr LLP. Former Member and Chairman of the Appellate Body of the World Trade Organization, Former Director-General of the Directorate-General for Competition and of the Legal Service of the European Commission. Honorary Professor at the University of Hamburg and Former Professor at the European University Institute.

Ayşe Gizem Yaşar
Associate at ELIG, Attorneys-at-Law. Holds an LL.M. from Panthéon-Assas University, Paris Institute of Comparative Law. Qualified in Istanbul.

Alfonso Gutiérrez
Partner at Uría Menéndez. Law Degree, University of Salamanca; LLM in EU Law, College of Europe (Bruges) and K.U. Leuven). He was Ian's associate between 1997 and 1999 at Forrester Norall & Sutton / White & Case.

Patrick R. Hugg
John J. McAulay Distinguished Professor of Law, Loyola University College of Law. Serving as Director of the Law School's international programmes, Loyola's Foreign Studies Programme at the University of Vienna, and Field Studies to the Institutions of the European Union and to the Rome-Istanbul-based 'Origins of the Civil Law' programme.

Sir Francis G. Jacobs
Professor of Law, King's College London; formerly Advocate General, Court of Justice of the European Communities.

Assimakis P. Komninos
Partner at White & Case LLP. Visiting fellow of University College London and Senior Associate Fellow of the Institute for European Studies at the Vrije Universiteit Brussels. Former Commissioner-Member of the Board of the Hellenic Competition Commission.

Colin MacKay
Journalist and Broadcaster, BBC Radio Scotland; formerly Political Editor and Lobby Correspondent of Scottish Television plc. Anchorman of 11 British General Elections. Major Interviewer of 9 British Prime Ministers. Author of The Scottish Dimension in Canada.

Jacquelyn MacLennan
Partner at White & Case LLP. Honorary Fellow, Europa Institute, University of Edinburgh.

Paul Mahoney
Judge of the European Court of Human Rights. He was the first President of the European Union Civil Service Tribunal (2005–2011). Former lecturer at University College London. Visiting professor at the University of Saskatchewan, Saskatoon.

Niamh Nic Shuibhne
Professor of European Union Law, School of Law, University of Edinburgh. Visiting Professor, College of Europe (Bruges). Joint Editor, Common Market Law Review.

Isao Noishiki
Former professor of law at Hannan University in Osaka, and visiting lecturer of several universities. Graduate of Kyoto University, Former Councilor of Matsushita Electric Industrial Co. Ltd., currently Panasonic Corp.

Christopher Norall
Retired lawyer, former partner of Forrester Norall & Sutton.

José Pérez Santos
Emeritus partner of Uría Menéndez. He was a colleague of Ian Forrester when they were both working at the Brussels office of Cleary Gottlieb Steen & Hamilton.

Pauline Tart
Assistant to Ian Forrester since 1976. Born British, by marriage also Belgian, hails from Earby, a small town once in Yorkshire, now in Lancashire.

Robert B. Reich
Chancellor's Professor at the University of California at Berkeley. He has served in three US administrations, most recently as Secretary of Labor under President Bill Clinton, and is the author of fourteen books.

Sir Konrad Schiemann
Former judge of the Court of Justice of the European Communities (2004-2012) and the English and Welsh Court of Appeal (1995).

Dean Spielmann
President of the European Court of Human Rights since 2012 and Judge since 2004. He has taught at universities in Luxembourg and France and is a certified member of the Grand-Ducal Institute. Honorary Fellow of Fitzwilliam College, Cambridge; Honorary Professor of University College London; Honorary Bencher of Gray's Inn, London; Doctor honoris causa of the State University of Yerevan, of the University Babeş-Bolyai of Cluj-Napoca and the University of Bucharest.

Michel Waelbroeck
Former member of the law firm Liedekerke Wolters Waelbroeck & Kirkpatrick. Emeritus professor of European law at the Université Libre de Bruxelles. Emeritus member of the Institute of International Law. Former President of the Belgian Competition Commission. Doctor honoris causa of the University of Neuchâtel.

Jo Weiss
Head of Social Responsibility for White & Case LLP globally, which encompasses the Firm's global pro bono practice, charitable contributions, volunteering and environmental sustainability initiative. Former consultant at McKinsey & Co.

e-Competitions
Antitrust Case Laws e-Bulletin

e-Competitions Bulletin

CASE LAW DATABASE

e-Competitions is the only online resource that provides consistent coverage of antitrust cases from 55 jurisdictions, organized into a searchable database structure. e-Competitions concentrates on cases summaries taking into account that in the context of a continuing growing number of sources there is a need for factual information, i.e., case law.

- 12,000 case summaries
- 2,600 authors
- 55 countries covered
- 24,000 subscribers

SOPHISTICATED EDITORIAL AND IT ENRICHMENT

e-Competitions is structured as a database. The editors make a sophisticated technical and legal work on all articles by tagging these with key words, drafting abstracts and writing html code to increase Google ranking. There is a team of antitrust lawyers – PhD and judges clerks - and a team of IT experts. e-Competitions makes comparative law possible. Thanks to this expert editorial work, it is possible to search and compare cases.

PRESTIGIOUS BOARDS

e-Competitions draws upon highly distinguished editors, all leading experts in national or international antitrust. Advisory Board Members include: Sir Christopher Bellamy, Ioanis Lianos (UCL), Eleanor Fox (NYU), Damien Géradin (Tilburg University), Barry Hawk (Fordham University) Fred Jenny (OECD), Jacqueline Riffault-Silk (Cour de cassation), Wouter Wils (DG COMP), etc.

LEADING PARTNERS

- Association of European Competition Law Judges: The AECLJ is a forum for judges of national Courts specializing in antitrust case law. Members timely feed e-Competitions with just released cases.
- Academics partners: Antitrust research centres from leading universities write regularly in e-Competitions: University College London, King's College London, Queen Mary University, etc.
- Law firms: Global law firms and antitrust niche firms write detailed cases summaries specifically for e-Competitions: Allen & Overy, DLA Piper, Jones Day, Norton Rose Fulbright, Skadden Arps, White & Case, etc.

INSTITUTE of Competition Law
Antitrust databases and resources

The Institute of Competition Law

The Institute of Competition Law is a publishing company, founded in 2004 by Dr. Nicolas Charbit, based in Paris and New-York. The Institute cultivates scholarship and discussion about antitrust issues though publications and conferences. Each publication and event is supervised by editorial boards and scientific or steering committees to ensure independence, objectivity, and academic rigor. Thanks to this management, the Institute has become one of the few think tanks in Europe to have significant influence on antitrust policies.

AIM

The Institute focuses government, business and academic attention on a broad range of subjects which concern competition laws, regulations and related economics.

BOARDS

To maintain its unique focus, the Institute relies upon highly distinguished editors, all leading experts in national or international antitrust: Bill Kovacic, Mario Monti, Eleanor Fox, Barry Hawk, Laurence Idot, Fred Jenny, etc.

AUTHORS

3,800 authors, from 55 jurisdictions.

PARTNERS

- Universities: University College London, King's College London, Queen Mary University, Paris Sorbonne Panthéon-Assas, etc.
- Law firms: Allen & Overy, Cleary Gottlieb Steen & Hamilton, DLA Piper, Hogan Lovells, Jones Day, Norton Rose Fulbright, Skadden Arps, White & Case, etc.

EVENTS

More than 250 events since 2004 in Brussels, London, New York, Paris, Singapour and Washington, DC.

ONLINE VERSION

Concurrences website provides all articles published since its inception.

PUBLICATIONS

The Institute publishes Concurrences Journal, a print and online quarterly peer-reviewed journal dedicated to EU and national competitions laws. e-Competitions is a bi-monthly antitrust news bulletin covering 55 countries. The e-Competitions database contains over 12,000 case summaries from 2,600 authors.

www.ingramcontent.com/pod-product-compliance
Lightning Source LLC
LaVergne TN
LVHW051937290926
849162LV00014B/1868/J